Lecture Notes in Computer Sc

T0238157

Commenced Publication in 1973
Founding and Former Series Editors:
Gerhard Goos, Juris Hartmanis, and Jan van Leeuwen

Paolo Ciancarini   Herbert Wiklicky (Eds.)

Coordination Models and Languages

8th International Conference, COORDINATION 2006
Bologna, Italy, June 14-16, 2006
Proceedings

 Springer

Volume Editors

Paolo Ciancarini
Università di Bologna, Dipartimento di Scienze dell'Informazione
Mura Zamboni 7, 40127 Bologna, Italy
E-mail: cianca@cs.unibo.it

Herbert Wiklicky
Imperial College, Department of Computing
Huxley Building, 180 Queen's Gate, London SW7 2AZ, UK
E-mail: herbert@doc.ic.ac.uk

Library of Congress Control Number: 2006926827

CR Subject Classification (1998): D.2.4, D.2, C.2.4, D.1.3, F.1.2, I.2.11

LNCS Sublibrary: SL 2 – Programming and Software Engineering

ISSN   0302-9743
ISBN-10   3-540-34694-5 Springer Berlin Heidelberg New York
ISBN-13   978-3-540-34694-4 Springer Berlin Heidelberg New York

Springer is a part of Springer Science+Business Media

springer.com

© Springer-Verlag Berlin Heidelberg 2006
Printed in Germany

Typesetting: Camera-ready by author, data conversion by Scientific Publishing Services, Chennai, India
Printed on acid-free paper   SPIN: 11767954   06/3142   5 4 3 2 1 0

Preface

This volume contains the proceedings of the 8th International Conference on Coordination Models and Languages, Coordination 2006. This year the conference was part of a set of federated conferences named DisCoTec 2006, held in Bologna in June 2006. It was held in the series of successful conferences whose proceedings were also published in LNCS, in volumes 1061, 1282, 1594, 1906, 2315, 2949, and 3454.

The conference was born in 1996, as a forum for researchers working on programming models, formalisms, and platforms for describing or supporting concurrent and distributed computations. Contemporary information systems increasingly rely on combining concurrent and distributed, and now also mobile, reconfigurable and heterogeneous components. New models, architectures, languages, and verification techniques are necessary to cope with the complexity induced by the demands of today's software industry. Coordination languages have emerged as a successful approach, in that they provide abstractions that cleanly separate behavior from communication, thereby supporting modular design, simplifying reasoning, and ultimately enhancing software development. Research on coordination models and languages is still playing a crucial role in addressing the technological concerns of widely distributed applications and services.

We received 50 submission. All papers were reviewed by four reviewers. The Program Committee used a tool for collaborative conference management to select 18 regular papers. The Program Committee invited Chris Hankin and Pierpaolo Degano to give talks.

The conference and this volume would not have been possible without the intellectual contributions of all the authors, the careful reviews and advice by members of the Program Committee, and the additional referees who helped us to evaluate the papers. We thank Gianluigi Zavattaro, the General Chair of DisCoTec 2006, for his helpful support with the conference management system.

April 2006

Paolo Ciancarini
Herbert Wiklicky

Organization

Coordination 2006, the 8th International Conference on Coordination Models and Languages, is part of the set of federated conferences DisCoTec 2006, also including DAIS 2006, the 6th IFIP International Conference on Distributed Applications and Interoperable Systems, and FMOODS 2006, the 8th IFIP International Conference on Formal Methods for Open Object-Based Distributed Systems, as well as three workshops organized by the department of Computer Science,
University of Bologna.

Program Committee

Conference Chair:	Gianluigi Zavattaro, University of Bologna, Italy
Program Chairs:	Paolo Ciancarini, University of Bologna, Italy
	Herbert Wiklicky, Imperial College London, UK
Members:	Farhad Arbab, CWI Amsterdam, The Netherlands
	Luis Barbosa, Universidade do Minho, Portugal
	Antonio Brogi, University of Pisa, Italy
	Wolfgang Emmerich, University College London, UK
	Frank de Boer, CWI & Utrecht University, The Netherlands
	Jean-Marie Jacquet, University of Namur, Belgium
	Joost Kok, Leiden University, The Netherlands
	Toby Lehman, IBM Almaden, USA
	D.C. Marinescu, University of Central Florida, USA
	Ronaldo Menezes, Florida Institute of Technology, USA
	Andrea Omicini, University of Bologna, Italy
	Paolo Petta, OeFAI, Austria
	Gian Pietro Picco, Politecnico di Milano, Italy
	Ernesto Pimentel, University of Malaga, Spain
	Rosario Pugliese, University of Florence, Italy
	Gruia Catalin Roman, Washington University, USA
	Robert Tolksdorf, FU Berlin, Germany
	Emilio Tuosto, University of Leicester, UK
	Carlos Varela, Rensselaer Polytechnic Institute, USA
	Alan Wood, University of York, UK

Table of Contents

Stochastic Reasoning About Channel-Based Component Connectors

Christel Baier[1] and Verena Wolf[2]

[1] Universität Bonn, Germany
baier@cs.uni-bonn.de
[2] Universität Mannheim, Germany
wolf@informatik.uni-mannheim.de

Abstract. Constraint automata have been used as an operational model for component connectors that coordinate the cooperation and communication of the components by means of a network of channels. In this paper, we introduce a variant of constraint automata (called continuous-time constraint automata) that allows us to specify time-dependent stochastic assumptions about the channel connections or the component interfaces, such as the arrival rates of communication requests, the average delay of enabled I/O-operations at the channel ends or the stochastic duration of internal computations. This yields the basis for a performance analysis of channel-based coordination mechanisms. We focus on compositional reasoning and discuss several bisimulation relations on continuous-time constraint automata. For this, we adapt notions of strong and weak bisimulation that have been introduced for similar stochastic models and introduce a new notion of weak bisimulation which abstracts away from invisible non-stochastic computations as well as the internal stochastic evolution.

1 Introduction

Coordination models and languages provide a formalization of the *glue-code* that binds individual components and organizes the communication and cooperation between them. In the past 15 years, various types of coordination models have been proposed that they yield a clear separation between the internal structure of the components and their interactions. See e.g. [19, 24, 13, 25, 15].

The purpose of this paper is to introduce an operational model for reasoning about *stochastic properties* of coordination languages similar to the approaches of Priami [27] and Di Pierro et al. [16]. In contrast to these approaches our focus is on exogenous channel-based coordination languages, such as Reo [2] (see also [5, 29, 1, 17, 14]) and stochastic models with nondeterminism. The rough idea of Reo is that complex component connectors are synthesized from channels via certain composition operators, thus yielding a *network of channels* (called Reo connector circuit) that coordinates the interactions between the components. An operational semantics of Reo connector circuits has been provided by means of *constraint automata* [4]. These are variants of labelled transition systems and encode the configurations of the network by their states and the possible data flow at the ports of the components and the nodes "inside" the network by their transitions. Extensions of constraint automata have been presented in [3] to study real-time constraints of component connectors and in [6] to reason about

P. Ciancarini and H. Wiklicky (Eds.): COORDINATION 2006, LNCS 4038, pp. 1–15, 2006.

channels with a probabilistic effect. The latter approach is time-abstract and deals with discrete probabilities, e.g., to model the faulty behaviours of buffered channels that might loose or corrupt stored messages, while the former approach focusses on a purely timed setting, e.g., to reason about hard deadlines, but does not deal with probabilities. The contribution of this paper is orthogonal to the extensions proposed in [3, 6] as it introduces a stochastic variant of constraint automata where transitions might have a certain delay according to some probability distribution over a continuous time domain. This model, called continuous-time constraint automata (CCA for short), combines the features of ordinary constraint automata with the race conditions in continuous-time Markov chains. CCA are close to *interactive Markov chains* (IMCs), which have been introduced by Hermanns [20] for specifying reactive systems with internal stochastic behaviours. CCA can be used – as ordinary constraint automata – to formalize the step-wise behaviour of the interfaces of the components and the channels connecting them, as well as an operational model for the composite system. In addition, CCA provide the possibility to specify, e.g., the average rate of communication requests of a certain component or the mean time that have to be passed between two consecutive I/O operations at a certain channel. Thus, CCA yield a simple and intuitive model that allow for a performance analysis of channel-based coordination mechanisms.

In this paper, we concentrate on compositional reasoning by means of *bisimulation* relations on CCA. We first consider strong and weak bisimulation, that have been introduced for interactive Markov chains [20]. These notions adapted to CCA yield equivalences that are congruences for the two basic operators (product and hiding) for generating the CCA for a complex component connector out of the CCA for its channels and the component interfaces. Furthermore, we introduce a new notion of weak bisimulation, called *very weak bisimulation* which abstracts away from the stochastic branching behaviour and cumulates the effect of sequences of stochastic transitions. Very weak bisimulation equivalence is coarser than weak bisimulation equivalence, but preserves the probabilities for trace-based linear time properties and can be checked in polynomial-time.

Organization. Section 2 recalls the basic concepts of ordinary constraint automata. CCA and a product and hiding operator on CCA are introduced in Section 3. Section 4 deals with bisimulation relations on CCA. Section 5 concludes the paper. Due to length restrictions, proofs for the theorems are omitted. They can be found in the full version (see http://pi2.informatik.uni-mannheim.de/HomePages/vwolf/cca.ps).

2   Constraint Automata

This section summarizes the basis concepts of constraint automata [4] and their use as operational model for channel-based component connectors. Constraint automata, CA for short, are variants of labelled transition systems where transitions are augmented with pairs $\langle N, g \rangle$ rather than action labels. The states of a constraint automata stand for the network configurations, e.g., the contents of the buffers for FIFO channels. The transition labels $\langle N, g \rangle$ can be viewed as *sets of I/O-operations* that will be performed *in parallel*. More precisely, N is a set of nodes in the network where data-flow is observed simultaneously, and g is a boolean condition on the observed data items. Thus, transitions going out of a state q represent the possible data-flow in the corresponding configuration and its effect on the configuration.

Data assignments and data constraints. CA use a finite set $\mathcal{N}$ of nodes. The nodes can play the role of input and output ports of components, but they can appear outside the interfaces of components as "intermediate" stations of the network where several channels are glued together and the transmission of data items can be observed. For the purposes of this paper, there is no need to distinguish between write and read operations at the nodes. Instead CA only refer to the data items that can be "observed" at a node. Throughout the paper, we assume a fixed, non-empty and finite data domain *Data* consisting of the data items that can be transmitted through the channels. A data assignment for $N \subseteq \mathcal{N}$ means a function $\delta : N \rightarrow Data$. We write $\delta.A$ for the data item assigned to node $A \in N$ under δ and $DA(N)$ for the set of all data assignments for node-set N. CA use a symbolic representation of data assignments by data constraints which mean propositional formulae built from the atoms "$d_A = d_B$", "$d_A \in P$" or "$d_A = d$" where A, B are nodes, d_A is a symbol for the observed data item at node A and $d \in Data$, $P \subseteq Data$. The symbol $\models$ stands for the obvious satisfaction relation which results from interpreting data constraints over data assignments. Satisfiability and logical equivalence $\equiv$ of data constraints are defined as usual. We write $DC(N)$ to denote the set of satisfiable data constraints using only the symbols d_A for $A \in N$, but not d_B for $B \in \mathcal{N} \setminus N$.

Constraint automata (CA) [4]. A CA is a tuple $\mathcal{A} = (Q, \mathcal{N}, \longrightarrow, Q_0)$ where Q is a set of states, also called configurations, $\mathcal{N}$ a finite set of nodes, $Q_0 \subseteq Q$ the set of initial states and $\longrightarrow$ a subset of $\bigcup_{N \subseteq \mathcal{N}} Q \times \{N\} \times DC(N) \times Q$, called the transition relation.

We write $q \xrightarrow{N,g} p$ instead of $(q, N, g, p) \in \longrightarrow$ and refer to N as the node-set and g the guard. Transitions where the node-set N is non-empty are called *visible*, while transitions with the empty node-set are called *hidden*. Each transition represents a set of possible interactions given by the *transition instances* that result by replacing the guard g with a data assignment δ where g holds. The intuitive behaviour of a CA is as follows. The automaton starts in an initial state. If the current state is q then an instance $q \xrightarrow{N,\delta} p$ of the outgoing transitions from q is chosen, the corresponding I/O-operations are performed and the next state is p. If there are several outgoing transitions from state q the next transition is chosen nondeterministically. A formalization of the possible (finite or infinite) observable data flow of a constraint automaton is obtained by the notion of a run. A run in $\mathcal{A}$ denotes a (finite or infinite) sequence of consecutive transition instances $q_0 \xrightarrow{N_0,\delta_0} q_1 \xrightarrow{N_1,\delta_1} q_2 \xrightarrow{N_2,\delta_2} \ldots$ where $q_0 \in Q_0$. For finite runs we require that the last state q does not have an outgoing hidden transition. This can be understood as a *maximal progress assumption* for hidden transitions, i.e., steps that do not require any interaction with the environment.

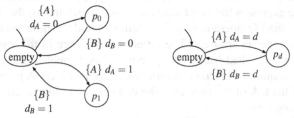

The picture above shows a CA for a FIFO1 channel with the node-set $\mathcal{N} = \{A, B\}$ and $Data = \{0, 1\}$. Node A serves as input port where data items can be written into the channel, while node B can be regarded as an output port where the stored data element is taken from the buffer and delivered to the environment.

State "empty" stands for the configuration where the buffer is empty, while state p_d encodes the configuration where d is stored in the buffer. Often, we use simplified parametric pictures for CA with meta symbols for data items as in the right of the picture (and formally explained in [4]).

For another example, we regard a simple system consisting of a producer and a consumer which are linked via a synchronous channel for transmitting the generated products from the producer's output port B to the consumer's input port C.

We model both components (producer and consumer) and the synchronous channel BC by CA. Parametric pictures are shown below. We assume here that the producer is activated by obtaining an input value d from the environment at its input port A. It then generates a certain product $f(d)$ which is synchronously delivered to the consumer. After having received $e = f(d)$, the consumer starts the consume-phase and finally sends a signal via output port D to the environment. We assume here that the value send off at D is arbitrary, that is, we deal with the valid guard true (which is omitted in the picture).

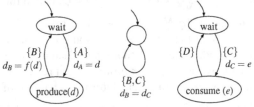

Product. To obtain a constraint automata for the composite producer-consumer-system, we apply a product construction to the three CA. The product of two CA $\mathcal{A}_1 = (Q_1, \mathcal{N}_1, \longrightarrow_1, Q_{0,1})$ and $\mathcal{A}_2 = (Q_2, \mathcal{N}_2, \longrightarrow_2, Q_{0,2})$ is defined as follows. $\mathcal{A}_1 \bowtie \mathcal{A}_2$ is a CA with the components $(Q_1 \times Q_2, \mathcal{N}_1 \cup \mathcal{N}_2, \longrightarrow, Q_{0,1} \times Q_{0,2})$ where $\longrightarrow$ is given by the following rules:

- If $q_1 \xrightarrow{N_1, g_1}_1 p_1$, $q_2 \xrightarrow{N_2, g_2}_2 p_2$, $N_1 \cap \mathcal{N}_2 = N_2 \cap \mathcal{N}_1 \neq \emptyset$ then $\langle q_1, q_2 \rangle \xrightarrow{N_1 \cup N_2, g_1 \wedge g_2} \langle p_1, p_2 \rangle$, provided that $g_1 \wedge g_2$ is satisfiable.
- If $q_1 \xrightarrow{N, g}_1 p_1$ where $N \cap \mathcal{N}_2 = \emptyset$ then $\langle q_1, q_2 \rangle \xrightarrow{N, g} \langle p_1, q_2 \rangle$.
- If $q_2 \xrightarrow{N, g}_2 p_2$ where $N \cap \mathcal{N}_1 = \emptyset$ then $\langle q_1, q_2 \rangle \xrightarrow{N, g} \langle q_1, p_2 \rangle$.

The former rule expresses the synchronization case which means that both automata have to "agree" on the I/O-operations at their common nodes, while the I/O-operations at their individual nodes is arbitrary. The latter two rules are in the style of classical interleaving rules for labelled transition systems. They formalize the case where no synchronization is required since no common nodes are involved. A parametric picture for the product of the CA of the producer, the consumer and the synchronous channel BC has the following form:

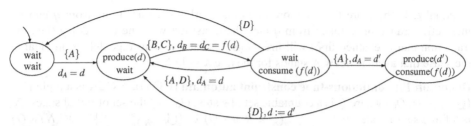

Hiding. Another operator that is helpful for abstraction purposes and can be used in Reo to built components from networks by declaring the internal structure of the network as hidden (i.e., invisible for the environment) is the hiding operator. It takes as input a CA $\mathcal{A} = (Q, \mathcal{N}, \longrightarrow, Q_0)$ and a non-empty node-set $M \subseteq \mathcal{N}$. The result is a CA hide$(\mathcal{A}, M)$ that behaves as $\mathcal{A}$, except that data flow at the nodes $A \in M$ is made invisible. Formally, hide$(\mathcal{A}, M) = (Q, \mathcal{N} \setminus M, \longrightarrow_M, Q_{0,M})$ where

$$q \xrightarrow{\bar{N}, \bar{g}}_M p \text{ iff there exists a transition } q \xrightarrow{N, g} p \text{ such that } \bar{N} = N \setminus M \text{ and } \bar{g} = \exists M[g].$$

$\exists M[g]$ stands short for $\bigvee_{\delta \in DA(M)} g[d_A/\delta.A \mid A \in M]$, where $g[d_A/\delta.A \mid A \in M]$ denotes the syntactic replacement of all occurrences of d_A in g for $A \in M$ with $\delta.A$. Thus, $\exists M[g]$ formalizes the set of data assignments for $\bar{N} = N \setminus M$ that are obtained from a data assignment δ for N where g holds by dropping the assignments for the nodes $A \in N \cap M$. For example, hiding nodes B and C in the CA $\mathcal{A}$ for the producer-consumer system yields a CA $\mathcal{A}' = $ hide$(\mathcal{A}, \{B, C\})$ with node-set $\{A, D\}$. $\mathcal{A}'$ has the same structure as $\mathcal{A}$, the only difference being that the $\{B, C\}$-transition in $\mathcal{A}$ becomes a hidden transition in $\mathcal{A}'$.

3 Continuous-Time Constraint Automata

We now present a stochastic extension of constraint automata that yields the basis for a performance analysis of channel-based component connectors, e.g. to reason about expected response times, the average number of messages that are stored in a buffer of a FIFO channel, the stochastic long-run behaviour or verifying soft deadlines such as "there is a 95% chance to obtain a message at input port B within 10 time units after having sent a request from output port A". Continuous-time constraint automata (CCA for short) rely on the assumption that hidden transitions are performed as soon as possible, while enabled I/O-operations at (non-hidden) nodes can occur at any moment or even can be refused. The idea is that the environment might connect to the non-hidden nodes and might either agree to perform a communication immediately, might cause a delay of a certain communication or might even be not willing to cooperate. CCA are most in the spirit of interactive Markov chains (IMC) that have been introduced by Hermanns [20] and that are closely related to continuous-time Markov decision processes [28]. As in IMCs we have two types of transitions:

- *interactive* transitions $q \xrightarrow{N, g} p$ as in ordinary constraint automata, and
- *Markovian transitions* $q \xrightarrow{\lambda} p$ where λ is a positive real number, called rate.

The interpretation of the rates is as in continuous-time Markov chains, see e.g. [22], i.e., with probability $1 - e^{-\lambda t}$ the delay of a Markovian transition with rate λ is less or equal t. If there are two or more outgoing Markovian transitions from q and no interactive transition is taken from q then the transition with the least delay (i.e., the transition that is enabled first) will fire. Note that rates and average delays are dual in the sense that average delay Λ stands for the rate $\lambda = 1/\Lambda$.

Definition 1 (Continuous-time constraint automata (CCA)). A CCA is a tuple $C = (Q, \mathcal{N}, \longrightarrow, Q_0)$ where Q is a countable set of states, $Q_0 \subseteq Q$ the set of initial states, $\mathcal{N}$ is a finite set of nodes and $\longrightarrow \subseteq (Q \times \mathbb{R}_{>0} \times Q) \cup \left(\bigcup_{N \subseteq \mathcal{N}} Q \times \{N\} \times DC(N) \times Q \right)$ such that for all states q and p there is at most one Markovian transition from q to p. $\square$

We write $\mathbf{R}(q, p) = \lambda$ if $q \xrightarrow{\lambda} p$ and $\mathbf{R}(q, p) = 0$ if there is no Markovian transition from q to p. For mathematical reasons, we require that for each state the exit rate $E(q)$ defined by $\sum_{p \in Q} \mathbf{R}(q, p)$ is finite and that there does not exist an infinite path consisting of consecutive interactive transitions. (The latter assumptions are irrelevant for the purposes of this paper, but they are necessary to ensure non-zenoness.) When state q is entered then either *immediately* a hidden transition instance is taken or the system stays in state q until one of the Markovian transitions becomes enabled and fires or a visible interactive transition is taken. A visible transition instance $q \xrightarrow{N,\delta} p$ can only be taken if all involved nodes $A \in N$ agree to perform the I/O-operations specified by (N, δ). If N is non-empty then this agreement depends on the (unknown) environment which might refuse to provide the required I/O-operations at the nodes $A \in N$. Thus, none of the visible transitions might be taken. If, however, the current state q has one or more outgoing hidden transitions there is a *nondeterministic choice* which selects one of the interactive (visible or hidden) transitions. Thus, Markovian transitions can only be taken from state q if there is no hidden transition that starts in q, in which case q is called a *Markovian state*.

The possible stepwise behaviours of a CCA can be made precise by means of the runs and the induced stochastic processes. A run in a CCA C is a sequence of consecutive transition instances $q_0 \xrightarrow{\alpha_0} q_1 \xrightarrow{\alpha_1} q_2 \xrightarrow{\alpha_2} \ldots$ where the α_i's are either triples (t, N, δ) such that $q_i \xrightarrow{N,\delta} q_{i+1}$ is an instance of an interactive transition and $t \geq 0$ (the time passage between entering state q_i and performing the I/O-operations specified by (N, δ)) or $\alpha_i \in \mathbb{R}_{>0}$ and there is a Markovian transition from q_i to q_{i+1}. In the latter case, α_i stands for the amount of time the system spends in state q_i until the first Markovian transition fires. According to the maximal progress assumption we require that Markovian transitions and that $\alpha_i = (t, N, \delta)$ for some $t > 0$ can only occur if no hidden transition can be taken in q_i and that finite runs end in a state where all outgoing transitions are visible. To reason about the probabilities of runs, the concept of schedulers, also often called policy, strategy or adversary, is needed. The details, which can be found e.g. in [28], are not of importance here. We just mention that a scheduler takes as input the history of the system, formalized by a finite prefix of a run, and either selects one of the enabled interactive transition instances or, if no hidden transition can be taken, decides to take a visible transition instance with some delay t unless a Markovian transition fires first or decides to take no interactive transition and to wait for the first enabled Markovian transition. For any given scheduler a probability measure on the induced runs can be defined which, for instance, allows to speak about the probability to reach a certain configuration within t time units or the expected time until a certain communication takes place.

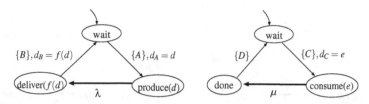

Example 1. The picture above shows a stochastic variant for the CA of the producer and the consumer. Here, we assume that the production time takes in average $1/\lambda$ time units, while the mean time of the consume phase is $1/\mu$. The data-abstract behavior of the composite system can then be specified by the CCA shown below. This CCA can now be subject of a stochastic analysis. For example, it can be verified that the average time of one production-consume cycle is $1/\lambda + 1/\mu$, or that the probability for the event "after being activated through an input at A, the time for delivering the product via channel BC is less or equal t" is given by $1 - e^{-\lambda t}$.   □

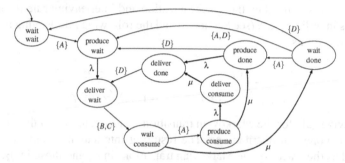

Beside specifying stochastic phenomena that are internal to certain components, also channels might have stochastic behaviours and can be modelled by CCA. E.g., if a component Comp, that is linked to the sink end of a FIFO1 channel c, is waiting for a message along c then Comp cannot immediately read when a message is written at the source end. Instead it has to wait for a certain (possibly very small) amount of time until the read operation can be performed. As long as we consider any channel in isolation these delays might be very small or even negligible. However, for complex networks where several channels are composed, the effect of delays becomes less clear and can play a crucial role for performability issues. Assume a FIFO channel c with 1.000 buffer cells is composed from 1.000 copies of FIFO1 channel with average delay Λ then the mean time passage between writing a data item d into c's source end and the instant where d can be taken at the sink end is $1.000 \cdot \Lambda$.

Example 2. A FIFO1 channel with average delay $1/\lambda$ between the read and write operations can be modelled by one of the CCA shown below. In both CCA, after the write operation at the source A the state $wait(d)$ is reached where a Markovian transition with rate λ is emanating, leading to state $take(d)$ where the sink B can take the element. In the CCA on the left, no proper delay between the read operation at sink B and the next write operation at A is specified, while the automaton on the right relies on the assumption that the physical properties of the buffer yield an average delay $1/\mu$ for enabling a write operation after a read operation.   □

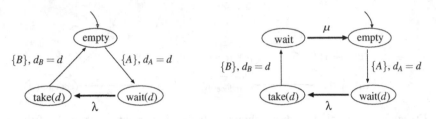

We now explain how to construct a CCA for a given network, generated from channels and component interfaces with CCA-semantics, in a compositional manner. We assume here a calculus of channels, such as Reo [2], where networks are created via product (join) and hiding. In the following definition of the product of CCA we assume that the common nodes are those where data flow has to be synchronized.

Definition 2 (Product of CCA). The product of two CCA $C_1 = (Q_1, \mathcal{N}_1, \longrightarrow_1, Q_{0,1})$ and $C_2 = (Q_2, \mathcal{N}_2, \longrightarrow_2, Q_{0,2})$ is the CCA $C_1 \bowtie C_2 = (Q_1 \times Q_2, \mathcal{N}_1 \cup \mathcal{N}_2, \longrightarrow, Q_{0,1} \times Q_{0,2})$ where $\longrightarrow$ is defined by the synchronization and interleaving rule for interactive transitions as in ordinary CA (see Section 2) and the following interleaving rules for the Markovian transitions:

$$\frac{q_1 \xrightarrow{\lambda}_1 p_1}{\langle q_1, q_2 \rangle \xrightarrow{\lambda} \langle p_1, q_2 \rangle} \qquad \frac{q_2 \xrightarrow{\lambda}_2 p_2}{\langle q_1, q_2 \rangle \xrightarrow{\lambda} \langle q_1, p_2 \rangle}$$

The interleaving rule for the Markovian transition is adequate due to the memory-less property of exponential distributions. The resulting interleaving diamond for a state $\langle q_1, q_2 \rangle$ models the "race" of the Markovian transitions in q_1 and those in q_2.

The product-operator $\bowtie$ is associative and commutative (up to isomorphism). Thus, when starting with a network where several components are linked via channels then the CCA for the composite system is obtained by applying the binary operator $\bowtie$ to the CCA for the channels and component interfaces in any order.

Example 3 (Triple modular redundancy). Let us look for a CCA that models a fault tolerant system relying on von Neumann's concept of triple modular redundancy. The task is to compute a certain boolean function value $f(d)$ for an input value $d \in \{0, 1\}$ provided by a user and to return $f(d)$. Three unreliable modules are available that attempt to calculate $f(d)$, but may fail to compute the correct value. Thus, after having obtained the computed values $f_1, f_2, f_3 \in \{0, 1\}$ by the modules, a majority decision will be made and the value $MAJ(f_1, f_2, f_3)$ will be returned to the user.

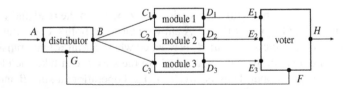

The system consists of five components as shown above. The distributor gets the input value d via its input port A and delivers it to the three modules via synchronous channels connecting the distributor's output port B with the input ports C_i of the modules. The modules operate independently from each other and calculate a values f_i that will be delivered via a synchronous channel D_iE_i. The voter then makes the majority decision and returns the obtained value via its output port H. To avoid that the distributor reads the next input value before the voter has returned a value, the voter and the distributor are linked via a synchronous channel FG. Assuming that the average time for the internal computation of the modules is $1/\lambda$ and all other transitions are immediate the interfaces of the distributor, modules and voter can be modelled by the following CCA:

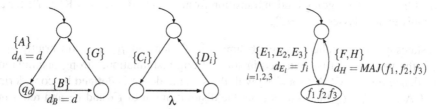

Composing these CCA with the automata for the involved synchronous channels via the product-operator $\bowtie$ yields the CCA shown below. □

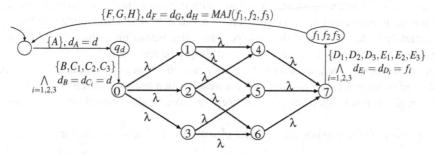

Definition 3 (Hiding in CCA). Let $C = (Q, \mathcal{N}, \longrightarrow, Q_0)$ be a CCA and $\emptyset \neq M \subseteq \mathcal{N}$. The CCA $\text{hide}(C,M)$ is the tuple $(Q, \mathcal{N} \setminus M, \longrightarrow_M, Q_{0,M})$ where the transition relation $\longrightarrow_M$ is given by the following two rules:

$$\frac{q \xrightarrow{N,g} p, \ \bar{N} = N \setminus M, \ \bar{g} = \exists M[g]}{q \xrightarrow{\bar{N},\bar{g}}_M p} \quad \text{and} \quad \frac{q \xrightarrow{\lambda} p, \lambda > 0}{q \xrightarrow{\lambda}_M p}$$

where $\exists M[g]$ is defined as in the non-probabilistic case. □

4 Bisimulation on CCA

Since CCA are slight variants of interactive Markov chains (IMCs), we may adapt the bisimulation techniques suggested in [20] for IMCs. Bisimulation equivalence for IMCs arises through a combination of standard bisimulation [23] for the interactive transitions and lumping equivalence [12, 21, 9, 8] for the Markovian transitions. We now adapt these notions of strong and weak bisimulation for CCA and introduce a new (coarser) variant of weak bisimulation equivalence on CCA.

For $P \subseteq Q$, $\mathbf{R}(q,P) = \sum_{p \in P} \mathbf{R}(q,p)$ denotes the total rate to move from q to P via Markovian transitions.

Definition 4 (Strong bisimulation for CCA). Let C be a CCA as in Def. 1. A strong bisimulation on C is an equivalence $\mathcal{R}$ on Q such that for all $(q_1,q_2) \in \mathcal{R}$:

(S1) If $q_1 \xrightarrow{N,\delta} p_1$ then there is a transition instance $q_2 \xrightarrow{N,\delta} p_2$ such that $(p_1,p_2) \in \mathcal{R}$.
(S2) If there is no outgoing hidden transition from q_1 then $\mathbf{R}(q_1,P) = \mathbf{R}(q_2,P)$ for all equivalence classes $P \in Q/\mathcal{R}$.

Two states q_1, q_2 are called strongly bisimilar in C, denoted $q_1 \sim_C q_2$ (or briefly $q_1 \sim q_2$), if the pair (q_1,q_2) is contained in some strong bisimulation. Strong bisimulation equivalence for two CCA C_1 and C_2 with the same node-set is defined by considering the CCA $C = C_1 \uplus C_2$ that results from the disjoint union of C_1 and C_2 and requiring that for each initial state q_1 in C_1 there exists an initial state $q_2 \in C_2$ such that $q_1 \sim_C q_2$, and vice versa. We write $C_1 \sim C_2$ to denote that C_1 and C_2 are strongly bisimilar.   □

Condition (S2) makes no restrictions on the Markovian transitions if q_1 (and hence also q_2 by (S1)) has an interactive transition with the empty node-set. In fact, any state that has such an internal move (which represents data flow at some hidden nodes) will immediately be left by one of the enabled interactive transitions. Thus, the Markovian transitions are irrelevant for them, and could simply be removed.

In an analogous way, we adapt Hermans's notion of weak bisimulation for IMCs [20] to our setting. CCA C is said to have a weak hidden transition from q to p, denoted $q \Longrightarrow p$, if p is reachable from q in C via zero or more hidden transitions. Furthermore,

$$q \xrightarrow{N,g} p \text{ iff there exists states } q' \text{ and } p' \text{ with } q \Longrightarrow q', q' \xrightarrow{N,g} p' \text{ and } p' \Longrightarrow p.$$

We refer to $q \xRightarrow{N,\delta} p$ as a weak interactive transition instance in C. For $P \subseteq Q$, the backward closure of P in C, denoted $bc(P)$, is the set of all states $q \in Q$ such that $q \Longrightarrow p$ for some state $p \in P$. Thus, $bc(P)$ contains exactly those states that can reach a P-state via hidden transitions. Since hidden transitions are always enabled, the states $q \in bc(P)$ are those that can reach P without any delay. State q is called Markovian if there is no outgoing hidden transition from q.

Definition 5 (Weak bisimulation for CCA). Let C be a CCA as in Def. 1. A weak bisimulation on C is an equivalence $\mathcal{R}$ on Q such that for all $(q_1,q_2) \in \mathcal{R}$:

(W1) Each weak interactive transition instance of q_1 can be matched by a weak interactive transition instance of q_2 in the following sense:

(W1.1) If $q_1 \xRightarrow{N,\delta} p_1$ where $N \neq \emptyset$ then $q_2 \xRightarrow{N,\delta} p_2$ for some state p_2 where $(p_1,p_2) \in \mathcal{R}$.
(W1.2) If $q_1 \Longrightarrow p_1$ then $q_2 \Longrightarrow p_2$ for some state p_2 such that $(p_1,p_2) \in \mathcal{R}$.
(W2) If q_1 is Markovian then there exists a Markovian state r_2 with $q_2 \Longrightarrow r_2$, $(q_1,r_2) \in \mathcal{R}$ and $\mathbf{R}(q_1,bc(P)) = \mathbf{R}(r_2,bc(P))$ for all $\mathcal{R}$-equivalence classes P.

Two states q_1, q_2 are called weakly bisimilar in C, denoted $q_1 \approx_C q_2$ (or briefly $q_1 \approx q_2$), if the pair (q_1, q_2) is contained in some weak bisimulation. Weak bisimilarity for two CCA is defined as in the case of strong bisimulation equivalence.   □

Example 4 (Triple modular redundancy). Let us look for the product-CCA for TMR in Example 3. States 1,2,3 are weakly bisimilar, as well as states 4,5,6. This simply follows by the fact that none of these states has a weak interactive transition and that $\mathbf{R}(i, \{4,5,6\}) = 2\lambda$ for $i = 1,2,3$ and $\mathbf{R}(i, \{7\}) = \lambda$ for $i = 4,5,6$. After hiding all nodes except for A and H, also states states q_d and 0 as well as states 7 and $\langle f_1 f_2 f_3 \rangle$ are weakly bisimilar. Note that e.g. for q_d and 0, conditions (W1.1) and (W1.2) are obviously fulfilled since none of these states has a weak visible transition and $q_d \Longrightarrow 0$.

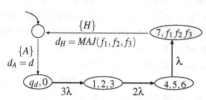

To mimic the Markovian transitions of state 0, state q_d may first take the hidden transition from q_d to 0 and then perform the CTMC-like race in state 0. By collapsing weakly bisimilar states, we obtain a CCA with four states (see the picture on the left) that is weakly bisimilar to the original one.   □

Bravetti [11] introduced a slightly coarser notion of weak bisimulation on IMCs, which relaxes condition (W2) by the requirement that $\mathbf{R}(q_1, bc(P)) = \mathbf{R}(r_2, bc(P))$ for all $\mathcal{R}$-equivalence classes P, except for the $\mathcal{R}$-equivalence class of q_1. Bravetti's weak bisimulation, denoted $\approx^B$, agrees with the coarsest equivalence satisfying condition (W1) and the following condition (W2'):

(W2') If q_1 is Markovian then $q_2 \Longrightarrow r_2$ for some Markovian state r_2 with $(q_1, r_2) \in \mathcal{R}$
and $\Pr(q_1 \stackrel{\leq t}{\Longrightarrow} bc(P)) = \Pr(r_2 \stackrel{\leq t}{\Longrightarrow} bc(P))$ for all $t \geq 0$ and $P \in Q/\mathcal{R}$ with $q_1 \notin P$.

where, for $t \geq 0$, $q \in Q$ and $P \subseteq Q$, $\Pr(q \stackrel{\leq t}{\Longrightarrow} P)$ denotes the probability to move from q to P via Markovian transitions emanating from Markovian states within at most t time units.[1]

Theorem 1 (Compositionality of strong and weak bisimulation). *Let C_1, C_1', C_2, C_2' be CCA such that C_i and C_i' have the same node-set, $i = 1, 2$. Moreover, let $\cong$ be one of the three equivalences $\sim$, $\approx$ or $\approx^B$. Then, $C_1 \cong C_1'$ and $C_2 \cong C_2'$ implies $C_1 \bowtie C_2 \cong C_1' \bowtie C_2'$ and $\mathrm{hide}(C_1, M) \cong \mathrm{hide}(C_1', M)$.*

The congruence result stated in Theorem 1 yields that strong and weak bisimulation are adequate for the compositional design of complex component connectors. However, for the analysis coarser equivalences that abstract away from sequences of non-observable (hidden or Markovian) transitions, but still preserve the probabilities of the observable data flow are desirable.

We now present a new notion of bisimulation equivalence for CCA, called *very weak bisimulation*, which relies on the assumption that the given CCA models the "complete"

---

[1] The Markovian states together with their Markovian transitions yield an ordinary continuous-time Markov chain with state space Q. Thus, we may deal here with the standard sigma-algebra and probability measure on CTMCs, see e.g. [22, 26].

closed system where the enabledness of visible transitions no longer depend on the environment and can be taken as soon as possible. This view is adequate, even for systems that are open in nature provided that stochastic assumptions are available for the environment which allow to model the environment by a CCA. The CCA that is subject for the (stochastic) analysis then arises through the product of the CCA for the channels, the component interfaces and the environment.

In the sequel, let C be a CCA as in Def. 1. State q is called *purely Markovian* if q is Markovian and has no (hidden or visible) outgoing interactive transition. State q is called *vanishing* if q has exactly one hidden transition and no visible transitions. Let C^M be the CTMC that results from C after the following two transformations: 1) First, all vanishing states are replaced by their (unique) successor which is not vanishing, i.e. either purely Markovian, has more than one hidden transitions or has at least one visible transition. Note that the successor is not necessarily a direct one since a maximal sequence of vanishing states is replaced by the direct successor of the last state of this sequence. After this transformation there might still be states with hidden transitions (namely those that have at least one interactive transition in addition or two or more hidden transitions). 2) Next, all states that have at least one outgoing interactive transition are made absorbing, i.e. we remove all outgoing Markovian transitions of states that are not purely Markovian.

Then, for a purely Markovian state $q \in Q$, $P \subseteq Q$ and $t \geq 0$, $\mathrm{Pr}^M(q \overset{\leq t}{\Longrightarrow} P)$ denotes the probability to move from q to a state $p \in P$ in the CTMC C^M within at most t time units.

Definition 6 (Very weak bisimulation). A very weak bisimulation on a CCA C is an equivalence relation $\mathcal{R}$ on Q such that for all $(q_1, q_2) \in \mathcal{R}$:

(V1) Each weak interactive transition instance of q_1 can be matched by a weak interactive transition instance of q_2 in the sense of (W1.1) and (W1.2) of Definition 5.

(V2) If q_1 is purely Markovian then there exists a purely Markovian state r_2 with $q_2 \Longrightarrow r_2$, $(q_1, r_2) \in \mathcal{R}$ and

$$\mathrm{Pr}^M(q_1 \overset{\leq t}{\Longrightarrow} bc(P)) = \mathrm{Pr}^M(r_2 \overset{\leq t}{\Longrightarrow} bc(P))$$

for all $\mathcal{R}$-equivalence classes P that contain no purely Markovian states.

States q_1, q_2 are called very weakly bisimilar in C, denoted $q_1 \approx_C^{vw} q_2$ (or briefly $q_1 \approx^{vw} q_2$), if the pair (q_1, q_2) is contained in $\mathcal{R}$ for some very weak bisimulation $\mathcal{R}$. Very weak bisimilarity for two CCA is defined as for strong bisimulation equivalence. $\square$

The rationale behind (V2) is that $\approx^{vw}$-equivalent states can reach the set $bc(P)$ after some time passage t (obtained by sequences of Markovian and hidden transitions leading to a state p that is in the backward closure of P) with equal probability.

Note that there are no restrictions on Markovian transitions of states that are not purely Markovian. The relation $\approx^{vw}$ abstracts away from those transitions which is a useful abstraction for closed models where visible transitions will never be delayed due to the product operator and can be considered as immediate. Clearly, $\approx$ is strictly finer than $\approx^B$ which again is finer than $\approx^{vw}$ since for each weak bisimulation $\mathcal{R}$ à la Bravetti $\mathcal{R}$ is also a very weak bisimulation.

For the CCA C_1, C_2 in the following picture we have $C_1 \approx^{vw} C_2$, while $C_1 \not\approx^B C_2$, provided that $\lambda, \mu > 0$, $\lambda \neq \mu$ and $N \neq 0$.

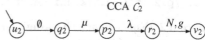

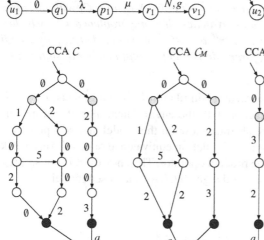

Example 5. Consider CCA C in the picture on the left that originates from linking several simple subsystems via synchronous channels. Each subsystem introduces a certain delay and some nodes are hidden (hidden transitions are denoted by $\emptyset$) whereas others are visible (visible transitions have label $a = \langle N, g \rangle$). CCA C_M is the result of the transformation where vanishing states are melt with their respective successor state. The CTMC C_M that gives the probabilities for condition (V2) in Definition 6 can be obtained by considering only the Markovian transitions of CCA C_M. It holds that $C \approx^{vw} C_M \approx^{vw} C'$ because the probability to reach a dark shaded state within $t > 0$ time units from a light shaded state is equal in all three depicted CCA. This comes from the fact that the underlying CTMCs have the same distribution when considering the time until an absorbing state (the dark shaded state) is entered. All initial states are in same equivalence class, all light shaded states form an equivalence class, all dark shaded states form another class and the states reached via the visible a-transition are in the same class. All remaining states form singletons.   □

For automatic reasoning with CCA in bisimulation framework, one aims at efficient algorithms for checking the equivalence of two finite CCA. Algorithms for checking strong and weak bisimulation equivalence have been proposed by Hermanns [20] for IMCs and can easily be adapted for CCA. These algorithms operate with a partition-splitter technique for computing the bisimulation quotient.

The treatment of very weak bisimulation is more difficult since it requires reasoning about *phase-type distributions* rather than (rates of) exponential distributions. The algorithm for checking $\approx^{vw}$ also relies on a partitioning splitter technique as it is standard for other bisimulation relations. In the sequel, we concentrate only on the rough ideas of a polynomial time algorithm. Several optimizations are possible to obtain a more efficient implementation.

First, vanishing states are replaced by their successor. Let n be the number of all involved states. Then as a preprocessing step for each pair (q, r) of states where q is purely Markovian and r not, the first n moments of the distribution of the time until absorption in r when q is the initial state are computed. This can be done in polynomial time. Since these distributions are uniquely determined by their first n moments during the partition-splitter algorithm the distributions for the time until the backward closure of a certain equivalence class is reached can be checked for equality in an efficient way. For details we refer to the full version which can be found at our website (see http://pi2.informatik.uni-mannheim.de/HomePages/vwolf/cca.ps).

Theorem 2 (Equivalence checking). *Given two finite CCA C_1 and C_2 with the same node-set and over fixed data domain, the equivalence checking problem asking whether "Does $C_1 \cong C_2$ hold?" where $\cong$ is $\sim$, $\approx$, $\approx^B$ or $\approx^{vw}$ can be decided in polynomial time with respect to the total number of transitions and the total number of states in C_1 and C_2.*

We suggest to use Bravetti's notion of weak bisimulation for open models, i.e. models containing ports that require interaction with the environment. For closed models the coarser relation $\approx^{vw}$ gives a more abstract view on the model and still preserves linear-time properties [30]. Unlike weak bisimulation equivalence $\approx$ or $\approx^B$ very weak bisimulation is not a congruence for the product operator. This, however, is not surprising since its definition relies on the view of the given CCA as a closed model.

5 Conclusion

The goal of the paper was to provide an operational model for reasoning about component connectors under stochastic assumptions about the channels and component interfaces. We introduced CCA for this purpose, together with notions of strong and weak bisimulation that are preserved by the composition operators product and hiding. Since the latter are the only operators needed for the compositional generation of (static) networks in the channel-based calculus Reo, our framework fits well in this context and provides the basis for a performance analysis of Reo component connectors. In this paper, we concentrated on the issue of bisimulation relations for CCA. However, since CCA are close to standard stochastic models (such as continuous-time Markov decision processes), also other validation techniques are applicable, such as simulation on the basis of MoDeST [10] or reasoning about expectations [18] or verifying time-bounded reachability properties [7]. Vice versa, our new notion of weak bisimulation equivalence $\approx^{vw}$ can also be helpful for reasoning about IMCs and similar stochastic models.

References

1. F. Arbab. Abstract behavior types: A foundation model for components and their composition. In *[15]*, pages 33–70, 2003.
2. F. Arbab. Reo: A channel-based coordination model for component composition. *Mathematical Structures in Computer Science*, 14(3):1–38, 2004.
3. F. Arbab, C. Baier, F. de Boer, and J. Rutten. Models and temporal logics for timed component connectors. In *Proc. SEFM'04*. IEEE CS Press, 2004.
4. F. Arbab, C. Baier, J.J.M.M. Rutten, and M. Sirjani. Modeling component connectors in reo by constraint automata. *Science of Computer Programming*, special issue on Foundations of Coordination Languages and Software Architectures (to appear), 2005.
5. F. Arbab and J.J.M.M. Rutten. A coinductive calculus of component connectors. In *Proc. WADT 2002*, volume 2755 of *LNCS*, pages 35–56, 2003.
6. C. Baier. Probabilistic models for reo connector circuits. *Journal of Universal Computer Science*, 11(10):1718–1748, 2005.

7. C. Baier, B. Haverkort, H. Hermanns, and J.-P. Katoen. Efficient computation of time-bounded reachability probabilities in uniform continuous-time markov decision processes. In *Proc. TACAS*, volume 2988 of *Lecture Notes in Computer Science*, pages 61–76, 2004. Full version to appear in Theoretical Computer Science.
8. C. Baier, H. Hermanns, J.-P. Katoen, and V. Wolf. Comparative branching time semantics for Markov chains. In *Proc. CONCUR 2003*, number 2761 in LNCS, pages 492–507, 2003. Full version to appear in Information and Computation.
9. M. Bernardo and R. Gorrieri. Extended Markovian process algebra. In *Proc. CONCUR 1996*, number 1119 in LNCS, pages 315–330. Springer, 1996.
10. H. Bohnenkamp, H. Hermanns, J.-P. Katoen, and R. Klaren. The modest modeling tool and its implementation. *Computer Performance Evaluation/TOOLS*, pages 116–133, 2003.
11. M. Bravetti. Revisiting interactive Markov chains. In *Proc. Models for Time-Critical Systems*, volume 68(5) of *Electr. Notes Theor. Comput. Sci.*, 2003.
12. P. Buchholz. Exact and ordinary lumpability in finite markov chains. *Journal of Applied Probability*, 31:59–75, 1994.
13. P. Ciancarini. Coordination models and languages as software integrators. *ACM Comput. Surv.*, 28(2):300–302, 1996.
14. D. Clarke, D. Costa, and F. Arbab. Modeling coordination in biological systems. In *Proc. of the Int. Symposium on Leveraging Applications of Formal Methods (ISoLA 2004)*, 2004.
15. F.S. de Boer, M.M. Bonsangue, S. Graf, and W.-P. de Roever, editors. *Formal Methods for Components and Objects*, volume 2852 of *LNCS*. Springer, 2003.
16. A. Di Pierro, C. Hankin, and H. Wiklicky. Continuous-time probabilistic klaim. *Electr. Notes Theor. Comput. Sci.*, 128(5):27–38, 2005.
17. N. Diakov and F. Arbab. Compositional construction of web services using Reo. In *Proc. International Workshop on Web Services: Modeling, Architecture and Infrastructure (ICEIS 2004), Porto, Portugal, April 13-14*, 2004.
18. E. Feinberg. Continuous time discounted jump markov decision processes: A discrete-event approach. *Math. Oper. Res.*, 29(3):492–524, 2004.
19. D. Gelernter and N. Carriero. Coordination languages and their significance. *Commun. ACM*, 35(2):97–107, 1992.
20. H. Hermanns. *Interactive Markov Chains*, volume 2428 of *Lecture Notes in Computer Science*. Springer Verlag, 2002.
21. J. Hillston. *A compositional approach to performance modelling*. Cambridge University Press, 1996.
22. J. G. Kemeny, J. L. Snell, and A. W. Knapp. *Denumerable Markov Chains*. D. Van Nostrand Co., Princeton, NJ, USA, 1966.
23. R. Milner. *Communication and Concurrency*. Prentice Hall International Series in Computer Science. Prentice Hall, 1989.
24. O. Nierstrasz, S. Gibbs, and D. Tsichritzis. Component-oriented software development. *Commun. ACM*, 35(9):160–165, 1992.
25. A. Omicini, F. Zambonelli, M. Klusch, and R. Tolksdorf, editors. *Coordination of Internet Agents: Models, Technologies, and Applications*. Springer, 2001.
26. P. Panangaden. Measure and probability for concurrency theorists. *Theoretical Computer Science*, 253(2):287–309, 2001.
27. Corrado Priami. Stochastic pi-calculus. *Comput. J.*, 38(7):578–589, 1995.
28. M. L. Puterman. *Markov Decision Processes—Discrete Stochastic Dynamic Programming*. John Wiley & Sons, Inc., New York, 1994.
29. J.J.M.M. Rutten. Component connectors. In *[?]*, chapter 5, pages 73–87. Oxford University Press, 2004.
30. V. Wolf, C. Baier, and M. Majster-Cederbaum. Trace semantics for stochastic systems with nondeterminism. In *Proc. QAPL*, 2006. to appear.

Atomic Commit and Negotiation in Service Oriented Computing[*]

Laura Bocchi[1] and Roberto Lucchi[2]

[1] Department of Computer Science, University of Leicester
University Road, Leicester LE1 7RH, UK
bocchi@mcs.le.ac.uk
[2] Dipartimento di Science dell'Informazione, University of Bologna
Mura Anteo Zamboni 7, 40127 Bologna, Italy
lucchi@cs.unibo.it

Abstract. In this paper we investigate the relationship between two problems, related to distributed systems, that are of particular interest in the context of Service Oriented Computing: atomic commit and negotiation. We will show that there exists a rather strict interdependency between the two problems by discussing how negotiation could be expressed as an instance of the atomic commit problem, and vice versa. To this end we exploit the Contract Net Protocol, a well known negotiation protocol, that will be described by means of the asynchronous pi calculus (Pi-CNP). Besides modeling CNP we also formally describe some basic properties of the CNP protocol.

1 Introduction

Distributed state synchronization is a general problem concerning Service Oriented Computing (SOC). Specifically, in the Web Services scenario some recent efforts addressed the states synchronization of distributed participants. Some examples are the Tentative Hold Protocol (THP) [1], the Business Transaction Protocol (BTP) [2], and WS-Transaction [3]. These protocols rule the enactment of a multi-step interaction among a number of participants, in order to achieve an agreement on the outcome of the distributed transaction. In order to address the requirements of real e-business scenarios over the Web a number of challenges come into play. A key challenge consists of supporting the dynamic automated composition of Web services, for example through the definition of protocols that support negotiation activities.

These issues present analogies with the notion, well known in the context of Multi Agent Systems, of distributed problem solving. In a scenario of distributed problem solving some knowledge-sources (KS) have to find a cooperative solution to a problem, in a decentralized way. Each knowledge source is not able to autonomously achieve the solution; the problem is decomposed in sub-tasks that are delegated to some other KSs. A KS can decompose the assigned task

---

[*] Research partially funded by EU Integrated Project Sensoria, contract n. 016004.

P. Ciancarini and H. Wiklicky (Eds.): COORDINATION 2006, LNCS 4038, pp. 16–27, 2006.
© Springer-Verlag Berlin Heidelberg 2006

in further sub-tasks. [4, 5] discuss the relationship between negotiation and distributed problem solving and propose the Contract Net Protocol as a solution to distributed problem solving.

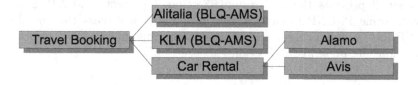

Fig. 1. A usage scenario involving negotiation activities

The following scenario shows how CNP is used to negotiate a contract amongst a travel agent and flight/cars providers: (1) the initiator sends a *call for proposal* (CFP) to many potential contractors, (2) the initiator awaits for proposals for a certain amount of time, (3) the initiator chooses a number of bids to award. Participants can subcontract. Figure 1 illustrates the usage scenario involving negotiation activities of a travel booking service (e.g., on the Web Service Architecture) that encloses multiple distributed and inter-organizational transactions. *Travel Booking* tries to book different alternative flights and to rent a car. *Travel Booking* succeeds if at least one of the airlines has available flights. Car rental is not necessary. In case both airlines have available flights, *Travel Booking* commits and rejects the reservation of the most expensive flight. The example underlines also the possibility for a service (e.g., the Car Rental) of engaging sub-services (e.g, single car rental companies) in order to satisfy a request (i.e., sub-contracting).

BTP and WS-transactions also address similar issues. For instance BTP introduces *cohesions* [6] to address use cases involving a negotiation on the particular service provided by each participant. BTP supports two types of transaction: *atoms* and *cohesions*. Atoms are a loosely coupled version of the classic ACID transaction: it commits only if and only if all its sub-entities commit. Atoms are representable as instances of atomic commit [7]. The atomic commit is a well known problem addressing the agreement of a number of distributed participants (distributed consensus) to achieve a global outcome, typically commit or abort. With cohesions the consensus is no longer required. A cohesion can decide to commit even if some of its sub-entities are unable to commit. Furthermore in case of commit, a cohesion can decide to reject the commitment of some of its sub-entities, causing their failure.

Contribution and Content. The main contribution of this work is the formal investigation, based on the pi calculus [8], of the inter-dependencies between the negotiation and atomic commit problems. In particular, we present an implementation of CNP with the asynchronous pi calculus, namely Pi-CNP, for which we prove some basic properties. We also study how to solve the atomic commit problem by means of Pi-CNP and how to express a negotiation of Pi-CNP by composing a number of generic solutions to the atomic commit problem.

The pi calculus is a message-based formalism and is natural for the representation and formal analysis of distributed protocols, that are also based upon message exchange in a distributed setting. Moreover this choice implies a straightforward implementation with Web service languages.

Section 2 presents the background. Section 3 presents Pi-CNP. Section 4 presents some Pi-CNP properties. Sections 5 and 6 discuss the encoding of Pi-CNP into atomic commit and of atomic commit into Pi-CNP respectively. Conclusions are presented in Section 7.

2   Background

The present section discusses the basics concepts that are used in the rest of this paper. Section 2.1 gives an overview of CNP. Section 2.2 gives an overview on the asynchronous pi calculus, that is used in Section 3 to model CNP. Section 2.3 presents a pi calculus based high level semantic for the atomic commit, that is used in Section 5 and Section 6 to compare atomic commit and CNP basing of their representations with the pi calculus.

2.1   Bidding Negotiation: The CNP

Negotiation is '*a discussion in which the interested parties exchange information and come to an agreement*' [4]. In the most general significance the *discussion* is a process involving parties that can be either human or software agents. In [9] negotiation is described by means of a number of orthogonal issues:

protocol the pattern of information exchange between the parties,
strategy the evaluation rules to decide whether to sign an agreement,
objects description the description of the objects that have to be sold/bought.

The protocol has to be known and applied by all the parties in order to perform a correct conversation. On the contrary a strategy is embodied within each single party; the evaluation is done according to a single party's perspective. In this work we put the focus on a classic protocol for bidding negotiation, namely CNP [5]. The interaction between agents involved in a CNP has been described by the Foundation for Intelligent Physical Agents (FIPA) [10] by means of the following steps: (1) the Initiator sends a CFP, (2) each Participant reviews the received CFP's (possibly from different initiators) and bids (i.e., sends a proposal) on the feasible ones accordingly, (3) the Initiator chooses the best bid and awards the Contract to the respective Participant, (4) the Initiator rejects the other bids.

Time is a relevant aspect to consider when implementing a CNP; [11] proposes a meta-model for CNP (i.e., the Time-Bounded Negotiation Framework), describing three different variants: the Nothing-Guaranteed Protocol (NGP) where the bidder does not give any grant about the future availability of its proposal (i.e., the grant holds for an interval $t = 0$), the Acceptance-Guaranteed Protocol (AGP) where the bidder is forced to keep its proposal available until it receives a notification (i.e., $t = \infty$) and the Finite-Time Guarantee Protocol (FGP) where the proposal is valid just for a certain period of time. In this paper we take into account the AGP. A further discussion about the relation of atomic commit with the other two approaches is left as a future work. We assume that, once the initiator takes a decision, all the parties have to respect it.

2.2 An Overview of the Asynchronous Pi Calculus

The asynchronous pi calculus assumes distributed entities called *processes* which exchange messages over channels, named $u, v, \ldots, z$. The content of a message is also a channel name. A process can send a message z along a channel u with the non-blocking output action $\overline{u}\, z$. A process can also receive a message on channel u with the blocking input action $u(v).P$. The parallel execution of two processes P and Q can be expressed as $P \mid Q$. Parallel processes can communicate by performing an input and an output action on the same channel. Communication along u is described by the reaction $\overline{u}\, z \mid u(v).P \xrightarrow{\tau} P\{z/v\}$. Its effects are visible to the receiver as name substitution of the actual parameter z for the formal parameter v. The continuation P of the input process can be executed after the input on u has been received. In the polyadic pi calculus a message is a string of names $\tilde{v}$ instead of a single name v. The process $\nu u.P$ declare a local variable u with scope P. The process $P + P$ represents the choice, $!P$ can create an arbitrary number of copies of P. The pi calculus is summarized in Table 1:

Table 1. The asynchronous pi calculus

Terms P in the asynchronous pi calculus are as follows. In $u(\tilde{x})$ the names $\tilde{x}$ are bound, as is x in $\nu x.P$. We identify terms up to alpha-renaming of bound names.

$$P \quad ::= \quad 0 \quad \mid \quad \overline{u}\,\tilde{x} \quad \mid \quad u(\tilde{x}).P \quad \mid \quad P|P \quad \mid \quad \nu x.P \quad \mid \quad P + P \quad \mid \quad !P$$

Labelled transitions are as follows, where labels μ range over $u(\tilde{x})$, $\nu \tilde{z}.\overline{u}\,\tilde{x}$ and τ. Symmetrical rules for (SUM), (PAR), and (COM) are omitted.

$$\overline{u}\,\tilde{x} \xrightarrow{\overline{u}\,\tilde{x}} 0 \quad \text{(OUT)} \qquad u(\tilde{x}).P \xrightarrow{u(\tilde{x})} P \quad \text{(IN)} \qquad \frac{P \xrightarrow{\mu} P'}{P + Q \xrightarrow{\mu} P'} \quad \text{(SUM)} \qquad \frac{Q \xrightarrow{\mu} Q'}{P + Q \xrightarrow{\mu} Q'} \quad \text{(SUM)}$$

$$\frac{P \xrightarrow{\mu} P'}{!P \xrightarrow{\mu} P' \,|\, !P} \quad \text{(REP)} \qquad \frac{P \xrightarrow{\mu} P' \quad x \notin \mu}{\nu x.P \xrightarrow{\mu} \nu x.P'} \quad \text{(RES)} \qquad \frac{P \xrightarrow{\nu \tilde{z}.\overline{u}\,\tilde{y}} P' \quad x \neq u, x \in \tilde{y} \backslash \tilde{z}}{\nu x.P \xrightarrow{\nu \tilde{z}x.\overline{u}\,\tilde{y}} P'} \quad \text{(OPEN)}$$

$$\frac{P \xrightarrow{\mu} P' \quad \mathrm{bn}(\mu) \cap \mathrm{fn}(Q) = \emptyset}{P \mid Q \xrightarrow{\mu} P' \mid Q} \quad \text{(PAR)} \qquad \frac{P \xrightarrow{\nu \tilde{z}.\overline{u}\,\tilde{y}} P' \quad Q \xrightarrow{u(\tilde{x})} Q' \quad \tilde{z} \cap \mathrm{fn}(Q) = \emptyset}{P \mid Q \xrightarrow{\tau} \nu \tilde{z}.(P' \mid Q'\{\tilde{y}/\tilde{x}\})} \quad \text{(COM)}$$

Simulation is as follows. We write $\overset{\tau}{\Rightarrow}$ for $\xrightarrow{\tau}{}^{*}$, and $\overset{\mu}{\Rightarrow}$ for $\xrightarrow{\tau}{}^{*}\xrightarrow{\mu}\xrightarrow{\tau}{}^{*}$ when $\mu \neq \tau$, and $P \overset{\mu}{\Rightarrow}$ for $\exists P' : P \overset{\mu}{\Rightarrow} P'$. A symmetric relation S is a *weak ground simulation* if whenever PSQ then $P \xrightarrow{\mu} P'$ implies there exists Q' such that $Q \overset{\mu}{\Rightarrow} Q'$ and $P'SQ'$.

Write $\lesssim$ for the largest ground simulation. Write $\approx$ for the largest ground bisimulation (S is a *weak ground bisimulation*, if both S and S^{-1} are weak ground simulations).

---

labelled transitions define the possible reactions of a process. *Simulation* is a relation characterizing when two processes have the same behavior.

We write $\tilde{x}_C$ for an arbitrary sequence $x_1, \ldots, x_n$ of the elements in set C. The external choice is $P \oplus Q = \nu c.(\overline{c} \,|\, c.P \,|\, c.Q)$. We use the shorthand $x[P,Q] = \nu u, v.(\overline{x}\, u, v \,|\, u.P \,|\, v.Q)$ with u, v fresh, $\overline{x}\,\text{left} = x(u,v).\overline{u}$ and $\overline{x}\,\text{right} = x(u,v).\overline{v}$.

2.3   The Atomic Commit

The generic problem of atomic commit can be described by the following scenario. Let us consider a transaction that is distributed across n parties. Each party executes some local computation and eventually reaches a state in which it is either able or unable to commit. The parties have to enact some protocol to agree on the outcome (i.e., either commit or abort). It is assumed that a party can not pass from an unable state to an able one; if at least one party is unable, then the transaction must abort.

In this paper we use a particular formulation of the atomic commit proposed in [12], that presents an analogy between the problem of atomic commit and the synchronous rendezvous of process calculi. In particular the basic rendezvous mechanism *itself* is already a special case of atomic commit between two parties. Since the problem of the atomic commit typically involves n parties, it is introduced a multi-parties rendezvous: $\overline{u} \,|\, \overline{v} \,|\, \overline{w} \,|\, u()\wedge v()\wedge w().P \rightarrow P$. We use the notation $u(x)\wedge v(y)\wedge w(z).P$ to refer, at a high level, the atomic commit among the parties u, v, z. The generic solution to the atomic commit is expressed as an implementation of the higher level description that follows. The high level description has been achieved in [12] by enabling only the transitions where a certain set of properties defined in literature, that atomic commit protocols guarantee, hold.

The protocol is defined as a set of states with transitions $\rightarrow$ among them. The transitions might correspond to transmission and receipt of a message, or an instance of failure. All the possible states are partitioned into the following disjoint and exhaustive partitions. Write (x,y) for a state where x parties have committed and y aborted. Let i, j range over $1 \ldots N{-}1$. A state $(x,y)w$ denotes a case in which all the parties are able to commit (willing) and $(x,y)u$ the case in which at least one party is unable (unwilling). The properties defined in literature, characterizing atomic commit protocols, have been used in [12] to define the high level semantic for correct atomic commit protocols that follows:

Theorem 1 (Correctness). *A transition system* $(P, \rightarrow, \downarrow)$ *is an atomic commit protocol iff it is bisimilar to the following diagram (where $\Rightarrow$ refers to one or more moves $\rightarrow$):*

$$
\begin{array}{ccc}
(0,0)w & & (0,0)u \\
\Downarrow \searrow & & \Downarrow \\
(N,0)w \quad (0,N)w & & (0,N)u
\end{array}
$$

Theorem 1, proved in [12], is used in Section 5 to prove that the encoding of atomic commit with Pi-CNP is correct.

3   Negotiation and the Pi-CNP

In this section we model CNP with the asynchronous pi calculus. Each instance of the protocol has one initiator I that involves a number of bidders. Each bidder can possibly subcontract. The whole interaction can be represented by a tree structure. Let $\mathcal{I}$ be the set of participants to the negotiation. The tree-like hierarchy of these transactions is denoted by a relation $\text{par}: \mathcal{I} \mapsto \mathcal{I}$ which indicates the immediate parent of a transaction; writing $\text{par}^n(i)$ for n applications of the pair function, we assume that if $i = \text{par}^m(j)$ then do not exists n such that $j = \text{par}^n(i)$. Define the set of i's children $C(i) = \{j : \text{par}(j) = i\}$ and the set of i's descendants $D(i) = \{j : \exists n.i = \text{par}^n(j)\}$.

In the initial state T_i already sent its CFP: the identity of the participants $C(i)$ is fixed. Let *Proposals* be the set of possible proposals, where $a \in$ *Proposals* represents a non-proposal. *Proposal* has empty intersection with the channels used in the protocol (i.e., $bn(T_i)$ and $\{ok_i, abort_i, d_i, a_i, v_i\}$).

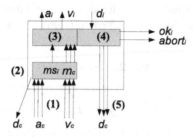

Fig. 2. The usage of the channels from T_i's perspective

The intuition of the channels usage in T_i is summarized in Fig. 2. In **(1)** the children make their proposals: a message along v_c represents a valid proposal, and a message along a_c represents the choice from c not to participate to the agreement (i.e., *non-proposal*). In **(2)** each valid proposal forwarded along m_c. In **(3)** depending on the strategy T_i decides whether it is able to succeeds or not. Success is indicated to the parent over the channel v_i, failure over a_i. **(4)** Eventually the parent will know whether to accept i, or to refuse it. This decision is communicated to i via the 'decision' channel d_i, and so determines i's final state. The transaction i can indicate its final state via the messages $ok_i/abort_i$. **(5)** Finally, the decision is propagated to all the children c along the channels $\tilde{d}_{C(i)}$. The accepted children, according to the internal choice strategy, will be told the same decision as i received. The rejected children and the latecomers, will be told to abort/undo regardless.

The problem of defining and managing a specific strategy is not addressed in detail here but, since it induces choices that influence the execution of the protocol, we represent it as a parameter of T_i. A strategy s has the following influences on the protocol execution, where A is the set of bidders that sent a valid proposal:

s.outcome. On the basis of the valid proposals from the children, T_i decides whether to send a proposal or a non-proposal to its parent.

s.children. Decides which valid proposals to include in the agreement.

s.merge. It is the final proposal from T_i to its parent, considering the self-proposal and the proposals of the sub-contractors.

T_i is composed by different processes summarized in Table 3. T_i's children are implemented by $\prod_{c \in C(i)} T_c$ and the self proposal by $\overline{m}_s(x_s)$ with $x_s \in Proposals$.

$Timer^\emptyset_{C(i)}$ receives the votes from all the participants in $C(i)$, that are assumed as non local entities. Its main roles are to convert external messages (i.e., the bids) into internal messages, to manage a deadline for bids arrivals, and to store the valid bidders with a recursive definition of the set A.

$Stop^B_A$ enforces the deadline expiration by triggering $T_i.\mathrm{col}^A$. Latecomers and bidders that sent a non-proposal are not included in A.

$T_i.\mathrm{col}^A$ receives the internal votes and decides, depending on the strategy, embodied in *s.outcome^A*, whether to perform local success (i.e., $T_i.\mathrm{localc}^A$) or local failure (i.e., $T_i.\mathrm{localf}^A$). *s.outcome^A* decides on the basis of the set of children proposals $\tilde{x}_{C(i)}$ and the self-proposal. $\forall c \in C(i)$, if $c \notin A$ then $x_c = a$.

Table 2. The strategy

$$s.outcome^A : \{\mathcal{P}^{|C(i)|+1}\} \to \{T_i.\mathrm{localc}^A, T_i.\mathrm{localf}^A\}$$

$$s.merge^A : (\mathcal{P}^{|C(i)|+1}) \to Proposals \setminus \{a\}$$

$$s.children^A : \{P^{|C(i)|+1}\} \to \mathcal{P}(A).$$

Table 3. The generic Pi-CNP node

$$T_i(s) = \nu \tilde{v}_{C(i)}, \tilde{a}_{C(i)}, \tilde{m}_{C(i)}, ms_i, \tilde{d}_{C(i)}.(\overline{ms}_i(x_s) \mid Timer^\emptyset_{C(i)} \mid \prod_{c \in C(i)} T_c)$$

$$Timer^B_A = \sum_{c \in A}((v_c(x).(\overline{m}_c(x) \mid Timer^B_{A \setminus \{c\}}) + (a_c.Timer^{B \cup \{c\}}_{A \setminus \{c\}}))) \oplus Stop^B_A$$

$$Stop^B_A = T_i.\mathrm{col}^{C(i) \setminus (A \cup B)} \quad \text{with} \quad T_i.\mathrm{col}^A = ms_i(x_s).\tilde{m}_A(\tilde{x}_A).(s.outcome^A)$$

$$T_i.\mathrm{localc}^A = \overline{v}_i(s.merge^A(\tilde{x}_{C(i)}, x_s)) \mid d_i[T_i.\mathrm{ok}^A, T_i.\mathrm{fail}^A]$$

$$T_i.\mathrm{localf}^A = \overline{a}_i \mid T_i.\mathrm{fail}^A$$

$$T_i.\mathrm{ok}^A = \overline{ok}_i \mid \prod_{c \in s.children^A} \overline{d}_c left \mid \prod_{c \in C(i) \setminus s.children^A} \overline{d}_c right$$

$$T_i.\mathrm{fail}^A = \overline{abort}_i \mid \prod_{c \in C(i)} \overline{d}_c right$$

$T_i.\text{localc}^A$ is executed if bids are satisfactory. In this case T_i sends its proposal $v_i(s.merge^A)$ to the parent, and awaits the parent's final verdict along d_i. $s.merge^A$ merges the self-proposal with the sub-contractors proposals.

$T_i.\text{localf}^A$ is executed if the bids do not satisfy T_i. In this case a failure a_i is signaled to i's parent, and $T_i.\text{fail}$ is executed to propagate the refusal to all the children.

$T_i.\text{ok}^A$ manages the achievement of a successful agreement. An arbitrary number of bidders is selected according to the function $s.children^A$ and is notified of the success. All the other participants (latecomers, non-proposal senders, parties rejected by $s.children^A$) are sent a failure message.

$T_i.\text{fail}^A$ notifies the failure of the agreement to all the participants.

The overall tree of transactions is collected in a test harness that we refer to as initiator (I). We suppose the root of the tree is transaction i:

$$I = \nu v_i, a_i, d_i.\left(T_i \mid (v_i(x).(\overline{d}_i left + \overline{d}_i right) + a_i)\right).$$

4   The Properties of Pi-CNP

In this section we illustrate some properties of Pi-CNP: the outcome of a party is persistent (Durability), each party eventually reaches an outcome (Eventuality), and the failure of a party implies the failure of all its sub-contractors (Local Atomicity). Table 4 illustrates the most general representation of the strategy within the protocol: the non deterministic choice of all the possibilities. We considered $T_i(nd)$ in order to prove that the properties hold for each possible strategy. For each possible s we observe that $s.outcome^A \lesssim nd.outcome^A$ and $s.children^A \lesssim nd.children^A$. It follows that $T_i(strategy) \lesssim T_i(nd)$. The properties are illustrated above, together with some lemmas used in the following sections. The proofs, not reported for lack of space are available in [13].

Table 4. Non determinism as the most general strategy

$$nd.outcome^A = T_i.\text{localc}^A \oplus T_i.\text{localf}^A$$

$$nd.children^A = \prod_{c\in A} \overline{d}_c left \oplus \overline{d}_c right$$

Lemma 1. If $C(i) = \emptyset$, then $T_i(nd) \approx (\overline{v}_i \mid d_i[\overline{ok}_i, \overline{abort}_i]) \oplus (\overline{a}_i \mid \overline{abort}_i)$.

Lemma 2.   If $T_i(nd) \xrightarrow{\overline{v}_i} T_i'$ then $T_i' \xrightarrow{d_i left} \nu\tilde{z}.(T_i.\text{ok} \mid P)$ for some P and $T_i' \xrightarrow{d_i right} \nu\tilde{z}.(T_i.\text{fail} \mid Q)$ for some Q.

Theorem 2 (Durability). $I \lesssim \prod_{i\in\mathcal{I}}(\overline{abort}_j \oplus \overline{ok}_j)$.

Theorem 3 (Eventuality). $\forall I : I \Longrightarrow \tau I'$ then, $\forall j \in \mathcal{I}$, then $I' \xrightarrow{\overline{ok}_j}$ or $I' \xrightarrow{\overline{abort}_j}$.

Theorem 4 (Local Atomicity). If $I \xrightarrow{\overline{abort}_i} I'$ then $\not\exists j \in D(i)$ such that $I' \xrightarrow{\overline{ok}_j}$.

5   Expressing Atomic Commit with CNP

In order to express an atomic commit protocol by means of Pi-CNP we define a strategy (see Table 5) for which Pi-CNP satisfies Theorem 1 $ac.outcome^A$ allows a state of local success only if all the children voted a valid proposal before the expiration, local failure otherwise. $ac.children^A$ defines the children either all confirmable or all rejectable depending on the local outcome. In case of local success the transaction can also fail; in this case all the children are rejected. We define $ac.merge^A = x_s$ as the empty message (messages along v_i and a_i are empty signals). Let $I(ac)$ denote an instance of Pi-CNP with the strategy of Table 5. A preliminary lemma and correctness of the encoding are presented below.

Table 5. The strategy for atomic commit

$$ac.outcome^A = \begin{cases} T_i.\mathrm{localc}^{C(i)} \oplus T_i.\mathrm{localf}^{C(i)} & \text{if } A = C(i); \\ T_i.\mathrm{localf}^A & \text{otherwise.} \end{cases}$$

$$ac.children^A = \begin{cases} C(i) & \text{if } ac.outcome^A = T_i.\mathrm{localc}^{C(i)} \oplus T_i.\mathrm{localf}^{C(i)}; \\ \emptyset & \text{otherwise.} \end{cases}$$

Lemma 3. *If $T_i(ac) \overset{\overline{v}_i}{\Longrightarrow} T_i'(ac)$ then $\forall j \in \{i\} \cup D(i)$, $T_i' \mid \overline{d}_i left \overset{\overline{ok}_j}{\Longrightarrow}$.*

Proof. Let us reason by induction on the depth of the level of i.
Base Case. $C(i) = \emptyset$. By Lemma 1, $T_i = (\overline{v}_i \mid d_i[\overline{ok}_i, \overline{abort}_i]) \oplus (\overline{a}_i \mid \overline{abort}_i)$. If a message along v_i was sent, then the left hand term was previously chosen, and $T_i' = d_i[\overline{ok}_i, \overline{abort}_i]$. Trivially $T_i' \mid \overline{d}_i left \overset{\overline{ok}_i}{\Longrightarrow}$.
Inductive Case. If $T_i(ac) \overset{\overline{v}_i}{\Longrightarrow} T_i'(ac)$ then for Lemma 2, $T_i(ac) \mid \overline{d}_i left \Longrightarrow T_i.ok \mid P$. The execution of $T_i.ok$ triggers the output $\overline{ok}_i$ and the messages $\prod_{c \in C(i)} \overline{d}_c left$. $\forall c \in C(i)$, by inductive hypothesis, we have $\forall j \in D(c)$ the outcome $\overline{ok}_j$.

Proposition 1. *$I(ac)$ is an atomic commit protocol.*

Proof sketch. It is sufficient to show that $I(ac)$ is bisimilar to the diagram of Theorem 1 in order to prove that it is an atomic commit protocol. We observe that I(ac) eventually reaches a state in which either all the parties already voted or the deadline expires. In this state, $Timer_{C(i)}^{\emptyset} \to^* \prod_{c \in A} \overline{m}_c(x_c) \mid ms_i.\widetilde{m}_A(x_A).(ac.outcome^A)$ where A is the set of parties for which a valid proposals was received in time. It holds that either $A = C(i)$ or $A \subset C(i)$. We associate $A = C(i)$ to the state $(0,0)w$, and $A \subset C(i)$ to the state $(0,0)u$ of the diagram. Starting from both $(0,0)w$ and $(0,0)u$, a number of τ steps are performed (i.e., $\overline{ms}_i(x_s) \mid \prod_{c \in A} \overline{m}_c(x_c) \mid ms_i.\widetilde{m}_A(x_A).(ac.outcome^A) \to^* ac.outcome^A$) that are also associated to states $(0,0)w$ and $(0,0)u$ respectively.

In $(0,0)u$, $ac.outcome^A = T_i.\text{localf}^A$. The subprocess $T_i.\text{fail}^A$ of $T_i.\text{localf}^A$ enables a message $\overline{abort}_i$ and, for Eventuality (Theorem 3) and Local Atomicity (Theorem 4), all the participants abort: $(0,0)u \Rightarrow (0,N)u$.

In $(0,0)w$, $ac.outcome^{C(i)} = T_i.\text{localc}^{C(i)} \oplus T_i.\text{localf}^{C(i)}$. If $ac.outcome^{C(i)} \to T_i.\text{localf}^{C(i)}$ then $\text{fail}^{C(i)}$ enables a message $\overline{abort}_i$ and, for Eventuality (Theorem 3) and Local Atomicity (Theorem 4), all the participants have to abort (i.e., $(0,0)w \Rightarrow (0,N)w$). If $ac.outcome^{C(i)} \to T_i.\text{localc}^{C(i)}$ then (1) a message along v_i unblocks the process $\overline{d}_i left + \overline{d}_i right$ in the harness, (2) it is possible to execute either $T_i.\text{ok}^{C(i)}$ or $T_i.\text{fail}^{C(i)}$ depending on the parent decision. For Lemma 3, the message $\overline{d}_i left$ assures an outcome $\prod_{j \in D(i)} \overline{ok}_j$, corresponding to the transition $(0,0)w \Rightarrow (N,0)w$. If the message $\overline{d}_i right$ is chosen from the harness, $T_i.\text{fail}^C(i)$ is executed assuring, for Local Atomicity, an outcome $\prod_{j \in D(i)} \overline{abort}_j$ (i.e., $(0,0)w \Rightarrow (0,N)w$).

For Durability (Theorem 2), $(0,N)$ and $(N,0)$ are final states.

6 Expressing CNP with Atomic Commit

In this section we study how to overcome the differences between atomic commit and CNP: votes collection (i.e., atomic commit waits for the vote of all the participants, CNP allows participants to ignore the CFP), outcome achievement and propagation (i.e., atomic commit succeeds if and only if all the votes are successful, CNP does not), vote type (i.e., yes/no vote type of atomic commit versus the CNP proposals).

Votes Collection. A participant to CNP can decide whether to reply or not to a CFP, basing on other possible CFPs received and its own convenience. The initiator waits for proposals until the expiration of a deadline. Atomic commit waits for all the votes. According to [7] atomic commit should consider unreliability (i.e., message loss among the distributed parties and temporary node crash). A solution to the atomic commit should cope with the problem of missing votes due to message loss. In general message loss is overcame with the usage of timers in the wait for votes phase. The case, in CNP, in which a party does not answer to a CFP corresponds, in the essence, to the loss of its vote.

Outcome Achievement and Propagation. We consider a simplified scenario where a proposal can be *yes* or *no*, similarly to the vote of atomic commit. We address generalized proposals later. According to [12], an instance of atomic commit is representable by a generalized rendezvous (e.g., $a_1 \wedge \ldots \wedge a_n.P_n$).

In a negotiation there are different combination of proposals from i's children that may lead to an agreement. We can represent each of these combinations as a set $N(i) \subseteq C(i)$. $N(i)$ encloses all the participants that are required to propose *yes* in a particular combination of proposals. For instance if we need to book a travel including transport and hotel room we can start a negotiation with a flight company, the railway company and a hotel. There are two combinations in this case: (Plane $\wedge$ Hotel) and (Train $\wedge$ Hotel). In [12] this behavior is expressed by mean of a *choice* among instances of atomic commit. For example, writing $p()$ for the plane, $t()$ for the train and $h()$ for the hotel we can have $\overline{p}\,|\overline{h}\,|p()_\wedge h().S_1 + t()_\wedge h().S_2 \rightarrow S_1$ or $\overline{t}\,|\overline{h}\,|p()_\wedge h().S_1 + t()_\wedge h().S_2 \rightarrow S_2$.

Let J_j, with $j \in \{1, \ldots, n\}$, be an instance of atomic commit expressed as multiparty rendezvous. J_j represents a set $N_j(i)$ of necessary votes for i's success. The overall behavior is represented by the choice $J_1 + \ldots + J_n$.

We denote with $A(i) \subseteq N(i)$ the set of confirmed proposals in a particular combination. According to the proposed encoding of negotiation as a choice of atomic commit, we can express a scenario where $N(i) = A(i)$: all the parties in J_j are necessary and accepted.

The possibility that, in case of success, only some of the proposals are confirmed, is expressed by the choice operator. Recalling the example above, $p()_\wedge h() + t()_\wedge h().S_2$, either plane or train is confirmed even if they are both available.

There is a further aspect to consider. A negotiation can commit even if some parties are not available. Let us consider, for instance, the case in which hotel h and plane p are necessary and taxi t is not. We can represent this scenario with two instances of atomic commit: with and without t (i.e., $h_\wedge p_\wedge t + h_\wedge p$). The case in which a necessary party is not eventually confirmed is not represented (e.g., 'book the flight just if there is a free hotel, but do not book the hotel'). This seems a reasonable limitation according to the use cases of the negotiation problem.

The Vote Type. We considered so far a proposal that can have values within a limited set, namely $\{yes, no\}$. Let us extend the set of proposals to a generic set *Proposals*. If *Proposals* is finite, then it is possible to represent the scenario with a number $|Proposals|$ of yes/no-negotiations (i.e., $J_1 + \ldots + J_n$): one for each possible value of *Proposals*. There is no a priori limitation to the cardinality of *Proposals* but to express CNP it is necessary a finite number of values.

The Encoding. Let us consider a negotiation with a set $C(i)$ of participants. Each element of $\mathcal{P}(C(i))$ represents a set of necessary elements in one instance of atomic commit. A negotiation is associated to a subset of $\mathcal{P}(C(i))$. The presence of an unnecessary element i can be described by the repetition of the same set with and without i. The negotiation about a set of values extending the simple set $\{yes, no\}$ is representable by the repetition of $|Proposals|$ protocols on the $\{yes, no\}$ set.

7 Conclusion

We modeled CNP with the asynchronous pi calculus and we illustrated some basic properties. We studied the relationship between CNP and atomic commit. On the one hand we have shown that the atomic commit is a particular case of CNP: a particular strategy exists that allows to satisfy the atomic commit requirements. On the other hand we have shown how the atomic commit can be exploited to implement negotiation protocols, with some limitations. The limitations are: (1) considering atomic commit protocols that address message loss, (2) excluding the case in which a necessary party is not eventually confirmed

(3) defining *Proposals* as a finite set. Furthermore, in a negotiation scenario the choice is a done a posteriori with respect to the votes arrival. We represented it as the non deterministic choice among an a priori planned set of possibilities. Non determinism does not represent the preference among the possibilities. We conclude that: i) negotiation is a wider problem w.r.t. atomic commit, ii) atomic commit, for which a number of solutions have been proposed and implemented, can be exploited to model a meaningful subset of the negotiation features.

We consider this work as a first step towards the definition of a taxonomy of conversation protocols whose aim is to reach a form of multi-party agreement. An ontology, defined on the basis of such a taxonomy, could be used to characterize the different features of business protocols in a machine-readable way, thus enabling the run time enactment of multiparty negotiation protocols in a dynamically reconfigurable scenario.

References

1. Roberts J. and Srinivasan K. Tentative Hold Protocol Part 1: White Paper. http://www.w3.org/TR/tenthold-1/, 2001.
2. OASIS. Business Transaction Protocol. http://www.oasis-open.org/committees/download.php/1184/2002-06-03.BTP_cttee_spec_1.0.pdf, 2002.
3. Cabrera F., Copeland G., Cox B., Freund T., Klein J., Storey T., and Thatte S. Web Services Transaction (WS-Transaction). http://www-106.ibm.com/developerworks/webservices/library/ws-transpec/.
4. Davis R. and Smith R. G. Negotiation as a Metaphor for Distributed Problem Solving. In *Readings in Distributed Artificial Intelligence*, pages 333–356. Morgan Kaufmann Publishers Inc., 1988.
5. Smith R. G. The Contract Net Protocol: High-Level Communication and Control in a Distributed Problem Solver. In *Readings in Distributed Artificial Intelligence*, pages 357–366. Morgan Kaufmann Publishers Inc., 1988.
6. Dalal S., Temel S., Little M., Potts M., and Webber J. Storey T. Coordinating Business Transactions on the Web. *IEEE Internet Computing*, 7(1):30–39, 2003.
7. Hadzilacos V. On the Relationship Between the Atomic Commitment and Consensus Problems. In B. Simons and A.Z. Spector, editors, *Fault Tolerant Distributed Computing*, volume 448 of *Lecture Notes in Computer Science*, pages 201–208. Springer-Verlag, 1990.
8. Milner R. *Communicating and Mobile Systems: the Pi-Calculus*. Cambridge University Press, 1989.
9. Jennings N. R., Parsons, S., Sierra C., and Faratin P. Automated Negotiation. In *Proceedings of 5th Int Conf. on Practical Application of Intelligent Agents and Multi-Agent Systems (PAAM-2000)*, pages 23–30, 2000.
10. FIPA. *FIPA Contract Net Interaction Protocol Specification*. FIPA, 2001.
11. Lee K. J. and Chang Y. S. Time-Bounded Negation Framework for Multi-Agent Coordination. In *Selected papers from the First Pacific Rim International Workshop on Multi-Agents, Multiagent Platforms*, pages 61–75. Springer-Verlag, 1999.
12. Bocchi L. and Wischik L. A Process Calculus of Atomic Commit. *Electronic Notes in Theoretical Computer Science*, 105:119–132, 2004.
13. Bocchi L., Ciancarini P., and Lucchi R. Atomic Commit and Negotiation in Service Oriented Computing. Technical Report UBLCS-2005-16, University of Bologna, Italy, 2005. ftp://ftp.cs.unibo.it/pub/techreports/2005/2005-16.pdf.

Synthesizing Concurrency Control Components from Process Algebraic Specifications

Edoardo Bontà[1], Marco Bernardo[1], Jeff Magee[2], and Jeff Kramer[2]

[1] Istituto di Scienze e Tecnologie dell'Informazione,
Università di Urbino
[2] Department of Computing, Imperial College London

Abstract. Process algebraic specifications can provide useful support for the architectural design of software systems due to the possibility of analyzing their properties. In addition to that, such specifications can be exploited to guide the generation of code. What is needed at this level is a general methodology that accompanies the translation process, which in particular should help understanding whether and when it is more appropriate to implement a software component as a thread or as a monitor. The objective of this paper is to develop a systematic approach to the synthesis of correctly coordinating monitors from arbitrary process algebraic specifications that satisfy some suitable constraints. The whole approach will be illustrated by means of the process algebraic specification of a cruise control system.

1 Introduction

Although process algebras were originally conceived as a means for producing abstract views of concurrent programs and reasoning about their properties [13,9,3], due to their compositional nature it was soon realized their adequacy for modeling complex systems [6]. More recently process algebras have been integrated within the software architecture design level [14,15], because they provide support for the early assessment of the gross system properties. This has resulted in a family of process algebraic ADLs, for which several techniques based on equivalence checking have been developed for the component-oriented verification and diagnosis of architectural mismatch freedom [2,12,11,10,7,1].

At the software architecture design level, process algebras have turned out to be useful also for code generation purposes. In [12] it is shown how a disciplined process algebraic modeling is beneficial at subsequent stages for guiding the implementation of Java software. In [4,5] an automatic code generator is presented, which translates process algebraic architectural descriptions into multithreaded Java programs on the basis of a transparent Java package called Sync that ensures the correct thread synchronization.

In a process algebraic description, the behavior of a software component is specified through a sequence of action-based equations, which define possibly alternative execution traces composed of local actions and actions interacting with other components. In this framework two natural candidates for the target

P. Ciancarini and H. Wiklicky (Eds.): COORDINATION 2006, LNCS 4038, pp. 28–43, 2006.

of the translation of the process algebraic description of a component are a thread and a monitor.

What is needed at this level is a general methodology that accompanies the translation process, which in particular should help understanding whether and when it is more appropriate to implement a software component as a thread or as a monitor. This would overcome some limitations that are present in the current process algebraic approaches. With respect to [12] generality would be gained, as it would become possible to undertake the translation of arbitrary process algebraic descriptions. With respect to [4, 5], where only threads are taken into account, the performance of the generated code may be improved thanks to the synthesis of monitors as they would reduce the thread context switch frequency. Moreover the presence of monitors would result in a lightweight concurrency control management with respect to package Sync, with the monitors themselves constituting explicit coordination areas that were not available before to the developer adopting the approach of [4, 5].

The objective of this paper is to develop a systematic approach to the synthesis of correctly coordinating Java monitors from arbitrary process algebraic component descriptions that satisfy some suitable constraints. The constraints are related to the fact that a monitor is a passive entity, which typically encapsulates data in a way that guarantees a mutually exclusive access. In other words, a monitor coordinates the access of the threads to its methods, but its statements are executed by the entering threads. As we shall see, in order to enforce a correct concurrency control when using a monitor, it is sufficient that a thread taking the control of the monitor can perform neither interacting actions nor infinitely many local actions while inside the monitor.

Once these constraints are satisfied, the process algebraic description of a component can systematically be transformed into a canonical form that we call monitor normal form, from which it is easy to synthesize a Java monitor. The constraints and the approach will be illustrated by means of the process algebraic specification of a cruise control system taken from [12], which will be used as a running example throughout the paper.

This paper is organized as follows. In Sect. 2 we present the constraints that guarantee the derivability of a monitor from a process algebraic component description. In Sect. 3 we show how to transform into monitor normal form a process algebraic component description that satisfies all the constraints. In Sect. 4 we describe how to synthesize a Java monitor from a monitor normal form. Finally, in Sect. 5 we provide some remarks on related and future work.

2   Monitor Constraints

In this section we present a set of constraints under which it is possible to synthesize a correctly coordinating monitor from the process algebraic description of a software component. Before doing so, we introduce some terminology and we recall the way in which threads and monitors interact with each other in an object-oriented language like Java.

2.1 Terminology

In our process algebraic view, both thread and monitor classes should be modeled as architectural element types [1]. An architectural element type representing a Java class that extends or implements a thread base class will be called *native-thread type* and will be translated into a *native-thread component*. An architectural element type representing a Java monitor class will instead be called *monitor type* and will be translated into a *monitor component*.

Furthermore, we distinguish between two kinds of interacting actions, which we simply call interactions from now on. An *active-control interaction* is performed by an architectural element whenever it starts communicating with another architectural element. A *passive-control interaction* is executed by an architectural element whenever it is waiting for another architectural element to start communicating with it. In particular the entry points (and hence implicitly the exit points) of the monitor types will be described through passive-control interactions.

2.2 Thread-Monitor Interaction

Given a native-thread component T and a monitor component M, the interaction between them takes place by means of the component control switch depicted in the sequence diagram of Fig. 1. When T intends to interact with M, T invokes a synchronized method of M – which corresponds to performing an active-control interaction – so that the thread t leaves T and waits until M is ready to interact.

More precisely, in a synchronous model t waits outside M if another thread is currently running inside M, otherwise it immediately enters M and possibly blocks, which happens when t has to wait for a notification related to a condition synchronization of M that does not hold upon entering M. In an asynchronous model, instead, an exception is raised if a condition synchronization for t does not hold and either there is no thread running inside M or the thread currently running inside M leaves it without notifying such a condition synchronization. We recall from [12] that a condition synchronization permits a monitor to block threads until a particular condition holds, such as e.g. a count becoming non-zero, a buffer becoming empty, or new input becoming available.

When M is ready, t takes its control and executes a sequence of statements of M corresponding to local actions, at the end of which t possibly notifies one of the threads blocked inside M about the validity of a condition synchronization and leaves the monitor. The end of such a statement sequence coincides either with the monitor termination or with the execution of the last local action before a passive-control interaction.

In order to achieve a correct concurrency control, it suffices that the thread taking the control of the monitor executes finitely many statements without moving to another monitor or invoking a method of another thread before leaving the monitor in which it is running[1]. In this way a thread will stay within the monitor for a finite amount of time (up to possible condition synchronizations

---

[1] Note that this does not prevent the monitor from invoking methods of the Java library and creating new non-thread objects.

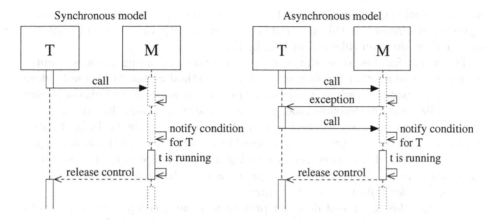

Fig. 1. Component control switch from native-thread T to monitor M

that will never hold), and will not cause any interference between the monitor and other monitors.

From the considerations above, we derive that the avoidance of (i) endless executions of local actions and (ii) active-control interactions guarantees that a correctly coordinating monitor can be obtained from the process algebraic specification of a component. For the sake of completeness, a third technical constraint, related to the avoidance of (iii) non-disjoint hybrid choices between sets of local actions and sets of interactions, must be satisfied.

2.3   Constraint 1: No Endless Executions of Local Actions

Since a monitor is a passive entity that coordinates other components, it is desirable that a thread taking the control of the monitor runs inside the monitor only for a finite amount of time. In the worst case, it may happen that the thread blocks forever inside the monitor because of a condition synchronization that will never hold. However, this does not prevent other threads from entering the monitor and running.

In order to achieve finiteness, we need to enforce that the maximum number of consecutive local actions that can be performed inside a candidate monitor type is finite. This can easily be checked on the process algebraic description of a candidate monitor type by verifying the absence of cycles of local actions.

As we shall see in Sect. 4, each local action will be translated into a method to be manually filled in later on. If we adhere to the guidelines of [5], according to which non-terminating statements should be avoided within these methods, a finite sequence of local actions will be executed in a finite amount of time. In this way the absence of cycles of local actions proved at the process algebraic level is guaranteed to be preserved at the Java code level.

2.4   Constraint 2: No Active-Control Interactions

A monitor coordinates other components but should not invoke methods of other monitors or threads. Therefore, a candidate monitor type should not possess any active-control interaction. This can trivially be verified at the level of the process algebraic description if this is suitably annotated with information about the control flow direction (like e.g. in PADL [1]).

The reason for this constraint is to prevent a thread running inside a monitor from moving to another monitor or invoking a method of another thread before finishing its execution within the monitor in which it is running. This constraint thus implies that interferences among monitors are avoided and that any monitor component can passively interact only with thread components. In particular, deadlock cannot occur because of a possible invocation of methods belonging to the same thread that is currently running inside the monitor. Moreover, this constraint ensures, together with the previous one, that a thread runs inside a monitor only for a finite amount of time.

Note that this constraint does not prevent a monitor component from invoking methods of the Java library and creating new non-thread objects. In fact, the methods translating the local actions of the monitor component are free to create local objects and to interact with them. However, this should not alter the topology prescribed by the process algebraic architectural description.

2.5 Constraint 3: No Non-disjoint Hybrid Choices

A *hybrid choice* in the process algebraic description of a component is a choice between a non-empty set of interactions and a non-empty set of local actions. The problem with hybrid choices is that they may hamper the detection of the action sequence corresponding to the statement sequence that should be executed by a thread running inside a monitor.

In fact, recalled that the monitor entry and exit points are described through passive control interactions, to automatically detect the beginning and the end of the action sequence in a candidate monitor type we need that the sequence is comprised between two passive-control interactions. A choice between a passive-control interaction and a local action would make it impossible to decide whether the currently running thread has completed its task or not, unless the two actions are preceded by two disjoint conditions.

As a consequence of this constraint, a candidate monitor type can contain only choices among all interactions or all local actions. This can easily be checked at the process algebraic description level. In addition, hybrid choices are admitted provided that the involved actions are preceded by disjoint boolean conditions, i.e. the logical conjunction of the condition of any involved interaction and the condition of any involved local action must be false.

3   Syntactic Transformation into Monitor Normal Form

Once the three constraints defined in the previous section are satisfied by the process algebraic description of a candidate monitor type, it is possible to proceed to the transformation of the description itself into monitor normal form. Starting from this canonical form, it will be possible to straightforwardly synthesize the Java implementation of the monitor type.

In order to facilitate the derivation of each method of the targeted Java monitor class, a good idea may be to rewrite the process algebraic specification of the monitor type in such a way that all the interacting actions are collected into a single equation. Due to constraint 2, each such interaction is a passive-control one, so if we place all of them at the beginning of a different branch of a choice, we exactly characterize the point at which the monitor is waiting for a thread to take its control.

The process algebraic specification in monitor normal form obtained at the end of the rewriting process will be formed by:

- An *interacting choice equation*, which is composed of a choice in which every branch starts with an interaction possibly followed by local actions only.
- A group of *local equations*, which are original equations of the monitor type that include only local actions.
- A group of *setting equations*, which are the original non-local equations whose branches that have been moved to the interacting choice equation are replaced by an invocation of the latter equation with suitably set parameters.

This monitor normal form can be achieved through a sequence of five steps, which will be exemplified on the process algebraic description of a cruise control system taken from [12].

3.1 Example: A Cruise Control System

An automobile cruise control system is governed by means of three buttons – on, off, and resume – and takes into account two pedals – accelerator and brake. When the engine is running and on is pressed, the cruise control system records the current speed and maintains the car at this speed. When accelerator, brake or off is pressed, the cruise control system disengages but retains the speed setting. If resume is pressed, the system accelerates or de-accelerates the car back to the previously-recorded speed.

The kernel of the cruise control system is provided by a cruise controller, which includes a speed control that is initially disabled. While the latter clears and records the speed setting and, when enabled, sets the throttle according to the current speed and the recorded speed, the behavior of the former is more complex. When the engine is switched on (engineOn), speed clearing is triggered (clearSpeed) and the cruise controller becomes active. When active, pressing on triggers the recording of the current speed (recordSpeed) and enables the speed control (enableControl). The system is then cruising. Pressing on again triggers the recording of the new current speed and the system remains cruising. Pressing off, brake or accelerator disables the speed control (disableControl) and sets the system to standby, from which the system can return to the cruising state whenever resume or on is pressed. Switching the engine off (engineOff) at any time makes the cruise controller inactive and the speed control disabled.

We now provide the FSP specification [12] of the cruise controller:

```
INACTIVE = (engineOn->clearSpeed->
                (engineOff->INACTIVE
                |on->recordSpeed->enableControl->CRUISING
                )
           ),
CRUISING = (engineOff->disableControl->INACTIVE
            |{off,brake,accelerator}->disableControl->STANDBY
            |on->recordSpeed->enableControl->CRUISING
           ),
STANDBY  = (engineOff->INACTIVE
            |resume->enableControl->CRUISING
            |on->recordSpeed->enableControl->CRUISING
           ).
```

where:

- INACTIVE, CRUISING, and STANDBY are the names of the three process algebraic equations that formalize the behavior of the cruise controller.
- engineOn, engineOff, on, off, brake, accelerator, and resume are the interactions.
- clearSpeed, recordSpeed, enableControl, and disableControl are the local actions.
- The symbol "->" is the action prefix operator: $\{a_1, \ldots, a_n\}$ -> P executes an action from the set and then behaves as P.
- The symbol "|" is the choice operator: P_1 | P_2 behaves as either P_1 or P_2.

If engineOn, engineOff, on, off, brake, accelerator, and resume are considered as passive-control interactions, it is not difficult to observe that all the three monitor constraints defined in Sect. 2 are satisfied by the FSP description of the cruise controller.

3.2 Step 1: Rewriting Complex Choices

If the process algebraic specification of a monitor type contains some choices among interactions that are written in an abbreviated notation, such choices must be expanded. Likewise, if the specification contains some nested choices among interactions, such choices must be flattened. By doing so, it will be easier to handle the branches of the choices among interactions as we shall see in the subsequent steps.

In the FSP specification of the cruise controller, the equations INACTIVE and STANDBY do not contain complex choices, while the equation CRUISING contains the abbreviated FSP notation {◁action list▷}, hence it is expanded into:

```
CRUISING = (engineOff->disableControl->INACTIVE
            |off->disableControl->STANDBY
            |brake->disableControl->STANDBY
            |accelerator->disableControl->STANDBY
            |on->recordSpeed->enableControl->CRUISING
           )
```

3.3   Step 2: Splitting the Equations

Since in the interacting choice equation of the monitor normal form any branch must start with an interaction, every interaction or choice among interactions that does not occur at the beginning of the body of an equation must be moved together with what follows it into a new equation. The moved block is replaced in the original equation by an invocation of the new equation. At the end of this splitting process, any interaction will be at the beginning of some equation.

In the FSP specification of the cruise controller, only the first equation needs to be transformed, because in the equations CRUISING and STANDBY all the occurrences of interactions are already at the beginning of some branch. The equation INACTIVE thus becomes:

```
INACTIVE         = (engineOn->clearSpeed->SPLIT_1_INACTIVE),
SPLIT_1_INACTIVE = (engineOff->INACTIVE
                   |on->recordSpeed->enableControl->CRUISING
                   )
```

3.4   Step 3: Building the Interacting Choice Equation

The interacting choice equation can now be built by suitably merging into a single equation the equation body branches that start with an interaction.

In order to preserve the semantics of the original equations of the monitor type, the resulting interacting choice equation needs several parameters representing the current interacting state of the monitor. Such a state can be encoded through the non-local equation (among the ones present at the end of step 2) describing the current behavior – bounded integer parameter eq – and the set of interactions that are currently enabled – boolean parameters g_ representing guards associated with the enabledness of the interactions. Note that parameter eq is strictly necessary because the same set of interactions may be enabled in several different non-local equations. On the other hand, the guards g_ are necessary to decide the branch to be undertaken in the current interacting state and, as we shall see, useful to implement the condition synchronizations.

The body of the interacting choice equation is thus a guarded choice among all the merged equation body branches. In particular, if one of the involved bodies started with a single interaction, the whole body becomes a branch of the interacting choice equation. Instead, if it started with a choice among all interactions, each branch of such a choice becomes a branch of the interacting choice equation. Finally, if it started with a disjoint hybrid choice, only the branches starting with an interaction move to the interacting choice equation[2].

Each branch of the interacting choice equation is preceded by a boolean expression composed of the logical conjunction of: the control that the value of eq corresponds to the value associated with the non-local equation body that contained the considered branch, the guard g_ associated with the first interaction

---

[2] We shall see later on that this does not disrupt the semantics of the disjoint hybrid choice, hence of the original process algebraic specification.

of the branch itself, and other possible conditions inherited from the original branch.

In the FSP specification of the cruise controller, the bodies of the equations INACTIVE, SPLIT_1_INACTIVE, CRUISING, and STANDBY are represented by the values 0, 1, 2, and 3 of parameter eq, respectively, and their branches are merged into the following interacting choice equation:

```
INTER_CH_EQ[eq:0..3]        [g_engineOn:Boolean]    [g_engineOff:Boolean]
          [g_on:Boolean]    [g_off:Boolean]         [g_resume:Boolean]
          [g_brake:Boolean][g_accelerator:Boolean]  =
  (when((eq==0) && g_engineOn)  engineOn->clearSpeed->SPLIT_1_INACTIVE
  |when((eq==1) && g_engineOff)                      engineOff->INACTIVE
  |when((eq==1) && g_on)        on->recordSpeed->enableControl->CRUISING
  |when((eq==2) && g_engineOff)    engineOff->disableControl->INACTIVE
  |when((eq==2) && g_off)                  off->disableControl->STANDBY
  |when((eq==2) && g_brake)              brake->disableControl->STANDBY
  |when((eq==2) && g_accelerator) accelerator->disableControl->STANDBY
  |when((eq==2) && g_on)        on->recordSpeed->enableControl->CRUISING
  |when((eq==3) && g_engineOff)                      engineOff->INACTIVE
  |when((eq==3) && g_resume)       resume->enableControl->CRUISING
  |when((eq==3) && g_on)        on->recordSpeed->enableControl->CRUISING
  )
```

3.5   Step 4: Rewriting Non-local Equations into Setting Equations

The interacting choice equation built in step 3 does not replace the original equations. This refers not only to local equations and equations with disjoint hybrid choices – which are not completely involved in the construction of the interacting choice equation – but also to the other equations, as invocations to them are still around.

The body of each non-local equation is thus rewritten in such a way that its possible local branches are preserved. By contrast, its branches that have been moved to the interacting choice equation are replaced by a single invocation of the latter equation with suitably set actual values for parameters eq and g_. So, we refer to such a rewritten equation as a setting equation.

The actual value of eq passed to the interacting choice equation has to be the value associated with the setting equation body. The actual values of the boolean guards are set as follows. If an interaction does not occur at the beginning of any moved branch of the original non-local equation, then the corresponding guard g_ is set to false. If it occurs instead and at least one of its occurrences was not guarded by any condition in the original branch that contained it, the corresponding guard g_ is set to true. Finally, if it occurs and all of its occurrences were guarded by some condition in the original branches that contained them, the corresponding guard g_ is set to the logical disjunction of these conditions (if at least one of them holds true, then the interaction is enabled).

If an original non-local equation started with a single interaction or a choice among interactions only, its body is entirely replaced by an invocation of the interacting choice equation having the above-mentioned actual values for eq and g_. In the case in which the original equation contained a disjoint hybrid choice, instead, its body preserves all the local branches. The other (interacting) branches, moved together with their conditions to the interacting choice equation, are replaced by a single branch. This branch contains the invocation of the interacting choice equation preceded by the logical disjunction of all the conditions associated with the interacting branches. In this way the semantics of the selection between the group of local branches and the group of interacting branches is preserved, with the selection within the latter group being deferred to the interacting choice equation.

In the FSP specification of the cruise controller, the non-local equations INACTIVE, SPLIT_1_INACTIVE, CRUISING, and STANDBY are rewritten into the following setting equations:

```
INACTIVE =
  INTER_CH_EQ[0] [True] [False][False][False][False][False][False],
SPLIT_1_INACTIVE =
  INTER_CH_EQ[1] [False][True] [True] [False][False][False][False],
CRUISING =
  INTER_CH_EQ[2] [False][True] [True] [True] [False][True] [True],
STANDBY =
  INTER_CH_EQ[3] [False][True] [True] [False][True] [False][False]
```

3.6   Step 5: Rearranging the Interacting Choice Equation

As a final step, the interacting choice equation undergoes to a sorting of its branches as well as to a number of optimizations. On the one hand, the branches are lexicographically sorted on the basis of their guards g_ associated with their starting interactions. The reason is that all the branches starting with the same interaction will be translated into a single synchronized method of a Java monitor class, hence this sorting should facilitate the code generation.

On the other hand, some optimizations are useful to simplify the structure of the interacting choice equation and thus of the monitor to be synthesized. First, if an interaction occurs at the beginning of only one of the branches associated with a same value of eq, in that branch the possible condition inherited from the original branch can be removed. In fact, the same condition is already contained in the guard g_ associated with the considered branch.

Second, if all the branches with the same initial interaction are associated with a single value of eq, the check on eq can be removed from these branches. In fact, this means that the initial interaction was present only in a single non-local equation body of the original specification, and the guard g_ associated with the action can be true only when eq has that value.

Third, if several branches are identical up to their boolean expressions – i.e. checks on different values of eq and possibly other different conditions inherited from the original specification – these branches can be collapsed into a single one. This new branch is preceded by an expression which includes, besides the checks on g_ and the different values that eq can take on, the logical disjunction of the conditions of the collapsed branches. If the interaction occurs only at the beginning of such a new branch, by virtue of the first two optimizations the disjunction of the inherited conditions and the check on eq can be removed.

In the FSP specification of the cruise controller, the second optimization can be applied to the branches starting with engineOn, off, brake, accelerator, and resume. The third optimization can be applied to the branches beginning with engineOff and corresponding to the values 1 and 3 of eq, and to the branches beginning with on and corresponding to the values 1, 2, and 3 of eq. In the latter case the check on the different values of eq can be removed. After applying such optimizations, the interacting choice equation becomes:

```
INTER_CH_EQ[eq:0..3]        [g_engineOn:Boolean]      [g_engineOff:Boolean]
            [g_on:Boolean]    [g_off:Boolean]           [g_resume:Boolean]
            [g_brake:Boolean] [g_accelerator:Boolean]   =
  (when(g_engineOn)                      engineOn->clearSpeed->SPLIT_1_INACTIVE
  |when(g_engineOff && ((eq==1) || (eq==3)))          engineOff->INACTIVE
  |when(g_engineOff && (eq==2))    engineOff->disableControl->INACTIVE
  |when(g_on)                 on->recordSpeed->enableControl->CRUISING
  |when(g_off)                        off->disableControl->STANDBY
  |when(g_brake)                    brake->disableControl->STANDBY
  |when(g_accelerator)        accelerator->disableControl->STANDBY
  |when(g_resume)                  resume->enableControl->CRUISING
  )
```

3.7   Correctness of the Transformation

The syntactic transformation of the process algebraic description of a monitor type into monitor normal form is correct in the following sense.

Theorem 1. *Let M be the process algebraic description of a monitor type and let M' be the process algebraic description of the monitor normal form obtained by applying to M the syntactic transformation. Then the LTS underlying M' is isomorphic to the LTS underlying M.* ∎

4   Monitor Implementation

The application of the steps illustrated in the previous section allows an arbitrary process algebraic description of a monitor type to be rewritten into its semantically equivalent monitor normal form. In this section we show how to synthesize a monitor component as a Java class from a monitor normal form.

In the Java monitor class, the interacting choice equation will be translated into a set of public synchronized methods each corresponding to a different interaction. Instead, the setting and local equations will be translated into non-public methods of the monitor. Finally, the constructor of the Java monitor class will invoke the method corresponding to the first equation of the process algebraic description.

The synthesis of the monitor will be exemplified below by translating into Java code the monitor normal form of the process algebraic description of the cruise controller. This is accomplished through a sequence of four steps, which guide the automated generation of the Java code.

4.1   Translating Local Actions into Stub Class Methods

On the basis of the approach proposed in [5], each local action of the process algebraic description of a monitor type will be synthesized in the Java monitor class as an invocation of a non-completely specified public method of an auxiliary class, which we call *stub class*. In this way the software developer can subsequently fill in the methods associated with the local actions, without any intervention on the main monitor class. The stub class will be instantiated by the constructor of the Java monitor class.

Recalled that the FSP specification of the cruise controller contains the local actions `clearSpeed`, `recordSpeed`, `enableControl`, and `disableControl`, the related Java stub class `LocalActionsController` is synthesized as follows:

```
class LocalActionsController {
  public LocalActionsController() {/* FILL IN THE CONSTRUCTOR BODY */}
  public void clearSpeed()      {/* FILL IN THE METHOD BODY */}
  ...
  public void disableControl()  {/* FILL IN THE METHOD BODY */}
}
```

4.2   Synthesizing the Monitor Class Constructor

The first-executed method of the Java monitor class, i.e. the constructor, is in charge of the instantiation of the stub class for the local actions and of the invocation of the method corresponding to the (local or setting) equation of the monitor normal form associated with the first equation of the original process algebraic description.

Besides the definition of the constructor, at the beginning of the monitor class there is the declaration/definition of some private members. The first private member is an object of the stub class for the local actions that will be instantiated by the constructor. Then, an integer variable `eq` and a boolean array `guard[]` are declared, which translate the parameters of the interacting choice equation, together with the definition of some integer constants associated with the setting equations, which represent the values that `eq` can take on.

Referring to the monitor normal form of the cruise controller, the Java monitor class starts as follows:

```
private LocalActionsController laController;
private int eq;
private boolean guard[];
private final static int INACTIVE        = 0,
                         SPLIT_1_INACTIVE = 1,
                         CRUISING         = 2,
                         STANDBY          = 3;
```

```
public Controller() {
  laController = new LocalActionsController();
  inactive();
}
```

4.3 Translating Setting and Local Equations

The setting and local equations of the monitor normal form are translated into non-public methods of the Java monitor class. Since these equations do not contain interactions, only sequences of/choices among local actions have to be considered during their translation.

While a sequence of local actions can easily be synthesized as a sequence of invocations of the associated stub methods, a choice among local actions has to be treated carefully. In fact, even if the branches of the choice can be guarded by some conditions, it is not necessarily the case that such conditions are disjoint. One possibility is to translate such nondeterministic choices by means of the selection statements provided by Java, with the software developer subsequently removing nondeterminism at the code level. Another possibility is to synthesize a probabilistic mechanism to randomly select a branch whose associated condition holds true. This solution may be appropriate for the implementation of simulation software and randomized concurrent algorithms.

An invocation of a setting or local equation is turned into an invocation of the monitor class method translating the equation itself. Each setting equation contains in turn an invocation of the interacting choice equation, which corresponds to the fact that the thread currently running inside the monitor is on the verge of leaving it. This invocation is translated into a sequence of assignment statements in which eq and guard[] are set to the corresponding actual parameters specified in the invocation. Since before leaving the monitor the thread has to notify the other threads possibly blocked inside the monitor, the assignment statement sequence is followed by an invocation of the Java method notifyAll() to wake up all the threads waiting inside the monitor. The unblocking conditions, which have just been updated by setting guard[], will be handled by the synchronized methods translating the interacting choice equation.

Referring to the monitor normal form of the cruise controller, the translation of the setting equation INACTIVE is implemented as follows:

```
protected synchronized void inactive() {
  eq = INACTIVE;
  guard = new boolean[] {true, false, false, false, false, false, false};
  notifyAll();
}
```

4.4 Translating the Interacting Choice Equation

Any group of branches of the interacting choice equation that start with the same interaction is translated into a public synchronized method of the monitor class.

The resulting methods basically translate the communication of the passive-control interactions of the monitor type with the active-control interactions of native-thread types to which the passive-control ones are attached.

At the beginning of each such method, the boolean guard associated with the related interaction is translated into a condition synchronization statement:

```
while (!<guard>)
  wait();
```

If the boolean guard is true, a thread can enter the monitor without blocking. Otherwise it blocks on the Java method `wait()` until another thread leaves the monitor by setting the guard to true and notifying about this event.

The condition synchronization is implemented in a different way whenever the related interaction is asynchronous. The reason is that in this case, if the condition synchronization is false, an entering thread has to exit the monitor without blocking. This is implemented as follows:

```
if (!<guard>)
  throw new AsyncInteractionNotReadyException();
```

After the condition synchronization, within the method associated with an interaction we have an `if-else` statement, which handles the selection among the branches (starting with the considered interaction) based on the value of `eq`. For those branches sharing the same value of `eq` a nested selection statement is necessary, which is based on inherited conditions.

Referring to the monitor normal form of the cruise controller, the branches of the interacting choice equations starting with `engineOff` are translated into the following method (index 1 of `guard[]` is associated with `engineOff`):

```
public synchronized void engineOff()
    throws AsyncInteractionNotReadyException {
  if (!guard[1])
    throw new AsyncInteractionNotReadyException();
  if ((eq == SPLIT_1_INACTIVE) || (eq == STANDBY))
    inactive();
  else /* if (eq == CRUISING) */ {
    laController.disableControl();
    inactive();
  }
}
```

5   Conclusion

In this paper we have addressed the problem of synthesizing concurrency control components, in the form of Java monitor classes, from arbitrary process algebraic specifications. The problem of synthesizing Java monitors has been previously addressed in [16, 8] outside the process algebra field.

In [16] a tool equipped with a model checker automatically generates Java monitor classes from monitor descriptions written in Action Language. The correctness of the synchronization and of the behavior of the generated Java monitor is guaranteed by construction, independently of the context of the monitor description. Unlike our approach, this approach requires that the monitor description conforms a priori to a specific monitor template.

In [8] implementations of synchronization policies are generated in Java through synchronized methods and lock objects. While in the previously described approaches the generated Java monitors are obtained from formal specifications and are correct by construction, in this approach the code is generated from critical regions delimited by the developer with high-level synchronization directives and the correctness of the implemented synchronization policies is verified at the code level via model checking.

For the future we plan to conduct further investigations on the monitor constraints, in particular with respect to specific contexts, and to develop a tool – to be hopefully integrated inside the automatic code generator PADL2Java [4, 5] – that synthesizes a Java monitor class from any process algebraic specification that satisfies the three constraints.

References

1. A. Aldini and M. Bernardo, *"On the Usability of Process Algebra: An Architectural View"*, in Theoretical Computer Science 335:281-329, 2005.
2. R. Allen and D. Garlan, *"A Formal Basis for Architectural Connection"*, in ACM Trans. on Software Engineering and Methodology 6:213-249, 1997.
3. J.A. Bergstra, A. Ponse, and S.A. Smolka (eds.), *"Handbook of Process Algebra"*, Elsevier, 2001.
4. M. Bernardo and E. Bontà, *"Generating Well-Synchronized Multithreaded Programs from Software Architecture Descriptions"*, in Proc. of the *4th Working IEEE/IFIP Conf. on Software Architecture (WICSA 2004)*, IEEE-CS Press, pp. 167-176, Oslo (Norway), 2004.
5. M. Bernardo and E. Bontà, *"Preserving Architectural Properties in Multithreaded Code Generation"*, in Proc. of the *7th Int. Conf. on Coordination Models and Languages (COORDINATION 2005)*, LNCS 3454:188-203, Namur (Belgium), 2005.
6. T. Bolognesi and E. Brinksma, *"Introduction to the ISO Specification Language LOTOS"*, in Computer Networks and ISDN Systems 14:25-59, 1987.
7. C. Canal, E. Pimentel, and J.M. Troya, *"Compatibility and Inheritance in Software Architectures"*, in Science of Computer Programming 41:105-138, 2001.
8. X. Deng, M.B. Dwyer, J. Hatcliff, and M. Mizuno, *"Invariant-based Specification, Synthesis, and Verification of Synchronization in Concurrent Programs"*, in Proc. of the *24th Int. Conf. on Software Engineering (ICSE 2002)*, ACM press, pp. 442-452, Orlando (Florida), 2002.
9. C.A.R. Hoare, *"Communicating Sequential Processes"*, Prentice Hall, 1985.
10. P. Inverardi and S. Uchitel, *"Proving Deadlock Freedom in Component-Based Programming"*, in Proc. of the *4th Int. Conf. on Fundamental Approaches to Software Engineering (FASE 2001)*, LNCS 2029:60-75, Genova (Italy), 2001.
11. P. Inverardi, A.L. Wolf, and D. Yankelevich, *"Static Checking of System Behaviors Using Derived Component Assumptions"*, in ACM Trans. on Software Engineering and Methodology 9:239-272, 2000.

12. J. Magee and J. Kramer, *"Concurrency: State Models & Java Programs"*, Wiley, 1999.
13. R. Milner, *"Communication and Concurrency"*, Prentice Hall, 1989.
14. D.E. Perry and A.L. Wolf, *"Foundations for the Study of Software Architecture"*, in ACM SIGSOFT Software Engineering Notes 17:40-52, 1992.
15. M. Shaw and D. Garlan, *"Software Architecture: Perspectives on an Emerging Discipline"*, Prentice Hall, 1996.
16. T. Yavuz-Kahveci and T. Bultan, *"Specification, Verification, and Synthesis of Concurrency Control Components"*, in ACM SIGSOFT Software Engineering Notes 27:169-179, 2002.

Automated Evaluation of Coordination Approaches

Tibor Bosse, Mark Hoogendoorn, and Jan Treur

Vrije Universiteit Amsterdam, Department of Artificial Intelligence
De Boelelaan 1081, 1081 HV Amsterdam, The Netherlands
{tbosse, mhoogen, treur}@cs.vu.nl
http://www.cs.vu.nl/~{tbosse, mhoogen, treur}

Abstract. How to coordinate the processes in a complex component-based software system is a nontrivial issue. Many different coordination approaches exist, each with its own specific advantages and drawbacks. To support their mutual comparison, this paper proposes a formal methodology to automatically evaluate the performance of coordination approaches. This methodology comprises (1) creation of simulation models of coordination approaches, (2) execution of simulation experiments of these models applied to test examples, and (3) automated evaluation of the models against specified requirements. Moreover, in a specific case study, the methodology is used to evaluate some coordination approaches that originate from various disciplines.

1 Introduction

Coordinating processes in a complex software system is a nontrivial issue. By a component-based approach to software systems, a divide and conquer strategy can be used to address the various aspects involved. This may lead to a possibly large number of components, which each can be analysed and designed independently. However, a designer may still be left with the problem how all these fragments can be combined into a coherent system. To solve such a problem, many different coordination approaches have been proposed, each having its advantages and drawbacks. Important questions when choosing such a coordination approach are the suitability, correct functioning, and efficiency of the approach for the particular component-based system.

This paper presents a methodology to enable a comparison of such factors for the different coordination approaches in a series of test examples. First of all, this methodology allows for the creation of simulation models for each of the coordination approaches. Secondly, it comprises an engine which simulates the different coordination approaches for a variety of test examples. Finally, the methodology consists of an automatic evaluation of the outcome of the simulations against specified requirements (e.g. successfulness and efficiency).

The problem of coordination of component-based software systems has crucial aspects in common with the problem of coordination in natural (biological), cognitive (human and animal mind) or societal systems (organisational structures). Evolution processes over long time periods have generated solutions for the coordination problem in these areas. Therefore, it may make sense to analyse in more detail how

P. Ciancarini and H. Wiklicky (Eds.): COORDINATION 2006, LNCS 4038, pp. 44–62, 2006.

these solutions work. Some literature is available that describes theories for coordination in these areas. This literature can be used as a source of inspiration to obtain new approaches to coordination of complex component-based software systems. As a first step, this paper evaluates a number of such approaches in a specific case study, to see to what extent they provide satisfactory solutions.

First, in Section 2 the methodology and supporting software tools are described. In Section 3 a number of coordination approaches obtained from the literature in various disciplines are briefly introduced. Section 4 describes a set of test examples that can be used as input for the evaluation of the coordination approaches. In Section 5 the simulations that were undertaken to evaluate the usefulness of the coordination approaches for the test examples are briefly discussed. Section 6 presents the results, and Section 7 is a final discussion.

2 Evaluation Method

To explore possibilities to address the coordination problem, an evaluation methodology, supported by a software environment, has been created: (a) a number of *coordination approaches* are selected, (b) a number of *test examples* representing specific software component configurations are chosen, (c) based on each of these coordination approaches a *simulation model* is formally specified, (d) related to the test examples, relevant *requirements* are formally specified in the form of relevant dynamic properties, (e) *simulations* are performed where selected coordination approaches are applied to the chosen test examples, resulting in a number of simulation traces, and (f) the simulation traces are *evaluated* (automatically) for the specified requirements.

To evaluate a given coordination approach, adequate test examples of component-based software configurations are needed. One may be tempted to use a real-life component-based software system as a test example, e.g., consisting of hundreds of components. However, such type of testing for one case would take a lot of effort, and to get a reasonable idea it should be repeated for a representative number of software systems at least. For this stage of the exploration this would not be appropriate. Instead, a number of smaller but representative test examples have been identified. As a source, the library of workflow patterns described in [1] has been used. The examples given there have been extended with input and output data and information flow channels.

To test the selected coordination approaches on the chosen examples, implement-tations have to be made. One way to do this would be to create specific imple-mentations for each of the (abstract) test examples, by explicitly defining the internal functioning of the components involved. Next, one would add to these implement-tations one by one implementations of the coordination approaches, and then run each of these implementations. The resulting log data, which should include a registration of the processing time, for example, in terms of processor time or number of computation steps, can then be evaluated. Such an evaluation at an implementation level, however, has some drawbacks: the specific implementations chosen may affect the results, and the specific underlying software/hardware combination may affect the processing times measured; e.g., think of aspects of concurrency that within a software/hardware environment may have to be mapped onto a form of interleaving of processes. Therefore a different approach is chosen. All the testing is done within one given simulation environment. Within this environment, one by one the processing of a software system based on one example and one coordination approach is simulated. In that case, the examples are defined at an abstract level (i.e., only in terms of input-output relations, ignoring the internal functioning). The measured time then is simulated time, not processing time. In simulated time, processes can easily be active in parallel. The simulation environment chosen is logic-based, so that the simulation models and the resulting simulation traces can be logically analysed, supported by another software environment.

To evaluate the resulting simulation traces, in the first place it is needed to identify the relevant properties, serving as requirements, on which such an evaluation should be based. A number of aspects can be covered in such requirements. A first aspect is effectiveness or successfulness to provide the desired output for the example system. When a coordination approach does not involve the right components at the right times, and therefore is not able to generate the desired output, then it is not effective. A second aspect to evaluate is efficiency: to what extent time is wasted in the process to obtain the eventual goals. A third aspect is to what extent the coordination approach is able to generate the possible activation traces one has in mind for the given example. Such properties can be formally specified and automatically checked for the simulation traces.

To support the evaluation method described a software environment is used: to logically specify simulation models and to execute these models in order to get simulation traces, and to specify relevant dynamic properties and to check such properties against simulation traces. For the simulation part, the language LEADSTO is used [6], based on a variant of Executable Temporal Logic [4]. The basic building blocks of this language are causal relations of the format $\alpha \rightarrow\!\!\!\rightarrow_{e, f, g, h} \beta$, which means:

> if   state property α holds for a certain time interval with duration g,
> then   after some delay (between e and f) state property β will hold
>   for a certain time interval of length h.

where α and β are state properties of the form 'conjunction of literals' (where a literal is an atom or the negation of an atom), and e, f, g, h non-negative real numbers. For the analysis part the language TTL is used [7]. This predicate logical language supports formal specification and analysis of dynamic properties, covering both qualitative and quantitative aspects. TTL is built on atoms referring to states, time points and traces. A *state* of a process for (state) ontology Ont is an assignment of truth values to the set of ground atoms in the ontology. The set of all possible states for ontology Ont is denoted by STATES(Ont). To describe sequences of states, a fixed *time frame* T is assumed which is linearly ordered. A *trace* γ over state ontology Ont and time frame T is a mapping $\gamma : T \rightarrow$ STATES(Ont), i.e., a sequence of states γ_t (t $\in$ T) in STATES(Ont). The set of *dynamic properties* DYNPROP(Ont) is the set of temporal statements that can be formulated with respect to traces based on the state ontology Ont in the following manner. Given a trace γ over state ontology Ont, the state in γ at time point t is denoted by state(γ, t). These states can be related to state properties via the formally defined satisfaction relation $\models$, comparable to the Holds-predicate in the Situation Calculus: state(γ, t) $\models$ p denotes that state property p holds in trace γ at time t. Based on these statements, dynamic properties can be formulated in a formal manner in a sorted first-order predicate logic, using quantifiers over time and traces and the usual first-order logical connectives such as $\neg$, $\wedge$, $\vee$, $\Rightarrow$, $\forall$, $\exists$. A special software environment has been developed for TTL, featuring both a Property Editor for building and editing TTL properties and a Checking Tool that enables formal verification of such properties against a set of (simulated or empirical) traces.

3 Coordination Approaches

As mentioned earlier, the coordination problem in software systems has crucial aspects in common with the problem of coordination in natural (biological), cognitive (human and animal mind) or societal systems (organisational structures). Therefore, a large body of literature is available that describes coordination approaches in these areas. In this section, some of the most well-known approaches are discussed. Section 3.1 focusses on the *behavior networks* approach by Pattie Maes [17]. Section 3.2 describes Selfridge's *pandemonium* model [22], and Section 3.3 addresses the decision-making techniques known as *voting methods* [18]. These approaches were chosen for two reasons. First, because they are well-known approaches in the (wider) literature in various disciplines on coordination. Second, because together they more or less cover the area of different coordination approaches: the behavior networks use a rather *global* and sequential strategy (i.e., the approach determines which component is activated based on global information concerning all components), whereas voting methods and (especially) the pandemonium model use a *local* and possibly nonsequential strategy (i.e., the components involved only use information about themselves or their direct neighbours to determine which component is activated).

3.1 Behavior Networks

Behavior networks have been introduced by Pattie Maes in 1989. She distinguishes *competence modules* within a system, where each module is specified by a tuple containing four elements: (1) a list of preconditions to be fulfilled before a competence module can become active; (2) the competence module's action in terms of an add list; (3) the competence module's actions in terms of a delete list; (4) a level of activation. A competence module is said to be executable in case the list of preconditions is fulfilled. A network of competence modules is created via three types of links: successor links (a link from x to y for every element on the add list of x which is on the preconditions list of y), predecessor links (a link from x to y for every element on the precondition list of x which is on y's add list), and conflictor links (a link from x to y for every element on the precondition list of y which is on x's delete list). Through these links the competence modules activate and inhibit each other, so that "after some time the activation energy accumulates in the modules that represent the 'best' actions to take given the current situation and goals" [17]. The patterns of these spreading activations among modules, as well as the input of new activation energy into the network, is determined by the state of the environment and goals via three ways: activation by state (add activation to modules that (partially) match the current state), activation by goals (add activation to modules which (partially) achieve the goals), and inhibition by protected goals (remove activation from modules that (partially) remove the protected goals). Thereafter, activation spreads through the network via activation of successors, activation of predecessors, and inhibition of conflictors. After having spread the activation, a decay phase makes sure the overall activation remains constant within the network. Once performed, a competence module fires in case it is executable, the activation is over the threshold that has been set, and it is the competence module with the highest activation. In case the module indeed fires, its activation goes to 0, and all thresholds return to their normal value. In case no module fires, the threshold is reduced by 10%. For more mathematical details, see [17].

3.2 The Pandemonium Model

In 1958, Selfridge proposes an approach he calls pandemonium, to enable pattern recognition [22]. This is a system composed of primitive constructs called *demons*, each representing a possible pattern. Once an image is presented, each of the demons computes the similarity of the image with the pattern it represents, and gives an output depending monotonically on that similarity. Finally, a decision demon selects the pattern belonging to the demon whose output is largest.

Jackson [14] extends this idea to a theory of mind. Besides demons involved in perception, he also identifies demons that cause external actions and demons that act internally on other demons. Jackson pictures the demons as living in a stadium. Almost all of them are the crowd, cheering on the performers. The remainder of the demons are down on the playing field, exciting the crowd in the stands. Demons in the stands respond selectively to these attempts to excite them. Some are more excited than others; some shout louder. The loudest demon in the stands replaces one of those currently performing which is sent back to the stands. The loudness of the shouting of a demon is dependant upon being linked with the demon that must excite. Stronger links produce louder responses. The system starts off with initial built-in links between the demons. New links are made between demons, and existing links are strengthened in proportion to the time they have been together on the field, plus the gain of the system (i.e., when all is going well, the gain is higher).

3.3 Voting Methods

The concept of *voting* refers to a wide collection of techniques that are used to describe decision-making processes involving multiple agents. Although originating from political science, voting methods are currently used within a number of domains, including game theory (where they are used as methods for conflict resolution) and pattern recognition (where they are used to combine classifier outputs).

The general idea of voting methods is rather intuitive, and is comparable to the techniques used in elections. Consider a set of agents N, and a set of possible outcomes S of an election. Each agent $i \in N$ has preferences over the outcomes: $\leq_i \subseteq$ S x S. The voting approach uses a function F that selects a candidate outcome S, given the preferences of the voters. A simple instance of F would be to count all votes, and to select the outcome with the highest amount of votes. However, a large number of (more complex) voting approaches exist. These can roughly be divided into three classes: *unweighed voting methods* in which each vote carries equal weight, *confidence voting methods* in which voters can express a degree of preference for a candidate, and *ranked voting methods* in which the voters are asked for a preference ranking over the candidates. See [18] for an overview of different voting methods.

As mentioned above, voting methods are currently used in many different domains, such as game theory and pattern recognition. In this paper it will be explored whether they are of any use to solve coordination problems in complex (component-based) software systems. To this end, the electorate will be filled in by certain components, and the candidates by the possible activations of components.

4   Test Examples

Test examples have been identified to test the different coordination approaches. The examples were inspired by the workflow patterns defined by van der Aalst [1]. These patterns can be seen as building blocks for more complex patterns occurring in real-life component-based systems. In total, seven test examples have been described, two of which are discussed below. A test example consists of a number of components, called {C1, C2,..}, and several types of data, called {d1, d2,..}. Different components need different data as input, and create different data as output. The complete set of test examples is described in [5].

Pattern 1 - Sequence
The first pattern is straightforward: it involves three components. After completion of the first component, the second component is activated, and after completion of the second, the third component is activated.

On the basis of this pattern, a next step was to create a corresponding test example. In principle, this means defining an example (in terms of components and data) in such a way that, if provided as input to a coordination approach, pattern 1 will come out. A visualisation of such an example is given in Figure 1. In this case component C1 needs data d1 as input, and creates data d2 as output. Moreover, as indicated in the box on the right, the *input data* (the data that is initially available to the system) is d1, and the *goal data* (the data that the system needs to create in order to be successful) is d4. Given this situation, the expectation is that if any coordination approach is applied to the example, the result will be a trace in which the components are activated in sequence (i.e., first C1, then C2, and then C3). Note that it is assumed that data is shared, i.e., whenever a component generates output data, this data is immediately available to all other components in the system. This could be implemented, for example, by incorporating a *shared repository*, where all components store their output data and read their input data from. Another assumption is that data cannot be

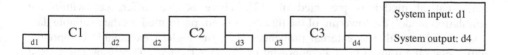

Fig. 1. Test example 1 – Sequence

removed. Thus, once data is written to the shared repository, it will stay there. Other approaches such as explicit communication channels can however easily be incorporated into the methodology.

Pattern 7 - Synchronizing Merge
Pattern 7 involves four components. After completion of the first component, there is a choice between the second and third component: either one of them can be activated, or both. In case one of them is activated, the fourth component is activated after this component has completed. In case both of them are activated, the fourth component is activated after both have completed.

The test example that was created on the basis of this pattern is shown in Figure 2. As can be seen in the figure, in this example both a conjunction in a component's output data and a disjunction in a component's input data occur. Furthermore, note that, when formalising this example in LEADSTO, the disjunction on the input side of C4 is modelled by defining three separate variants of C4: one variant (called C4) with d4 as input, one variant (called C5) with d5 as input, and one variant (called C6) with d4 and d5 as input.

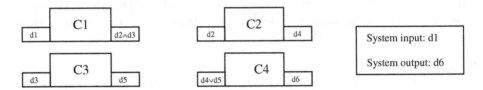

Fig. 2. Test example 7 - Synchronizing Merge

5 Simulation

To compare the coordination approaches described in Section 3 against the above test examples, a number of simulation experiments have been performed. First, the three selected coordination approaches have been implemented in the LEADSTO simulation language, see [5]. Next, the implemented simulation models have been applied to the test examples. The simulation models for the behavior networks, the pandemonium, and the voting method, are addressed, respectively, in Section 5.1, 5.2, and 5.3. For each simulation model, an example simulation trace (resulting from applying the model to test example 7) is provided.

5.1 Behavior Networks Simulation

The simulation model for Maes' behavior networks is created on the basis of the mathematical model as presented in [17]. There is one difference: within the simulation model, the lowering of the threshold is not performed, as the available data does not change due to external influences (i.e., the highest executable component will remain the highest until a component has been activated). Therefore, the highest executable component is simply selected, avoiding unnecessary computation. The

LEADSTO specification for the approach roughly corresponds to the description in Section 3.1.

Figure 3 presents a simulation trace that has resulted from executing the approach on test example 7. Initially, the data present is set to d1: data(d1). Furthermore, the goal is set to d6 for this particular scenario: goal(d6). Before starting, the activation value, referred to as the alpha value of the components currently present in the system are set to 0 for the time point before the current time point (i.e. time point 0): alpha(0, c1, 0), alpha(0, c2, 0), alpha(0, c3, 0), alpha(0, c4, 0), alpha(0, c5, 0), and alpha(0, c6, 0). Thereafter calculations are performed to determine the activity within the different components: The input from the current state is calculated (i.e. given the current data available, calculate the activation caused for the different components) as well as the input from the goals. Since only C4, C5, and C6 have a goal as an output, these components are

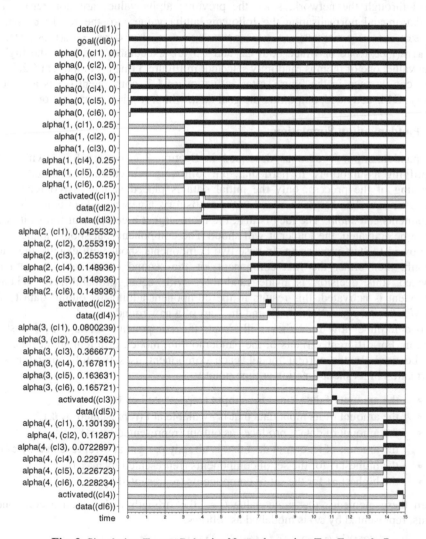

Fig. 3. Simulation Trace - Behavior Networks against Test Example 7

the only ones to receive activation through this source. Due to the fact that the previous alpha value is 0, no activation is spread around the network. The next alpha value for the six components present in the system is therefore obtained by simply summing up the input from the goals and state per component, and normalizing it to 1: alpha(1, c1, 0.25), alpha(1, c2, 0), alpha(1, c3, 0), alpha(1, c4, 0.25), alpha(1, c5, 0.25), and alpha(1, c6, 0.25). As a result, component C1 is activated, as this is the executable component with the highest alpha value: activated(c1). Due to the activity of component C1, its output data is generated, which is shown in the trace: the presence of data d2 and d3: data(d2) and data(d3).

A new round of computation is performed; the input from the goals remains the same, as these have not changed. However, the input from the current state changes, due to the additional data d2 and d3 being present. Furthermore, activation is now spread through the network, since the previous alpha values are non-zero. After calculation and normalisation the following alpha values are the result: alpha(1, c1, 0.0425532), alpha(1, c2, 0.255319), alpha(1, c3, 0.255319), alpha(1, c4, 0.148936), alpha(1, c5, 0.148936), and alpha(1, c6, 0.148936). Since both C2 and C3 are executable and have the highest alpha value, one of them is randomly selected; in Figure 3 this is component C2.

As can be seen in the figure, after activation of C2, component C3 is activated. Finally, C4 is activated, outputting the goal data, which results in termination.

5.2 Pandemonium Simulation

The pandemonium is used as described in Section 3.2, but modified with some simplifying assumptions. In particular, the following procedure is assumed: at the beginning of the process, only the initial data is placed at the shared repository. Whenever new data has been added to the repository, a new round starts in which all components can *shout*. The idea is that, the more urgent a component thinks it is for him to be activated, the louder it will shout. The component that shouts loudest will be allowed to start processing. In case two components shout with exactly the same strength, then either the first component, or the second component, or both are activated (this decision is made randomly, with equal probabilities). When a component is activated, this results in the component adding its output data to the *shared repository* (see Section 4), and the start of a new round.

To determine how loud they will shout, the components make use of a shout function. For different variants of the pandemonium model, different shout functions may be used. In the current model, each component uses the following types of information in its shout function at time point t:

- the amount of data it needs as input (represented by $i1$)
- the amount of its input data that is available at t (represented by $i2$)
- the amount of data it produces as output (represented by $o1$)
- the amount of its output data that is already present at t (represented by $o2$)
- the highest $i1$ for the set of components (represented by max_i)
- the highest $o1$ for the set of components (represented by max_o)

Given these elements, the shout value (i.e., the strength with which a component shouts, represented by sv) is modelled as follows:

$$sv = (i2/i1)^{\beta 1} * (1 - o2/o1)^{\beta 2} * (i1/max\_i)^{\beta 3} * (o1/max\_o)^{\beta 4}$$

Here, β1, β2, β3, and β4 are real numbers between 1 and 1.5, indicating the importance of the corresponding factor. Several settings have been tested for these parameters. In the examples shown here, β1=1.4, β2=1.3, β3=1.1, and β4=1.2. Since the factors can never exceed 1, the shout value sv will be a value between 0 and 1.

Figure 4 depicts the simulation trace that has resulted from applying the pandemonium approach to test example 7. As the figure shows, initially the only data that is present is d1: data(d1). Based on this data, every component starts shouting. Component C1 shouts loudest (with strength 0.47, whilst the others shout with strength 0.0): shout(c1, 0.466516), shout(c2, 0.0), ..., shout(c6, 0.0). Thus, component C1 is selected to become active: active_component(c1). As a result, C1 creates data d2 and d3, which are stored at the repository as well: data(d2), data(d3). Then again, every component starts shouting. This time, both component C2 and C3 shout loudest (with strength 0.20, whilst the others shout with strength 0.0): shout(c1, 0.0), shout(c2, 0.203063), shout(c6, 0.0). As a result, both component C2 and C3 are selected to become active: active_component(c2), active_component(c3). Note that this selection is based on the assumption that multiple components may be activated at the same time. If this is not allowed, the approach would select one of the components at random. Next, component C2 creates data d4, and component C3 creates data d5. These data are stored at the repository: data(d4), data(d5). Again, every component starts shouting. Component C6 (which is a specific variant of C4, see the description of the example) shouts loudest (with strength 0.44): shout(c1, 0.0), shout(c2, 0.0), shout(c6, 0.435275). Thus, component C6 is selected to become active: active_component(c6). Eventually, component C6 creates data d6, which is stored at the repository: data(d6). Since d6 is the goal data, at this point the process terminates.

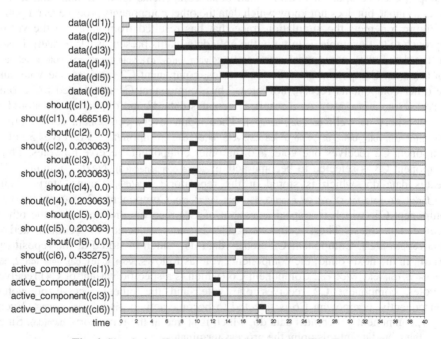

Fig. 4. Simulation Trace - Pandemonium against Test Example 7

5.3 Voting Simulation

The simulation of the voting method uses the same assumptions as the pandemonium method, with one difference: instead of shouting, all components can *vote*. The idea is that each component can vote on only one component (possibly on itself). After all components have voted, the votes are counted, and the component with most votes will be allowed to start processing. To determine on whom they will vote, the components make use of a *voting procedure*. For different variants of the voting method, different voting procedures may be used. In the current model, each component follows the following procedure:

1. if my input is present, and my output is not, then I vote for myself
2. if my input is not present, and this input is generated by one other component, vote for that component
3. if my input is not present, and this input is generated by $n>1$ other components, vote for one of those components (at random)
4. if my output is present, and this output is used by one other component, vote for that component
5. if my output is present, and this output is used by $n>1$ other components, vote for one of those components (at random)
6. if my output is present, and this output is used by no other components (i.e., it is part of the goal data), do not vote

Note that this approach assumes a *local* perspective of the components. This means that each component only has knowledge about itself and its direct neighbours. For example, each component knows which other components need the data that it produces as input, but does not know which data the other components produce as output.

Figure 5 depicts the simulation trace that has resulted from applying the voting approach to test example 7. Initially the only data that is present is d1: data(d1). Based on this data, every component starts voting: vote_for(c1, c1), vote_for(c2, c1), vote_for(c3, c1), vote_for(c4, c2). Component C1 receives 3 votes, component C2 receives one vote, and the other components receive no votes. Thus, component C1 is selected to become active: active_component(c1). As a result, C1 creates data d2 and d3, which are stored at the repository as well: data(d2), data(d3). Then again, every component starts voting: vote_for(c1, c3), vote_for(c2, c2), vote_for(c3, c3), vote_for(c4, c3). Component C3 receives 3 votes, component C2 receives one vote, and the other components receive no votes. Thus, component C3 is selected to become active: active_component(c3). Next, component C3 creates data d5, which is stored at the repository: data(d5). Voting starts again: vote_for(c1, c2), vote_for(c2, c2), vote_for(c3, c5), vote_for(c4, c2). Component C2 receives 3 votes, component C5 (which is a specific variant of C4) receives one vote, and the others receive no votes. Thus, component C2 is now selected to become active: active_component(c2). Component C2 creates data d4, which is stored at the repository: data(d4). In the next round, the components vote as follows: vote_for(c1, c2), vote_for(c2, c6), vote_for(c3, c6), vote_for(c4, c6). Component C6 (which is a specific variant of C4) receives 3 votes, component C2 receives one vote, and the others receive no votes. Consequently, component C6 is selected to become active: active_component(c6). Eventually, component C6 creates data d6, which is stored at the repository: data(d6). Since d6 is the goal data, at this point the process terminates.

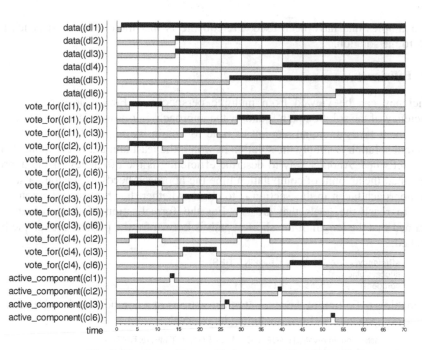

Fig. 5. Simulation Trace - Voting against Test Example 7

6 Evaluation

This section addresses the evaluation of the performance for the different approaches that have been simulated as described above. This evaluation can be performed from multiple perspectives. First of all, the achievement of the goals that have been set for the system are an important evaluation criterion. Secondly, an element in the evaluation is the efficiency of the approach. Finally, patterns can be specified which are (allowed) to occur in the component configurations used as test examples, and it can be checked whether a coordination approach indeed identifies these patterns. To enable automated checking of the results of the approaches, a formal specification of the different types of properties is required. For this purpose, the language TTL introduced in Section 2 is used. After such a formal description has been obtained, the automated TTL-checker can be used to see how well the approach performs.

6.1 Successfulness

The first property to be checked is called successfulness. Informally, this property states that in the trace γ all goal data d will eventually be derived. Formally:

successfulness(γ:TRACE) $\equiv$
$\forall$t:TIME, d:DATA [state(γ, t) = goal(d) $\Rightarrow$
$\exists$t2:TIME [t2 $\geq$ t $\wedge$ state(γ, t2) |= data(d)]]

The results of automatically checking this property against the traces that were generated in the simulation show that all approaches eventually find the solution for the examples that have been used. Prerequisite is that there must exist at least one path to the solution.

6.2 Efficiency

Efficiency can be viewed from multiple perspectives. First, one can look at the efficiency of the solution path found by the approach. For now, it is assumed that each component takes an equal amount of time to obtain its output. Therefore, the most efficient solution is simply the solution in which the least amount of components have been activated. Another way to describe efficiency is the efficiency of the approach itself, i.e., the amount of computation time the approach needs to generate a solution. The approach taken in this section is to check whether the shortest activation path is used to reach the goals that are set. For the formalisation of this property, it is assumed that the length of the shortest path is known for the particular example being checked:

efficiency(γ:TRACE, shortest_path:INTEGER) $\equiv$
successfulness(γ) $\wedge$
component_activations(γ, shortest_path)

To enable a definition of the amount of activations of a component, first the activation of one component is defined, including its interval:

has_activation_interval(γ:TRACE, c:COMPONENT, tb:TIME, te:TIME) $\equiv$
tb < te $\wedge$ state(γ,te) $\not\models$ activated(c) $\wedge$
[$\forall$t tb$\leq$t<te $\Rightarrow$ state(γ,t) $\models$ activated(c)] $\wedge$
$\exists$t1<tb [$\forall$t2 t1$\leq$t2<tb $\Rightarrow$ state(γ,t2) $\not\models$ activated(c)]

An example of a definition for a trace with one component activation is shown below.

component_activations(γ:TRACE, 1) $\equiv$
$\exists$c:COMPONENT, tb:TIME, te:TIME
has_activation_interval(γ, c:COMPONENT, tb:TIME, te:TIME) $\wedge$
[$\forall$c2:COMPONENT, tb2:TIME, te2:TIME
[has_activation_interval(γ, c2:COMPONENT, tb2:TIME, te2:TIME) $\Rightarrow$ c = c2 $\wedge$ tb = tb2 $\wedge$ te = te2]]

Table 1 shows the outcome of checking the property efficiency in the TTL Checker for the generated traces. A plus indicates that in all generated traces the efficient solution was found; a minus indicates that no efficient solution is found in at least one of the generated traces.

Table 1. Efficiency of the different approaches on the examples

Example	Behavior Networks	Pandemonium	Voting
Sequence	+	+	+
Parallel Split	+	+	-
Synchronization	+	+	+
Exclusive choice	+	+	+
Simple Merge	+	+	+
Multi Choice	-	-	+
Synchronizing merge	-	-	-

For the first five examples, both the behavior networks and the pandemonium always find the optimal path to the solution. For voting, the optimal solution for the parallel split is not always found: apparently, there are situations when this approach is not efficient. This is mainly due to the fact that the voting components have only *local* information. As a result, their voting behaviour is not always fully rational. This problem could be solved by allowing a more global perspective for the components.

For the synchronizing merge and the multi-choice (which can be described as the synchronizing merge without component C4), the behavior networks approach fails to find the optimal solution in some cases. For the first, it activates both C2 and C3 whereas only one of the components is required to obtain the goal data. Adapting the parameters of the approach could probably prevent this from occurring. Furthermore, in the synchronizing merge case, both C2 and C3 are activated whereas C4 only needs one input to generate output.

Also the pandemonium model is not always efficient for the multi-choice and synchronizing merge. For the multi-choice, this is the case because the model sometimes generates traces where first C1 is activated, and then C2 and C3 are activated simultaneously. Although this solution is efficient in terms of activation rounds (i.e., only two rounds), it is not efficient in terms of component activations: three components are activated in total, where two activations would have been sufficient (i.e., C1 followed by C2, or C1 followed by C3). For the synchronizing merge, in some cases the same situation occurs as with the behavior networks: sometimes both C2 and C3 are activated simultaneously, whilst only one of them is required.

The voting method however succeeds in always finding the efficient solution for the multi-choice. Here, the aforementioned situation that both C2 and C3 are activated never occurs, because there is always one component that receives more votes than the others. However, like the other approaches, the voting method is sometimes inefficient with respect to the synchronizing merge. Here, again the same situation occurs as with the behavior networks and the pandemonium: sometimes both C2 and C3 are activated, where only one of them is necessary.

6.3 Specifying and Checking Patterns

As has been mentioned, certain expected patterns can be specified for component configuration examples, and it can be checked whether these patterns are indeed found by the different approaches. For the test examples used in this document, the component configuration specifications originate from workflow patterns. Therefore, the patterns taken for the test examples are precisely the workflow patterns from which these examples have been derived. Specification of patterns can be done from two perspectives: (1) exhaustively summing up all possible outcomes; (2) specifying the constraints between activation intervals of different components. For the second approach, the interval relations as identified by Allen [2] were used and specified in TTL, for example the before relation:

before(b1:TIME, e1:TIME, b2:TIME, e2:TIME) ≡ e1 < b2

Below, workflow patterns 1 and 7 are specified using TTL expressions. For both patterns, all traces are first summed up in an informal fashion (according to perspective 1 above). After that, the formal TTL expressions specifying the const-raints between the activation intervals of the different components are shown (according to perspective 2). The complete set of seven TTL expressions can be found in [5].

Pattern 1 - Sequence

Possible traces: ABC.

Activation interval constraints in TTL:

```
∃bA,eA,bB,eB,bC,eC:TIME
has_activation_interval(trace1, A, bA, eA) ∧
has_activation_interval(trace1, B, bB, eB) ∧
has_activation_interval(trace1, C, bC, eC) ∧
before(bA, eA, bB, eB) ∧
before(bB, eB, bC, eC)
```

Pattern 7 - Synchronizing Merge

Possible traces: ABD, ACD, ABCD, ABCD, A B|C D.
Here, "B|C" indicates that B and C are activated simultaneously.

Activation interval constraints in TTL:

```
[∃bA,eA,bB,eB,bD,eD:TIME
has_activation_interval(trace1, A, bA, eA) ∧
has_activation_interval(trace1, B, bB, eB) ∧
has_activation_interval(trace1, D, bD, eD) ∧
before(bA, eA, bB, eB) ∧
before(bB, eB, bD, eD)]
 ∨
[∃bA,eA,bC,eC,bD,eD:TIME
has_activation_interval(trace1, A, bA, eA) ∧
has_activation_interval(trace1, C, bC, eC) ∧
has_activation_interval(trace1, D, bD, eD) ∧
before(bA, eA, bC, eC) ∧
before(bC, eC, bD, eD)]
 ∨
[∃bA,eA,bB,eB,bC,eC,bD,eD:TIME
has_activation_interval(trace1, A, bA, eA) ∧
has_activation_interval(trace1, B, bB, eB) ∧
has_activation_interval(trace1, C, bC, eC) ∧
has_activation_interval(trace1, D, bD, eD) ∧
before(bA, eA, bB, eB) ∧
before(bA, eA, bC, eC) ∧
before(bB, eB, bD, eD) ∧
before(bC, eC, bD, eD)]
```

Automated checks have pointed out that the behavior networks, pandemonium, and voting approaches always find the patterns that have been identified. In the parallel split case, the success of the voting approach however is debatable. The reason for this is that besides the expected patterns (A[BC]) also patterns such as A-B-B-C appear. According to personal communication with van der Aalst this is however not a violation of the pattern. Following his perspective, a trace satisfies a pattern when the components as prescribed by the patterns occur being active in the trace in the specified sequence. It is however allowed for other components (either a different component or activation of the same component at another time point) to be active within the same trace. For checking the more strict version (i.e. exactly the prescribed sequence without other activations) a *closed world assumption* version of the property has been specified as well.

Since the abstract way of modelling used here is not computationally expensive, checking a property against a trace on average took no more than one second. For more information about the complexity of checking TTL expressions, see [7].

7 Discussion

To conclude, this paper presented a formal methodology to evaluate and compare the performance of different coordination approaches. The methodology comprises the creation of simulation models for the coordination approaches, the execution of simulation experiments of these models applied to test examples, and their automated evaluation against specified requirements. In a specific case study, the methodology was used to evaluate three well-known coordination approaches from the literature. During this case study, the simulation approach turned out quite beneficial. Within a reasonable time, a nontrivial number of approaches have been tested against a nontrivial number of cases: $3 \times 7 = 21$ combinations have been explored. Furthermore, the automated checks of dynamic properties against generated traces have turned out useful to evaluate the simulations for the different approaches against requirements. Finally, an existing library of workflow patterns [1] turned out an appropriate source for cases to be explored, although their specification also needs to cover data flow aspects. It was not too difficult to add such data flow aspects.

Concerning the specific case study performed, the voting, pandemonium and behavior networks approach have been thoroughly evaluated with respect to a number of relevant performance indicators, namely successfulness, efficiency, and pattern checks. All approaches turned out effective in finding the solution in all cases. However, none of the approaches is always efficient for all patterns. The behavior networks and pandemonium approaches perform equally well; they succeed for the "simple" cases and sometimes fail to be efficient for the two complicated cases (i.e. multi-choice and synchronizing merge). Surprisingly, the voting approach always finds the most efficient solution for one of the complicated cases, namely the multi-choice. It does however fail in the rather trivial case of the parallel split. All approaches also find the patterns specified for each of the component configuration examples.

All in all, when comparing the different coordination approaches, the performance based on the criteria specified above is almost similar. The way in which they find the component activation sequences is however completely different. The behavior networks approach needs a global overview of the system: it needs to know for each component what data it needs as input and what data it generates as output. Such a global view might not always be available or might be inconvenient. On the other hand, for the pandemonium a completely local view is sufficient: each component only needs information about its own input and output data. In between is the voting approach, which needs information about itself and its direct neighbours. When comparing the approaches on required computation time, the behavior networks approach takes far more computation time than the other approaches. This has two causes: first, due to the fact that all global information is used within the approach, it has a lot more information to take into consideration. Second, both for the voting and pandemonium approach the calculations per component can be performed in parallel, which can not be done in the behavior networks approach.

Work related to the approach presented in this paper can, first of all, be found in the field of action selection mechanisms (also called behaviour coordination mechanisms) in robotics. Pirjanian [19] presents an overview of several mechanisms used in that particular field, including a classification of these mechanisms. He identifies two main streams: arbitration and command fusion. In the arbitration approach, one behaviour is arbitrarily selected from a group of competing ones, giving it the ultimate control. For command fusion mechanisms however, recommendations are combined from multiple behaviours to form a control action that represents their consensus. The behaviour networks approach as presented by Maes [17] is an example of an arbitration mechanism, whereas both voting and the pandemonium model can be placed in the command fusion category. Tyrrell [23] presents a comparison between several mechanisms for action selection, using a simulator of an animal world. The comparison approach is however not formal like the approach presented in this paper. Furthermore, the framework for comparison is not generic, but developed for a specific case study, making it hard to generalise the results obtained. Another related field can be found within multi-agent systems, where coordination mechanisms play an essential role to ensure a proper functioning of the system as a whole. These coordination mechanisms address types of interactions and agreements between the different agents that were not considered in this paper. For a comparison between different coordination mechanisms in agent systems, see for example [8]. Concerning other related work, coordination models and languages for interfacing between components often focus on how different components within a software system can interact, see for example [3]. Due to the assumption of data being available and interpretable for all components, these component interaction models have not been considered in this paper, but can easily be incorporated in the methodology.

The methodology presented in this paper is supported by two software environments: the LEADSTO environment for simulation [6], and the TTL environment for verification of properties [7]. For simulation, various other approaches exist, such as the Dynamical Systems Theory [20], Executable Temporal Logic [4], PLC automata [9], qualitative reasoning (see, e.g., [10]), and stochastic pi-calculus (as used in [12]). For verification of properties, alternative approaches are standard temporal languages such as LTL and CTL [13], and calculi like the situation calculus [21] and the event calculus [15]. See, respectively, [6] and [7] for an extensive comparison of LEADSTO and TTL with these approaches.

Finally, the work as reported has led to a number of ideas for further research. While the specific coordination approaches borrowed from other disciplines were found to have value, no attempts have been made yet to come up with refinements, extensions or improvements of these approaches, or, inspired by these approaches, to design completely new (and possibly better) approaches. Some possible future extensions are allowing *preference* for certain components, allowing a *dynamic environment*, and enabling the components to process *partial data*.

Acknowledgements

This work has been performed as part of a project funded by CAMS-Force Vision, the software development company associated with the Royal Netherlands Navy. Moreover, the authors are grateful to Egon van den Broek, Rob Duell, Andy van der Mee, and Bas Vermeulen for various fruitful discussions.

References

1. Aalst, W.M.P. van der, Hofstede, A.H.M. ter, Kiepuszewski, B., and Barros, A.P. Workflow Patterns. QUT Technical report FIT-TR-2002-02, Queensland University of Technology, Brisbane, 2002.
2. Allen, J. F. Maintaining knowledge about temporal intervals. In: *Communications of the ACM*, 26, 1983, pp. 832-843.
3. Arbab, F. Reo: A Channel-based Coordination Model for Component Composition, *Mathematical Structures in Computer Science*, Cambridge University Press, vol. 14, No. 3, 2004, pp. 329-366.
4. Barringer, H., Fisher, M., Gabbay, D., Owens, R., and Reynolds, M. *The Imperative Future: Principles of Executable Temporal Logic*, John Wiley & Sons, 1996.
5. Bosse, T., Hoogendoorn, M., and Treur, J. Coordination Approaches for Complex Software Systems. Technical report 06-04ASRAI, Vrije Universiteit Amsterdam, Amsterdam, 2006. URL: http://hdl.handle.net/1871/9195.
6. Bosse, T., Jonker, C.M., Meij, L. van der, and Treur, J. LEADSTO: a Language and Environment for Analysis of Dynamics by SimulaTiOn. In: Eymann, T., et al. (eds.), *Proc. of the Third German Conference on Multi-Agent System Technologies, MATES'05*. Lecture Notes in Artificial Intelligence, vol. 3550. Springer Verlag, 2005, pp. 165-178.
7. Bosse, T., Jonker, C.M., Meij, L. van der, Sharpanskykh, A, and Treur, J. A Temporal Trace Language for the Formal Analysis of Dynamic Properties. Technical Report, Vrije Universiteit Amsterdam, Department of Artificial Intelligence, 2006.
8. Bourne, R., Shoop, K., and Jennings, N. Dynamic evaluation of coordination mechanisms for autonomous agents. In P. Brazdil and A. Jorge, editors, *Progress in Artificial Intelligence*, Lecture Notes in Artificial Intelligence. Springer Verlag, 2001, pp. 155-168.
9. Dierks, H. PLC-automata: A new class of implementable real-time automata. In M. Bertran and T. Rus, editors, Transformation-Based Reactive Systems Development (ARTS'97), volume 1231 of Lecture Notes in Computer Science. Springer-Verlag, 1997, pp. 111-125.
10. Forbus, K.D. *Qualitative process theory*. Artificial Intelligence, vol. 24, no. 1-3, 1984, pp. 85-168.
11. Franklin, S. Artificial Minds, MIT Press, Cambridge Massachusetts, 1997.
12. Gardelli, L., Viroli, M., Omicini, A.: On the Role of Simulations in Engineering Self-Organizing MAS: the Case of an Intrusion Detection System in TuCSoN. In: *3rd International Workshop "Engineering Self-Organising Applications" (ESOA)*, 2005, pp. 161-175.
13. Goldblatt, R. *Logics of Time and Computation*, 2nd edition, CSLI Lecture Notes 7, 1992.
14. Jackson, J.V. Idea for a Mind, *SIGGART Newsletter*, no 181, 1987, pp. 23-26.
15. Kowalski, R. and Sergot, M.A. A logic-based calculus of events, *New Generation Computing*, 4, 1986, pp. 67-95.

16. Lindsay, P. H., and Norman, D. A. *Human Information Processing: An Introduction to Psychology.* Academic Press, Inc., New York, 1977.
17. Maes, P. How to do the right thing. *Connection Science*, 1989. 1(3): pp. 291-323.
18. Ordeshook, P. *Game theory and political theory: An Introduction.* Cambridge: Cambridge University Press, 1986.
19. Pirjanian, P. *Behavior coordination mechanisms -- state-of-the-art.* Technical Report IRIS-99-375, Institute of Robotics and Intelligent Systems, School of Engineering, University of Southern California, October 1999.
20. Port, R.F., and Gelder, T. van (eds.) *Mind as Motion: Explorations in the Dynamics of Cognition.* MIT Press, Cambridge, Mass, 1995.
21. Reiter, R. Knowledge in Action: Logical Foundations for Specifying and Implementing Dynamical Systems, Cambridge MA: MIT Press, 2001.
22. Selfridge, O. G. Pandemonium: a paradigm for learning in mechanization of thought processes. In *Proceedings of a Symposium Held at the National Physical Laboratory*, London, November 1958, pp. 513-526.
23. Tyrrell, T. *Computational Mechanisms for Action Selection*, PhD thesis, University of Edinburgh, 1993.

Choreography and Orchestration Conformance for System Design*

Nadia Busi, Roberto Gorrieri, Claudio Guidi,
Roberto Lucchi, and Gianluigi Zavattaro

Department of Computer Science,
University of Bologna, Italy
{busi, gorrieri, cguidi, lucchi, zavattar}@cs.unibo.it

Abstract. In a previous work we have presented a formal framework devoted to show the relevance of choreography and orchestration in the design of service oriented applications. Even if useful to start a formal investigation of the relationship between choreography and orchestration, the proposed framework was not suitable to specify real case studies. In fact, it simply permitted to specify all possible computations abstracting away from the conditions driving the choice of the actual behaviour. In this paper we tackle this problem by introducing the notion of state variables. The addition of state requires a substantial modification of the entire framework because the same state variable, at the level of choreography, can be actually stored in distributed orchestrators that will need to synchronize in order to maintain consistent views. In order to faithfully investigate this problem we also need to modify the formal model at the orchestration level, moving from synchronous to asynchronous communication as the latter is the communication modality of the ordinary communication infrastructures.

1 Introduction

Choreography and orchestration languages are used for composing service-based applications. The former ones allow to manage applications composed of a number of services in a top view manner, that is the conversation rules which govern the interactions between the services involved in the applications, whereas the latter ones provide a mean to program the internal executable behaviour of some specific service, called orchestrator, responsible to coordinate the collaborating services. These approaches have been separately developed by industrial consortia and international organizations as W3C and OASIS. In particular, WS-CDL [W3C] and WS-BPEL [OAS] specifications represent the most credited languages for the Web Services technology which deal with choreography and orchestration respectively.

Our work aims at synergically exploiting both languages for designing service-based applications where choreography and orchestration can be used for giving different views of the same system. The former one abstracts away from single

* Research partially funded by EU Integrated Project Sensoria, contract n. 016004.

P. Ciancarini and H. Wiklicky (Eds.): COORDINATION 2006, LNCS 4038, pp. 63–81, 2006.

service peculiarities and, by means of *roles*, describes the behaviours of system participants focusing on their access points and the interactions they perform. The latter one is centered on single services by allowing to design their internal activities by means of workflow operators and message exchange capabilities.

In this context the challenge is to identify the interdependencies between the two views and, in particular, a relationship which allows to verify whether a choreography and an orchestrated system describe the same application. A first effort in this direction has been presented in [BGG+05] where a formal framework, devoted to express the relationship between choreography and orchestration, was introduced. The framework is composed by two calculi, inspired by WS-CDL and WS-BPEL, which capture the peculiarities of choreography and orchestration and a notion of conformance between them. In particular, all the framework is centered on the basic interaction mechanisms and the compositional operators exploited to program more complex patterns. Even if the compositional operators are the same at the choreography and the orchestration levels, the basic interaction mechanisms are significantly different. At the choreography level, the basic interaction mechanisms are atomic synchronizations that permit an instantaneous flow of information between two roles. At the orchestration level, on the contrary, the basic interaction mechanisms consider the act of sending (executed by one process) separated from the act of receiving (executed by another independent process). Finally, conformance is a relationship between the two calculi, inspired to bisimulation, which allows us to verify whether the interactions performed by an orchestrated system behave in accordance with the interactions expressed by a given choreography.

Although the interaction mechanisms that can be described with the framework that we have proposed in [BGG+05] are relevant for managing service-oriented applications, they are insufficient for describing complex systems. The main lack of expressiveness is concerned with the impossibility to describe the choices that are performed depending on the contents of the exchanged messages. For instance, let us consider a electronic shop that allows payments via services provided by either Visa or Master Card depending on the kind of credit card used by the buyer. In this example, the interaction pattern that can be expressed with the choreography calculus in [BGG+05] is an alternative choice between a basic interaction involving the electronic shop and the Visa service, or a basic interaction involving the electronic shop and the Marter Card service. The condition governing this choice cannot be specified. Nevertheless, this condition is definitely relevant when conformance comes into play; for instance, an orchestrator that randomly sends the request for payment to either Visa or Master Card is conformant if we abstract away from this aspect.

The aim of this paper is to tackle this lack of expressiveness of our previous version of the framework. The main idea we follow is to introduce state variables both in the choreography and in the orchestration calculi. This extension requires a substantial redefinition of the entire framework. Intuitively, the main problem is concerned with the fact that a state variable at the choreography level could be distributed among different and possibly distributed processes at the orchestration level. For instance, an airplane reservation role could be embodied by a travel agency and several airplane company services. In this case, a state variable associated to the airplane reservation role (e.g. the departure date) is distributed among the travel agency and the airplane companies contacted to complete the reservation. Moreover, in order to faithfully model at the orchestration level the problem of synchronizing the distributed views on the shared state variables, we need to consider asynchronous communication[1] as this is the communication modality provided by the ordinary communication infrastructures.

Many technical novelties are necessary to model faithfully state variables; here we simply recall the most relevant ones. In the calculi, choices are now expressed with two distinct operators: an external non-deterministic choice guarded by basic interaction operations and a conditional construct depending on the state of variables. The operational semantics of the orchestration language is strongly influenced by the asynchronous communication mechanism; in fact, in order to model the basic request-response communication pattern, it is necessary to keep track of the relationship between an asynchronous request message and the corresponding asynchronous response message. The main novelties are in the definition of the conformance relation. In particular it deals with the initial internal state of processes and then introduces different kinds of silent actions for distinguishing between internal and coordinating interactions. The former one is used to describe internal synchronization while the latter one expresses the interactions the orchestrators exploit for respecting the constraints of the choreography and that are not considered in it.

There are other works that consider both choreography and orchestration as complementary approaches for managing service oriented systems. In [CHYa] and [CHYb] Honda et al. present two process calculi: one inspired to WS-CDL and the other to pi-calculus, they formalize the two calculi without presenting any formal relation between them. In [DD04] Dijkman and Dumas exploit Petri nets for describing choreography, orchestration and service interface behaviours focusing on the relationship between a single orchestrator w.r.t. a given choreography. In [BBM+05] Schifanella et al., by means of automaton, defines a conformance notion which allows them to test whether interoperability is guaranteed by limiting the notion to systems involving only two peers. Some other papers about conformance exist like [HM05] and [BGJ+05]. The former focuses on automated testing of behavioural contracts provided by a service, whereas the latter deals only with systems composed by two peers.

The paper is structured as follows. Section 2 presents the language for describing choreography whereas in Section 3 we present the orchestration one. In Section 4 the conformance notion is defined and in Section 5 a business application case study is reported. Section 6 concludes the paper by reporting some final remarks and future work.

---

[1] The formal framework in [BGG+05] considers synchronous communication both for choreography and for orchestration.

2   A Formal Model for Choreography

In this section we introduce the formal model for representing choreography. Intuitively, a choreography is described by three main components: the roles, the initial state constraints on variables and the conversations.

A role represents the behaviour that a participant has to exhibit in order to fulfill the activity defined by the choreography. Each role, which is identified by a name, is equipped with a set of variables and a set of operations.

Operations represent the access point and can have one of the following interaction modalities: *One-Way* or *Request-Response*. Indeed, in WSDL specifications, the most significant types of operations are the *One-Way*, where only the incoming message is defined, and the *Request-Response*, where both the incoming message and the response one are defined.

Let us now introduce the formalization of *roles*, *variables* and *operations*. Let Var be the set of variables ranged over by x, y, z, k. We denote with $\tilde{x}$ tuples of variables, for instance, we may have $\tilde{x} = \langle x_1, x_2, ..., x_n \rangle$. Let $OpName$ be the set of operation names, ranged over by o, and $OpType = \{ow, rr\}$ be the set of operation types where ow denotes a One-Way operation whereas rr denotes the Request-Response one. An operation is described by its operation name and operation type. Namely, let $Op = \{(o, t) \mid o \in OpName, t \in OpType\}$ be the set of operations where each operation is univocally identified by its name. Let $RName$ be the set of the role names, ranged over by ρ and $Role$, defined as $\{(\rho, \omega, V) \mid \rho \in RName, \omega \subseteq Op, V \subseteq Var\}$, be the set which contains all the possible roles.

The state of a choreography describes the variable values and it is represented by a function $\mathcal{S}_C : Var \rightarrow Val \cup \{\bot\}$ from variables to the set $Val \cup \{\bot\}$ ranged over by w. Val, ranged over by v, is a generic set of values on which it is defined a total order relation[2]. $\mathcal{S}_C(x)$ represents the value of variable x in the state $\mathcal{S}_C$ ($\mathcal{S}_C(x) = \bot$ means that x is not yet initialized), while $\mathcal{S}_C[v/x]$ denotes the state $\mathcal{S}_C$ where x holds value v (we use $\mathcal{S}_C[\tilde{v}/\tilde{x}]$ when dealing with tuples of variables), formally:

$$\mathcal{S}_C[v/x] = \mathcal{S}'_C \qquad \mathcal{S}'_C(x') = \begin{cases} v & \text{if } x' = x \\ \mathcal{S}_C(x') & \text{otherwise} \end{cases}$$

A choreography can be designed by considering the fact that some variables can hold only a limited set of values within the initial state. This is the case, for example, of a binary variable which can assume only the values 0 or 1. The following grammar allows us to generate logic conditions on variables which we will exploit for expressing the constraints of the initial state and conditional constructs:

$$\chi ::= x \leq e \mid e \leq x \mid \neg \chi \mid \chi \wedge \chi$$

where e denotes an expression which can contain variables references and which can be evaluated into a value v or, when some variables within the expression

---

[2] we extend such an order relation on the set $Val \cup \{\bot\}$ considering $\bot < v$, $\forall v \in Val$

are not instantiated, into the symbol $\perp$. In the following we use $e \hookrightarrow_{\mathcal{S}_C} w$ to denote that, when the state is $\mathcal{S}_C$, the expression e is evaluated into the value w. It is worth noting that constraints such as $x = v$, $x \neq v$ and $v_1 \leq x < v_2$ can be defined as abbreviations. We exploit the notation $\mathcal{S}_C \vdash \chi$ for denoting that the state $\mathcal{S}_C$ satisfies the condition χ. The satisfaction relation for $\vdash$ is defined by the following rules:

1. $\mathcal{S}_C(x) = \perp \Rightarrow \mathcal{S}_C \vdash (x \leq \perp \wedge \perp \leq x)$
2. $e \hookrightarrow_{\mathcal{S}_C} v, \mathcal{S}_C(x) \leq v \Rightarrow \mathcal{S}_C \vdash x \leq e$
3. $e \hookrightarrow_{\mathcal{S}_C} v, v \leq \mathcal{S}_C(x) \Rightarrow \mathcal{S}_C \vdash e \leq x$
4. $\mathcal{S}_C \vdash \chi' \wedge \mathcal{S}_C \vdash \chi'' \Rightarrow \mathcal{S}_C \vdash \chi' \wedge \chi''$
5. $\neg(\mathcal{S}_C \vdash \chi) \Rightarrow \mathcal{S}_C \vdash \neg\chi$

We highlight the fact that rule 1 states that when a variable x is defined with value $\perp$ the only condition which can be satisfied on such a state is $x = \perp$.

The conversations among the roles are defined by using a conversation language whose definition follows where we intend I as a finite non-empty subset of natural numbers:

$$C ::= \mathbf{0} \mid \eta \mid C; C \mid C|C \mid \sum_{i \in I}^{+} \eta_i; C_i \mid \sum_{i \in I}^{\oplus} \chi_i?\eta_i; C_i$$
$$\eta ::= (\rho_A, \rho_B, o, \widetilde{x}, \widetilde{y}, dir) \mid x := e$$

In the following we use CL_P, ranged over by C, to denote the set of conversations. η represents the basic building block of a conversation which can be an interaction or an assignment. $(\rho_A, \rho_B, o, \widetilde{x}, \widetilde{y}, dir)$ means that an interaction from role ρ_A to role ρ_B is performed. In particular, o is the name of the operation $(o, t) \in Op$ on which the message exchange is performed. Variables $\widetilde{x}$ and $\widetilde{y}$ are those used by the sender and the receiver, respectively and $dir \in \{\uparrow, \downarrow\}$ represents if the interaction is a request ($\uparrow$) or a response ($\downarrow$) one. $x := e$ means that the result of the evaluation of the expression e is assigned to the variable x. Coherently with the grammar of logic conditions, here we abstract away from the syntax of expression e and we exploit the evaluation function $\hookrightarrow_{\mathcal{S}_C}$ introduced above. A conversation can be the null one ($\mathbf{0}$), a basic operation (η), the sequential composition ($C; C$), the parallel composition ($C \mid C$) or two different kind of choices: the non-deterministic choice ($\sum_{i \in I}^{+} \eta_i; C_i$) and the deterministic one ($\sum_{i \in I}^{\oplus} \chi_i?\eta_i; C_i$). The former non-deterministically selects a conversation to execute independently from the state of the choreography whereas in the latter the selection is driven by guard conditions χ. The choice is deterministic because the guards are evaluated in a sequential order.

The semantics of CL_P is defined in terms of a labelled transition system [Kel76] which describes the evolution of a conversation joined with a state. Let $Act_C = \{\mu \mid \mu = (\rho_A, \rho_B, o, \widetilde{v}, dir)\} \cup \{\tau\}$ be the set of actions ranged over by ν where μ represents parameterized interactions. $(C, \mathcal{S}_C) \xrightarrow{\nu} (C', \mathcal{S}_C')$ means that the conversation C in the state $\mathcal{S}_C$ evolves in one step in a configuration $(C', \mathcal{S}_C')$ performing the action ν. Let Γ_C be the set of all possible states over the variables in Var. We define $\rightarrow \subseteq (CL_P, \Gamma_C) \times Act_C \times (CL_P, \Gamma_C)$ as the least relation which

Table 1. Semantics of CL_P

(INTERACTION 1)

$$((\rho_A, \rho_B, o, \tilde{x}, \tilde{y}, \uparrow), \mathcal{S}_C) \xrightarrow{\mu} (\mathbf{0}, \mathcal{S}_C[\tilde{w}/\tilde{y}]), \ \mu = (\rho_A, \rho_B, o, \tilde{w}, \uparrow), \ \tilde{w} = \mathcal{S}_C(\tilde{x})$$

(INTERACTION 2)

$$((\rho_A, \rho_B, o, \tilde{x}, \tilde{y}, \downarrow), \mathcal{S}_C) \xrightarrow{\mu} (\mathbf{0}, \mathcal{S}_C[\tilde{w}/\tilde{x}]), \ \mu = (\rho_A, \rho_B, o, \tilde{w}, \downarrow), \ \tilde{w} = \mathcal{S}_C(\tilde{y})$$

(ASSIGN)

$$\frac{e \hookrightarrow_{\mathcal{S}_C} v}{(x := e, \mathcal{S}_C) \xrightarrow{\tau} (\mathbf{0}, \mathcal{S}_C[v/x])}$$

(SEQUENCE)

$$\frac{(C, \mathcal{S}_C) \xrightarrow{\nu} (C', \mathcal{S}'_C)}{(C; D, \mathcal{S}_C) \xrightarrow{\nu} (C'; D, \mathcal{S}'_C)}$$

(PARALLEL)

$$\frac{(C, \mathcal{S}_C) \xrightarrow{\nu} (C', \mathcal{S}'_C)}{(C \mid D, \mathcal{S}_C) \xrightarrow{\nu} (C' \mid D, \mathcal{S}'_C)}$$

(CONGR)

$$\frac{C' \equiv C, (C, \mathcal{S}_C) \xrightarrow{\nu} (D, \mathcal{S}'_C), D \equiv D'}{(C', \mathcal{S}_C) \xrightarrow{\nu} (D', \mathcal{S}'_C)}$$

(CHOICE 1)

$$\frac{(\eta_i; C_i, \mathcal{S}_C) \xrightarrow{\nu} (C'_i, \mathcal{S}'_C), i \in I}{(\sum_{i \in I}^{+} \eta_i; C_i, \mathcal{S}_C) \xrightarrow{\nu} (C'_i, \mathcal{S}'_C)}$$

(CHOICE 2)

$$\frac{\mathcal{S}_C \vdash \chi_i, (\eta_i, \mathcal{S}_C) \xrightarrow{\nu} (\mathbf{0}, \mathcal{S}'_C), \mathcal{S}_C \nvdash \chi_j, j \in I, j < i}{(\sum_{i \in I}^{\oplus} \chi_i?\eta_i; C_i, \mathcal{S}_C) \xrightarrow{\nu} (C_i, \mathcal{S}'_C)}$$

(STRUCTURAL CONGRUENCE)

$$\mathbf{0}; C \equiv C \qquad C \mid \mathbf{0} \equiv C$$
$$C \mid D \equiv D \mid C \qquad (C \mid D) \mid F \equiv C \mid (D \mid F)$$

---

satisfies the axioms and rules of Table 1 and closed w.r.t. $\equiv$, where $\equiv$ is the least congruence relation satisfying the axioms at the end of Table 1.

The structural congruence $\equiv$, which equates the conversations whose behaviour cannot be distinguished, expresses that $(C, \mid)$ is an abelian monoid where $\mathbf{0}$ is the null element. Furthermore, the rule $\mathbf{0}; C \equiv C$ means that when a conversation completes then the other one which follows in sequence can be performed.

The description of axioms and rules follows. The axioms INTERACTION describe that an interaction, which is a request or a response one depending on the value of dir, is performed. When a request is performed ($dir = \uparrow$) the information contained in the variables $\tilde{x}$ within the sender role ρ_A are passed to the variables $\tilde{y}$ within the receiver role ρ_B exploiting the operation o of the role ρ_B. When a response is performed ($dir = \downarrow$) the information contained in the variables $\tilde{y}$ within the receiver role ρ_B are passed to the variables $\tilde{x}$ within the sender role ρ_A exploiting the operation o of the role ρ_B. The rule ASSIGN states that the resulting value of the expression e, evaluated within the state $\mathcal{S}_C$, is assigned to a variable x thus updating the state of the choreography. Rules SEQUENCE, PARALLEL and CONGR are standard. Rule CHOICE 1 deals with the non-deterministic choice which is independent of the state. It is worth noting that the construct $\eta_i; C_i$ guarantees that the conversation can always move. Rule CHOICE 2, on the contrary, deals with deterministic choice depending on the state $\mathcal{S}_C$. Here, we want to highlight that guards are sequentially evaluated and the first which is satisfied in the state $\mathcal{S}_C$ is selected.

Now we are ready to define a choreography. A choreography, denoted by $\mathcal{C}$, is defined by the tuple (C, Σ, X) where $C \in CL_P$, $\Sigma \subseteq Role$ is a finite set containing all involved roles and X is a logic condition which expresses the variables constraints of the initial state. The constraint expressed by X is strictly pertaining to the choreography because it expresses the set of possible values that variables can hold at the initial state. It is worth noting that such a constraint is not considered when the system evolves.

We say that a choreography $\mathcal{C} = (C, \Sigma, X)$ is *well-formed* if: i) the sets of variables used by roles are disjoint, ii) the variables appearing in each guard condition and each assignment in C involve variables of a single role. In the following we consider only well-formed choreographies.

3   A Formal Model for Orchestration

An orchestrator can be seen as a process, associated to an identifier, that can exchange information, represented by variables, with other processes. Let ID be the set of possible orchestrator identifiers ranged over by id. The language is defined as it follows where we intend I as a finite non-empty set of indexes:

$$P ::= \mathbf{0} \mid \bar{o} \mid \bar{o}(\tilde{y}) \mid \bar{o}(\tilde{x}, \tilde{y}) \mid \epsilon \mid x := e \mid P; P \mid P \mid P \mid \sum_{i \in I}^{+} \epsilon_i; P_i \mid \sum_{i \in I}^{\oplus} \chi_i ? P_i$$
$$\epsilon ::= o \mid o(\tilde{x}) \mid o(\tilde{x}, \tilde{y}, P)$$
$$E ::= [P, \mathcal{S}]_{id} \mid E \parallel E$$

An orchestrated system E consists of the parallel composition of orchestrators. An orchestrator $[P, \mathcal{S}]_{id}$ is a process P identified by id whose variables state is $\mathcal{S}$. The variables state of an orchestrator is described by a function $\mathcal{S} : Var \rightarrow Val \cup \{\bot\}$ mapping variables to values as defined for the choreography. Informally, the idea is that orchestrators are executed on different locations, thus they can be composed by using only the parallel operator ($\parallel$). Processes can be composed in parallel ($\mid$), sequence (;) and with two different alternative composition operators: one is composed of input guarded processes and the other one is composed of processes guarded by conditions on variables state (such processes are of the form $\chi ? P$ where χ is the condition associated to P).

$\mathbf{0}$ represents the null process. Communication mechanisms model Web Services One-Way and Request-Response operations. In particular, we have three kinds of primitives for synchronization, one for the internal synchronization and two for the external one. The former simply consists of a channel o that different threads of the process running in parallel can use to coordinate their activities. In this case no message is exchanged; this is because the orchestrator variables are shared by all threads running on that orchestrator. The primitives for external synchronization, that is between different orchestrators, are the following ones: $o(\tilde{x})$ and $\bar{o}(\tilde{y})$ represent the input and the output of a single message whereas the primitives $o(\tilde{x}, \tilde{y}, P)$ and $\bar{o}(\tilde{x}, \tilde{y})$ represent coupled messages exchanges. In particular we have that $o(\tilde{x})$ represents a One-Way operation whose name is o where the received information is stored in the tuple of variable $\tilde{x}$ of the receiver.

Table 2. Axioms over P

(IN)
$$(o, \mathcal{S}) \xrightarrow{o} (\mathbf{0}, \mathcal{S})$$

(OUT)
$$(\bar{o}, \mathcal{S}) \xrightarrow{\bar{o}} (\mathbf{0}, \mathcal{S})$$

(ONE-WAYOUTASYN)
$$(\bar{o}(\tilde{y}), \mathcal{S}) \xrightarrow{\tau} (\langle \bar{o}(\mathcal{S}(\tilde{y})) \rangle, \mathcal{S})$$

(ONE-WAYOUT)
$$(\langle \bar{o}(\tilde{v}) \rangle, \mathcal{S}) \xrightarrow{\bar{o}(\tilde{v})} (\mathbf{0}, \mathcal{S})$$

(ONE-WAYIN)
$$(o(\tilde{x}), \mathcal{S}) \xrightarrow{o(\tilde{v})} (\mathbf{0}, \mathcal{S}[\tilde{v}/\tilde{x}])$$

(REQ-OUTASYN)
$$(\bar{o}(\tilde{x}, \tilde{y}), \mathcal{S}) \xrightarrow{\tau} (\langle \bar{o}(\mathcal{S}(\tilde{x}), \tilde{y}) \rangle, \mathcal{S})$$

(REQ-OUT)
$$(\langle \bar{o}(\tilde{v}, \tilde{y}) \rangle, \mathcal{S}) \xrightarrow{\bar{o}(\tilde{v}, \tilde{y})(n)} (o_n(\tilde{y}), \mathcal{S})$$

(RESP-OUTASYN)
$$(\bar{o}_n(\tilde{y}), \mathcal{S}) \xrightarrow{\tau} (\langle \bar{o}_n(\mathcal{S}(\tilde{y})) \rangle, \mathcal{S})$$

(RESP-OUT)
$$(\langle \bar{o}_n(\tilde{v}) \rangle, \mathcal{S}) \xrightarrow{\bar{o}_n(\tilde{v})} (\mathbf{0}, \mathcal{S})$$

(REQ-IN)
$$(o(\tilde{x}, \tilde{y}, P), \mathcal{S}) \xrightarrow{o(\tilde{v}, \tilde{y})(n)} (P; \bar{o}_n(\tilde{y}), \mathcal{S}[\tilde{v}/\tilde{x}])$$

(RESP-IN)
$$(o_n(\tilde{x}), \mathcal{S}) \xrightarrow{o_n(\tilde{v})} (\mathbf{0}, \mathcal{S}[\tilde{v}/\tilde{x}])$$

$\bar{o}(\tilde{y})$ represents a One-Way invocation whose name is o and the sent information is stored in the tuple $\tilde{y}$ of the sender. $o(\tilde{x}, \tilde{y}, P)$ represents a Request-Response operation whose name is o. In this case the process receives a message and stores the received information in $\tilde{x}$ then it executes the process P and, at the end, sends the information contained in $\tilde{y}$ as a response message to the invoker. Finally, $\bar{o}(\tilde{x}, \tilde{y})$ represents the invocation of a Request-Response operation whose name is o. The process sends the information contained in $\tilde{x}$ as a request message and stores the information of the response message in $\tilde{y}$. The processes $x := e$ deal with variable assignment.

Let OL be the set of all the orchestrated system ranged over by E. The semantics of OL is defined in terms of a labelled transition system which describes the evolution of an orchestrated system. To this end we exploit the syntax of the language enhanced with terms we use to describe asynchronous communication as it follows:

$$P ::= \ldots \mid \langle \bar{o}(\tilde{v}) \rangle \mid \langle \bar{o}(\tilde{v}, \tilde{y}) \rangle \mid \langle \bar{o}_n(\tilde{v}) \rangle$$

We define $\rightarrow$ as the least relation which satisfies the axioms and rules of Tables 2, 3 and 4. Let $Act_{OL} = \{\bar{o}, o, \bar{o}(\tilde{v}), o(\tilde{v}), \bar{o}(\tilde{v}, \tilde{k})(n), o(\tilde{v}, \tilde{z})(n), \bar{o}_n(\tilde{v}), o_n(\tilde{v}), \sigma, \tau\}$ be the set of actions ranged over by γ. σ is a parameterized action of the form $(id, id', o, \tilde{v}, dir)$ where id, id' are orchestrators ids, o is an operation name, $\tilde{v}$ are tuples of values and $dir \in \{\uparrow, \downarrow\}$.

Table 2 deals with IN, OUT, ONE-WAYOUT, ONE-WAY-IN, REQ-OUT, REQ-IN, RESP-OUT, RESP-IN axioms. It is worth noting that the processes $\langle \bar{o} \rangle$, $\langle \bar{o}(\tilde{y}) \rangle, \langle \bar{o}(\tilde{x}, \tilde{y}) \rangle, \langle \bar{o}_n(\tilde{v}) \rangle$ model asynchronous communication which characterize Service Oriented Computing and in particular Web Services. Indeed, every time an outcoming message process is performed, they "freeze" the value of the variable to be sent and, by exploiting the structural congruence rules of Table 3, they

Table 3. Rules over P

(ASSIGN)
$$\frac{e \hookrightarrow_S v}{(x := e, \mathcal{S}) \xrightarrow{\tau} (\mathbf{0}, \mathcal{S}[v/x])}$$

(INT-SYNC)
$$\frac{(P, \mathcal{S}) \xrightarrow{o} (P', \mathcal{S}) \, , \, (Q, \mathcal{S}) \xrightarrow{\bar{o}} (Q', \mathcal{S})}{(P \mid Q, \mathcal{S}) \xrightarrow{\tau} (P' \mid Q', \mathcal{S})}$$

(CONGRP)
$$\frac{P \equiv_P P' \, , \, (P', \mathcal{S}) \xrightarrow{\gamma} (Q', \mathcal{S}'), \, Q' \equiv_P Q}{(P, \mathcal{S}) \xrightarrow{\gamma} (Q, \mathcal{S}')}$$

(PAR-INT)
$$\frac{(P, \mathcal{S}) \xrightarrow{\gamma} (P', \mathcal{S}')}{(P \mid Q, \mathcal{S}) \xrightarrow{\gamma} (P' \mid Q, \mathcal{S}')}$$

(SEQ)
$$\frac{(P, \mathcal{S}) \xrightarrow{\gamma} (P', \mathcal{S}')}{(P; Q, \mathcal{S}) \xrightarrow{\gamma} (P'; Q, \mathcal{S}')}$$

(CHOICE 1)
$$\frac{(\epsilon_i; P_i, \mathcal{S}) \xrightarrow{\gamma} (P', \mathcal{S}') \quad i \in I}{(\sum_{i \in I}^{+} \epsilon_i; P_i, \mathcal{S}) \xrightarrow{\gamma} (P', \mathcal{S}')}$$

(CHOICE 2)
$$\frac{\mathcal{S} \vdash \chi_i \quad \mathcal{S} \not\vdash \chi_j, j \in I, j < i}{(\sum_{i \in I}^{\oplus} \chi_i ? P_i, \mathcal{S}) \xrightarrow{\tau} (P_i, \mathcal{S})}$$

(STRUCTURAL CONGRUENCE OVER P)

$$P \mid \mathbf{0} \equiv_P P \quad \mathbf{0}; P \equiv_P P \quad (P \mid Q) \equiv_P (Q \mid P) \quad (P \mid Q) \mid R \equiv_P P \mid (Q \mid R)$$
$$(\langle \bar{o} \rangle \, ; Q) \equiv_P (\langle \bar{o} \rangle \mid Q) \quad (\langle \bar{o}(\tilde{v}) \rangle \, ; Q) \equiv_P (\langle \bar{o}(\tilde{v}) \rangle \mid Q)$$
$$(\langle \bar{o}(\tilde{v}, \tilde{y}) \rangle \, ; Q) \equiv_P (\langle \bar{o}(\tilde{v}, \tilde{y}) \rangle \mid Q) \quad (\langle \bar{o}_n(\tilde{v}) \rangle \, ; Q) \equiv_P (\langle \bar{o}_n(\tilde{v}) \rangle \mid Q)$$

goes in parallel with the other processes. In the REQ-IN rule, after the reception of a request on a Request-Response operation the process P must be executed before sending the response.

In Table 3 there are the rules over P where the ASSIGN one deals with variables assignment within the orchestrators. Rule INT-SYNC deals with internal synchronization whereas CONGRP with internal structural congruence denoted by $\equiv_P$. PAR-INT and SEQ describe the behaviour of processes composed in parallel and sequentially, respectively. Finally CHOICE1 and CHOICE2 describe the behavior of the two alternative composition operators. The former one non-deterministically selects among the processes guarded by inputs which can be consumed, while the latter one resembles the deterministic choice, depending on variables state, used in choreography.

In Table 4 the rules at the level of orchestrator system are considered. Rule ONE-WAYSYNC deals with the synchronization on a One-Way operation between two orchestrators whereas the rules REQ-SYNC and RESP-SYNC deal with that on a Request-Response one. Rule REQ-SYNC exploits a fresh label n which is generated in order to univocally link the response synchronization defined in rule RESP-SYNC. Considering the axioms REQ-OUT and REQ-IN indeed, the Request-Response primitives will be transformed into two ONE-WAY (invocation and reception) identified by the label n which is unique and univocally

Table 4. Rules over E

(RULES OVER E)

(ONE-WAYSYNC)

$$\frac{[P,\mathcal{S}]_{id} \overset{\bar{o}(\tilde{v})}{\rightarrow} [P',\mathcal{S}']_{id} \ , \ [Q,\mathcal{T}]_{id'} \overset{o(\tilde{v})}{\rightarrow} [Q',\mathcal{T}']_{id'} \ , \sigma = (id, id', o, \tilde{v}, \uparrow)}{[P,\mathcal{S}]_{id} \parallel [Q,\mathcal{T}]_{id'} \overset{\sigma}{\rightarrow} [P',\mathcal{S}']_{id} \parallel [Q',\mathcal{T}']_{id'}}$$

(REQ-SYNC)

$$\frac{[P,\mathcal{S}]_{id} \overset{\bar{o}(\tilde{v},\tilde{y})(n)}{\rightarrow} [P',\mathcal{S}']_{id} \ , \ [Q,\mathcal{T}]_{id'} \overset{o(\tilde{v},\tilde{y})(n)}{\rightarrow} [Q',\mathcal{T}']_{id'}}{[P,\mathcal{S}]_{id} \parallel [Q,\mathcal{T}]_{id'} \overset{\sigma}{\rightarrow} [P',\mathcal{S}']_{id} \parallel [Q',\mathcal{T}']_{id'}} \ , \ \begin{array}{c} n \ fresh \\ \sigma = (id, id', o, \tilde{v}, \uparrow) \end{array}$$

(RESP-SYNC)

$$\frac{[P,\mathcal{S}]_{id} \overset{o_n(\tilde{v})}{\rightarrow} [P',\mathcal{S}']_{id} \ , \ [Q,\mathcal{T}]_{id'} \overset{\bar{o}_n(\tilde{v})}{\rightarrow} [Q',\mathcal{T}']_{id'} \ , \sigma = (id, id', o, \tilde{v}, \downarrow)}{[P,\mathcal{S}]_{id} \parallel [Q,\mathcal{T}]_{id'} \overset{\sigma}{\rightarrow} [P',\mathcal{S}']_{id} \parallel [Q',\mathcal{T}']_{id'}}$$

(PAR-EXT)

$$\frac{E_1 \overset{\gamma}{\rightarrow} E_1'}{E_1 \parallel E_2 \overset{\gamma}{\rightarrow} E_1' \parallel E_2}$$

(CONGRE)

$$\frac{E_1 \equiv E_1' \ , \ E_1' \overset{\gamma}{\rightarrow} E_2' , \ E_2' \equiv E_2}{E_1 \overset{\gamma}{\rightarrow} E_2}$$

(INT-EXT)

$$\frac{(P,\mathcal{S}) \overset{\gamma}{\rightarrow} (P',\mathcal{S}')}{[P,\mathcal{S}]_{id} \overset{\gamma}{\rightarrow} [P',\mathcal{S}']_{id}}$$

(STRUCTURAL CONGRUENCE OVER E)

$$\frac{P \equiv_P Q}{[P,\mathcal{S}]_{id} \equiv [Q,\mathcal{S}]_{id}}$$

$$E_1 \parallel E_2 \equiv E_2 \parallel E_1 \qquad E_1 \parallel (E_2 \parallel E_3) \equiv (E_1 \parallel E_2) \parallel E_3$$

determined during the synchronization. It is worth noting that all the synchronizations which are performed between different orchestrators are labelled with an action σ. This fact will be fundamental for the definition of the conformance notion presented in the next section. PAR-EXT deals with external parallel composition and CONGRE is for external structural congruence denoted by $\equiv$. INT-EXT expresses the fact that an orchestrator behaves in accordance with its internal processes.

4 Conformance Between Choreography and Orchestration

Our proposal defines a conformance notion based on a relation between the labelled transition system of choreography and the labelled transition system of another model obtained from the orchestration system by associating choreography roles to the orchestrators. In particular, let $\mathcal{C} = (C, \Sigma, X)$ be a choreography and E be an orchestrated system. We define a *joining function*, named Ψ, for associating the orchestrators and the variables of E to the roles of $\mathcal{C}$ and we test the conformance, up to Ψ, of E and $\mathcal{C}$ by using a relation where the σ labels of the former are compared with the μ ones of the latter.

Definition 1 (joining functions). *A joining function is an element of the set*

$$\{\Psi \mid \Psi : ID \to RName \cup \{\bot\} \times (Var \to Var \cup \{\bot\})\}$$

containing functions which associate to each orchestrator identifier a pair composed of a choreography role (or the $\bot$ value in case no role is associated) and a function from orchestrator variables to choreography variables (or the $\bot$ value in case no variable is associated). We denote with Ψ^1 the projection of Ψ on the first element of the pair (the associated role), with Ψ^2 the projection on the second element (the variable mapping function).

Given a joining function Ψ and an action $\sigma = (id, id', o, \tilde{v}, dir)$ of a given orchestrated system where id and id' are orchestrator identifiers, o is an operation, $\tilde{v}$ are tuples of values and $dir \in \{\uparrow, \downarrow\}$, we denote with

$$\Psi[\sigma] = (\Psi^1(id), \Psi^1(id'), o, \tilde{v}, dir)$$

the renaming of the orchestrator identifiers with the joined roles. The projection Ψ^2 will be exploited for joining the initial values of the choreography variables to the related ones of the orchestrated system.

Now we introduce the *conformance notion* between a choreography and an orchestrated system which exploits a relation, named *conformability relation*, inspired to bisimulation [Mil89]. Given a choreography $C = (C, \Sigma, X)$ an orchestrated system E and a joining function Ψ, the idea is to consider all the possible choreography states which satisfy the initial constraint X and for each of them test, up to Ψ, the conformability ($\triangleright_\Psi$) between the labelled transition system of the choreography and a new labeled transition system for the orchestrated systems that we call the *joined labelled transition system*. In particular, in this new transition system the initial values of the variables of the orchestrated system are joined with the choreography ones up to Ψ^2. Furthermore, some hiding operators are applied to the orchestrated system in order to observe only those interactions which are relevant for the choreography. Hiding consists of replacing labels with τ or with a special label $\tilde{\tau}$ and it is applied to three kinds of actions: (i) the interactions that involve an orchestrator not joined with any role are replaced with $\tilde{\tau}$; (ii) the interactions performed on operations not declared in the choreography are replaced with $\tilde{\tau}$; (iii) the interactions which are performed between orchestrators joined with the same role are replaced with τ. The case (iii) is concerned with interactions that corresponds to internal operation within the same role at the level of choreography, while cases (i) and (ii) correspond to coordinating actions that are introduced only at the level of orchestration in order to coordinate distributed orchestrators. For this reason we distinguish these two kinds of actions introducing the new label $\tilde{\tau}$. Formally, such a difference comes into play in the conformability relation.

Definition 2 (Joined labelled transition system). *Given a choreography $C = (C, \Sigma, X)$, an orchestrated system $E \in OL$ and a joining function Ψ such that $Im^1(\Psi) = \Sigma \cup \{\bot\}^3$, let ω_C be the set of operations involved within the*

---

^{3} $Im^1(\Psi) = \{\Psi^1(id) \mid id \in ID\}$

choreography C, let ω_o be the set of operations exhibited by the processes of E and let $E_{OP} = \omega_o/\omega_C$ be the set of operations exhibited by E and which do not appear within the roles of C. Let $E_\perp$ be the set of orchestrator identifiers id of E for which $\Psi(id) = \perp$. We denote the joined labelled transition system with:

$$E ^\frown \Psi^2 / E_{OP} /\!/ E_\perp /\!/\!/ E_{id}$$

where:

- *$E ^\frown \Psi^2$ is an operator which associates the values of the choreography variables in $\mathcal{S}_C$ to the corresponding variables in the states of E up to the joining function Ψ^2. Formally let $\tilde{x}_{id}$ and $\tilde{y}_{id}$ be the tuples of variables in Var which belong to the state of the orchestrator id and for which the following conditions hold respectively: $\Psi^2(id)(\tilde{x}_{id}) \neq \perp$, $\Psi^2(id)(\tilde{y}_{id}) = \perp$ and let $\tilde{v}_{id}$ be the tuple of values of the choreography variables joined with the variables $\tilde{x}_{id}$ that is $\tilde{v}_{id} = \mathcal{S}_C(\Psi^2(id)(\tilde{x}_{id}))$. We have that the $E ^\frown \Psi^2$ is inductively defined as follows:*

  - *$[P, \mathcal{S}]_{id} ^\frown \Psi^2 = [P, \mathcal{S}[\tilde{v}_{id}/\tilde{x}_{id}, \perp/\tilde{y}_{id}]]_{id}$*
  - *$E ^\frown \Psi^2 = [P, \mathcal{S}[\tilde{v}_{id}/\tilde{x}_{id}, \perp/\tilde{y}_{id}]]_{id} \parallel E' ^\frown \Psi^2$*

- *$/E_{OP}$ is a hiding operator which hides, replacing with $\tilde{\tau}$ moves, all the transitions which contain operations contained in E_{OP}*
- *$/\!/ E_\perp$ is a hiding operator which hides, replacing with $\tilde{\tau}$ moves, all the transitions which contain orchestrators not joined with any role.*
- *$/\!/\!/ E_{id}$ hides, replacing with τ moves, all the interactions between the same role (the id of the sender is the same of the receiver).*

In the following we present the conformability relation between the labelled transition system of the choreography and the orchestrated system one. Conformability is inspired by bisimulation but some differences exist. In particular, conformability considers $\tilde{\tau}$ and τ moves differently. Indeed, in order to abstract away from coordinating interactions on the orchestration side, we will exploit the particular arrows $\overset{\sigma}{\Rightarrow}$ and $\overset{\tau}{\Rightarrow}$ for representing the concatenation of the following transitions $\overset{\tilde{\tau}^*}{\rightarrow}\overset{\sigma}{\rightarrow}\overset{\tilde{\tau}^*}{\rightarrow}$ and $\overset{\tilde{\tau}^*}{\rightarrow}\overset{\tau}{\rightarrow}\overset{\tilde{\tau}^*}{\rightarrow}$ respectively. This means that we focus on observable interactions which are represented by σ for the orchestrated system and by $\mu = \Psi^1[\sigma]$ for the choreography. Furthermore, τ actions in choreography, which correspond to assignments, are related to internal role actions in orchestration. It is worth noting that here, we are not interested to distinguish between deadlock and termination states both in choreography and orchestration which are related in conformability by introducing the set of states $C_\delta(\mathcal{S}_C)$ and E_δ defined in the following.

Definition 3 (Conformability). *Let Ψ be a joining function. A relation $\mathcal{R}_\Psi \subseteq ((CL_P, \Gamma_C) \times OL)$ is a conformability relation if $((C, \mathcal{S}_C), E) \in \mathcal{R}_\Psi$ implies that $C \in C_\delta(\mathcal{S}_C)$ and $E \in E_\delta$ or, for all $\mu \in Act_C$ and for all $\sigma \in Act_{OL}$, the following conditions hold:*

1. $(C, \mathcal{S}_C) \xrightarrow{\mu} (C', \mathcal{S}'_C) \Rightarrow E \xrightarrow{\hat{\tau}}^* E' \wedge E' \xrightarrow{\sigma} E'' \wedge E'' \xrightarrow{\hat{\tau}}^* E'''$
   $\wedge \, ((C', \mathcal{S}'_C), E''') \in \mathcal{R}_\Psi \wedge \Psi^1[\sigma] = \mu$

2. $(C, \mathcal{S}_C) \xrightarrow{\tau} (C', \mathcal{S}'_C) \Rightarrow E \xrightarrow{\hat{\tau}}^* E' \wedge E' \xrightarrow{\tau} E'' \wedge E'' \xrightarrow{\hat{\tau}}^* E'''$
   $\wedge \, ((C', \mathcal{S}'_C), E''') \in \mathcal{R}_\Psi$

3. $E \xrightarrow{\sigma} E' \Rightarrow (C, \mathcal{S}_C) \xrightarrow{\tau}^* (C', \mathcal{S}'_C) \wedge (C', \mathcal{S}'_C) \xrightarrow{\mu} (C'', \mathcal{S}''_C) \wedge$
   $\wedge \, (C'', \mathcal{S}''_C) \xrightarrow{\tau}^* (C''', \mathcal{S}'''_C) \wedge ((C''', \mathcal{S}'''_C), E') \in \mathcal{R}_\Psi \wedge \Psi^1[\sigma] = \mu$

4. $E \xrightarrow{\tau} E' \Rightarrow ((C, \mathcal{S}_C), E') \in \mathcal{R}_\Psi \vee ((C, \mathcal{S}_C) \xrightarrow{\tau} (C', \mathcal{S}'_C) \wedge ((C', \mathcal{S}'_C), E') \in \mathcal{R}_\Psi)$

where $\hat{\tau} \in \{\tau, \tilde{\tau}\}$, the arrow $\xRightarrow{\gamma}$ means the concatenation of the following transitions: $\xrightarrow{\tilde{\tau}}^* \xrightarrow{\gamma} \xrightarrow{\tilde{\tau}}^*$ and $C_\delta(\mathcal{S}_C)$ and E_δ are defined as follows:

- $C_\delta(\mathcal{S}_C) = \{C \in CL_P \mid \forall C' \in CL_P \, \nexists \nu, \mathcal{S}'_C \text{ s.t. } (C, \mathcal{S}_C) \xrightarrow{\nu} (C', \mathcal{S}'_C)\}$
- $E_\delta = \{E \in OL \mid \nexists E' \in OL \text{ s.t. } E \xrightarrow{\sigma} E' \vee E \xrightarrow{\tilde{\tau}} E' \vee E \xrightarrow{\tau} E'\}$

We write $(C, \mathcal{S}_C) \triangleright_\Psi E$ if there exists a conformability relation $\mathcal{R}_\Psi$ such that $((C, \mathcal{S}_C), E) \in \mathcal{R}_\Psi$.

We can now conclude this section reporting the formal definition of our conformance notion.

Definition 4 (Conformance). *Given a choreography $C = (C, \Sigma, X)$, an orchestrated system $E \in OL$ and a joining function Ψ such that $Im^1(\Psi) = \Sigma \cup \{\bot\}$, let ω_C be the set of operations involved within the choreography C, let ω_o be the set of operations exhibited by the processes of E and let $E_{OP} = \omega_o / \omega_C$ be the set of operations exhibited by E and which do not appear within the roles of C. Let $E_\bot$ be the set of orchestrator identifiers id of E for which $\Psi(id) = \bot$. We say that E is conformant to C if the following condition holds:*

$$\forall \mathcal{S}_C \in \Gamma_C \text{ s.t. } \mathcal{S}_C \vdash X, (C, \mathcal{S}_C) \triangleright_\Psi E^{\frown \Psi^2} / E_{OP} \| E_\bot \| E_{id}$$

Observe that on the right hand side of $\triangleright_\Psi$ the joined labelled transition system of the orchestrated system defined in Definition 2 is considered.

5 Example

Here we reason about the meaning of conformance by using an example. Let us now consider a business scenario where a customer invokes a market service in order to buy some goods and it receives the price as a response. Considering the price, the customer will buy or not the goods (in this case, for the sake of clarity, we have choosen 100 as a constant for discriminating the price but, in order to abstract away from this value, it could be possible to use a variable with a range of values). If the customer sends a message for buying the market will invoke a supplier service for making the order. The supplier service will accept or not the order. In the case the order can be fulfilled, the market service will invoke a bank service for the payment and will return a positive answer to the customer, the bank service concurrently will send a receipt to the cutomer.

In order to define the choreography let us consider four roles: ρ_C which represents the customer behaviour, ρ_M which represents the market service, ρ_B which represents the bank service for credit card payment and ρ_S which represents the supplier service. For each role we define the following operations and sets of variables:

$$\omega_C = \{(\text{RESULT}, ow), (\text{RECEIPT}, ow)\}, \quad \omega_M = \{(\text{PRICE}, rr), (\text{BUY}, ow)\},$$
$$\omega_S = \{(\text{ORDER}, rr)\}, \quad \omega_B = \{(\text{PAY}, ow)\}.$$
$$V_C = \{good_C, num_C, buy_C, card_C, ncard_C, price_C, outcome_C, receipt_C\}$$
$$V_M = \{good_M, num_M, buy_M, card_M, ncard_M, price_M, outcome_M\}$$
$$V_S = \{good_S, num_S, price_S, outcome_S\}$$
$$V_B = \{card_B, ncard_B, receipt_B, price_B\}$$

Let Σ be the set of roles defined in the following way:
$$\Sigma = \{(\rho_C, \omega_C, V_C), (\rho_M, \omega_M, V_M), (\rho_S, \omega_S, V_S), (\rho_B, \omega_B, V_B)\}.$$

Let Con be the following conversation:

$$Con ::= (PriceReq; BuyReq; (buy_C = accepted?Order; BuyResp)) \mid$$
$$\mid \quad outcome_M = OK?Payment$$

$$PriceReq ::= (\rho_C, \rho_M, \text{PRICE}, good_C \circ num_C, good_M \circ num_M, \uparrow)$$
$$; \quad (\rho_C, \rho_M, \text{PRICE}, price_C, price_M, \downarrow)$$

$$BuyReq ::= ((price_C \geq 100?buy_C := cancelled; card_C := null; ncard_C := null)$$
$$\oplus \quad (price_C < 100?buy_C := accepted))$$
$$; \quad (\rho_C, \rho_M, \text{BUY}, buy_C \circ card_C \circ ncard_C, buy_M \circ card_M \circ ncard_M, \uparrow))$$

$$Order ::= (\rho_M, \rho_S, \text{ORDER}, good_M \circ num_M, good_S \circ num_S, \uparrow)$$
$$; \quad (\rho_M, \rho_S, \text{ORDER}, outcome_M, outcome_S, \downarrow)$$

$$BuyResp ::= (\rho_M, \rho_C, \text{RESULT}, outcome_M, outcome_C, \uparrow)$$

$$Payment ::= (\rho_M, \rho_B, \text{PAY}, card_M \circ ncard_M \circ price_M, card_B \circ ncard_B \circ price_B, \uparrow)$$
$$; \quad (\rho_B, \rho_C, \text{RECEIPT}, receipt_B, receipt_C, \uparrow)$$

Finally, we define the following initial constraints over the variables:

$$X = good_C \in \{apple, banana\} \wedge$$
$$\wedge \ 0 \leq num_C \leq 200 \wedge$$
$$\wedge \ card_C \in \{visa, mastercard\} \wedge$$
$$\wedge \ ncard_C = price_C = buy_C = receipt_C = outcome_C = \bot \wedge$$

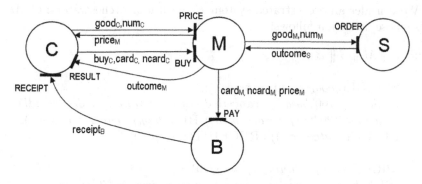

Fig. 1. Interactions among the roles

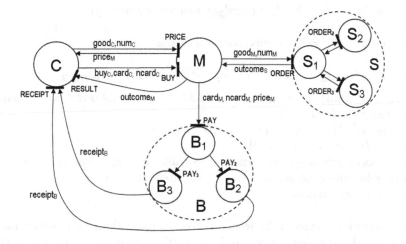

Fig. 2. Orchestration system E_2

$\wedge\ good_M = num_M = card_M = ncard_M = buy_M = outcome_M = \perp \wedge$
$\wedge\ 50 \leq price_M \leq 200 \wedge$
$\wedge\ goods_S = nums_S = cards_S = \perp \wedge$
$\wedge\ outcome_S \in \{OK, REJECTED\} \wedge$
$\wedge\ receipt_B = ReceiptDoc \wedge$
$\wedge\ card_B = ncard_B = price_B = \perp$

We consider the choreography $Chor = (Con, \Sigma, X)$. In Fig. 1 are graphically represented the interactions among the roles set by Con without showing the order they are performed. The circles are the roles, the bold segments are the operations and the arrows are the interactions. In the following we present two possible orchestrated systems both conformant with the choreography $Chor$. Here we intend to show that the orchestrated system can have different levels of refinement without loosing the conformance with a given choreography.

1. We consider an orchestrated system E_1 with four orchestrators: C, M, S and B whose definition follows:

$$E_1 ::= C \parallel M \parallel S \parallel B$$

$$
\begin{aligned}
C ::= &[(\overline{\text{PRICE}}(good_C \circ num_C, price_C); \\
; \quad &((price_C \geq 100?buy_C := cancelled; card_C := null; ncard_C := null) \\
\oplus \quad &(price_C < 100?buy_C := accepted)); \overline{\text{BUY}}(buy_C \circ card_C \circ ncard_C) \\
; \quad &\text{RESULT}(outcome_C)) \mid \text{RECEIPT}(receipt_C)]_C
\end{aligned}
$$

$$
\begin{aligned}
M ::= &[\text{PRICE}(good_M \circ num_M, price_M, \mathbf{0}) \\
\mid \quad &(\text{BUY}(buy_M \circ card_M \circ ncard_M)); buy_M = accepted?Ord)]_M \\
Ord ::= &\overline{\text{ORDER}}(good_M \circ num_M, outcome_M); (\overline{\text{RESULT}}(outcome_M) \\
\mid \quad &outcome_M = OK?\overline{\text{PAY}}(card_M \circ ncard_M \circ price_M))
\end{aligned}
$$

$$S ::= [\text{ORDER}(good_S \circ num_S, outcome_S, \mathbf{0})]_S$$

$$B ::= [\text{PAY}(card_B \circ ncard_B \circ price_B); \overline{\text{RECEIPT}}(receipt_B)]_B$$

We consider a joining function Ψ where C, M, S and B embody roles ρ_C, ρ_M, ρ_S and ρ_B, respectively that is:
$\Psi^1(C) = \rho_C, \Psi^1(M) = \rho_M, \Psi^1(S) = \rho_S, \Psi^1(B) = \rho_B$,
$\Psi^1(id) = \perp$ for $id \notin \{C, M, S, B\}$.
As far as the variables are concerned we consider a joining function projection Ψ^2 which joins the orchestrated system variables with the choreography ones that have the same name.

2. We consider a system E_2 where there are more than four orchestrators. In particular the supplier service and the bank service are splitted into three orchestrators which are joined to the same role.

$$E_2 ::= C \parallel M \parallel S_1 \parallel S_2 \parallel S_3 \parallel B_1 \parallel B_2 \parallel B_3$$

$$
\begin{aligned}
C ::= &[(\overline{\text{PRICE}}(good_C \circ num_C, price_C); \\
; \quad &((price_C \geq 100?buy_C := cancelled; card_C := null; ncard_C := null) \\
\oplus \quad &(price_C < 100?buy_C := accepted)); \overline{\text{BUY}}(buy_C \circ card_C \circ ncard_C)) \\
; \quad &\text{RESULT}(outcome_C)) \mid \text{RECEIPT}(receipt_C)]_C
\end{aligned}
$$

$$
\begin{aligned}
M ::= &[\text{PRICE}(good_M \circ num_M, price_M, \mathbf{0}) \mid \\
\mid \quad &(\text{BUY}(buy_M \circ card_M \circ ncard_M)); buy_M = accepted?Ord))]_M \\
Ord ::= &\overline{\text{ORDER}}(good_M \circ num_M, outcome_M); (\overline{\text{RESULT}}(outcome_M) \\
\mid \quad &outcome_M = OK?\overline{\text{PAY}}(card_M \circ ncard_M \circ price_M))
\end{aligned}
$$

$$
\begin{aligned}
S_1 ::= &[\text{ORDER}(good_{S1} \circ num_{S1}, outcome_{S1}, SelS)]_{S1} \\
SelS ::= &good_{S1} = apple?\overline{\text{ORDER}}_2(good_{S1} \circ num_{S1}, outcome_{S1}) \\
\oplus \quad &good_{S1} = banana?\overline{\text{ORDER}}_3(good_{S1} \circ num_{S1}, outcome_{S1})
\end{aligned}
$$

$$S_2 ::= [ORDER_2(goods_{S2} \circ num_{S2}, outcome_{S2}, \mathbf{0})]_{S2}$$
$$S_3 ::= [ORDER_3(goods_{S3} \circ num_{S3}, outcome_{S3}, \mathbf{0})]_{S3}$$

$$B_1 ::= [PAY(card_{B1} \circ ncard_{B1} \circ price_{B1});$$
$$; (card_{B1} = visa?\overline{PAY_2}(card_{B1} \circ ncard_{B1} \circ price_{B1})$$
$$\oplus\ card_{B1} = mastercard?\overline{PAY_3}(card_{B1} \circ ncard_{B1} \circ price_{B1}))]_{B1}$$
$$B_2 ::= [PAY_2(card_{B2} \circ ncard_{B2} \circ price_{B2}); \overline{RECEIPT}(receipt_{B2})]_{B2}$$
$$B_3 ::= [PAY_3(card_{B3} \circ ncard_{B3} \circ price_{B3}); \overline{RECEIPT}(receipt_{B3})]_{B3}$$

We consider the following joining function: $\Psi^1(C) = \rho_C, \Psi^1(M) = \rho_M, \Psi^1(S_1)$ $= \rho_S, \Psi^1(S_2) = \rho_S, \Psi^1(S_3) = \rho_S, \Psi^1(B_1) = \rho_B, \Psi^1(B_2) = \rho_B, \Psi^1(B_3) = \rho_B$ $\Psi^1(id) = \perp$ for $id \notin \{C, M, S_1, S_2, S_3, B_1, B_2, B_3\}$.

As for as the variables are concerned we exploit the same rule used for example 1 but with the following differences:

$$\Psi^2(S_1)(goods_{S1} = goods_S)$$
$$\Psi^2(S_1)(num_{S1} = num_S)$$
$$\Psi^2(B_1)(card_{B1} = card_B)$$
$$\Psi^2(B_1)(price_{B1} = price_B)$$
$$\Psi^2(S_2)(outcome_{S2} = outcome_S)$$
$$\Psi^2(S_3)(outcome_{S3} = outcome_S)$$
$$\Psi^2(B_2)(receipt_{B2} = receipt_B)$$
$$\Psi^2(B_3)(receipt_{B3} = receipt_B)$$

The first orchestrated system joins strongly the choreography because there is an orchestrator for each role and all the variables are the same, furthermore all the communications follow the choreography conversation. On the contrary, the second one shows how roles can be splitted on more than one orchestrator without loosing the conformance with the choreography. In particular it is worth noting that interactions within roles S and B are irrelevant to the end of conformance because they are performed between orchestrators joined with the same role. Such a kind of interaction are hidden by the $/\!/\!/ E_{id}$ operator.

6 Conclusion

In this work we continue the line of research initiated in [BGG+05] devoted to the formalization of the notion of conformance between a choreography and an orchestrated system, as well as the formalization of the notion of orchestration and choreography languages. More precisely, we extend our formal framework with the notion of state and asynchronous communication. The introduction of state is fundamental to specify the dependencies of system behavior on actual values, for instance, the fact that a customer selects one seller because it offers the best price. The second modification is useful to have a closer modeling of the way orchestrators actually communicate on, e.g., the Internet.

From a technical point of view, these extensions have required a considerable amount of work related to an appropriate modeling of nondeterminism. In particular, we had to significantly rephrase the notion of conformance. Moreover, the new notion of conformance supports the distributed implementation at the orchestration level of choreography roles. For instance, an abstract role for credit card payment can be actually implemented by means of a group of orchestrators that support the interaction between banks and credit card institutions.

The conformance notion we have defined between these two concrete languages is a powerful mechanism for designing and developing complex systems. The designer can start the design phase by programming the choreography and, in a second stage, to program and refine orchestrated systems testing, step by step, its conformance w.r.t. the choreography thus obtaining a correct implementation of the system.

As future work we intend to develop a mathematical machinery for extracting the interfaces and the workflow skeleton of the orchestrators starting from a given choreography. This will permit to verify the conformance even when the whole set of orchestrator is not completely known (the unknown orchestrators will be synthesized directly from the the choreography). As far as process calculi are concerned we intend to make a closer comparison between the two languages we propose and the most interesting proposals like WS-BPEL for orchestration and WS-CDL for choreography. In [GGL05] we present a partial comparison which investigates the interactions patterns by drawing a parallel between WS-CDL and our choreography language.

References

[BBM+05]   M. Baldoni, C. Badoglio, A. Martelli, V. Patti, and C. Schifanella. Verifying the conformance of web services to global interaction protocols: a first step. In *Proc. of Web Services and Formal Methods Workshop (WS-FM'05)*, volume 3670 of *LNCS*, pages 257–271. Springer-Verlag, 2005.

[BGG+05]   Nadia Busi, Roberto Gorrieri, Claudio Guidi, Roberto Lucchi, and Gianluigi Zavattaro. Choreography and orchestration: A synergic approach for system design. In *ICSOC (International Conference of Service Oriented Computing)*, pages 228–240, 2005.

[BGJ+05]   T. Berg, O. Grinchtein, B. Jonsson, M. Leucker, H. Raffelt, and B. Steffen. On the Correspondence Between Conformance Testing and Regular Inference. In *Proc. of Fundmental Approaches to Software Engineering (FASE'05)*, volume 3442 of *LNCS*, pages 175–189. Springer-Verlag, 2005.

[CHYa]   Marco Carbone, Kohei Honda, and Nabuko Yoshida. Programming interaction with types. [http://www.w3.org/2002/ws/chor/5/06/ F2FJune14.pdf], W3C WS-CDL WG London F2F, June 14 2002.

[CHYb]   Marco Carbone, Kohei Honda, and Nabuko Yoshida. A theoretical basis of communication-centred concurrent programming. Posted at w3-chor mailing list, November 2005.

[DD04]   Remco Dijkman and Marlon Dumas. Service-oriented design: A multiviewpoint approach. *Int. J. Cooperative Inf. Syst.*, 13(4):337–368, 2004.

[GGL05]   R. Gorrieri, C. Guidi, and R. Lucchi. Reasoning on the interaction patterns
in choreography. In *Proc. of Web Services and Formal Methods Workshop
(WS-FM'05)*, volume 3670 of *LNCS*, pages 333–348. Springer-Verlag, 2005.

[HM05]   R. Heckel and L. Mariani. Automatic Conformance Testing of Web
Services. In *Proc. of Fundmental Approaches to Software Engineering
(FASE'05)*, volume 3442 of *LNCS*, pages 34–48. Springer-Verlag, 2005.

[Kel76]   Robert M. Keller. Formal verification of parallel programs. *Commun.
ACM*, 19(7):371–384, 1976.

[Mil89]   Robin Milner. *Communication and Concurrency*. Prentice Hall, 1989.

[OAS]   OASIS. *Web Services Business Process Execution Language Version 2.0,
Working Draft.* [http://www.oasis-open.org/committees/download.php/
10347/wsbpel-specification-draft-120204.htm].

[W3C]   W3C. *Web Services Choreography Description Language Version
1.0. Working draft 17 December 2004.* [http://www.w3.org/TR/2004/
WD-ws-cdl-10-20041217/].

Workflow Patterns in Orc

William R. Cook, Sourabh Patwardhan, and Jayadev Misra

Department of Computer Sciences, University of Texas at Austin
{wcook, sourabh, misra}@cs.utexas.edu

Abstract. Van der Aalst recently proposed a set of *workflow patterns* to characterize the kinds of control flow that appear frequently in workflow processes. These patterns are useful for evaluating the capabilities of workflow systems and models. In this paper we provide implementations of the workflow patterns in Orc, a new process calculus for orchestrating wide-area computations. A key feature of the Orc implementations is that they are expressed as *definitions* that can be reused as needed.

1 Introduction

The concept of workflow is familiar to anyone who has worked in an organization: achieving almost any goal requires coordination of multiple activities involving multiple participants. These activities are typically subject to many constraints and dependencies governing the order of activities and the capabilities of participants. Exceptional situations, interrupts, and failures must also be handled without losing sight of the end goal.

Despite the familiar and prosaic nature of workflow, developing formal models and languages for expressing workflows has proven to be a significant research challenge. The Workflow Management Coalition defines workflow informally as "The computerised facilitation or automation of a business process, in whole or part." [14] Their reference model defines vocabulary and identifies the interfaces into and out of a workflow system, but it does not provide a formal model of workflow.

Formal models of concurrency are being applied to the analysis of workflow. Petri Nets, which are a variant of finite state automata, have been used to model workflows for many years [1, 5]. Others have proposed using the π-calculus as a workflow model [9]. UML activity diagrams, which are a form of flowchart, have also been used extensively in analysis and design of workflows [4, 6]. There is as yet no widely-accepted formal model of workflow. The lack of a fundamental model of workflow makes it difficult to compare different models.

Recently van der Aalst proposed a set of workflow patterns [2] to characterize the kinds of control flow that appear frequently in workflow processes. The patterns facilitate comparison of very different workflow products and models: products can be compared quantitatively by counting the number of workflow patterns they can express directly, and qualitatively by examining the complexity of each pattern's implementation. The patterns have been implemented in a wide range of systems, providing surprising range of solutions to these common problems [2, 11, 13, 9].

P. Ciancarini and H. Wiklicky (Eds.): COORDINATION 2006, LNCS 4038, pp. 82–96, 2006.
© Springer-Verlag Berlin Heidelberg 2006

This paper shows how Orc [8], a new orchestration language, can be used to implement the workflow patterns. Orc is a process calculus in which basic services, like user interaction and data manipulation, are implemented by primitive *sites*. Orc provides constructs to orchestrate the concurrent invocation of sites to achieve a goal – while managing time-outs, priorities, and failure of sites or communication. Orc has already been used to implement a variety of traditional concurrent programming patterns [8], some of which overlap with the workflow patterns.

One difficulty in using van der Aalst's patterns is that the patterns are not formally defined. The informal descriptions are suggestive but in many cases admit several interpretations. The implementations in this paper are based on a study of the original pattern descriptions [2] and their implementation in [11].

2 Overview of Orc

An Orc program consists of a set of definitions and a *goal* expression which is to be evaluated. The evaluation of the goal expression calls sites (see below) and defined expressions, and *publishes* values. In this section, we give an informal overview of the programming model. For more a more detailed discussion and a formal semantics, see [8].

2.1 Syntax

In the following syntax, E is an expression name, M a site name, x a variable, c a constant, $\bar{p}$ a list of actual parameters and $\bar{q}$ a list of formal parameters.

$$
\begin{array}{rl}
e, f, g, h \in Expression & ::= M(\bar{p}) \parallel E(\bar{p}) \parallel f >x> g \parallel f \mid g \parallel f \text{ where } x :\in g \parallel x \\
p \in Actual & ::= x \parallel M \parallel c \parallel f \\
q \in Formal & ::= x \parallel M \\
Definition & ::= E(\bar{q}) \; \underline{\Delta} \; f
\end{array}
$$

An expression can be a site call $M(\bar{p})$, or a call to a defined expression $E(\bar{p})$. There are only three operators: $>x>$ for sequential composition, $\mid$ for parallel composition, and **where** for asymmetric parallel composition. The operators are listed in decreasing order of precedence, so that $f >x> g \mid h$ means $(f >x> g) \mid h$. The following sections discuss each kind of expression in turn. The syntax of Orc is extended here to include expressions as arguments in calls to definitions, using the same substitution semantics given in [8].

2.2 Site Call

The simplest Orc expression is a *site* call $M(\bar{p})$, where M is a site name and $\bar{p}$ is a list of actual parameters. A site is a separately defined procedure, like a web service. The site may be implemented on the client's machine or a remote machine. A site call elicits at most one response; it is possible that a site never responds to a call.

A site call $CNN(d)$, where CNN is a news service and d is a date, may download the newspage for the specified date. Calling $Email(a, m)$ sends message m to address a, causing permanent change in the state of the recipient's mailbox, and returns a signal to the client to denote completion of the operation. Calling an airline flight-booking site returns the booking information and causes a tentative state change in the airline database.

Site calls are *strict*, i.e., a site is called only if all its parameters have values.

We define a few sites in Table 1 that are fundamental to effective programming in Orc. Additionally, **0** represents a site which never responds; it may be used to terminate certain parts of a computation. Orc expressions can use $Rtimer$ to manage time, although none of the current workflow patterns require this ability.

Table 1. Fundamental Sites

$let(x, y, \cdots)$	Returns argument values as a tuple.
$if(b)$	Returns a signal if b is true, and it does not respond if b is false.
$Signal$	Returns a signal. It is same as $if(true)$.
$Rtimer(t)$	Returns a signal after exactly t time units.

We have made very few assumptions about the behaviors of sites because we want to orchestrate sites which may have unpredictable delays, including infinite delays, i.e., failing to respond. This generality allows us to regard humans (and their communication devices) as sites and include them in orchestrations. An Orc program may act as the director of a coordinated activity, such as 9-11 dispatching, in which it instructs humans (police, medical personnel) and listens to their responses.

A site M can have multiple entry points, denoted by $M.n$ where n is the name of a method in the site.

2.3   Composition Operators

As we have described earlier, evaluation of an Orc expression calls some sites and *publishes* a set of values. In Section 2.2, we considered simple expressions like $CNN(d)$; evaluation of this expression calls site CNN and publishes the value, if any, returned by the site. In this section, we discuss the syntax and semantics of general Orc expressions in informal terms.

There are three composition operators in Orc to combine expressions. Symmetric composition of f and g, written as $f \mid g$, evaluates f and g independently. The sites called by f and g are the ones called by $f \mid g$ and a value published by either f or g is a value published by $f \mid g$. Expressions f and g are evaluated independently. There is no direct communication or interaction between these two computations; the computations may interact only by accessing a common site. For example, f may write into a cell by calling site $Write$ and g may read that cell by calling $Read$.

Condition : *set, wait*

A condition allows multiple activities to wait until an event happens. Before *set* is called, all calls to *wait* block. When *set* is called, all waiting activities are enabled and future calls to *wait* return immediately.

Buffer : *put, get*

The result of *Buffer* is a local buffer site with two operations, *put* and *get*. The *put* operation adds values to the buffer and publishes a signal on completion. The *get* operation returns an item from the buffer – it blocks until an item is available.

Lock : *acquire, release*

A lock has exactly one owner. When the lock is created it is not owned. An expression that acquires the lock becomes its owner, and all subsequent calls to *acquire* will block until the owner calls *release*. At that point, one of the blocked expressions, if any, will be given ownership and unblocked.

Fig. 1. Definition of three factory sites used in the workflow implementations. Each factory site returns a local site that implements one or more methods. The method names are listed in italics after the factory name.

In $f >x> g$, expression f is evaluated, each value published by it initiates a fresh evaluation of g as a separate computation, and the value published by f is called x in g's computation. Variable x may be a parameter in a site call in g. Evaluation of f continues while (possibly several) evaluations of g are run. This is the only mechanism in Orc similar to spawning threads. If f is *silent* (i.e. publishes no value), g is never evaluated. If f publishes a single value, there is strict sequencing in the evaluations of f and g. The values published by the executions of g are the values published by $f >x> g$. As an example, the following expressions calls sites *CNN* and *BBC* in parallel to get the news for date d. Any results from either of these sites are bound to x and then site *email* is called to send the information to address a.

$$(CNN(d) \mid BBC(d)) >x> email(a, x)$$

The expression $f \gg g$ is a short-hand for $f >x> g$ when the variable x is not needed.

To evaluate $(g \textbf{ where } x :\in f)$, start by evaluating both f and g in parallel. Evaluation of parts of g which do not depend on x can proceed, but site calls in which x is a parameter are suspended until it acquires a value. In $((M \mid N(x)) \textbf{ where } x :\in R)$, for example, evaluation M can proceed even before x has a value. If f publishes a value, then x is assigned this value, f's evaluation is terminated and the suspended parts of g can proceed. This is the only mechanism in Orc to block and terminate parts of a computation.

2.4   Definitions

Declaration $E(\bar{q}) \;\triangleq\; f$ defines expression E whose formal parameter list is $\bar{q}$ and body is expression f. A call $E(\bar{p})$ is evaluated by replacing the formal parameters $\bar{q}$ by the actual parameters $\bar{p}$ in the body of the definition f. Sites are called by value, while definitions are called by name.

2.5   Local Sites

A *local site* is a site that is created during execution of an expression. A local site is constructed by a *factory* site, which publishes a site when called. The factory sites used in the workflow implementations are defined in Fig. 1. The sites returned by the factory contain multiple methods. For example, the *Buffer* factory returns a site with *put* and *get* methods.

The following Orc expression illustrates the use of local sites. It creates a buffer, then executes three expressions in parallel, two of which insert numbers into the buffer while the other attempts to read from the buffer:

$$Buffer >b> \; (b.put(3) \mid b.put(5) \mid b.get)$$

The value obtained by $b.get$ is either 3 or 5. Expression $b.get$ is blocked until one of the first two expressions is completed.

2.6   Synchronous Execution

We impose the following constraints on the Orc semantics: (1) a site is called as soon as possible, and (2) response from a site is processed only if there is no pending site call to be made. Therefore, initially, Orc calls all sites which can be called, and then it waits to receive a response. On receiving a response, it may publish some values and call some sites and waits for the next response. An expression publishes a (possibly empty) stream of values (position in the stream depends on the time of publication). The synchronous semantics ensures that in $(g \;\textbf{where}\; x :\in f)$, the first value published by f is assigned to x.

3   Workflows in Orc

A workflow consists of a set of activities generating output in the form of data or events which may trigger further actions. These activities can be executed in sequential or parallel order. A workflow can be represented by a composition of elementary patterns as discussed in the subsequent sections. These patterns are modeled by composition of basic Orc expressions and Orc site calls. An Orc expression or site call may publish (produce) zero or more values as output.

We will use the workflow term "activity" to refer to an Orc expression that publishes at most one value and stops execution after this value is produced: an activity is complete when it publishes its value. Orc expressions that produce more then one value, or continue to call sites after producing a value, are not considered well-formed activities, but they can be converted into proper form by terminating them after the first value is produced.

Some patterns also use activities to signal *events*. In this case the event occurs when the activity publishes its value.

The following sections correspond to the patterns defined by van der Aalst [2]. We assume that f and g represent well-formed activities, unless stated otherwise.

WP 1: Sequence. "An activity in a workflow process is enabled after the completion of another activity in the same process. Example: After the activity *order registration* the activity *customer notification* is executed." [11]

Sequential execution is a built-in feature of Orc.

$$Seq(f,g) \; \underline{\Delta} \; f \gg g$$

If f and g are activities, then the sequential composition is an activity. Note that if f is not an activity (i.e. it produces more than one value) g will be executed more than once.

WP 2: Parallel Split. "A point in the process where a single thread of control splits into multiple threads of control which can be executed in parallel, thus allowing activities to be executed simultaneously or in any order. Example: After activity *new cellphone subscription order* the activity *insert new subscription in Home Location Registry application* and *insert new subscription in Mobile answer application* are executed in parallel." [11]

The ability to run activities in parallel is an inherent feature of Orc.

$$Par(\bar{f}) \; \underline{\Delta} \; f_1 \mid \cdots \mid f_n$$

A bar over an expression $\bar{x}$ represents a list of items $x_1, \ldots, x_n$. The expression created by Par is not a well-formed activity, however, because it produces more than one value. The Discriminator pattern discussed in Section 3 can be used to model a well-formed activity by ensuring termination after the first value has been produced.

WP 3: Synchronization. "A point in the process where multiple parallel branches converge into one single thread of control, thus synchronizing multiple threads. ... Example: Activity *archive* is executed after the completion of both activity *send tickets* and activity *receive payment*." [11]

Synchronization is a standard pattern in concurrent systems; its implementation in Orc was presented in [8].

$$Sync(\bar{f}) \; \underline{\Delta} \; let(x_1) \gg \cdots \gg let(x_n)$$
$$\textbf{where } x_1 :\in f_1$$
$$\cdots$$
$$\textbf{where } x_n :\in f_n$$

This expression uses asymmetric parallel composition to run the expressions f_i in parallel. The output of each expression is captured in a corresponding variable x_i,

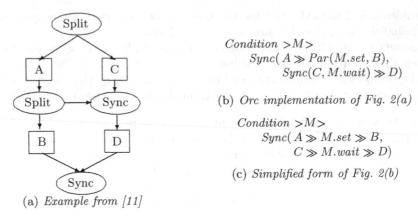

Condition $>M>$
  Sync($A \gg Par(M.set, B)$,
        Sync($C, M.wait$) $\gg D$)

(b) *Orc implementation of Fig. 2(a)*

Condition $>M>$
  Sync($A \gg M.set \gg B$,
        $C \gg M.wait \gg D$)

(c) *Simplified form of Fig. 2(b)*

(a) *Example from [11]*

Fig. 2. Unstructured workflow example

which is undefined until f_i publishes its value. The body of the **where** expression calls *let* on each variable: since site calls are strict, the sequence of calls will block until all the variables $\bar{x}$ are defined – that is, it will block until all the activities f_i are complete.

Synchronization of multiple activities is always a well-formed activity, even if f_i may produce more than one value. This is because *Sync* takes just the first value of each sub-expression and then terminates the sub-expression.

The previous example is a *structured* workflow, because the structure of synchronization matches the control flow structure: the expressions being synchronized are defined within the same composition operator. In an *unstructured* workflow, the expressions being synchronized appear in different places in the flow of control. Unstructured workflows are frequently more difficult to describe than structured workflows. Van der Aalst gives an example of an unstructured workflow, reproduced in Fig. 2(a), in which the synchronization path does not follow the structure of sub-expressions. This workflow cannot be expressed using only structured workflow constructs. In Orc, it requires a local site to express the communication between parallel branches, as defined in Fig. 2(b). The expression first creates a *Condition*, a local site defined in Section 2.5. The first *Sync* expression represents the Split/Sync nodes at the top and bottom of Fig. 2(a). This is a structured synchronization. The left path A/Split/B is implemented by $A \gg (M.set \mid B)$, which executes A and then sets the condition to true and executes B. The right path C/Sync/D is implemented by *Sync*($C, M.wait$) $\gg D$, which uses *Sync* to wait for C to complete and the condition to be set. When these two events have been synchronized, D is executed.

The expression in Fig. 2(b) corresponds closely to the diagram in Fig. 2(a), but it can be simplified to a more readable from in Fig. 2(c). This simplification replaces parallel execution with sequential execution. But the overall effect is the same if *set* and *wait* are instantaneous: instead of executing them in parallel with B or C, they can simply executed sequentially (before B and after C, respectively). Such transformations can be obtained through algebraic manipulation of Orc expressions.

WP 4: Exclusive Choice. "A point in the process where, based on a decision or workflow control data, one of several branches is chosen. Example: The manager is informed if an order exceeds $600, otherwise not."[11]

An exclusive choice is simply a conditional, or "if" statement.

$$XOR(b, f, g) \triangleq if(b) \gg f \mid if(\neg b) \gg g$$

The built-in *if* site (see Table 1) does not publish a value when the condition is false, so only one of the two parallel alternatives will execute. Exclusive choice, like other patterns above, naturally generalizes to a choice between a set of options, also known as a case statement. Nested conditional constructs can also be represented using XOR. An example is given below.

$$XOR(b_1, f, XOR(b_2, g, XOR(b_3, h, i)))$$

WP 5: Simple Merge. A *merge* is "a point in the workflow process where two or more alternative branches come together ... Example: After the payment is received or the credit is granted the car is delivered to the customer."[2] A simple merge assumes that only *one* of the expressions being merged is executing, so synchronization is not needed. Petri nets represent merges explicitly, while in Orc a merge is implicit in the structure of an expression. In the following, we assume that only of the f_i expressions will produce a value.

$$Merge(\bar{f}, h) \triangleq Par(\bar{f}) \gg h$$

WP 6: Multi-choice. "A point in the process, where, based on a decision or control data, a number of branches are chosen and executed as parallel threads. Example: After executing the activity *evaluate damage* the activity *contact fire department* or the activity *contact insurance company* is executed. At least one of these activities is executed. However, it is also possible that both need to be executed."[11]

A Multi-Choice is a non-exclusive choice. A separate condition controls the execution of each choice, and multiple conditions can be true.

$$MultiChoice(\bar{b}, \bar{f}) \triangleq IfDo(b_1, f_1) \mid \cdots \mid IfDo(b_n, f_n)$$
$$IfDo(b, f) \triangleq if(b) \gg f$$

WP 7: Synchronizing Merge. "A point in the process where multiple paths converge into one single thread. Some of these paths are active (i.e. they are being executed) and some are not. If only one path is active, the activity after the merge is triggered as soon as this path completes. If more than one path is active, synchronization of all active paths needs to take place before the next activity is triggered. ... Example: After either or both of the activities *contact fire department* and *contact insurance company* have been completed (depending on whether they were executed at all), the activity *submit report* needs to be performed (exactly once)."[11]

This pattern is implemented in Orc by modifying the *IfDo* expression to always publish a signal when it completes, even if the condition is false. The resulting conditional activities can then be synchronized.

$$SyncMerge(\bar{b}, \bar{f}) \triangleq Sync(IfSignal(b_1, f_1), \cdots, IfSignal(b_n, f_n))$$
$$IfSignal(b, f) \triangleq if(b) \gg f \mid if(\neg b)$$

Van der Aalst creates an unstructured example of synchronizing merge by replacing the Split at the top of Fig. 2(a) with a Multi-Choice, and the two Synchronize nodes with Synchronizing Merges. He says "then the process must somehow keep track of the activation of the left thread in order to determine whether activity D should be activated immediately after activity C completes, or whether it should also wait for activity A to complete."[11] Assuming that the left and right conditions for the Multi-Choice are α and β respectively, the resulting workflow can be expressed by making appropriate changes to workflow can be encoded easily in Orc:

$$Condition >M> Sync(XOR(\alpha, A \gg M.set \gg B, Signal \mid M.set),$$
$$IfSignal(\beta, C \gg M.wait \gg D))$$

The call to *XOR* (see WP 4) either executes the left path $A \gg M.set \gg B$ or else sets the condition M and signals completion, so that the condition is set in both alternatives. The right-hand path is the same as in Fig. 2(c) with the addition of the *IfSignal* (see WP 7) condition for β. This expression cannot be written using *SyncMerge* because of the additional call to $M.set$ when α is false. Orc cannot fully encapsulate this pattern as a definition. Some mechanism would be needed to track the collection of active synchronization variables, so that they can be *set* in the false branch of conditionals.

WP 8: Multi-merge. A multi-merge allows multiple branches to converge without synchronization. "If more than one branch gets activated, possibly concurrently, the activity following the merge is started for every activation of every incoming branch."[11] The sequential composition operator in Orc supports this behavior directly.

$$MultMerge(\bar{f}, h) \triangleq (f_1 \mid \cdots \mid f_n) \gg h$$
$$\equiv Par(\bar{f}) \gg h$$

WP 9: Discriminator. "A point in the workflow process that waits for one of the incoming branches to complete before activating the subsequent activity. From that moment on it waits for all remaining branches to complete and ignores them. ... Example: To improve query response time a complex search is sent to two different databases over the Internet. The first one that comes up with the result should proceed the flow."[11]

A discriminator returns the first value produced by a set of expressions but allows the remaining expressions to continue executing. To implement this behavior, Orc uses a local channel S created by a *Buffer* site.

$$Discr(\bar{f}) \triangleq Buffer >S> (Par(\bar{f}) >x> S.put(x) \mid S.get)$$

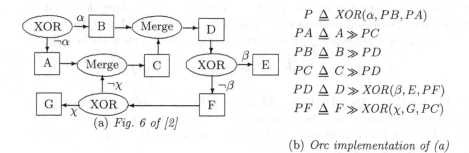

(a) *Fig. 6 of [2]*

$$P \triangleq XOR(\alpha, PB, PA)$$
$$PA \triangleq A \gg PC$$
$$PB \triangleq B \gg PD$$
$$PC \triangleq C \gg PD$$
$$PD \triangleq D \gg XOR(\beta, E, PF)$$
$$PF \triangleq F \gg XOR(\chi, G, PC)$$

(b) *Orc implementation of (a)*

Fig. 3. Arbitrary cycles example

The discriminator publishes only the first value that is placed in the buffer by $\bar{f}$, but allows $\bar{f}$ to continue running.

When applied to any expression $\bar{f}$, *First* terminates the computation of $\bar{f}$ after its first value is produced:

$$First(\bar{f}) \triangleq let(x) \text{ where } x :\in \bar{f}$$

First can be used to ensure termination of any expression f after it has produced its first value.

Van der Aalst uses discriminator to create another variation on the unstructured workflow in Fig. 2(a), by replacing the synchronize node between C and D with a discriminator. This means that D can start as soon as A or C completes. This example is easily defined in Orc, by simply replacing the corresponding *Sync* with *Discr*:

$$\text{Condition} >M> Sync(A \gg M.set \gg B,$$
$$Discr(C, M.wait) \gg D)$$

WP 10: Arbitrary Cycles. Workflows with arbitrary cycles and loops are easily created in Orc using recursive definitions. Fig. 3(a) gives a workflow from van der Aalst [2]. The diagram is a Petri Net, which can be understood as a form of flowchart. An XOR node is an exclusive choice in which the outgoing branches are labeled by a condition. A Merge node is a simple merge (WP 5).

Fig. 3(b) is an implementation of this flowchart in Orc. Each node is translated to a definition. An arc to a node in the flowchart is translated to a call to the corresponding definition. These expressions are equivalent to loops, because Orc is defined to optimize tail calls. Note that the Merge nodes are modelled implicitly.

Arbitrary cycles can be difficult to model when computations can only be structured as iterations with one entry and exit point [7]. Although Orc is highly structured, this example illustrates the use of recursion to define loops, which do not suffer from the problems of structured iteration.

Simple while loops can also be easily created. In the following definition, g publishes a boolean that controls execution of the loop. The call to *IfSignal* (see WP 7) evaluates $f \gg Loop(g, f)$ if b is true, and produces a signal otherwise.

$$Loop(g, f) \triangleq g >b> IfSignal(b, f \gg Loop(g, f))$$

WP 11: Implicit Termination. "A given subprocess should be terminated when there is nothing else to be done. In other words, there are no active activities in the workflow and no other activity can be made active (and at the same time the workflow is not in deadlock)." [2]

Implicit termination simply means that an expression continues running as long as there is more work to do, and that no explicit "stop" action is required. Since there is no explicit stop action in Orc, it supports implicit termination.

WP 12-15: Multiple Instances. There are three patterns covering creation of multiple instances of a workflow, one *without* synchronization, and two more with and without a priori *design time* knowledge.

The use of "process instance" in van der Aalst's patterns is probably influenced by his work on Petri nets: since Petri nets are (traditionally) understood as a form of finite state machine, they do not have the concept of block structure and instantiation as in process calculi like CCS, π-calculus and Orc.

Multiple threads are created using parallel composition *Par* (WP 12). If the list of instances is known at design time, then they can be synchronized by using *Sync* instead of *Par* (WP 13). For WP 14, the number of instances is known as a runtime quantity before the instances are created. We represent this runtime knowledge as a list in Orc, using a notation borrowed from Haskell [3]. An activity is started for each item in the list, and all the activities are synchronized using *Sync*.

$$SyncList(F, []) \triangleq Signal$$
$$SyncList(F, a : as) \triangleq Sync(F(a), SyncList(F, as))$$

Finally, WP 15 allows creation of instances where the number of instances is not known in advance: more instances may be created until some condition is satisfied. One implementation is a synchronized form of while loop. *ParLoop* is the same as *Loop* (see WP 10) except that iterations of the loop are performed in parallel and synchronized.

$$ParLoop(g, f) \triangleq g >b> IfSignal(b, Sync(f, ParLoop(g, f)))$$

WP 16: Deferred Choice. "A point in a process where one among several alternative branches is chosen based on information which is not necessarily available when this point is reached. This differs from the normal exclusive choice, in that the choice is not made immediately when the point is reached, but instead several alternatives are offered, and the choice between them is delayed until the occurrence of some event. Example: When a contract is finalized, it has to be reviewed and signed either by the director or by the operations manager, whoever is available first. Both the director and the operations manager would be notified that the contract is to be reviewed: the first one who is available will proceed with the review." [11]

Deferred choice happens when a set of *events* is used to select an alternative: the first event that fires causes its corresponding action to be activated. Deferred choice is called *arbitration* in [8]. Assume that the events are specified by a set of Orc expressions $\bar{e}$ and that the actions are defined by the Orc expressions $\bar{f}$. Note that, in Orc, the firing of an event is represented in terms of a site call to the environment. This enables the environment to participate in making a choice.

In the following definitions, *Which* produces an index identifying which event signalled; the call to *First* terminates the remaining events. The *Select* expression then runs the selected action.

$$DefChoiceTerm(\bar{e}, \bar{f}) \triangleq Which(\bar{e}) >k> Select(k, \bar{f})$$

$$Which(\bar{e}) \triangleq First(e_1 \gg let(1) \mid \cdots \mid e_n \gg let(n))$$

$$Select(k, \bar{f}) \triangleq if(k = 1) \gg f_1 \mid \cdots \mid if(k = n) \gg f_n$$

WP 17: Interleaved Parallel Routing. "A set of activities is executed in an arbitrary order: Each activity in the set is executed, the order is decided at run-time, and no two activities are executed at the same moment (i.e. no two activities are active for the same workflow instance at the same time)." [2]

This pattern is essentially an example of mutual exclusion between concurrent processes.

$$Interleave(\bar{f}) \triangleq Lock >M> (wait(M, f_1) \mid \cdots \mid wait(M, f_n))$$

$$wait(M, f) \triangleq M.acquire \gg f >x> M.release \gg let(x)$$

WP 18: Milestone. "A given activity can only be enabled if a certain milestone has been reached which has not yet expired. ... Example: After having placed a purchase order, a customer can withdraw it at any time before the shipping takes place." [2]

Consider three Orc activities f, g, and e. The completion of activity f enables g. Let e be an event that is raised when g is no longer allowed to run. Thus f precedes g and e, while e can interrupt g.

$$Milestone(f, g, e) \triangleq f \gg Interrupt(g, e)$$

$$Interrupt(g, e) \triangleq First(g \mid e)$$

This simple definition does not fully express the intent of the pattern: the intent is for f and e to be part of one workflow, while g is a part of another workflow. The workflows should communicate through channels, not be defined in a single expression. An improved definition uses two conditions, S and E. The S condition signals the start of the milestone, while E signals the end of the milestone.

$$Notify(f, S, E, e) \quad \underline{\Delta} \quad f \gg S.set \gg e \gg E.set$$
$$Listener(S, E, g) \quad \underline{\Delta} \quad S.wait \gg Interrupt(g, E.wait)$$
$$Milestone(f, e, g) \quad \underline{\Delta} \quad Condition >S> Condition >E>$$
$$(Notify(f, S, E, e) \mid Listener(S, E, g))$$

Van der Aalst also considers the case where g may be repeated arbitrarily after f and before e: this is done by replacing g by $Loop(true, g)$.

WP 19/20: Cancel Activity/Case. Cancelling can apply to an activity that is part of a workflow an entire workflow case. The *Interrupt* operator can be applied to a part of a workflow or the entire workflow to cancel part or all of the activity. This will cancel any activity immediately. *Interrupt* and *Condition* can be used in conjunction to model a set of cancellable activities.

4   Related Work

Orc implementations of the workflow patterns are most similar to BPML [11] and π-calculus. However, BPML is much more verbose than Orc. The mechanism for creating reusable definitions is also more cumbersome. There does not seem to be a mechanism analogous to local sites, so Interleaved Parallel Routing (WP 17) does not have a clean solution.

The π-calculus [9] versions of the workflow patterns are similar in structure to the Orc implementations. One significant difference is that π-calculus uses channels for all communication and synchronization. Orc expressions, on the other hand, embody structured forms of communication and control, so explicit channels (local sites) are needed only for unstructured workflows. The π-calculus explanation of the cancellation pattern is incomplete, because π-calculus does not provide built-in support for terminating a process, and the proposed encoding of a "global cancel trigger" is left undefined. The synchronizing merge pattern also does not specify how it is determined which processes are active.

Van der Aalst et al. defined a new workflow language, YAWL[10, 12], specifically to support the workflow patterns. The language is based on Petri nets, but is extended with special constructs for creating multiple instances and cancelling tokens in a group of nodes. The mechanism for multiple instantiation is analogous to Orc's sequential composition, but provides built-in synchronization. The node grouping and cancellation construct is similar to Orc's **where** operator. Rather than build specific workflow patterns into the language, Orc provides few fundamental primitives with a mechanism to define new operators for user-defined composition patterns.

5   Conclusion

We have implemented a set of standard workflow patterns using Orc, a new orchestration language. The solutions are generally easy to read and understand.

There is no reason to assume that the workflow patterns proposed by van der Aalst are complete. Orc has already been used to implement common concurrency patterns, like Priority and Timeout [8]. The Implicit Termination pattern suggests a need for an Explicit Termination pattern, in which an activity explicitly signals when it is complete. This pattern can also be implemented in Orc, although the machinery to do so is somewhat more complex.

One novelty of our approach is the encapsulation of pattern as *reusable definitions*. These definitions can be used to create larger programs; this technique is illustrated many times in this paper. Van der Aalst argues that all the workflow patterns should be expressed directly in the workflow language *without any encodings*. In his summary of the workflow patterns supported by various commercial systems, a pattern is marked as "not supported" if any form of encoding is required. In Orc some of the patterns require a combination of operators to implement – however, the pattern itself can be expressed as a *definition*, which can be reused whenever that pattern is required. Thus the pattern becomes another composition operator that can be used in larger programs. The operators that define patterns are reused extensively in this paper. This demonstrates the power of a language that can grow by adding new definitions, rather than requiring building a fixed set of primitives that cannot be easily extended by new definitions.

References

1. W. Aalst. The Application of Petri Nets to Workflow Management. *The Journal of Circuits, Systems and Computers*, 8(1):21–66, 1998.
2. W. M. P. V. D. Aalst, A. H. M. T. Hofstede, B. Kiepuszewski, and A. P. Barros. Workflow patterns. *Distrib. Parallel Databases*, 14(1):5–51, 2003.
3. R. Bird. *Introduction to Functional Programming using Haskell*. International Series in Computer Science, C.A.R. Hoare and Richard Bird, Series Editors. Prentice-Hall International, 1998.
4. M. Dumas and A. H. ter Hofstede. UML Activity Diagrams as a Workflow Specification Language. Technical report, Cooperative Information Systems Research Centre, Queensland University of Technology GPO Box 2434, Brisbane QLD 4001, Australia, Nov. 2003.
5. R. Eshuis and J. Dehnert. Reactive petri nets for workflow modeling. In W. M. P. van der Aalst and E. Best, editors, *Proceedings of the 24th International Conference on Applications and Theory of Petri Nets (ICATPN 2003)*, volume 2679 of *Lecture Notes in Computer Science*, pages 296–315. Springer-Verlag, June 2003.
6. R. Eshuis and R. Wieringa. Comparing petri net and activity diagram variants for workflow modelling - a quest for reactive petri nets. In H. Ehrig, W. Reisig, G. Rozenberg, and H. Weber, editors, *Petri Net Technology for Communication-Based Systems*, volume 2472 of *Lecture Notes in Computer Science*, pages 321–351. Springer-Verlag, November 2003.
7. B. Kiepuszewski, A. H. M. ter Hofstede, and C. Bussler. On structured workflow modelling. In *Conference on Advanced Information Systems Engineering*, pages 431–445, 2000.
8. J. Misra and W. R. Cook. Computation orchestration: A basis for wide-area computing. To appear in the Journal of Software & Systems Modeling, 2006.

9. F. Puhlmann and M. Weske. Using the π-calculus for formalizing workflow patterns. In *Proceedings of the 3rd International Conference on Business Process Management*, volume 3649 of *Lecture Notes in Computer Science*, 2005.

10. W. van der Aalst and A. ter Hofstede. YAWL: Yet Another Workflow Language. Technical report, Department of Technology Management, Eindhoven University of Technology P.O. Box 513, NL-5600 MB, Eindhoven, The Netherlands, Nov. 2003.

11. W. M. van der Aalst, M. Dumas, A. H. ter Hofstede, and P. Wohed. Pattern Based Analysis of BPML (and WSCI). Technical report, Department of Technology Management Eindhoven, University of Technology, The Netherlands, nov 2003.

12. W. M. P. van der Aalst, L. Aldred, M. Dumas, and A. H. M. ter Hofstede. Design and implementation of the yawl system. In A. Persson and J. Stirna, editors, *CAiSE*, volume 3084 of *Lecture Notes in Computer Science*, pages 142–159. Springer, 2004.

13. P. Wohed, W. M. van der Aalst, M. Dumas, and A. H. ter Hofstede. Pattern based analysis of BPEL4WS. Technical Report FIT-TR-2002-04, Queensland University of Technology, 2002.

14. The Workflow Reference Model. The Workflow Management Coalition, Jan. 1995.

Evolution On-the-Fly with Paradigm

Luuk Groenewegen[1] and Erik de Vink[1,2]

[1] LIACS, Leiden University, The Netherlands
[2] Department of Mathematics and Computer Science
Technische Universiteit Eindhoven, The Netherlands
luuk@liacs.nl, evink@win.tue.nl

Abstract. The coordination language Paradigm allows for a flexible and orthogonal modeling of interprocess relationships at the architectural level. It is shown how dynamic system adaptation can be captured in Paradigm by means of a special evolution component and associated evolution coordination scheme. The component, called McPal, drives the migration following a just-in-time strategy in its own view of the system, independent of other coordination relations. During migration, dynamic consistency between components remains assured, even for mixtures of old, intermediate and new behaviour. A restricted scheme of Mc-Pal that supports various forms of self-adaptation is presented. A simple but generic example of a scheduler and workers illustrates on-the-fly updating of coordination and run-time adaptation of scheduling policies using McPal.

Keywords: evolution on-the-fly, dynamic consistency, self-adaptation, migration, software architecture, Paradigm.

1 Introduction

Dynamic aspects of coordination arise naturally when considering evolution on-the-fly of systems at the architectural level. Here, evolution on-the-fly, such as dynamic software updating, is in contrast to other unanticipated system adaptation where components are first put to a halt, subsequently supplied with new behaviour, and finally restarted, likely with their state restored. In the setting here, the execution of the system should continue as much as possible. While running, the system will adapt itself and evolve into a new one via a number of migration steps, taken by the different components in a well-coordinated fashion.

The system architectures addressed in this paper are given as Paradigm models. Paradigm is a coordination language distinguishing detailed and global behaviour of processes (see [8, 12]). Coordination is achieved, by properly connecting the detailed and global views via so-called consistency rules. These rules relate detailed transitions between states of a process in a manager role to global change of subprocess constraints of other processes in an employee role. In Paradigm, separate coordination solutions for multiple collaborations can be relatively easily combined into one single architecture.

P. Ciancarini and H. Wiklicky (Eds.): COORDINATION 2006, LNCS 4038, pp. 97–112, 2006.

The paper's main contribution lies in showing how a specific component, called McPal –abbreviating Managing changing Processes ad libitum (or at leisure)– allows for modifying the dynamics of the system on-the-fly, while all components remain in execution in a dynamically consistent manner. The important intuition here is, a process within a model is viewed as a subprocess of an unknown larger process. As long as this subprocess constraint is valid, it is irrelevant whether the remainder of that process is known or not. This allows for defining new fragments of the process in a lazy manner, by modeling them just in time. After having such new fragments defined in a suitable manner, McPal can, on the basis of newly added dynamics, start to coordinate global level behaviour, eventually leading into a new evolutionary phase for each component. Thereby, the Paradigm notions guarantee enduring consistency between the components' behaviours before, during and after the migration, even for mixtures of old, intermediate and new behaviours.

To keep our explanation clear and sufficiently brief, we restrict this paper to a relatively simple form of McPal, not changing its own behaviour. This way, an evolution pattern for Paradigm models emerges, illustrated by an example of a scheduler and workers involved in different evolution scenarios. The starting point is a scheduler that excludes almost all overlapping of activity of the workers. As a first illustration, the coordination evolves to a situation where this restriction is significantly alleviated, allowing for more parallelism amongst the workers. A second illustration of the evolution pattern focuses on the scheduler, that migrates from a non-deterministic selection of workers to a round-robin selection policy.

In view of the above, the remainder of the paper has the following structure. Section 2 briefly describes Paradigm and introduces a small coordination example model. First, the model is extended in Section 3 with McPal for coordinating future self-adaptation of the model. Sections 4 and 5 present two different evolutionary continuations, one for reducing the critical sections, the other for changing the scheduling policy of workers. Both evolutionary changes are on-the-fly. Finally, Section 6 gives conclusions and discusses both related work and future research.

2   Paradigm

This section provides a very brief introduction to the coordination language Paradigm by means of a small example. The example serves two purposes, of illustrating the notions explained and of preparing the evolution to be addressed later. For more detailed explanation, including formal operational semantics, see e.g. [8, 12, 11]. Consider the following coordination situation. A scheduler is coordinating the activities of three workers. The workers are performing the same life-cycle simultaneously: alternating between not working and working. A worker is idle in the state free. The activity working actually consists of four smaller consecutive activities: nonCrit, pre, crit and post. The scheduler is coordinating their working. For the moment, the scheduler allows at most one

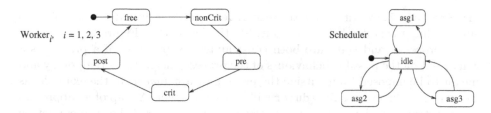

Worker$_i$ $i = 1, 2, 3$ Scheduler

Fig. 1. Processes Worker$_i$ and Scheduler

worker outside of free and nonCrit. The activities of the workers and of the scheduler can be described by a process or state transition diagram (STD).

In general, a *process* or *STD* S is a triple $\langle \mathsf{ST}, \mathsf{AC}, \mathsf{TS} \rangle$, with ST the set of *states*, with AC the set of *actions* or *labels*, and with $\mathsf{TS} \subseteq \mathsf{ST} \times \mathsf{AC} \times \mathsf{ST}$ the set of *transitions*. We write $x \xrightarrow{a} x'$ in case $(x, a, x') \in \mathsf{TS}$, or even $x \to x'$ if the precise action is irrelevant.

Figure 1 visualizes the processes of a worker and of the scheduler as directed graphs: transitions as edges and states as nodes. Activities have been mapped to states (as time spent for an activity coincides with a sojourn in a state); actions have been left empty. Each worker process, starts in state free, its non-working activity. After state free, Worker$_i$ continues to work: in nonCrit he does non-critical work, in pre he prepares the critical activity, in crit he does his critical work and in post he does its follow-up. Thereby he finishes working and continues in free with non-working. Process Scheduler starts in state idle where he does not allow any worker to do non-critical working. From state idle he can go non-deterministically to any of his states asg$_i$, $i = 1, 2, 3$, where he only allows Worker$_i$ to enter and leave states pre, crit and post for performing one full turn of critical activity.

The coordination exerted by the scheduler is formulated in terms of three global processes, each constituting a coarse-grained view of a worker process. Global processes are built from subprocesses and traps of the process it corresponds to. In general, a *subprocess* of a process $S = \langle \mathsf{ST}, \mathsf{AC}, \mathsf{TS} \rangle$ is a process $\langle \mathsf{st}, \mathsf{ac}, \mathsf{ts} \rangle$ such that $\mathsf{st} \subseteq \mathsf{ST}$, $\mathsf{ac} \subseteq \mathsf{AC}$ and $\mathsf{ts} \subseteq \{ (x, a, x') \in \mathsf{TS} \mid x, x' \in \mathsf{st}, a \in \mathsf{ac} \}$. Furthermore, a *trap* θ of a subprocess $S = \langle \mathsf{st}, \mathsf{ac}, \mathsf{ts} \rangle$ is a non-empty set of states $\theta \subseteq \mathsf{st}$ such that $x \in \theta$ and $x \xrightarrow{a} x' \in \mathsf{ts}$ imply that $x' \in \theta$. If $\theta = \mathsf{st}$, the trap is called trivial. For the worker processes we model two subprocesses,

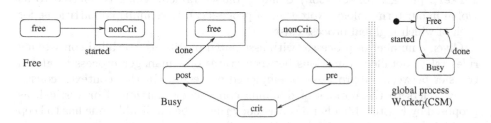

Fig. 2. Partition CSM and global worker process at the level of CSM

viz. Free and Busy with their traps started and done visualized as polygons surrounding the states belonging to it. See the left part of Figure 2.

Subprocesses and traps are both constraints: a subprocess of a process is a constraint on the possible behaviours of the process, meant to be temporary and meant to be imposed from outside the process by a *manager*. In the example, as we shall see, the process Scheduler will be the manager. A trap of a subprocess is a constraint on the subprocess' state space –once entered the trap cannot be left– valid only for the time the subprocess constraint holds, and committed to from inside the process in its *employee* role. So, a trap indicates a final stage of a subprocess.

To build suitable dynamics from such constraints, two more notions are needed: partition and connecting trap. In general, a *partition* π of a process $P = \langle \text{ST}, \text{AC}, \text{TS} \rangle$ is a collection $\{ (S_i, T_i) \mid i \in I \}$ of subprocesses $S_i = \langle \text{st}_i, \text{ac}_i, \text{ts}_i \rangle$ of P, each with a set T_i of its traps. Furthermore, for two subprocesses $S = \langle \text{st}, \text{ac}, \text{ts} \rangle$ and $S' = \langle \text{st}', \text{ac}', \text{ts}' \rangle$ of a partition π, a trap θ of S is called a *connecting* trap from S to S', if the states, of S, belonging to the trap θ are states in S' as well, i.e. $\theta \subseteq \text{st}'$. If such a connecting trap θ from S to S' exists, the triple (S, θ, S') is called a *subprocess change* or *transfer*. In Figure 2, the left part presents the elements of partition CSM (abbreviating critical section management) of a worker process, comprising the two subprocesses and the two traps. In this case, trap started of Free is connecting from Free to Busy as its state nonCrit belongs to Busy too. Similarly, trap done of Busy is connecting from Busy to Free as its state free belongs to Free too. A connecting trap provides a kind of overlap between two consecutive subprocess constraints.

On the basis of a partition π of a process P, we construct a new process, referred to as the *global process at the level of partition* π. This process is denoted by $P(\pi)$. Its states are the subprocesses from π, its actions are connecting traps from π and its transitions are the subprocess changes corresponding to these connecting traps. The one subprocess expressing the constraint valid at a certain moment, is referred to as the current subprocess of a partition at that moment. By construction, the current subprocess of a partition corresponds to the current state of the global process at the level of the partition. A process not being global, is referred to as detailed. Figure 2's right part presents the global process $\text{Worker}_i(\text{CSM})$, with its starting state Free chosen such that, as subprocess, it contains starting state free of process Worker_i. The process $\text{Worker}_i(\text{CSM})$ presents a behavioural view on the original Worker_i process; being less detailed than Worker_i, process $\text{Worker}_i(\text{CSM})$ is more coarse-grained, which is referred to as global in our terminology. Note that, a process can have multiple partitions, for each of which a global process exists.

Given a number of processes with associated partitions, so-called consistency rules relate detailed transitions between states of a manager process to global transfer between subprocesses of employee processes. (In this context, 'consistency' refers to the notions of dynamic consistency, horizontal or vertical, as proposed by Küster [14].) For a consistency rule to be applicable, one has to keep track of the current state of detailed as well as global processes. Any applicable consistency rule, no matter of what manager and partition, can be selected for application. In general, a consistency rule has the format

$$P: s \xrightarrow{a} s' \, * \, P_1(\pi_1): S_1 \xrightarrow{\theta_1} S_1', \dots, P_n(\pi_n): S_n \xrightarrow{\theta_n} S_n' \, . \tag{1}$$

In consistency rule (1), process P is the manager and process P_1 to P_n are the employees. Paradigm is restricted to having exactly one manager in a consistency rule. In case there are no employees, i.e. $n = 0$, we simply write $P: s \xrightarrow{a} s'$. Note that the local transition of P in (1) does not refer to a partition. The requirement on P for the consistency rule to apply is that the transition $s \xrightarrow{a} s'$ is possible in every current subprocess of process P, with respect to the various partitions of P. The requirements on P_1 to P_n with respect to consistency rule (1) is that each process P_i in its partition π_i has S_i as the current subprocess and within this subprocess trap θ_i has been entered. After application of the consistency rule the current state of manager P becomes s', the current subprocesses of employees P_1 to P_n become S_1' to S_n', respectively. Because of the demand of traps θ_i being connecting for subprocesses S_i and S_i', it does not matter in which detailed state the employees reside precisely. For each connecting trap, the whole of it is admitted in the new subprocess as a possible state to continue from.

For the scheduler process of our example, we provide the consistency rules

$$\texttt{Scheduler}: \texttt{idle} \rightarrow \texttt{asg}_i \, * \, \texttt{Worker}_i(\texttt{CSM}): \texttt{Free} \xrightarrow{started} \texttt{Busy}$$

$$\texttt{Scheduler}: \texttt{asg}_i \rightarrow \texttt{idle} \, * \, \texttt{Worker}_i(\texttt{CSM}): \texttt{Busy} \xrightarrow{done} \texttt{Free}$$

The first consistency rule expresses that `Scheduler` may change its current state `idle` into `asg`$_i$, provided the current subprocess constraint on `Worker`$_i$ is `Free` and the trap `started` has been entered, i.e. `Worker`$_i$'s current state belongs to the trap `started`. If `Scheduler` changes its current state from `idle` to `asg`$_i$ indeed, then, according to the rule, global process `Worker`$_i$(`CSM`) changes its current state from `Free` to `Busy`, or, put otherwise, the subprocess constraint of `Worker`$_i$ in partition `CSM` becomes `Busy` instead of `Free`. This is an example of horizontal dynamic consistency [14], as the rule couples behaviours from different components. Analogously, the second rule says, `Scheduler` may return from state `asg`$_i$ to state `idle`, provided the current subprocess constraint on `Worker`$_i$ is `Busy` and `Worker`$_i$'s current state belongs to trap `done`. If `Scheduler` indeed changes its current state from `asg`$_i$ to `idle`, then also global process `Worker`$_i$(`CSM`) changes its current state from `Busy` to `Free`. We see how both consistency rules couple one local scheduler transition to a (simultaneous) global `Worker`$_i$(`CSM`) transition. As `Scheduler` does not have a partition, it neither has any process at such a level, so `Scheduler`'s state transitions are not restricted by any current subprocess constraint from such a global level.

The workers have no employees. Therefore, their consistency rules are simpler than for the scheduler, each rule containing one of `Worker`$_i$'s detailed transitions only.

$$\texttt{Worker}_i: \texttt{free} \rightarrow \texttt{nonCrit} \qquad \texttt{Worker}_i: \texttt{crit} \rightarrow \texttt{post}$$

$$\texttt{Worker}_i: \texttt{nonCrit} \rightarrow \texttt{pre} \qquad \texttt{Worker}_i: \texttt{post} \rightarrow \texttt{free}$$

$$\texttt{Worker}_i: \texttt{pre} \rightarrow \texttt{crit}$$

A Worker$_i$ transition is possible only if it belongs to the current subprocess constraint of detailed process Worker$_i$ or, equivalently, to the current state of global process Worker$_i$(CSM). This is an example of vertical behavioural consistency in the sense of [14] between a detailed process and the global processes at the levels of its partitions.

In addition to the consistency rule format of (1), one can also have a so-called *change clause,* a consistency rule used here solely for changing the total set of consistency rules, instead of a consistency rule prescribing subprocess changes. A change clause is formulated as

$$P: s \xrightarrow{a} s' * [\, \texttt{var} := \texttt{expr} \,] \tag{2}$$

concerning a variable var, typically holding the list of consistency rules. It specifies that after application of the rule, process P has moved to state s' and the value of expr in s has been assigned to variable var. This way consistency rules can be added or deleted dynamically.

The initial configuration of a Paradigm model does not only comprise the starting states of the various detailed processes, but also those of the various global processes. Therefore, for every detailed process a starting state has to be specified, together with a subprocess to start from, for each of its partitions. Our example illustrates this as follows. The combined starting states are, grouped per detailed process and with $i = 1, 2, 3$:

$$(\texttt{Worker}_i, \texttt{Worker}_i(\texttt{CSM})) : (\texttt{free}, \texttt{Free}), \ \ \texttt{Scheduler} : \texttt{idle}$$

Note, each detailed starting state belongs indeed to each current subprocess constraint for that particular detailed process. The consistency rules guarantee the following property to be invariant: each current state of a detailed process belongs for each partition of that process to the current subprocess.

In summary, the above is an example of a Paradigm model. In general, a *Paradigm model* is a collection of detailed processes and global processes at the level of their given partitions, together with a set of consistency rules and a combination of detailed and global starting states. Dynamics within such a model stem from subsequent application of consistency rules. Any change of constraint specified by the particular consistency rule applied, then yields a number of global process transitions, i.e. subprocess transfers.

3   Self-adaptation and McPal

In this section we shall present a different model for the original coordination problem from the previous section. Apart from solving the same coordination problem, the model can modify itself and evolve, while remaining in execution, into another model, unknown in the beginning. For this we add the special process McPal. This McPal starts with not influencing the model as-is, nothing special to begin with. But our McPal, by its careful design, has the property to adapt the Paradigm model it belongs to. Process McPal is visualized in Figure 3.

Fig. 3. Process McPal

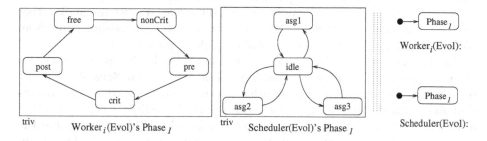

Fig. 4. Evolutionary phases and evolutionary processes to begin with

In state **obs**, **McPal** is observing the model as a whole and possibly computing or perhaps hearing from elsewhere how to change the model. As soon as
McPal arrives in state **startMigr**, it knows the new consistency rules according to which the executing model is going to migrate uninterruptedly towards
a new model. This migration is coordinated by **McPal** outside its state **obs**. To
support the migration, every other detailed process has an additional partition
called **Evol**. It contains the subprocesses reflecting the evolutionary phases so-far
of that particular detailed process. As long as **McPal** is in state **obs** for the first
time, each such partition consists of exactly one subprocess, here called **Phase₁**,
always being the full, unconstrained process itself, typically with the trivial trap
connecting from **Phase₁** towards an as yet unknown subprocess reflecting an intermediate migration phase. Figure 4 presents the **Evol** partitions for **Worker**$_i$ as
well as for **Scheduler** together with the degenerate global processes at the level
of these partitions. All other partitions are unchanged. The consistency rules for
the extended model are the original rules together with only one new rule for
McPal, viz. consistency rule (3) below, for the moment.

$$\text{McPal: obs} \rightarrow \text{startMigr} * \left[\, \text{CR} \; := \; \text{CR} \cup \text{CR}_{mig} \cup \text{CR}_{next} \,\right] \qquad (3)$$

This one rule is a change clause: as the set of consistency rules we start with,
is going to change during the migration, the set of consistency rules is bound
to a local variable of **McPal**, here denoted as **CR**. Change clause (3) should be
taken parametrically, i.e., at the very moment process **McPal** decides to take the
transition from its state **obs** to state **startMigr**, the collection of consistency
rules gets updated via the assignment in the change clause with the whole of
consistency rules in **CR**, **CR**$_{mig}$ and **CR**$_{next}$ at that moment. So the effect of the
change clause (3) fully depends on the actual values of its two parameters **CR**$_{mig}$
and **CR**$_{next}$. As we shall see later, **McPal** determines the pace of evolution.

With respect to the new detailed process **McPal** it is important to note, only
the first transition of **McPal**, from state **obs** to **startMigr** is supported by a

consistency rule. This means, in the first phase of the evolution the other transitions cannot occur. But, as a result of this, one possible transition in McPal, the set CR of consistency rules is extended with two more sets: one, CR_{mig}, for the intermediate phase proper and the other, CR_{next}, for the next evolutionary phase. In particular, once CR_{mig} is known, there are consistency rules for the other McPal transitions too, readily made, JIT-modeled (just in time), either by computational effort of McPal while in state obs, or by modeling effort from outside McPal and given as input to McPal while in state obs.

For this paper we shall keep process McPal unchanged. This means, we choose one particular form of sufficiently useful standard behaviour of McPal for actually coordinating the migration steps of other processes involved. By its first transition obs → startMigr, McPal extends via change clause (3) the rules, such that other processes' $Phase_1$ constraint is going to be relaxed, if necessary. For the examples we want to discuss here, three more migration steps will do: a transition startMigr → contMigr for continuing the migration, only if necessary, by adjusting the migration already begun; a transition contMigr → endMigr for restraining the other processes' constraints to the $Phase_2$ behaviours aimed at, thus closing their migration; the last one, transition endMigr → obs, for restraining the migrational freedom for McPal too, thus preventing McPal in some unknown future to repeat an old migration when a new one is in place. In the next two sections we present some concrete self-adapting Paradigm models and provide detail for McPal's remaining three transitions.

The combined starting states of the Paradigm model are grouped according to the five detailed processes:

$$(\text{Worker}_i, \text{Worker}_i(\text{CSM}), \text{Worker}_i(\text{Evol})) : (\text{free}, \text{Free}, \text{Phase}_1),$$
$$(\text{Scheduler}, \text{Scheduler}(\text{Evol})) : (\text{idle}, \text{Phase}_1),$$
$$\text{McPal} : \text{obs}.$$

4   Reducing the Extent of Exclusive Behaviour

The example variants presented in this section exhibit a restricted form of self-adaptation through step-wise modification of non-evolutionary global behaviours only, i.e. exclusively at the level of the three $\text{Worker}_i(\text{CSM})$ partitions. For the moment, the detailed worker and scheduler processes are not going to change at all, so their $Phase_1$ subprocess constraints remain unchanged during the evolution as discussed here. The non-evolutionary global processes $\text{Worker}_i(\text{CSM})$ do change, however.

To become more concrete, suppose we want to modify the original mutual exclusion management in two ways: by substantially restricting the exclusive behaviour as well as by making the return to non-critical working most asynchronous. These two improvements are realized by the new subprocesses OutCS and InCS, drawn in Figure 5, with their traps entering and left. Trap entering has been chosen as 'near' to state crit and as 'small' as possible. Trap left has been chosen as 'large' as possible –the larger the more asynchronous– and starting 'immediately after' state crit.

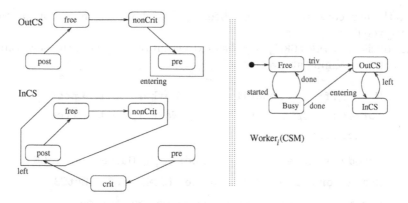

Fig. 5. Extensions of partition CSM and of global process Worker$_i$(CSM)

The trivial trap `triv` of subprocess `Free` is self-evident, so we do not redraw `Free` with its newly added trap. Nevertheless, it now also belongs to partition CSM. What is even more important, trap `triv` is connecting from `Free` to `OutCS` and the original trap `done` is connecting from `Busy` to `OutCS`. This is used for constructing the global process Worker$_i$(CSM) on the basis of the newly extended partition CSM. See Figure 5. The consistency rules in play are the original consistency rules in CR, the consistency rules CR$_{mig}$ that guide the migration, and the consistency rules CR$_{next}$ for the next evolutionary phase. The original consistency rules are bound to McPal's local variable CR, that is to say, CR has the rules mentioned in Section 3 as initial value. The consistency rules CR$_{mig}$ for the migration are the following.

McPal: `startMigr` → `contMigr`

McPal: `contMigr` → `endMigr` * Worker$_1$(CSM): `OutCS` $\overset{triv}{\to}$ `OutCS`

McPal: `endMigr` → `obs` * [CR := CR$_{next}$]

Scheduler: `asg`$_i$ → `idle` * Worker$_i$(CSM): `Busy` $\overset{done}{\to}$ `OutCS`,

    Worker$_{i-1}$(CSM): `Free` $\overset{triv}{\to}$ `OutCS`, Worker$_{i+1}$(CSM)`Free` $\overset{triv}{\to}$ `OutCS`

Here $i-1$ and $i+1$ denote the usual predecessor and successor values of i in the cyclic order of $1, 2, 3$.

The first rule for McPal above states that, in this migration, there is no coordination task for McPal in the first step. The second rule for McPal expresses that the migration has been completed, when the first worker runs restricted to the `OutCS` subprocess at the level of its CSM partition. Once in state `endMigr`, McPal cleans up the old and intermediate consistency rules by binding CR to CR$_{next}$ and comes back in state `obs` again. Here the actual migration is in the new rule for Scheduler. When returning from any of the states `asg`$_1$, `asg`$_2$, `asg`$_3$, all workers, including the Worker$_1$ that is checked by McPal, are transfered to subprocess `OutCS` of the next evolution phase. Note, the actual migration is not really enforced: Scheduler might carry on with the old coordination forever. As soon as the new consistency rule has been applied, however, migration has taken place irreversibly.

The consistency rules CR_{next} for the next evolutionary phase, the new solution we are actually aiming at, are

$$Worker_i: free \rightarrow nonCrit \qquad Worker_i: crit \rightarrow post$$

$$Worker_i: nonCrit \rightarrow pre \qquad Worker_i: post \rightarrow free$$

$$Worker_i: pre \rightarrow crit$$

$$Scheduler: idle \rightarrow asg_i * Worker_i(CSM): OutCS \xrightarrow{entering} InCS$$

$$Scheduler: asg_i \rightarrow idle * Worker_i(CSM): InCS \xrightarrow{left} OutCS$$

$$McPal: obs \rightarrow startMigr * [CR := CR \cup CR_{mig} \cup CR_{next}]$$

In the new evolution phase, the same scheduler continues to coordinate the same workers with more parallelism between the workers, now the extent of the exclusive, critical working interval has been reduced and trap `left` allows for a most asynchronous continuation of a worker after having finished his critical activity. The change clause for `McPal` for the transition from `obs` to `startMigr` caters for later evolution, at `McPal`'s leisure.

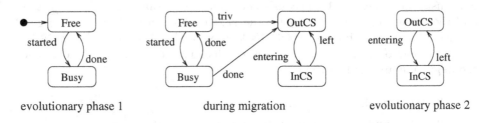

evolutionary phase 1   during migration   evolutionary phase 2

Fig. 6. Migration of process $Worker_i(CSM)$, first variant

Figure 6 might be viewed as a movie of global process $Worker_i(CSM)$ represented through three subsequent takes reflecting subsequent migration. The first take of the movie lasts until `McPal` leaves state `obs`. The second take lasts while `McPal` is in its three states `startMigr`, `contMigr` and `endMigr`. Upon arrival in state `endMigr` it is guaranteed that the worker process executes either subprocess `OutCS` or `InCS`. The third take starts when `McPal` returns in state `obs`.

An interesting variant, slightly different only, is `McPal`'s first migration rule in the above set CR_{mig} replaced by

$$McPal: startMigr \rightarrow contMigr * [CR := CR \backslash CR_{help}]$$

where CR_{help} has been computed or has been read from input in state `obs`, consisting of the 'migration avoiding' rules

$$Scheduler: asg_i \rightarrow idle * Worker_i(CSM): Busy \xrightarrow{done} Free$$

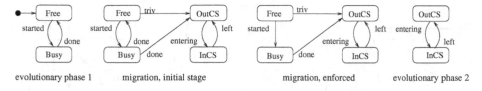

evolutionary phase 1   migration, initial stage   migration, enforced   evolutionary phase 2

Fig. 7. Migration of process $\text{Worker}_i(\text{CSM})$, second variant

The consequence thereof is, from McPal's arrival in state contMigr, the migration is more enforcing towards Phase_2, the actual evolutionary phase aimed at. The movie now consists of four takes, see Figure 7. The enforcing is an example of migration adjusting. Note, we have indeed specified the self-adaptation through new global behaviour at the level of $\text{Worker}_i(\text{CSM})$ only, leaving all detailed behaviours untouched.

5   Changing Scheduling Order

This section presents example variants of self-adaptation affecting a detailed process and involving non-trivial global behaviour at the level of partition Evol of that detailed process, really evolutionary behaviour in terms of subsequent phases.

To this aim, we reorganize the Paradigm model of Section 3 in a different way, namely by changing the non-deterministic selection policy of the scheduler into round robin selection. Figure 8 visualizes a combination of the original scheduler process and a new, envisaged one. The four upper states, of the seven states displayed, constitute the STD of the Scheduler process as in Figure 1. The six lower states, asg_1 to asg_3 and check_1 to check_3, will comprise the state space of the evolved Scheduler process. So, here we have a different type of change: a detailed process is going to get new behaviour. Round robin checking of a worker's wish to enter its critical section, is done in the states check_i, whereas the meaning of states asg_i is kept unchanged. The combined behaviours as presented in Figure 8 actually obscure what transitions could be taken during

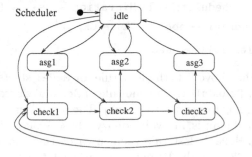

Fig. 8. Combined STD of two incarnations of Scheduler

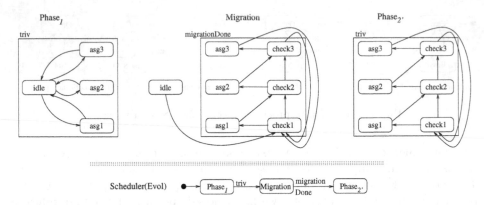

Fig. 9. Partition `Evol` of `Scheduler`, first variant

which evolutionary phase. At level of the partition `Evol` this becomes rather more clear from global process `Scheduler(Evol)`. Figure 9 presents the partition `Evol` of the extended process `Scheduler` under migration, together with global process `Scheduler(Evol)`. Without the traps and with `idle` added as starting state of the first evolutionary phase, it can be taken as a movie of process `Scheduler`'s evolution represented through three subsequent takes. Consistency rules for the migration as well as for the new way of scheduling are grouped into the two sets CR_{mig} and CR_{next}, like before. Remember, we start with `CR` as modeled in Section 3. As before, $i+1$ denotes the successor of i from the cyclic values $1, 2, 3$.

In addition, we use the negative side rule $P(\pi): S \xrightarrow{\theta}$ for the condition that within partition π of process P either S is not the current subprocess, or trap θ of subprocess S has not yet been entered. This condition is necessary for the corresponding manager transition to occur and it leaves the current subprocess at the level of partition π of P unchanged. The consistency rules for the migration are now the following.

$$\text{McPal}: \text{startMigr} \to \text{contMigr} *$$
$$\text{Scheduler(Evol)}: \text{Phase}_1 \xrightarrow{triv} \text{Migration}$$
$$\text{McPal}: \text{contMigr} \to \text{endMigr} *$$
$$\text{Scheduler(Evol)}: \text{Migration} \xrightarrow{migrationDone} \text{Phase}_2$$
$$\text{McPal}: \text{endMigr} \to \text{obs} * \left[\, \text{CR} := \text{CR}_{next} \,\right]$$
$$\text{Scheduler}: \text{idle} \to \text{check}_1$$

Please note, from the above list, the first rule for `McPal` starts the evolutionary migration phase for `Scheduler`. The one rule of `Scheduler` expresses the actual migration step, by going from `idle` to `check`$_1$. The second rule of `McPal` stabilizes the migration: `Scheduler` is in evolutionary phase `Phase`$_2$ from the moment the rule is applied. `McPal`'s last rule then discards rules no longer needed, by keeping those from CR_{next} only. It may happen, that the actual migration step to be taken by `Scheduler` does not occur, as `Scheduler`, while in asg_i, gets its phase `Migration` as the current subprocess constraint. In that case, `Scheduler` migrates right then implicitly, without taking an explicit step. As an aside, we have a non-trivial management relation: `McPal` manages the scheduler, while the scheduler manages the workers.

The consistency rules CR_{next} for the envisioned evolutionary phase are the following

$$\text{Worker}_i\text{: free} \rightarrow \text{nonCrit} \qquad \text{Worker}_i\text{: crit} \rightarrow \text{post}$$

$$\text{Worker}_i\text{: nonCrit} \rightarrow \text{pre} \qquad \text{Worker}_i\text{: post} \rightarrow \text{free}$$

$$\text{Worker}_i\text{: pre} \rightarrow \text{crit}$$

$$\text{Scheduler: check}_i \rightarrow \text{asg}_i \; * \; \text{Worker}_i(\text{CSM}): \text{Free} \stackrel{started}{\rightarrow} \text{Busy}$$

$$\text{Scheduler: asg}_i \rightarrow \text{check}_{i+1} \; * \; \text{Worker}_i(\text{CSM}): \text{Busy} \stackrel{done}{\rightarrow} \text{Free}$$

$$\text{Scheduler: check}_i \rightarrow \text{check}_{i+1} \; * \; \text{Worker}_i(\text{CSM}): \text{Free} \stackrel{started}{\nrightarrow}$$

$$\text{McPal: obs} \rightarrow \text{startMigr} \; * \; \left[\, \text{CR} := \text{CR} \cup \text{CR}_{mig} \cup \text{CR}_{next} \,\right]$$

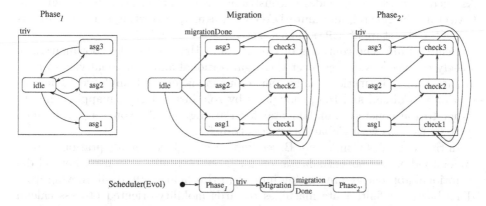

Fig. 10. Partition `Evol` of `Scheduler`, second variant

Figure 10 gives an alternative for partition `Evol` of the `Scheduler` process: during migration it allows for some extra delay of introducing the round robin approach, by a kind of last-orders possibility for at most one worker according to the old-fashioned non-deterministic selection mechanism. (See the transition from state `idle` to the states `asg`$_i$ in subprocess `Migration`.) Note that by thus changing the definition of subprocess `Migration`, i.e. the concrete constraint, we do not have to change our consistency rule formulations for achieving the evolution as depicted in Figure 10.

6   Conclusions, Related Work and Future Work

The scheduler and worker examples illustrate evolution on-the-fly as supported in Paradigm. The detailed transitions of the special component `McPal` mark the various migration steps from one evolutionary stage of the system to the next. Via consistency rules, new subprocesses of old or new behaviour can be introduced. Change clauses for McPal provide these consistency rules and dispose of coordination that is not desired any more. Although, the mechanism of subprocesses constrain the behaviour of components, the proposed evolution scheme itself does not require any component to stop, to be restarted later with new behaviour installed. In this sense, evolution is on-the-fly.

The evolution pattern as described allows for iterated evolution, as the McPal process is persistent in the model. A new migration can take place as soon as new consistency rules for intermediate and targeted behaviour and interaction are defined. With new semantics specified lazily, just-in-time, the self-adaptation is on-the-fly. In its present form, only one intermediate stage is foreseen in the evolution pattern, represented by the state contMigr of the detailed process of McPal. In the first evolution example variant, we have seen that this state was superfluous. The opposite, having more than one intermediate migration stage, is possible as well. Even stronger, the detailed behaviour of McPal can be specified just-in-time, determining the migration trajectory on-the-fly too. As such, our scheme provides unconstrained run-time selection of a migration trajectory. In general, any finite DAG with a unique starting state will do, as far as the structure of McPal is concerned.

Related work The contracts of Colman and Han [6] for the coordination of loosely coupled systems connect the organizational and functional views on an architecture, a distinction reminiscent to our managers and employees. The connection of Colman and Han, though, is by role instantiation, mapping the abstract to the concrete. Fundamental for Paradigm is the coupling of detailed state transitions with global subprocess transfer.

In the context of Component Based Software Engineering, adaptation is to be understood as component adaptation for interoperability purposes. Formal descriptional approaches are gaining impact in this field [2, 19, 16, 4], moving from IDLs based on finite state machines towards mobility-oriented process calculi and induced bisimulation equivalences. Although Paradigm is supported by a transition-based operational semantics [12], at present the behavioural theory to compare different evolutions or different stages within the same evolution, is not yet fully established. However, see [3, 13].

Oriol proposes to exploit asynchronous channels to drive unanticipated software evolution [17]. Leading principles are anonymity of entities, late binding and asynchronous communication in a setting of service-directed architectures. A variation geared towards tuple spaces has been reported in [18]. Because of the atomicity of the services involved, the granularity is more coarse-grained than in the approach presented here, however.

There is a vast amount of literature on dynamic updating at the code level, for example on concrete dynamic software updating systems design (see e.g. [15, 20]). In the context of declarative programming, dynamic logic programming (see [1] amongst others) involves sequences of logic programs to express the evolution of knowledge over time. Controls have to be put in place to deal with inconsistencies among separate programs and to fine-tune asserts and retracts of Horn clauses. However, as with the work on imperative programming languages mentioned above, as yet no migration pattern or architectural support is provided to guide the evolution.

In addition, we like to mention [9, 10] as examples reporting on self-adaptive systems on an architectural level. In these papers there is the same tendency as noted above (service atomicity) of concentrating on forms of self-adaptation referred to as: reconfiguration, structured reorganization, data-driven readjustment, canned workflows being triggered, recomposition and the like. The survey [5] compares fourteen different approaches to self-adaptation, none of which appears to achieve so-called unconstrained run-time selection. Our McPal pattern however, allows for exactly this: the outcome of our JIT-modeling, occurring while being in state **obs**, fully determines such run-time freedom: nothing happening during migration or during later evolutionary phases has been foreseen from the beginning. The paper [7] is coming closest to our approach. It draws attention to the dynamic consistency problem, which should be solved by coordination; details about how to do this, are not given however, contrarily to our McPal component which, based on Paradigm, specifies such coordination in detail.

Future work Further research will be devoted to more elaborate migration schemes. A case study of the dining philosophers evolving from deadlock to starvation and beyond is under way. For the treatment of more intricate evolution patterns, dynamic creation and deletion of complete detailed processes is involved, which requires extension of Paradigm's formal semantics. Larger software architectures, for example in a setting of changes at the business level requiring software adaptation of lower-level support-systems, are likely to become multi-tier. Concise models will benefit from higher-order consistency rules and coordination patterns. Thesis work is devoted to tooling that supports the analysis of extensive examples as well as refactoring, transformation and refinement strategies of Paradigm models.

Acknowledgment. We are indebted to our colleagues of the FaST-group, including Fahrad Arbab, Frank de Boer, Marcello Bonsangue, Jetty Kleijn, and Andries Stam for various stimulating discussions on the subject.

References

1. J.J. Alferes, J.A. Leite, L.M. Pereira, H. Przymusinska, and T. Przymusinski. Dynamic updates of non-monotonic knowledge bases. *Journal of Logic Programming*, 45:43–70, 2000.
2. R. Allen and G. Garlan. A formal basis for architectural connection. *ACM Transactions on Software Engineering Methodology*, 6:213–249, 1997.
3. J.C. Augusto and R.S. Gomez. A temporal logic view of Paradigm models. In *Proc. SEKE 2002, Ischia, Italy*, pages 497–503. ACM, 2002.
4. A. Bracciali, A. Brogi, and C. Canal. A formal approach to component adaptation. *Journal of Systems and Software*, 74:45–54, 2005.

5. J. Bradbury, J. Cordy, J. Dingel, and M. Wermelinger. A survey of self-management in dynamic software architecture specifications. In *[10]*, pages 28–33. ACM Press, 2004.
6. A. Colman and Jun Han. Coordination systems in role-based adaptive software. In J.-M. Jacquet and G.P. Picco, editors, *Proc. Coordination 2005*, volume 3454 of *LNCS*, pages 63–78, 2005.
7. L. Desmet, N. Janssens, S. Michiels, F. Piessens, W. Joonsen, and P. Verbaeten. Towards preserving coorectness in self-managed software systems. In *[10]*, pages 34–38. ACM Press, 2004.
8. G. Engels, L.P.J. Groenewegen, and G. Kappel. Coordinated Collaboration of Objects. In M. Papazoglou, S. Spaccapietra, and Z. Tari, editors, *Advances in Object-Oriented Data Modeling*, pages 307–331. MIT Press, 2000.
9. D. Garlan, J. Kramer, and A. Wolf, editors. *Proceedings of the 1st Workshop on Self-Healing Systems, Charleston SC*. ACM, 2002.
10. D. Garlan, J. Kramer, and A. Wolf, editors. *Proceedings of the 1st ACM SIGSOFT Workshop on Self-Managing Systems, Newport Beach CA*. ACM, 2004.
11. L. Groenewegen, N. van Kampenhout, and E. de Vink. Delegation Modeling with Paradigm. In J.-M. Jacquet and G.P. Picco, editors, *Proc. Coordination 2005*, volume 3454 of *LNCS*, pages 94–108, 2005.
12. L. Groenewegen and E. de Vink. Operational semantics for coordination in Paradigm. In F. Arbab and C. Talcott, editors, *Proc. Coordination 2002*, volume 2315 of *LNCS*, pages 191–206, 2002.
13. N. van Kampenhout. Systematic Specification and Verification of Coordination: towards Patterns for Paradigm Models. Master's thesis, LIACS, 2003.
14. J. Küster. *Consistency Management of Object-Oriented Behavioral Models*. PhD thesis, University of Paderborn, 2004.
15. S. Malabarba, R. Pandey, J. Gragg, E. Barr, and J.F. Barnes. Runtime support for type-safe dynamic Java classes. In E. Bertino, editor, *Proc. ECOOP 2000*, volume 1850 of *LNCS*, pages 337–361, 2000.
16. Sun Meng and L.S. Barbosa. On refinement of generic state-based software components. In C. Rattray, S. Maharaj, and C. Shankland, editors, *Proc. AMAST'04*, volume 3116 of *LNCS*, pages 506–520, 2004.
17. M. Oriol. *An Approach to the Dynamic Evolution of Software Systems*. PhD thesis, Department of Information Systems, University of Geneva, 2004.
18. M. Oriol and M.W. Hicks. Tagged sets: A secure and transparent coordination medium. In J.-M. Jacquet and G.P. Picco, editors, *Proc. Coordination 2005*, volume 3454 of *LNCS*, pages 252–267, 2005.
19. P. Poizat. *Korrigan: un formalisme et une méthode pour la spécification formelle et structurée de systèmes mixtes*. PhD thesis, IRIN, University of Nantes, 2000.
20. G. Stoyle, M.W. Hicks, G. M. Bierman, P. Sewell, and I. Neamtiu. Mutatis mutandis: safe and predictable dynamic software updating. In *Proc. POPL 2005, Long Beach, Calefornia*, pages 183–194. ACM, 2005.

Formalising Business Process Execution with Bigraphs and Reactive XML

Thomas Hildebrandt, Henning Niss, and Martin Olsen*

IT University of Copenhagen, Denmark
{hilde, hniss, mol}@itu.dk

Abstract. Bigraphical Reactive Systems have been proposed as a meta model for global ubiquitous computing generalising process calculi for mobility such as the pi-calculus and the Mobile Ambients calculus as well as graphical models for concurrency such as Petri Nets. We investigate in this paper how Bigraphical Reactive Systems represented as Reactive XML can be used to provide a formal semantics as well as an extensible and mobile platform independent execution format for XML based business process and workflow description languages such as WS-BPEL and XPDL. We propose to extend the formalism with primitives for XPath evaluation and higher-order reaction rules to allow for a very direct and succinct semantics.

1 Introduction

Recently proposed language standards for business process coordination such as WS-BPEL [2], XLANG [28], WSFL [18], and XPDL [7] have a syntax based on XML to facilitate exchange of process descriptions between different process execution engines and analysis tools. Business processes are so-called *long-lived* processes. This means that the *state* of a running process is continuously persisted, and also that mobility of *running* processes is highly relevant, for instance if an active business case is needed in a different part of the world or the process execution engine is updated. Interestingly, however, there is no standard representations of the state of processes and or the execution rules (i.e. the *semantics*) of business process languages relating the process description to the possible state changes. The state of a business process is usually assumed to be persisted in a proprietary format in a relational database [13] and the actual semantics, derived from an informal specification, is hidden in the implementation of a specific process tool. In other words, while the standards allow for exchange of process descriptions there is no platform independent standard for the mobility and exchange of running processes and execution rules, which limits the mobility of business processes in practice. The lack of formal semantics makes it difficult to guarantee consistency between different process tools, and the lack

---

* Authors listed alphabetically. This work was funded in part by the Danish Research Agency (grant no.: 2059-03-0031) and the IT University of Copenhagen (the Bigraphical Programming Languages project).

P. Ciancarini and H. Wiklicky (Eds.): COORDINATION 2006, LNCS 4038, pp. 113–129, 2006.

of an *extensible* format for the process language semantics makes it expensive to change tools when the process languages evolve.

In the present paper we describe a general approach to define an XML-based exchange and execution format for business process coordination, as well as an XML-based format for the process language semantics based on the meta process model of *Bigraphical Reactive Systems* (BRS) [10, 17, 20, 21]. The BRS meta model provides a format for specifying a signature for a process language and a set of reaction rules (rewrite rules) for its semantics and a general theory for deriving from the reaction rules a labelled bisimulation congruence for the process language [10]. Processes are represented as two graphs (explaining the name *bi*graphs), named the place graph and the link graph respectively, which are designed to generalise the pi-calculus [22] and the Mobile Ambients calculus [4]; bigraphs has been shown also to encompass Petri Nets [19].

Concretely, we investigate how BRSs, by exploiting similarities between Bigraphs and XML, can be used to provide a formal semantics and execution format for XML-based business process languages, using a small subset of WS-BPEL as an illustration of the idea. In spite of being just a small subset, the WS-BPEL case provides several benefits: Firstly, the case illustrates how an industry standard XML-based programming language can be extended to an XML-based execution format using ideas from process calculi. Secondly, we show how the semantics can be given as XML-based rewrite rules thereby both providing an extensible and interchangeable format for the semantics and narrowing the gap usually arising between a programming language and its formalisation, as it is the case for π-calculus formalisations of business processes. Finally, the case suggests an interesting extension of BRS to allow for (linear) higher-order reaction rules and tree logics, in this concrete case a subset of XPath. The higher-order reaction rules is essentially a format for wide reaction rules in which the different parts of the rule may be nested inside each other, and thus parameters of the reaction rules may be contexts. Subsequently, we employ XPath to constrain such context parameters, resulting in a kind of *context-dependent* reaction rules.

Our formalisation is presented as an instance of a distributed meta process calculus DiX, which at the same time can be regarded as a term language for a (generalisation of) pure open bigraphs and a process calculus notation for tuples of (unordered) XML, XML contexts and XML-rewrite rules. The DiX calculus and the theory of bigraphical reactive systems form the theoretical foundation for a distributed XML-centric model of computation. This has been implemented in a prototype called Distributed Reactive XML; it provides an extensible, distributed (peer-to-peer) process execution engine for the calculus directly based on the formalisation, and in particular a process engine for any concrete instance. Our approach thus constitutes a general approach to develop extensible and distributed process execution engines from formal process semantics.

The calculus with first-order reaction rules and its implementation as Distributed Reactive XML was presented in [15] based on the Reactive XML implementation given in [14, 31]. The case of WS-BPEL and the extension of the calculus and implementation to higher-order reaction rules and XPath is described in [23]. The present paper focus on the semantics; a follow up paper will address the implementation.

Related Work. Much work has been carried out recently on formalisations of workflow languages, in particular within the Petri Net [24] and pi-calculus formalisms. Indeed the question of which of these two formalisms is most suitable has raised a lively debate [30]. The work in [26] is the most comprenhensive, describing a complete Petri Net-semantics for WS-BPEL. Pi-calculus formalisations of business and workflow processes have been described in [25, 27]. With respect to comprehensibility and extensibility, all of these formalisations suffer from the fact that the business process language is formalised in very abstract models with few primitives for interaction. In comparison, the process semantics given in the present paper stays very close to the WS-BPEL language by utilizing the extensibility of bigraphical reactive systems and the similarities between bigraphs and XML. An argument for employing abstract minimalistic models such as the π-calculus and Petri Nets is of course to be able to perform formal reasoning and utilize verification tools. We retain this hope by relying on the formal theory for bigraphical reactive systems, notably the theory of bisimulation congruences, which will be pursued in future work.

Our representation of bigraphs as XML is inspired by the similarities between process calculi for mobility and semi-structured data observed in [3] and is closely related to the work in [9]. However the focus of [9] is to *represent XML as bigraphs* (and using bigraph-logics introduced by the same authors in [8] to describe properties of XML) as opposed to the present paper that have the opposite focus, namely to *represent bigraphs as XML*, and using XML as an platform independent execution format for bigraphical reactive systems. A possible joining point of the two lines of work would be to use bigraph-logics in place (and as a possibly semantics) of XPath.

The work on XML-based execution formats relates to the proactive XML-centric models of computation and coordination surveyed in [6], in which processes that manipulates XML-documents are embedded inside the documents themselves. In particular our work relates to the Workspaces approach [29] in which an XPDL process description is transformed into a set of XML documents representing the steps to be carried out, thus providing a distributed XML representation of the process state. The main difference between the Workspace approach and ours is that the computation steps in Workspaces are based on XSLT, which has the clear benefit of being an open and widely implemented standard. On the other hand, XSLT is in itself a complex programming language without a formal semantics.

2 Bigraphical Reactive Systems and Reactive XML

In this section we recall the extensible process and context calculus presented in [15] and its relationship to bigraphs and representation as Reactive XML.

Notation: We let n, m, i, j range over natural numbers and write $[m]$ for the set (ordinal) $\{1, \ldots m\}$.

2.1   Signatures and Process expressions

The starting point of our extensible process calculus is a general notion of signatures that encompasses both the signatures of XML documents and bigraph signatures. The terminology is partly borrowed from bigraph signatures.

Definition 1. *A signature is a tuple* $(\Sigma, \Xi \uplus \Delta \subseteq \Sigma, N_c \subseteq N, Att, ar)$, *where* Σ *is a set of* controls *ranged over by* κ, Ξ *and* Δ *are resp. the subsets of* active *and* atomic *controls,* N *is an infinite set of* names *ranged over by* n, N_c *is a set of* constant *names, Att is a set of finite* attribute index sets, *and* $ar : \Sigma \to Att$ *is a function assigning an attribute index set to each control.*   □

As a signature for XML, Σ is a set of XML *element names*, N is a set of XML *attribute values and variables* where N_c is the subset of attribute values (concretely the strings *not* beginning with a $\$$), and *Att* is the set of finite sets of XML *attribute names*. The subset of *active* controls Ξ in the signature determines where *reactions* (or rewrites) can take place as described below and the subset of *atomic* controls Δ are controls that can not have any children. Following [9] we assume the existence of an atomic control with no attributes for each possible $\#PCDATA$ node.

The notion of constant names is an extension of the notion of bigraph signatures and will be explained when we introduce contexts below. For bigraph signatures the attribute index set *Att* is the set $\omega = \{[n] \mid n \geq 0\}$ of finite ordinals and the attribute indexes $ar(\kappa)$ of a bigraph control κ are referred to as the *ports* of κ. The attributes of bigraph controls are thus simply a list of names indicating which name each port is *linked* to. In other words, bigraph signatures has the form $(\Sigma, \Xi \uplus \Delta \subseteq \Sigma, \emptyset, \omega, ar)$.

A distributed Σ-process is an ordered set of unordered trees for which each node is labelled by a control $\kappa \in \Sigma$ and a set of name attributes indexed by $ar(\kappa)$, which we write as $\kappa\{a_i : n_i\}_{a_i \in ar(\kappa)}$. If $ar(\kappa) = \{a_1, \ldots, a_k\}$ the control $\kappa\{a_i : n_i\}_{a_i \in ar(\kappa)}$ corresponds to the XML element $<\kappa\ a_1="n_1" \ldots a_k="n_k">$.

As formulated in Def. 2 below, we use a commutative and associative binary parallel composition $|$ to separate siblings and the prefix notation $\kappa\{a_i : n_i\}_{a_i \in ar(\kappa)}.p$ for a tree with root $\kappa\{a_i : n_i\}_{a_i \in ar(\kappa)}$ and sub tree p. For XML the prefix operator corresponds to surrounding p with the usual open and close elements as $<\kappa\ a_1="n_1" \ldots a_k="n_k"> p </\kappa>$. We collect trees into an ordered set of trees by an associative binary parallel composition $\|$. Using bigraph terminology, we refer to $|$ as the *prime* parallel composition and $\|$ as the *wide* parallel composition. We also refer to trees as *prime* processes and ordered collections of trees as *wide* processes (rather than distributed processes). We let 0 denote the empty collection of trees (i.e. wide process) and 1 the emtpy tree (i.e. prime process).

Definition 2. *For a signature* $\Sigma = (\Sigma, \Xi \uplus \Delta \subseteq \Sigma, N_c \subseteq N, Att, ar)$ *the* Σ-*processes are given by the grammar*

$$w ::= w \parallel w \mid p \mid 0 \qquad\qquad\qquad\qquad \text{wide } \Sigma\text{-processes}$$

$$p ::= \kappa\{a_i : n_i\}_{a_i \in ar(\kappa)}.p \mid \kappa_a\{i : n_i\}_{i \in ar(\kappa_a)}.1 \mid p \mid p \mid 1 \qquad \text{prime } \Sigma\text{-processes}$$

where $\kappa \in \Sigma \backslash \Delta$, $\kappa_a \in \Delta$, $n_i \in N$, and $j \geq 0$. Let $\equiv$ be the structural congruence defined as the least congruence with respect to the operators above that makes $|$ associative and commutative with identity 1 and $\|$ associative with identity 0.

Associativity of the parallel compositions allows us to leave out the parenthesis, writing respectively $\Pi_{i \in [n]} p_i$ and $I\!I\!I_{i \in [n]} p_i$ for the n times prime and wide parallel compositions and letting $\Pi_{i \in \emptyset} p_i = 1$ and $I\!I\!I_{i \in \emptyset} p_i = 0$. As usual we will often leave out trailing nil processes, writing $\kappa\{a_i : n_i\}_{a_i \in ar(\kappa)}$ for $\kappa\{a_i : n_i\}_{a_i \in ar(\kappa)}.1$. We say that the *width* of a wide process expression $I\!I\!I_{i \in [n]} p_i$ is n, i.e. the process is the *wide* parallel product of n primes.

2.2   Context Expressions and Reactions

To define reactions formally we first need to define *process contexts* formally.

Definition 3. *For a signature $\Sigma = (\Sigma, \Xi \uplus \Delta \subset \Sigma, N_c \subseteq N, Att, ar)$ the Σ-bigraph contexts are pairs $G = (W, \sigma)$, where $\sigma : N \to N$ is a finite substitution respecting constant names referred to as the* attribute context *and W is the* place context *defined by the grammar*

$$W ::= W \parallel W \mid P \mid 0$$

$$P ::= \kappa\{i : n_i\}_{i \in ar(\kappa)}.P \mid \kappa_a\{i : n_i\}_{i \in ar(\kappa_a)}.1 \mid P \mid P \mid 1 \mid [\ ]_j$$

where $\kappa \in \Sigma \backslash \Delta$, $\kappa_a \in \Delta$, $n_i \in N$, and $j \geq 0$. Define the names $n(W)$ of a place context W to be the set of attributes appearing at controls.

The first component of a context is what one may first expect of a (multi-hole) process context, namely a process expression with indexed holes $[\ ]_j$ in which processes can be placed. The second component, the finite name substitution σ, act as a context of the attribute variables. An attribute context thus allow renaming, fusion and instantiation of attribute variables. In bigraph terminology, the attribute context is called the link map and the place context is called the place graph. That the substitution σ is finite means that the set $dom(\sigma) = \{x \mid \sigma(x) \neq x\}$ is finite. That it respects contant names means that $dom(\sigma) \cap N_c = \emptyset$.

We type contexts $(W, \sigma) : (n, X) \longrightarrow (m, Y)$ if W has width m and for any hole $[\ ]_j$ in W the index j is in $[n]$, and the attribute context satisfies that $dom(\sigma) \subseteq X$ and $\sigma(X) \cup n(W) \subseteq Y$. Using bigraph terminology we refer to (n, X) and (m, Y) as interfaces, and (n, X) as the innerface and (m, Y) as the outerface of $(W, \sigma) : (n, X) \longrightarrow (m, Y)$. We write $(W, \sigma) \oplus X' : (n, X \uplus X') \longrightarrow (m, Y \cup X')$ for the extension of the interfaces with a set of names X' satisfying $X' \cap X = \emptyset$. The condition ensures that $X' \cap dom(\sigma) = \emptyset$ and thus well typedness.

We say that a context $(W, \sigma) : (n, X) \longrightarrow (m, Y)$ is *affine* if the same index appear at most once at a hole and that a context $(W, \sigma) : (n, X) \longrightarrow (m, Y)$ is *linear* if all indexes in $[n]$ appear exactly once. For bigraph signatures, the typed linear contexts given above is a term language for open pure bigraphs [10]. That the bigraphs are open and pure means respectively that we do not have the usual constructor for local names used to represent name binding in the pi-calculus nor the possibility of binding names within the attributes of controls, as e.g. used for the input prefix in the pi-calculus. Local names and binding is allowed in general, binding bigraphs but they are not needed for the work presented in this paper and is thus left for future work. We let 0 be short for the empty interface $(0, \emptyset)$. As usual, a process p can be viewed as a context $(p, id) : 0 \longrightarrow (m, Y)$ with the empty innerface, referred to as a *ground* context. We will often abbreviate the type of a ground context as $(p, id) : (m, Y)$.

Contexts $(W, \sigma) : (n, X) \longrightarrow (m, Y)$ and $(W', \sigma') : (m, Y) \longrightarrow (k, Z)$ compose as $(W', \sigma') \circ (W, \sigma) = (W'(W\sigma'), \sigma' \circ \sigma) : (n, X) \longrightarrow (k, Z)$ where $W\sigma'$ is the context obtained from W by substituting all attribute values n with $\sigma'(n)$ and $W'(W)$ is the context obtained by for all indexes $i \in [m]$ inserting the ith prime of W into every i-indexed hole of W'.

We say that a context is *active* if no holes are nested inside non-active controls. The dynamics of a process language is then defined by a set R of *parametric reaction rules*. A parametric reaction rule is a pair $(W_L : (n, X) \longrightarrow (m, Y), W_R : (n, X) \longrightarrow (m, Y))$ of wide contexts, where W_L is required to be linear. The set of process reactions is then defined by $W : (k, Z) \longrightarrow W' : (k, Z)$ if there exists a parametric rule $(W_L : (n, X) \longrightarrow (m, Y), W_R : (n, X) \longrightarrow (m, Y)) \in R$, an active context $W_A : (m, Y \cup X') \longrightarrow (k, Z)$ and a parameter process $W_P : (n, X \uplus X')$ such that $W \equiv W_A \circ W_L \oplus X' \circ W_P$ and $W' \equiv W_A \circ W_R \oplus X' \circ W_P$.

2.3 Reactive XML

Table 1 shows how processes and contexts are represented as XML, where ϵ denote the empty document. As indicated above we represent controls as XML elements (except for the #PCDATA controls represented as character data) and attributes as XML-attributes. We use the reserved[1] element names `wide`, `reg`, and `hole` for respectively the root of the wide process, the root of the primes (referred to as regions in bigraphs) and the holes. The `hole` element has an attribute `name` providing the index of the hole.

We represent the set of reaction rules as an XML document containing the rules encoded as pairs of contexts as well as an XPath representation of the active controls as will be described in Sec. 3. The technical report [16] contains the set of WS-BPEL reaction rules from [23] in Reactive XML format.

3   Formalising XML Business Process Execution

When representing WS-BPEL processes as bigraphs we leverage the fact that Reactive XML provides an XML-based syntax for bigraphs and that a bigraph-ical reactive system may tailor the exact expressions to the application. In other words, the representation makes it possible to view the original WS-BPEL process expression as a Reactive XML expression. In order to make the reaction rules simpler we have chosen to relax this a bit, and the translation from WS-BPEL process expressions to bigraphs may insert helper controls.

---

[1] Technically, this can be reserved using the notion of XML namespaces.

Table 1. Process contexts as XML

$$\llbracket \Pi_{i \in [n]}\, P_i \rrbracket \qquad\qquad = \texttt{<wide>}\,\texttt{<reg>}\llbracket P_1 \rrbracket\texttt{</reg>} \ldots \texttt{<reg>}\llbracket P_n \rrbracket\texttt{</reg>}\,\texttt{</wide>}$$

$$\llbracket \kappa\{a_i : x_i\}_{a_i \in ar(\kappa)}.P \rrbracket = \texttt{<}\kappa\;\; a_1\texttt{="}x_1\texttt{"} \ldots a_n\texttt{="}x_n\texttt{">}\;\llbracket p \rrbracket\;\texttt{</}\kappa\texttt{>}, \text{ for } |ar(\kappa)| = n$$

$$\llbracket \kappa_a \rrbracket \qquad\qquad = \kappa_a, \text{ for } \kappa_a \in \#PCDATA$$

$$\llbracket P \mid P' \rrbracket \qquad\qquad = \llbracket P \rrbracket \llbracket P' \rrbracket$$

$$\llbracket 1 \rrbracket \qquad\qquad\;\;\, = \epsilon$$

$$\llbracket\; [\;]_j\, \rrbracket \qquad\qquad = \texttt{<hole name="j"/>}$$

In this section we investigate how to formalise XML business process execution, concretely a subset of WS-BPEL, as bigraphical reactive systems. The contributions of this are twofold: on the one hand it gives a succint representation of the semantics of WS-BPEL subset, on the other hand it directly provides a subsequent implementation based on our earlier work on Reactive XML [15]. Due to space considerations the present paper addresses the first of these only; for the second we refer to [23]. For a bigraphical reactive system, one gets to specify not only process expressions in the formalism, but also the reaction rules. This makes bigraphical reactive systems particularly well-suited for representing the semantics of WS-BPEL as we can capture the semantics of each kind of WS-BPEL process as one or more bigraphical reaction rules.

3.1 A Subset of WS-BPEL as Processes

Figure 1 gives the grammar of the WS-BPEL process language we consider presented in the more compact DiX notation. The translation to XML (as described in Table 1) is straightforward. The corresponding signature Σ is defined in Table 2. The signature has the controls process, variables, variable, sequence, flow, while, assign, copy, from, to and invoke corresponding directly to elements in WS-BPEL and four additional controls: next, body, condition, and instance, to be described below.

We employ a simple kind of *sorting* (i.e. schema) restricting the allowed children of controls and the allowed names for attributes. We let q range over a subset of XPath expressions (including the contants *true* and *false*), defined below. We use sets in sorts to represent disjunction and let & represent conjunction. We use ? for zero or one, and * for zero or more. The process control thus have zero or one variables control as child and zero or one control from the set ACT (of actions). From a high-level perspective, a WS-BPEL process description consists of a number of processes in parallel

$$proc_1 \mid \ldots \mid proc_n$$

represented by *procs* in Figure 1. During execution, each of the processes $proc_i$ may get instantiated, eg., when it is being invoked. A process instance needs

$$
\begin{aligned}
system &::= procs \mid state \\
procs &::= proc \mid \ldots \mid proc \\
state &::= inst \mid \ldots \mid inst \\
proc &::= \mathsf{process}\{name : n\}.(vars \mid act) \\
vars &::= \mathsf{variables}.(var \mid \ldots \mid var) \\
var &::= \mathsf{variable}\{name : n\} \\
act &::= seq \mid while \mid flow \mid inv \mid rec \mid rep \mid assign \mid 1 \\
seq &::= \mathsf{sequence}.(act \mid \mathsf{next}.act) \\
while &::= \mathsf{while}\{condition : q\}.\mathsf{body}.act \\
flow &::= \mathsf{flow}.(act \mid \ldots \mid act) \\
inv &::= \mathsf{invoke}\{operation : n, inputVariable : n\} \\
rec &::= \mathsf{receive}\{operation : n, variable : n\} \\
rep &::= \mathsf{reply}\{operation : n, variable : n\} \\
assign &::= \mathsf{assign}.\mathsf{copy}.(from \mid to) \\
from &::= \mathsf{from}\{var : n\} \mid \mathsf{from\_expr}\{query : q\} \\
to &::= \mathsf{to}\{var : n\} \\
inst &::= \mathsf{instance}\{name : n\}.(instvars \mid act) \\
instvars &::= \mathsf{variables}.(instvar \mid \ldots \mid instvar) \\
instvar &::= \mathsf{variable}\{name : n\}.v
\end{aligned}
$$

Fig. 1. A grammar for the WS-BPEL subset

Table 2. BPEL process signature

Control	Activity	Attributes	Sort
process	passive	{name:n}	$\{variables\}^? \& ACT^?$
variables	passive		$\{variable\}^*$
variable	passive	{name:n}	$\#PCDATA$
sequence	active		$ACT^? \& \mathsf{next}$
flow	active		ACT^*
while	passive	{condition:q}	$\{condition\}^? \& \{body\}$
assign	passive		$\{copy\}$
copy	passive		$\{from\} \& \{to\}$
from	atomic	{var:n}	$\emptyset$
from_expr	atomic	{query:q}	$\emptyset$
to	atomic	{var:n}	$\emptyset$
invoke	atomic	{operation:n, inputVariable:n}	$\emptyset$
receive	atomic	{operation:n, variable:n}	$\emptyset$
reply	atomic	{operation:n, variable:n}	$\emptyset$
next	passive		$ACT^?$
body	passive		$ACT^?$
condition	passive		$ACT^?$
instance	active		$\{variables\}^? \& ACT^?$

where $ACT = \{\mathsf{sequence, flow, while, assign, invoke, receive, reply}\}$ and $\#PCDATA$ is the set of $\#PCDATA$ controls.

to maintain the current "program counter" indicating what activity is currently being executed and an assignment of values to the variables of the process. We shall refer to the representation of program counters and variable assignments for all process instances as the *execution state* of the WS-BPEL process description.

Traditionally, execution engines store execution state in proprietary formats, typically in a database. We propose to represent not only the WS-BPEL process description as XML, but also the execution state. This allows us to use Reactive XML to implement the execution steps taken by WS-BPEL processes. Reaction rules implement the semantics of WS-BPEL by rewriting the execution state appropriately. Again from a high-level perspective the current state of the execution of a WS-BPEL process description has the following form, represented by *system* in the grammar:

$$(proc_1 \mid \ldots \mid proc_n) \mid (inst_1 \mid \ldots \mid inst_m)$$

that is a set of process descriptions together with a set of the currently instantiated processes. We need the descriptions in order to be able to instantiate new processes; the instances capture the execution state, not as program program pointers but in the style of process calculi as descriptions of the current state and possible future behaviour. Process instances are represented using the control **instance** which is just like **process** except variables carry a current value.

Since process descriptions are only meant to be used when instantiating processes the **process** control is passive; dually, process instances are meant to be executed (ie., rewritten) and therefore the **instance** control is active.

Associated with each syntactic construct we present a number of reaction rules specifying how the execution state evolves for the construct in question. For example, there are two rules specifying how to execute while loops. The reaction rules rewrite the XML representation of the execution state; specifically, the process instance for which an execution step is to be taken. These reaction rules "capture" the semantics of WS-BPEL.

3.2 Combining Activities

WS-BPEL defines a number of *structural activities*; activities which combine smaller activities into a combined activity.

One of the most basic structural activities in WS-BPEL is that of parallel composition, known as flow. Activities prefixed by a flow are *concurrent* and thus may execute concurrently[2]. The execution of the flow activity ends when all parallel activities have finshed executing. By making the corresponding control flow active we ensure, appealing to the underlying bigraphical model, that the activities may execute in parallel. It would also have been possible to omit the explicit control completely, however, at the cost of more differences between the original WS-BPEL process and its encoding. We use a reaction rule to remove the flow control when all activities have ended

$$\textsf{flow}.1 \rightarrow 1 \tag{1}$$

---

[2] Future work will address the representation of *links* to constrain the execution order.

An equally important structural activity is sequential composition (using sequence). The activities are executed in the order in which they occur as children of the sequence control (ie., so-called "document order"). The execution of the sequence activity ends when the last activity in the sequence has finished executing. In contrast to flow its encoding has to address the fact that the children of a control are *unordered* in bigraphs. This means that we cannot just group two sequential activities under a sequence control which is active, as that would allow either of them to execute. Instead we introduce a new, passive control, next, to block execution of the second activity, and provide an explicit reaction rule for execution. That is, we represent two WS-BPEL activities in sequence `<sequence>` act_1 act_2 `</sequence>` by the process sequence.(act_1 | next.act_2) and use the following reaction rule to start execution of the second activity once the first has finished:

$$\text{sequence.next.}[\ ]_1 \rightarrow [\ ]_1. \tag{2}$$

The while structural activity provides for the repeated execution of an activity. The activity is executed repeatedly until the XPath condition no longer evalutes to true, in which case the execution of the while activity ends. To support basing conditions on XPaths we extend Reactive XML with a primitive for evaluating XPath expressions (rather than extending the underlying calculus, we could have written an XPath interpreter in DiX). Consider a rule containing $EvalXPath(query)$ on the right-hand side, Reactive XML rewrites using this rule by evaluating the XPath expression $query$ against the DiX context matching the left-hand side of the rule and inserting the result in place of $EvalXPath(query)$.

Equipped with this primitive we can easily specify the semantics of while by first appealing to the primitive (3) and then proceeding based on whether the condition evaluates to true (4) or false (5). As for sequence, we use a passive control body to block rewriting the body of the while; the control condition serves to delimit the results of XPath evaluation from WS-BPEL (in the event that the XPath generates valid WS-BPEL code).

$$\text{while}\{condition : \mathsf{q}\}.\text{body.}[\ ]_1 \tag{3}$$
$$\rightarrow \text{while}\{condition : \mathsf{q}\}.(\text{condition.}EvalXPath(q) \mid \text{body.}[\ ]_1)$$
$$\text{while}\{condition : \mathsf{q}\}.(\text{condition.}true \mid \text{body.}[\ ]_1) \tag{4}$$
$$\rightarrow \text{sequence.}([\ ]_1 \mid \text{next.while}\{condition : \mathsf{q}\}.\text{body.}[\ ]_1)$$
$$\text{while}\{condition : \mathsf{q}\}.(\text{condition.}false \mid \text{body.}[\ ]_1) \tag{5}$$
$$\rightarrow 1$$

The allowed XPath expressions are boolean and simple typed (i.e. integer) expressions over constants and the functions `bpws:getVariableData('`n`')` for extracting the value of a variable.

3.3   Variables

Assigning values to variables is one of the *primitive activities* of WS-BPEL (in the subset we consider the only other primitive activities are concerned with invoking processes as discussed in the next section). Variable assignments take the form assign.copy.(*from* | *to*).

The intention is to assign the value specified by *from* to the variable specified by *to*. In the WS-BPEL subset we consider in the present paper, *to* can only specify a variable as in to{*var* : x}. The value to assign to the *to* variable is specified by *from*: it can be either another variable, from{*var* : x}, or an XPath expression, from_expr{*expr* : q}. Below we describe how to define variable assignments of the form from{*var* : x}, the form from_expr{*expr* : q} is simpler as it appeals simply to $EvalXPath(q)$ rather than involving looking up the current binding of a variable.

Recall, that process instances record the current bindings of values to variables, as in

$$\text{instance.(variables.(variable}\{var : \text{x}\}.17 \mid \text{variable}\{var : \text{y}\}.\text{list.}(\ldots)) \mid \ldots) \quad (6)$$

binding the value 17 to x, and the XML element list.(...) to y.

Executing an assignment assign.copy.(*from* | *to*) is therefore a matter of manipulating the correct variables in the instance's variables control. In order to not let an assignment from one process instance affect the variables of another instance, we need to insist that the controls assign and variables are both located under the same instance control. Furthermore, since the assignment may occur within a structural activity, the reaction rule for variable-to-variable assignment takes the form:

$$
\begin{aligned}
&\text{instance}\{name : \$i\}.(C(\text{assign.copy.(from}\{var : \$f\} \mid \text{to}\{var : \$t\})) \\
&\quad \mid \text{variables.(variable}\{name : \$f\}.[\ ]_1 \mid \text{variable}\{name : \$t\}.[\ ]_2 \mid [\ ]_3)) \\
&\longrightarrow \text{instance}\{name : \$i\}.(C(1) \\
&\quad \mid \text{variables.(variable}\{name : \$f\}.[\ ]_1 \mid \text{variable}\{name : \$t\}.[\ ]_1 \mid [\ ]_3))
\end{aligned} \quad (7)
$$

(where $[\ ]_1$ is the value of the variable matched by $\$f$, $[\ ]_2$ is the value of the variable matched by $\$t$, and $[\ ]_3$ are the remaining bindings).

Intuitively, the context C above captures the fact that assign may be nested under active controls, i.e. flow, while, or a sequence. For example, considering again the process instance in (6) we could have

$$
\begin{aligned}
&\text{instance.(variables.}(\ldots) \\
&\quad \mid \text{sequence.(assign.copy.(from}\{var : \text{x}\} \mid \text{to}\{var : \text{y}\}) \mid \text{next.}(\ldots)))
\end{aligned} \quad (6')
$$

in which case C therefore is sequence.([] | next.(...)).

Formally, we want to have an infinite set of rules obtained by instatiating C with all possible active contexts. In the next sections we will suggest a format of higher-order parametric reaction rules that allow us to specify such rule sets.

3.4   Higher-Order Reaction Rules

Consider again the reaction rule for assignment. We wish to be able to abstract the context C in the reaction rule by a hole, writing:

instance$\{name : \$iname\}$.$([$ (assign.(copy.(from$\{var : \$f\}$ | to$\{var : \$t\}$))) $]_4$
$\quad$ | variables.(variable$\{name : \$f\}$.$[\ ]_1$ | variable$\{name : \$t\}$.$[\ ]_2$ | $[\ ]_3$))
$\longrightarrow$ instance$\{name : \$iname\}$.$([1]_4$
$\quad$ | variables.(variable$\{name : \$f\}$.$[\ ]_1$ | variable$\{name : \$t\}$.$[\ ]_1$ | $[\ ]_3$))

$$(8)$$

The parameters of holes 1, 2 and 3 are as usual prime processes, i.e. contexts $P_i : 0 \longrightarrow (1, X)$, but the parameter of the 4th hole is a prime context $C : (1, Z) \longrightarrow (1, Z)$ with a single hole and $Z = \{\$f, \$t\}$. That is, we wish to instantiate (8) with a wide process $W = P_1 \parallel P_2 \parallel P_3 \parallel C$ resulting in the ground rule

instance$\{name : \$iname\}$.$(C \circ ($assign.(copy.(from$\{var : \$f\}$ | to$\{var : \$t\}$))))
$\quad$ | variables.(variable$\{name : \$f\}$.$P_1$ | variable$\{name : \$t\}$.$P_2$ | P_3))
$\longrightarrow$ instance$\{name : \$iname\}$.$(C \circ 1$
$\quad$ | variables.(variable$\{name : \$f\}$.$P_1$ | variable$\{name : \$t\}$.$P_1$ | P_3))

Formally, we extend the types for interfaces with a limited function space considering types of the form $t ::= (\bar{t}, X)$, where $\bar{t}$ is a vector of types $t_1 t_2 \dots t_n$. The idea is, that if $(\bar{t}, X)$ is the innerface of a context W then every hole with index i is of the form $[W']_i$ where W' is a process of type t_i. A prime context C of type $t_i \longrightarrow (1, X)$ can be placed in the hole $[W']_i$, replacing the hole with the process $C \circ W'$. We will write 0 for the empty interface $(\epsilon, \emptyset)$ where ϵ is the empty vector, and we write (n, X) for the type $(\bar{t}, X)$ where $t_i = 0$ for all $i \in [|\bar{t}|]$. The type of the redex W_L and reactum W_R in the reaction rule above is then $(\bar{t}, Z) \longrightarrow (1, Z')$ where $t_1 = t_2 = t_3 = 0$, $t_4 = (1, Z)$ and $Z' = \{\$f, \$t, \$iname\}$.

However, note that the parameter $W = P_1 \parallel P_2 \parallel P_3 \parallel C$ above has type $(1, Z) \longrightarrow (4, X \cup Z)$, so it can not immediately be composed with W_L and W_R. Essentially, we need the hole to be part of the outerface. To this end, we define the *involution* of a process $(W)^-$ having the type $(W)^- : 0 \longrightarrow (\bar{t}, X)$ for $\bar{t} = t_1 t_2 \dots t_n$ if $W \equiv \Pi_{i \in [n]} P_i$ and P_i can be typed $t_i \longrightarrow (1, X)$. Now for $W = P_1 \parallel P_2 \parallel P_3 \parallel C$ we have $(W)^- : 0 \longrightarrow (\bar{t}, X \cup Z)$ for $t_1 = t_2 = t_3 = 0$ and $t_4 = (1, Z)$ matching the innerface of $W_L \oplus X \backslash Z$ and $W_R \oplus X \backslash Z$. We restrict ourself to only consider higher-order processes of type $(\bar{t}, X) \longrightarrow (n, Y)$ and $0 \longrightarrow (\bar{t}, X)$ given by the grammar below.

Definition 4. *For a signature* $\Sigma = (\Sigma, \Xi, N_c \subseteq N, Att, ar)$ *the* Higher-order Σ-bigraph contexts H *are defined by the grammar*

$$H \quad ::= (W_{ho}, \sigma) \mid (W_{ho}, \sigma)^-$$
$$W_{ho} ::= W_{ho} \parallel W_{ho} \mid P_{ho} \mid 0$$
$$P_{ho} ::= \kappa\{i : n_i\}_{i \in ar(\kappa)}.P_{ho} \mid P_{ho} \mid P_{ho} \mid 1 \mid [(W_{ho}, \sigma)]_j$$

where $\sigma : N \to N$ are finite substitutions, $\kappa \in \Sigma$, $n_i \in N$, and $j \geq 0$ as for 1st-order contexts. We will often write W_{ho} for (W_{ho}, id).

As indicated above, we type contexts $(W_{ho}, \sigma) : (\bar{t}, X) \longrightarrow (m, Y)$ for $\bar{t} = t_1 t_2 \ldots t_n$ if W_{ho} has width m, $dom(\sigma) \subseteq X$ and $\sigma(X) \cup n(W_{ho}) \subseteq Y$, and for any hole $[(W'_{ho}, \sigma')]_j, j \in [n]$ and $(W'_{ho}, \sigma')^-$ can be typed $0 \longrightarrow t_j$. We type contexts $(W_{ho}, \sigma)^- : 0 \longrightarrow (\bar{t}, X)$ for $\bar{t} = t_1 t_2 \ldots t_n$ if $W_{ho} \equiv \Pi_{i \in [n]} P_i$ and P_i can be typed $t_i \longrightarrow (1, X)$.

The higher-order contexts allow us to specify the reaction rule for assign as in (8) above. However, we wish to constrain the parameter of the 4th hole to only *active* contexts. In general the constraints may depend on attribute values, for instance to guarantee the existence of a certain path of controls between the root and the hole(s) as it is the case for the XPath addressing of sub contents of variables allowed in WS-BPEL. In the following section we address how this can be achieved.

3.5 XPath Attribute Values and Context Constraints

We consider a small subset of XPath given by the grammar

$$\phi \quad ::= naos \mid exp$$

$$naos \quad ::= \texttt{//*[not (ancestor-or-self::*[}nameset\texttt{])]} \mid \texttt{//*}$$

$$nameset ::= \texttt{name()='}n\texttt{'} \mid \texttt{name()='}n\texttt{'} \text{ or } nameset$$

$$exp \quad ::= \texttt{bpws:getVariableData('}n\texttt{')} \mid \ldots$$

The XPath expressions defined by *naos* are of the form

```
//*[not (ancestor-or-self::*[name()='n₁' or ... or name()='nₖ'])]
```

and selects nodes *not* nested within any of the controls n_i for $i \in [k]$. These expressions are for instance used to identify active contexts, by letting the set $\{n_1, \ldots, n_k\}$ be the set of passive controls. We will let ϕ_{active} denote this expression. The XPath expressions defined by *exp* are as for the while conditions, booleans and simple typed expressions.

Recall that an XPath expression evaluated with respect to a node (somewhat confusingly referred to as the context) in an XML-document and results in a nodeset. We define that a prime context P *satisfies* an XPath constraint if all of the holes are children of one of the nodes in the nodesets resulting from evaluating XPath on the children of the reserved reg control of $[\![P]\!]$ (the context represented as XML). The syntax of higher-order context holes is then extended to $[(W'_{ho}, \sigma')]_j^\phi$, where ϕ is an XPath expression belonging to the subset defined above. We extend the interface types accordingly to $t ::= (\bar{t}, \bar{\phi}, X)$ where $\bar{t}$ as before is a vector $t_1 \ldots t_n$ of types and $\bar{\phi}$ is a vector $\phi_1 \ldots \phi_n$ of limited XPath expressions as defined by the grammar above. We omit the XPath constraints from the type if they all are the expression //* that selects all contexts.

We extend the typing condition to require for $(W_{ho}, \sigma) : (\bar{t}, \bar{\phi}, X) \longrightarrow (m, Y)$ for $\bar{t} = t_1 t_2 \ldots t_n$ that for any hole $[(W'_{ho}, \sigma')]_j^\phi$ $\phi = \phi_j$ and for the involuted contexts with XPath constraints $(W_{ho}, \sigma)^- : 0 \longrightarrow (\bar{t}, \bar{\phi}, X)$ for $\bar{t} = t_1 t_2 \dots t_n$ and $\bar{\phi} = \phi_1 \dots \phi_n$ if $W_{ho} \equiv \Pi_{i \in [n]} P_i$ and P_i can be typed $t_i \longrightarrow (1, X)$ and satisfies ϕ_i.

Returning to the assign case, we can now add the constraint ϕ_{active} to the hole with index 4 and type the redex (and reactum) $W_L : (\bar{t}, \bar{\phi}, X) \longrightarrow (1, X)$ where $t_1 = t_2 = t_3 = 0$ and $t_4 = (1, Z)$ and $\phi_1 = \phi_2 = \phi_3 = //*$ and $\phi_4 = \phi_{active}$.

3.6 Process Communication

Communication amongst processes is the other form of *basic activities* of WS-BPEL we consider. The specification of communication takes up a large fraction of the WS-BPEL specification; here we shall focus on the basics of invoking a process and process communication. WS-BPEL addresses orchestration of web services and as such integrate features from WSDL (Web Services Description Language) [5]. In the present work, rather than working with web services, we consider a system as a collection of processes and interpret process invocation and communication as between the processes in the system. Furthermore, WS-BPEL also specifies how to correlate the messages between multiple (instances of) processes using so-called "correlation sets". See [23] for the details of representing this in Reactive XML.

A business process may invoke another process, thereby creating an instance of the invoked process, using operation{ *operation* : op, . . .}. This creates an instance of the process in the system which contains a set{ *operation* : op, . . .} activity. The invoking process instance may specify parameters to the receiving process by including a variable in the invoke attribute *inputVariable*. The intention is to look up the current value of the variable in the instance, and bind that value to the formal parameter specified in the receive's *variable* attribute (just as was done for variable assignment).

The above informal description can be expressed in the following reaction rule:

$$\mathsf{instance}\{name : \$i\}.([\ \mathsf{invoke}\{operation : \$o, inputVariable : \$in\} \ ]_3^{\phi_{active}}$$
$$| \ \mathsf{variables}.(\mathsf{variable}\{name : \$in\}.[\ ]_1 \ | \ [\ ]_2))$$
$$| \ \mathsf{process}\{name : \$p\}.([\mathsf{receive}\{operation : \$o, variable : \$var, \}]_6^{\phi_{active}}$$
$$| \ \mathsf{variables}.(\mathsf{variable}\{name : \$var\} \ | \ [\ ]_4) \ | \ [\ ]_5)$$

$$\longrightarrow$$

$$\mathsf{instance}\{name : \$i\}.([1]_3^{\phi_{active}} \ | \ \mathsf{variables}.(\mathsf{variable}\{name : \$in\}.[\ ]_1 \ | \ [\ ]_2))$$
$$| \ \mathsf{instance}\{name : \$p\}.(\mathsf{variables}.(\mathsf{variable}\{name : \$var\}.[\ ]_1 \ | \ [\ ]_4) \ | \ [\ ]_5)$$
$$| \ \mathsf{process}\{name : \$p\}.([\mathsf{receive}\{operation : \$o, variable : \$var\}]_6^{\phi_{active}}$$
$$| \ \mathsf{variables}.(\mathsf{variable}\{name : \$var\} \ | \ [\ ]_4) \ | \ [\ ]_5)$$

Observe (1) how the invoking process instance simply discards the invoke (in other words, it is asynchronous), (2) that the receiving process description remains unchanged (making it possible to create more instances), and (3) a new process instance has been added to the system with the correct variable binding and the "body" of the receiving process description ([ ]$_5$). We have used the same trick as for assign in order to locate the invoke under seq, flow, and while. One similarly needs a reaction that allows sending messages between two process instances (in WS-BPEL using reply and receive) following the pattern above:

$$\text{instance}\{name : \$rp\}.([\text{reply}\{operation : \$o, variable : \$out\}]_3^{\phi_{active}}$$
$$|\; \text{variables}.(\text{variable}\{name : \$out\}.[\,]_1 \;|\; [\,]_2))$$
$$|\;\; \text{instance}\{name : \$rv\}.([\text{receive}\{operation : \$o, variable : \$var\}]_6^{\phi_{active}}$$
$$|\; \text{variables}.(\text{variable}\{name : \$var\}.[\,]_4 \;|\; [\,]_5))$$
$$\longrightarrow$$
$$\text{instance}\{name : \$rp\}.([1]_3^{\phi_{active}} \;|\; \text{variables}.(\text{variable}\{name : \$out\}.[\,]_1 \;|\; [\,]_2))$$
$$|\;\; \text{instance}\{name : \$rv\}.([1]_6^{\phi_{active}} \;|\; \text{variables}.(\text{variable}\{name : \$var\}.[\,]_1 \;|\; [\,]_5))$$

4   Conclusion and Future Work

We have demonstrated how Bigraphical Reactive Systems, by exploiting the similarities of Bigraphs and XML, can be used to provide a formal semantics and a mobile and extensible XML execution format for XML-based business process languages. We used a small subset of WS-BPEL to illustrate how an industry standard XML-based programming language can be extended to an XML-based execution format using ideas from process calculi. By also representing the reaction rules as XML we provide an interchangeable format for the semantics and narrowing the gap usually arising between a programming language and its formalisation. The case suggested an interesting extension of BRS to allow for (linear) higher-order reaction rules constrained by tree logics, in this concrete case a subset of XPath, resulting in a kind of *context-dependent* reaction rules. We are currently working on expressing a more general category of higher-order contexts as a Geometry of Interaction [1, 11, 12] construction on the underlying category of bigraphs and show that the general theory of bisimulation congruences for bigraphs can be extended to this setting.

The WS-BPEL process calculus described in the previous sections is just a subset of a WS-BPEL process calculus which has been described and implemented as Distributed Reactive XML in [23]. We have so far only focussed on language primitives found in the XLANG subset. We leave for future work to demonstrate that the flow-graph primitives of the WFDL subset can be represented equally succinct.

The implementation of Distributed Reactive XML so far serves as a proof of concept. However, by representing the business process descriptions, their state and semantics of the process languages as XML and implementing it on top of a distributed peer-to-peer XML storage layer allowing concurrent reactions on shared processes and data, we achieve a middleware supporting many of the features of the ideal scenario described in [6]. We leave for future work to study the relationship between our approach and the approaches surveyed in [6], in particular the Workspaces approach.

References

[1] Samson Abramsky. Retracing some paths in process algebra. In *Proceedings of CONCUR'96*, volume 1119 of *LNCS*, pages 1–17, 1996.

[2] Tony Andrews and et al. Business process execution language for web services (version 1.1). Technical report, IBM, Microsoft, SAP and others, May 2003.

[3] Luca Cardelli. Semistructured computation. In *Proceedings of the 7th International Workshop on Database Programming Languages (DBPL)*, volume 1949 of *LNCS*, pages 1–16. Springer-Verlag, 2000.

[4] Luca Cardelli and Andrew D. Gordon. Mobile ambients. In *Proceedings of FoS-SaCS'98*, volume 1378, pages 140–155. Springer-Verlag, 1998.

[5] Roberto Chinnici, Jean-Jacques Moreau, Arthur Ryman, and Sanjiva Weerawarana. Web services description language (wsdl). Technical report, W3C, January 2006.

[6] P. Ciancarini, R. Tolksdorf, and F. Zambonelli. Coordination middleware for XML-centric applications. In *Proc. ACM/SIGAPP Symp. on Applied Computing (SAC)*. ACM Press, 2002.

[7] The Workflow Management Coalition. Process definition interface — XML process definition language (version 2.00). Technical Report WFMC-TC-1025, Workflow Management Coalition (WfMC), 2005.

[8] Giovanni Conforti, Damiano Macedonio, and Vladimiro Sassone. Bilogics: Spatial-nominal logics for bigraphs. 2004.

[9] Giovanni Conforti, Damiano Macedonio, and Vladimiro Sassone. Bigraphical logics for XML. In *Proceedings of the Thirteenth Italian Symposium on Advanced Database Systems (SEBD)*, pages 392–399, 2005.

[10] Ole Høgh Jensen and Robin Milner. Bigraphs and transitions. In *Proceedings of the 30th ACM SIGPLAN-SIGACT Symposium on Principles of Programming Languages (POPL)*, pages 38–49. ACM Press, 2003.

[11] J.Y. Girard. Geometry of interaction I: interpretation of system F. In *Proceedings Logic Colloquium*, number 88, pages 221–260. North-Holland, 1989.

[12] J.Y. Girard. Geometry of interaction II: deadlock free algorithms. In *Proceedings of COLOG 88*, number 417 in LNCS, pages 76–93. Springer-Verlag, 1989.

[13] Mike Havey. *Essential Business Process Modelling*. O'Reilly, 2005.

[14] Thomas Hildebrandt and Jacob W. Winther. Bigraphs and (Reactive) XML. Technical Report TR-2005-56, IT University of Copenhagen, 2005.

[15] Thomas Hildebrandt, Henning Niss, Martin Olsen, and Jacob W. Winther. Distributed Reactive XML. In *1st International Workshop on Methods and Tools for Coordinating Concurrent, Distributed and Mobile Systems (MTCoord)*, 2005.

[16] Thomas Hildebrandt, Henning Niss, and Martin Olsen. Business process execution languages as bigraphs and reactive xml. Technical Report TR 85, IT University of Copenhagen, 2006.

[17] Ole Høgh Jensen and Robin Milner. Bigraphs and mobile processes (revised). Technical Report UCAM-CL-TR-580, University of Cambridge, Computer Laboratory, February 2004.

[18] Frank Leymann. Web services flow language (WSFL). Technical report, IBM Software Group, 2001.

[19] Robin Milner. Bigraphs for petri nets. In *Lectures on Concurrency and Petri Nets*, pages 686–701, 2003.

[20] Robin Milner. Bigraphical reactive systems. In *Proceedings of 12th International Conference on Concurrency Theory (CONCUR)*, pages 16–35, 2001.

[21] Robin Milner. Axioms for bigraphical structure. Technical Report UCAM-CL-TR-581, University of Cambridge, Computer Laboratory, 2004.

[22] Robin Milner, Joachim Parrow, and David Walker. A calculus of mobile processes, I. *Information and Computation*, 100(1):1–40, 1992.

[23] Martin Olsen. Encoding mobile workflows in Reactive XML. Master's thesis, IT University of Copenhagen, 2006. In Danish.

[24] Carl Adam Petri. *Kommunikation mit Automaten*. PhD thesis, Bonn: Institut für Instrumentelle Mathematik, Schriften des IIM Nr. 2, 1962. Second Edition:, New York: Griffiss Air Force Base, Technical Report RADC-TR-65–377, Vol.1, 1966, Pages: Suppl. 1, English translation.

[25] Frank Puhlmanm and Mathias Weske. Using the pi-calculus for formalizing workflow patterns. In *Proceedings of BPM 2005*, number 2678 in LNCS. Springer-Verlag, 2005.

[26] Christian Stahl. A Petri net semantics for BPEL. Informatik-Berichte 188, Humboldt-Universität zu Berlin, jul 2005.

[27] Christian Stefansen. A declarative framework for enterprise information systems. Master's thesis, Dept. of Computer Science, University of Copenhagen (DIKU), 2005. Qualification Report.

[28] Satish Thatte. XLANG: Web services for business process design. Technical report, Microsoft Corporation, 2001.

[29] Robert Tolksdorf. Workspaces: A web-based workflow management system. *IEEE Internet Computing*, september 2002.

[30] Wil M.P van der Aalst. Pi calculus versus Petri nets: Let us eat "humble pie" rather than further inflate the "Pi hype". *BPTrends*, 3(5):1–11, 2005.

[31] Jacob W. Winther. Reactive XML. Master's thesis, IT University of Copenhagen, 2004.

Enabling Ubiquitous Coordination Using Application Sessions

Christine Julien and Drew Stovall

The Center for Excellence in Distributed Global Environments
The Department of Electrical and Computer Engineering
The University of Texas at Austin
{c.julien, dstovall}@mail.utexas.edu

Abstract. Enabling coordination among ubiquitous computing applications and resources requires programming abstractions and development tools tailored to this unique environment. This paper introduces a suite of coordination abstractions that enables expressive interaction between ubiquitous computing applications and dynamically available resources. In our model, applications express their coordination needs in terms of *application sessions* that are loosely defined by a set of interactions with remote resources. Our approach allows developers to delegate responsibility for the construction and maintenance of the communication links necessary to support the application's sessions to an underlying middleware. In this paper, we formalize a suite of session definitions for coordination in general classes of ubiquitous computing applications. We also present a middleware based on this coordination model that directly supports the software development task. Finally, we demonstrate the simplicity and flexibility of our approach using a real-world application.

1   Introduction

The increasing pervasiveness of computing capabilities has enabled new classes of ubiquitous applications that rely on interactions with dynamically available resources to provide an adaptive, responsive, and intuitive computing experience. Many applications have been built, but existing development tools are not flexible enough to meet the demands of interactive general-purpose applications. This paper undertakes a coordination approach to specifying and managing the interactions between application and resources. We leverage the benefits of this coordination to realize a programming framework that removes the need for an application programmer to be intimately familiar with the details of communication in pervasive computing. Our approach promises to simplify application development by promoting abstraction, reuse, and transparency.

Within this paper, we use two application domains that exemplify the unique challenges of building ubiquitous computing applications. In first responder applications, a dynamic set of participants is deployed in an emergency situation. People with differing tasks (e.g., paramedics, firemen, policemen, search and rescue personnel, etc.) converge on a geographic area, bringing with them computing, communicating, and sensing devices. Their applications benefit significantly

P. Ciancarini and H. Wiklicky (Eds.): COORDINATION 2006, LNCS 4038, pp. 130–144, 2006.
© Springer-Verlag Berlin Heidelberg 2006

from heightened degrees of cooperation involving pairs of participants or large dynamic groups of people. As a second example, construction sites are becoming increasingly loaded with sensing and computing capabilities. Supervisors and workers on the site desire to connect to local resources in real time to monitor and maintain safety or to track materials for planning.

This work defines new coordination mechanisms specifically tailored to pervasive computing applications. We define an application session to be *a temporary logical connection among two or more networked devices over which application data is exchanged*. We differentiate this application session from other connection mechanisms in that the state maintained involves an application-level dialog between the communicating entities and depends significantly on the application. As such, a session is further defined by the set of operations the application intends to perform over the logical connection, which is provided by an underlying physical connection between two (or more) distinct endpoints.

This paper's contributions are on two fronts, both focused on using coordination to simplify application development for ubiquitous computing. First, we define a coordination framework around the concept of application sessions and provide formal characterizations of a useful set of such sessions that clearly communicate the constructs' behavior to application developers. Second, we provide a middleware infrastructure that allows application developers to use these coordination constructs to create flexible and adaptive applications. Our framework is the first such programming environment to recognize applications' needs for diverse session semantics and to provide them in a unified manner.

This paper is organized as follows. Section 2 describes related projects. Section 3 introduces the new coordination constructs. In Section 4 we describe the programming interface and middleware implementation. Section 5 demonstrates the use of the framework in a real-world scenario, and Section 6 concludes.

2   Related Work

It has been shown that adopting a coordination approach to handling the unpredictability inherent in mobile computing can lead to solutions that simplify programming [1]. Several middleware solutions have taken this approach [2, 3, 4] but focus on exchanging data items in dynamic conditions and not on generic resource usage in pervasive computing situations. As ubiquitous computing has come to the forefront, projects have increasingly focused on providing dynamic access to a changing set of resources. Many efforts mediate quality of service requirements by leveraging object mobility to enhance application responsiveness and network-wide performance metrics [5, 6, 7]. These approaches focus on bringing objects closer to clients instead of on mobile clients that require inherently location-dependent resources.

Projects closer to our goals update bindings between clients and services as processing or environment dictates [8, 9]. A *follow-me session* [10] provides constant connectivity to services by transferring a connection from one provider to another. Context-Sensitive Bindings [10, 11] implement the follow-me session by defining a *context* and selecting resources from that context that match an application's specification. The approach favors complete transparency, and assumes that a resource binding should always be transferred, subject to an application's specified policies. *Service Oriented Network Sockets* [12] provide a similar abstraction but use well-accepted service discovery mechanisms to gather *all* matching services locally, then decide which services to connect to. This can incur significant amounts of overhead in networks that are dynamic, large in size, or contain numerous satisfactory services. iMash [13] presents a dynamic session hand-off scheme but relies on knowledgeable intermediaries that handle service switches on behalf of clients and resources. Similarly, Atlas [14] uses a central server to mediate the transfer of a service binding from one provider to another.

Our framework differs from these projects in several ways. First, we seek not to limit an application's sessions to a single type but to adapt to an application's needs, including simple queries, lasting connections, transparent resource migration, etc. Second, while we aim to decouple the semantics of application sessions from the implementation supporting the session, we recognize that the extreme scale and device constraints necessitate communication protocols tailored to particular session requirements. Instead of requiring all session types to use the same communication style, our framework incorporates a suite of novel protocols that efficiently support a variety of coordination semantics.

3   Defining Application Sessions

Our model introduces a set of application session definitions that coordinate interactions between ubiquitous computing applications and dynamic resources.

As shown in Fig. 1, we explicitly separate a user program (i.e., the application) from the session management infrastructure that manages coordination with available resources. The only knowledge shared between the session management and the user program are a *specification* (spec) that describes the resource(s) the application is looking for and an *object handle* (o) that allows the application to access the re-

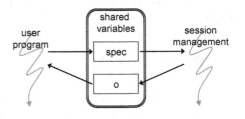

Fig. 1. Separation of Session Management from User Program

source(s) that the infrastructure connects it to. Through the coordination primitives this framework provides, the application completely delegates responsibility for maintaining resource connections to the infrastructure.

Substantial work has focused on allowing applications to abstractly define their resource needs through a variety of specification mechanisms. We assume resource requirements are described using semi-structured data [15], an approach common among description languages [16, 17, 18] and tuple based systems [2, 3, 19, 20]. Our approach can incorporate any of these schemes, so application developers can utilize specification languages with which they are familiar.

3.1 A Notation

Section 3.2 will introduce the sessions that provide varying coordination semantics between applications and resources. Each requires the application to provide a resource specification, and the session mechanics fill in and maintain the object handle on behalf of the application. In general, an application will invoke a session using code with semantics similar to those shown in Fig. 2.

The uninitialized value ($\perp$) indicates that a resource o declared by an application has not yet been modified by the session management scheme (i.e., a search is in progress). A null value (ϵ) indicates that a matching resource does not exist (or no longer exists). The $\langle \textbf{await}\, B \to S \rangle$ construct [21] allows a program to delay execution until the condition B holds. When B is true, the statements in S are executed in order. The angle brackets enclosing the construct indicate that the statement is executed atomically, i.e., no state internal to S is visible outside the execution of S. If S is omitted (as in Fig. 2), then the entire expression signifies a point of conditional synchronization.

```
spec = specification
[request session]
⟨await o ≠⊥⟩
if o ≠ ε then
    [use o]
fi
```

Fig. 2. Application Session Interaction

Throughout the next section, we will use some additional notational conventions. First, the *entails* ($\models$) relation expresses the fact that a resource satisfies a specification, i.e., $o \models spec$ indicates that the resource o satisfies the specification $spec$. The selection of a resource matching a specification will use the *non-deterministic assignment statement* [22]. A statement $x := x'.Q$ assigns to x a value x' nondeterministically selected from among the values satisfying the predicate Q. If an assignment is not possible, the statement aborts; we assume this results in assigning ϵ (a null value) to x. Within our model's semantics, we will use this notation to indicate that a resource is selected nondeterministically from any that satisfy the application's provided specification. Finally, we will also use a *three-part notation*: $\langle \textbf{op}\ quantified\_variables : range :: expression \rangle$, in which the variables from *quantified_variables* take on all possible values permitted by *range*. Each instantiation of the variables is substituted in *expression*, producing a multiset of values to which **op** is applied, yielding the value of the three-part expression. If no instantiation of the variables satisfies *range*, then the value of the three part expression is the identity element for **op**, e.g., *true* if **op** is $\forall$ or $\emptyset$ when **op** is set.

3.2 Basic Session Types

We next detail four basic sessions that form the foundation of our coordination framework. In Section 3.3, we describe a few generic extensions.

Query Session. Some application requests are simple data queries. For example, a first responder might request a copy of a nearby building's blueprints. After downloading the blueprints, the application may have no further need for interactions with the device providing the data. Using the constraints provided in the specification, the application should be connected to a single resource for the duration of the operation. Our first session type provides no long-lived interaction with the selected resource. This can be both beneficial (in terms of reduced network overhead) and limiting (in terms of capturing the environment's dynamics). We write the semantics of a query session as:

$$\boxed{o = spec}$$
$$\triangleq o = o'.(o' \models spec \land o'.\texttt{connected})$$

In these definitions, the expression in the box denotes the particular session semantic; in this case, the query semantic is expressed by assigning the specification to the shared object handle, o. The remainder of the expression defines the session's semantics. In a *query session*, the value assigned to o is nondeterministically selected from all objects that satisfy the specification *spec* and are connected. The connected relationship models the requirement that the application's device must be able to communicate with the selected resource's device. This abstraction allows the developer to delegate communication management to the middleware that implements the session constructs. In some cases, connectedness alone may not be enough to model usefulness of a resource; other characteristics can be handled as discussed in Section 3.3.

Provider Session. In many cases, once an application connects to a resource, it needs to perform several operations with that specific resource. For example, a paramedic may request a connection to a critical patient designated by a medical tag [23] placed by a triage worker. Once a patient is discovered, the paramedic may further query the patient's tag for injury information, vital signs, etc., and may wish to change and/or add information. As depicted in Fig. 3.2, to ensure data consistency, the paramedic must interact with the *same* tag that satisfied the initial request. The operational semantics for this session are:

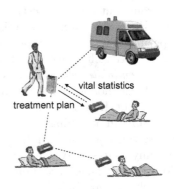

Fig. 3. Using a *Provider Session* in a first responder application.

$$\boxed{o \longleftarrow spec}$$
$$\triangleq o = o'.(o' \models spec \land o'.\texttt{connected})$$
$$\textbf{if } o \neq \epsilon \textbf{ then}$$
$$\langle \textbf{await } \neg o.\texttt{connected} \rightarrow o = \epsilon \rangle$$
$$\textbf{fi}$$

In a *provider session*, an application requests that the infrastructure maintains the connection to a particular resource given dynamics in the network topology. The application attaches the specification (*spec*) to the object handle o. If an object is found, the connection to it is monitored, and as long as the middleware can maintain communication between the application and the resource, it does so. This session is a two-way connection, so not only can the application make requests of the resource, but, if the resource changes, the client is also updated. If two paramedics are treating the same patient, and one changes the resource (e.g., updates the patient's record), this change is propagated to the second paramedic. The application's resource handle o is a local reflection of the remote resource. When the connection to the resource fails (i.e., when o.connected becomes false), the handle is assigned ϵ, which effectively notifies the application that the requested resource is no longer available.

Type Session. In other scenarios, an application may need persistent connection to *any* matching resource. On the construction site, safety applications may require that a device always knows its location (or an estimate of its location). Location servers around the site may periodically publish a region identifier, and a vehicle moving through the site can maintain a connection to a nearby location server. As Fig. 3.2 shows, as the vehicle moves, the particular server offering the location data may change,

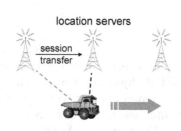

location servers

session transfer

Fig. 4. Using a *Type Session* on a construction site

but the application receives a steady stream of location updates. We express a *type session* as:

$$
\boxed{o \Leftarrow spec}
$$
$$
\triangleq\ o = o'.(o' \models spec \wedge o'.\text{connected})
$$
$$
\textbf{while } o \neq \epsilon \textbf{ do}
$$
$$
\langle \textbf{await } \neg o.\text{connected} \rightarrow o = o'.(o' \models spec \wedge o'.\text{connected}) \rangle
$$
$$
\textbf{od}
$$

This expression uses an open arrow ($\Leftarrow$) to represent the dynamic nature of a *type session*. When an attached resource becomes unavailable, the infrastructure attempts to locate a new resource that *is* connected and matches the specification. As long as such a resource is available, the application is connected to one, nondeterministically chosen from those that meet the requirements. If a match is not possible, the application's reference handle is assigned ϵ, which indicates that no matching resource is available. The above definition is a bit restrictive in that if a satisfactory resource is not available, the application must poll until one becomes available. This limitation will be addressed in Section 3.3.

Group Session. Some applications require a session with a *group* of resources. For example, an application may monitor the movement of workers and vehicles within the arc of a crane's movement. A device in the crane needs a session that includes the devices of workers and vehicles in this region, as shown in Fig. 3.2. In a *group session*, the application is connected to every resource that matches its specification, and the connections to matching resources are maintained as long as some resource matches. This session can be expressed as:

$$\boxed{o \Leftarrow_{\{\}} spec}$$
$$\triangleq\ o = \langle \text{set } o' : o' \models spec \wedge o'.\texttt{connected} :: o' \rangle$$
$$\textbf{while } o \neq \emptyset \textbf{ do}$$
$$\langle \textbf{await } group\text{-}change \rightarrow o = \langle \text{set } o' : o' \models spec \wedge o'.\texttt{connected} :: o' \rangle \rangle$$
$$\textbf{od}$$

where $group\text{-}change$ is defined by the following expression:

$$\boxed{group\text{-}change}$$
$$\equiv\ \langle \exists o' : o' \in o \wedge \neg o'.\texttt{connected} \rangle$$
$$\vee \langle \exists o' : o' \in o \wedge o \not\models spec \rangle$$
$$\vee \langle \exists o' : o' \notin o \wedge o'.\texttt{connected} \wedge o' \models spec \rangle$$

The object handle o is connected to a *set* of objects that match the specification, and the application can subsequently use set operations to interact with the resources. As this set changes (either because a matching resource disconnected, dynamics caused a matching resource to no longer satisfy *spec*, or because a new matching resource connected), the set reflects all of the connected matching resources. Some group definitions are easier to maintain than others, i.e., the communication constructs required for certain group definitions have acceptable performance under reasonable guarantees. The mechanisms our infrastructure uses to provide group communications are discussed in Section 4.

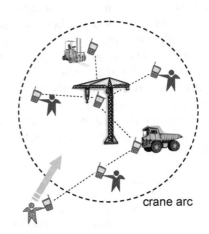

Fig. 5. Using a *Group Session* on a construction site

3.3   Session Extensions

We next describe generic extensions that add flexibility and expressiveness.

Specifications of Preference. In many instances, an application would like to express preferences that determine a partial ordering of matching resources. We allow programmers to specify a metric ($f(R)$) that selects a preferred resource over others. Generically, a metric accepts a resource's description (which can include information about the device where the resource is located) and generates an integer. Preferences may be specified for query sessions, provider sessions, or type sessions. The semantics of the augmented query session are:

$$\boxed{o = spec/f(R)}$$
$$\triangleq\ o = \langle \textbf{max } o' : o' \models spec \wedge o'.\texttt{connected} :: f(o') \rangle$$

This statement selects the resource with the largest metric value. If multiple resources have the same value, one is selected nondeterministically. For a provider session, the selection statement is very similar. In a type session, an additional change ensures that the connection is maintained to the most preferred resource:

$$\boxed{o \Leftarrow spec/f(R)}$$

$$\triangleq\ o = \langle \mathbf{max}\, o' : o' \models spec \wedge o'.\texttt{connected} :: f(o') \rangle$$
$$\mathbf{while}\ o \neq \epsilon\ \mathbf{do}$$
$$\qquad \langle \mathbf{await}\ \neg o.\texttt{connected} \vee \langle \exists o' : o'.\texttt{connected} \wedge o' \models spec \wedge f(o') > f(o) \rangle \rightarrow$$
$$\qquad\qquad o = \langle \mathbf{max}\, o' : o' \models spec \wedge o'.\texttt{connected} :: f(o') \rangle \rangle$$
$$\mathbf{od}$$

For brevity, the mechanics behind metric definition are omitted from this paper; an example is provided in Section 5. Useful metrics include:

- *relative mobility*: more stationary (i.e., less mobile) resources may be preferable due to their increased stability.
- *proximity*: closer resources (or resources in the same building) may often be preferable to more distant ones.
- *reliability*: resources with more consistent up-times are likely to be preferable.
- *error rate*: resources with smaller potential for error are more desirable.

These metrics can also be used to account for the cost or quality of service associated with using a particular resource, based on application-level definitions.

More Persistent Connections. In the basic session types, if an application's request cannot be satisfied, the infrastructure ceases looking for matches. This reduces communication overhead, but an application that cannot continue without a matching resource must poll on its own. For this reason we augment our type and group sessions with the ability to request that a session remain "active" even in the absence of a matching resource. As soon as a satisfactory resource does appear, it is connected. An active session ends only when the application explicitly shuts it down. The semantics for an *active type session* are:

$$\boxed{o \Leftarrow spec}$$

$$\triangleq\ o = o'.(o' \models spec \wedge o'.\texttt{connected})$$
$$\mathbf{while}\ \neg stop\ \mathbf{do}$$
$$\qquad \langle \mathbf{await}\ o = \epsilon \vee \neg o.\texttt{connected} \rightarrow o = o'.(o' \models spec \wedge o'.\texttt{connected}) \rangle$$
$$\mathbf{od}$$

This differs from the regular type session in a few subtle ways. First, the guard on the await statement now also attempts to reassign a resource when o is already ϵ. Second, the condition on the **while** loop is $\neg stop$, which references a third shared variable that is true when the session begins and set to false when the application quits the session. Without the *stop* variable, an application simply stops using the object handle o, which implicitly signals the end to the session. In the implementation, however, the underlying communication protocols should stop maintaining the session as soon as possible to ensure the best overall network performance, so our implementation uses the stop variable in all cases.

Maintenance and Migration of State. One aspect of sessions we have ignored so far is the migration of session state from one resource provider to another. This is significant in the case of the *type session* (as it directly involves moving an ongoing session from one provider to another) and may also affect group sessions (if a newcomer needs the history of an ongoing session). For now, our framework does not support the transfer of such session state and instead leaves its maintenance up to the application. Future work will include the formalization of such state transfers and their integration into our middleware.

4   Application Sessions: A Middleware

We provide our session constructs in a programming framework that enables rapid development of ubiquitous computing applications. We briefly detail the programming interface and our prototype implementation. Where appropriate, we also describe intended enhancements to the existing prototype.

4.1   Data Types

While our model does not restrict the format of descriptions and specifications, our implementation uses the ELIGHTS tuple space implementation [3]. Resources are provided as tuples that contain not only the resource (or its proxy) but also describe its properties. The `Resource` class serves as a wrapper for the `ETuple`; the `Specification` class is a wrapper of the `ETemplate` and provides restrictions over `Resource`s. The `Metric` interface allows applications to provide resource preferences and requires an implementing class to provide an `evaluate` method, which returns the metric's value for a provided `Resource`. Finally, we explicitly separate the properties of an application's group specification into two categories. The `Region` contains all those properties that can be used to restrict the communication *region* (e.g., distance, latency of communication, bandwidth, etc.). The remainder of the properties are placed in a regular `Specification`. We can use the `Region` to parameterize the communication protocols, thereby maximizing the application's performance.

4.2   The Session Factory

The major point of interaction between an application and the framework is the `SessionFactory`. A version of its interface (slightly simplified for presentation purposes) is shown in Fig. 6. The first three methods create basic sessions using a provided specification. The `active` boolean in the *type session* designates whether the middleware should monitor the available resources for a new match. The fourth method, `createGroupSession` uses information about the `Region` of communication. The next three methods allow a metric for preference in addition to the resource specification. The method `endSession` allows the application to determine when a session for a given `Specification` ends (instead of waiting until a resource is no longer available). The final method allows applications to make resources available to other components.

```
public class SessionFactory {
  public Resource createQuerySession(Specification spec);
  public Resource createProviderSession(Specification spec);
  public Resource createTypeSession(Specification spec, boolean active);
  public Resource[] createGroupSession(Region r, Specification spec,
                                       boolean active);
  public Resource createQuerySession(Specification spec, Metric m);
  public Resource createProviderSession(Specification spec, Metric m);
  public Resource createTypeSession(Specification spec, Metric m,
                                    boolean active);
  public void endSession(Specification spec);
  public void addResource(Resource r);
}
```

Fig. 6. Application Sessions Programming Interface

4.3   Middleware Support

Fig. 7 overviews our middleware's architecture. When requests arrive, the session factory determines whether a matching resource exists at this location (by looking in the local repository). Because our implementation represents resources and requests as tuples and templates, this matching occurs within ELIGHTS. While matching tuples against templates is straightforward, the complexity of checking $o \models spec$ depends on both the specification language used (e.g., ELIGHTS vs. another service description language) and the application. Future work will evaluate the difficulty associated with this aspect of the framework.

Efficiently discovering a resource in a dynamic pervasive computing environment can be very difficult. As Figure 7 shows, we use a package of discovery protocols. In relatively static environments, where the devices and resources change rarely, we use a registry method similar to Jini [18]. While such an approach is straightforward to implement, we have shown that a more application-aware protocol is more efficient in dynamic environments [24]. We have created Cross-Layer Discovery and Routing (CDR) [24] that uses information encapsulated in application requests to perform distributed resource discovery without a lookup

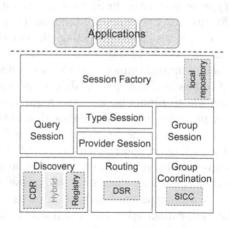

Fig. 7. Application Session Middleware

service. Our evaluations have further shown that an ideal discovery protocol may lie between the above two implementations. A hybrid protocol that combines the proactive style with the reactive style is under development. Currently, the selection of protocols associated with static or dynamic environments is performed off-line; future work will integrate context-awareness and adaptation into the middleware to allow it to switch between protocols as the environment dictates.

In our tuple based approach, descriptions contain "advertised" resource properties. Based on these properties and network conditions (e.g., latency, bandwidth, and mobility conditions), a session can use the application's preferences to determine which discovered resource best satisfies a request. In our prototype, the protocol waits for a predetermined time (based on the double of an estimate of the network's worst case round trip time) to ensure that it has received a response from the "best" resource. Currently, QoS requirements and preferences are sorted out as part of the resource matching process. In the future, using this information as part of the communication protocol may boost performance; we have seen promising results with the protocol for group communication (below) and are incorporating similar mechanisms into our CDR protocol.

To provide the long-lived connection required by a provider session, we use a mobile ad hoc routing scheme (DSR [25]) to maintain a route and discover when the route fails. In our current implementation, we provide a type session as a series of provider sessions. The connection to the first discovered resource is maintained as long as possible. When the connection to the resource breaks, the implementation attempts to launch another provider session. As long as this is successful, the application remains connected to a satisfactory resource. When applications specify preferences, the implementation must monitor the network for new resources that better satisfy the request. In this case, the middleware periodically reissues this initial request to determine whether a better resource exists. This polling implementation does not exactly match the semantics of the type session given in Section 3, and future work will develop reactive protocols for updating type session bindings that are not cost or performance prohibitive.

Our approach to providing efficient communication in group sessions is based on our Source-Initiated Context Construction (SICC) protocol [26] that creates and maintains connections to a set of devices that satisfy the application's region specification. Effectively, SICC creates a reverse multicast tree that allows information to funnel back to the requesting device from devices within the region. By providing the region abstraction to the developer, our framework ensures that the regions a programmer defines satisfy the underlying protocol's requirements. By issuing persistent queries over SICC's network structure, a group session receives notification of new resources and removes old resources as mobility and other conditions change the group membership.

A prototype implementation of this coordination middleware and its associated documentation are available at http://dstovall.org/servicesessions/.

5   An Application Scenario

To demonstrate how a developer uses our framework to build pervasive applications, we consider a team of first responders in an urban environment, tasked with search and rescue. A responder moves from building to building, looks for survivors, tags them with small sensors that emit information about their conditions and locations, and summons transportation. We take a few of the tasks that the responder's application supports and examine how these operations use our framework to find and coordinate with resources in the environment. To simplify the example code fragments, we use very simple resource specifications that search for resources based only on their types; most applications (including the ones we describe) will use more sophisticated requests.

Finding a Local Map. When the responder is first deployed, she may download a street map of the region. This map may be available on the device of a nearby responder who has already downloaded it or it may need to be downloaded from a central server. The application code that performs this action is:

```
Specification spec = new Specification();
spec.addConstraint(type, Specification.EQUALS, ''Map'');
Map localMap = (Map)sessionFactory.createQuerySession(spec);
if(localMap != null)
    [display map]
```

The Map class extends Resource and is defined within the application. The first two lines define the simple resource specification. The third line requires that the returned resource must be of type "Map" and calls the createQuerySession method to retrieve the specified resource. When a map has been discovered, localMap will reflect the map, and it can be displayed to the user.

Staying Connected to Local Blueprints. As the responder moves from one building to the next, she will likely want a copy of the blueprints of the local building if they are available. These blueprints could be stored in a device in the building itself (e.g., as part of the building's security system) or constructed by the device of a nearby responder. The application creates a type session:

```
Specification spec = new Specification();
spec.addConstraint(type, Specification.EQUALS, ''Blueprint'');
Metric local = new MyBuildingMetric();
Blueprint building =
        (Blueprint)sessionFactory.createTypeSession(spec, local, true);
[display blueprints when available]
```

The type session *prefers* blueprints for the current building over any others. This preference is encapsulated in MyBuildingMetric, whose evaluate method assigns "1" to resources in my building and "0" to any other resource. When the responder moves to a new building, a different set of blueprints are automatically attached to the building handle and can be displayed.

It is possible for the application's session to connect to a blueprint for a building other than the current one if a blueprint for the current building is unavailable. This disadvantage may be overcome by an extension of our approach that allows specifications to be based on contextual properties. In the above example, this would allow the specification to *require* that a matching resource is within the current building. Future work will investigate this approach.

Learning About Nearby Workers' Movements. Once the responder has a good picture of her environment, she wants to coordinate with other responders.

In our application, each responder keeps track of the buildings (and the rooms within the buildings) he or she has recently visited. Then the map (or the blueprint) can be overlaid with this information to ensure that our responder does not cover the same territory that has been searched by one of her colleagues. The code to discover and monitor these trajectories is:

```
Specification spec = new Specification();
spec.addConstraint(type, Specification.EQUALS,''Trajectory'');
Region r = DistanceRegion(100);
Trajectory[] trajectories =
       (Trajectory[])sessionFactory.createGroupSession(r, spec, true);
[display trajectories on map]
```

This code fragment defines a `DistanceRegion` that restricts the returned trajectories to those belonging to other first responders within 100 meters. This `DistanceRegion` class is provided within our framework and restricts a group to only those devices within the number of meters specified. Once this session is created, our responder's application will be constantly updated with respect to changes to the trajectories of other responders within 100 meters.

Summoning Evacuation Transportation. Once our responder has located a survivor, she tags him and loads information about the survivor's condition and location into the tag. She then needs to contact some form of evacuation vehicle to transport the survivor to safety. The responder would like to contact a particular vehicle, transfer the information about the survivor (including his location), and receive a confirmation that a particular vehicle will be retrieving the survivor. To ensure data consistency, the responder's device should connect to a proper vehicle and remain connected for the duration of the exchange:

```
Specification spec = new Specification();
spec.addConstraint(type, Specification.EQUALS, ''Ambulance'');
Vehicle ambulance = (Vehicle)sessionFactory.createProviderSession(spec);
[transfer information about survivor]
[receive confirmation]
sessionFactory.endSession(spec)
```

Because this session is defined by a discrete number of well-known tasks, when the session completes, the application invokes the `endSession` method to tear down the communication lines that were created for the session.

Sharing Resources. The previous discussions assume that another application component has made the requested resource available. When an application shares a resource, the resource and its description are placed in a local repository. For example, a first responder creates an instance of the `Trajectory` class (which extends the `Resource` class). As the responder moves, he updates his trajectory, changing the resource stored in the local repository. This change then propagates to a first responder who has requested a group session that monitors other nearby responders.

6 Conclusions

Simplifying the development of pervasive computing applications requires coordination abstractions that succinctly represent the interactions among applications and ubiquitous resources. In this paper, we have defined such a coordination model based on *application sessions* and demonstrated a novel set of such sessions that prove useful to a wide range of dynamic interactive applications. By subsequently capturing our rigorously defined sessions in a programming infrastructure, we present application developers with abstractions that ease their programming burdens and enable programmers to create complex, adaptive applications. By incorporating a suite of dynamic and adaptive communication protocols, the middleware that supports these session definitions provides appropriate, efficient, and scalable form of communication for different session types in varying environments. Such an integrative approach to abstraction and communication is imperative to meeting the rapidly growing demand for ubiquitous computing applications.

Acknowledgements

The authors would like to thank the Center for Excellence in Distributed Global Environments for providing research facilities and the collaborative environment. This research was funded, in part, by the National Science Foundation (NSF), Grant # CNS-0620245. The views and conclusions herein are those of the authors and do not necessarily reflect the views of the sponsoring agencies.

References

1. Roman, G.C., Murphy, A.L., Picco, G.P.: Coordination and mobility. In Omicini, A., Zambonelli, F., Klusch, M., Tolksdorf, R., eds.: Coordination of Internet Agents: Models, Technologies and Applications. (2000) 254–273
2. Murphy, A.L., Picco, G.P., Roman, G.C.: LIME: A middleware for physical and logical mobility. In: Proc. of the 21st Int'l. Conf. on Distributed Comput. Sys. (2001) 524–533
3. Julien, C., Roman, G.C.: Egocentric context-aware programming in ad hoc mobile environments. In: Proc. of the 10th Int'l. Symp. on the Foundations of Software Engineering. (2002) 21–30
4. Fok, C.L., Roman, G.C., Hackmann, G.: A lightweight coordination middleware for mobile computing. In: Proc. of the 6th Int'l. Conf. on Coordination Models and Languages. (2004) 135–151
5. Grimm, R., Davis, J., Lemar, E., MacBeth, A., Swanson, S., Anderson, T., Bershad, B., Borriello, G., Gribble, S., Wetherall, D.: System support for pervasive applications. ACM Trans. on Computer Sys. **22**(4) (2004) 421–486
6. Holder, O., Ben-Shaul, I., Gazit, H.: Dynamic layout of distributed applications in FarGo. In: Proc. of the 21st Int'l. Conf. on Software Engineering. (1999) 163–173
7. Ryan, C., Westhorpe, C.: Application adaptation through transparent and portable object mobility in java. In: Proc. of OTM Federated Conf. (2004) 1262–1284

8. Bellavista, P., Corradi, A., Montanari, R., Stefanelli, C.: Dynamic binding in mobile applications: A middleware approach. IEEE Internet Comput. **7**(2) (2003) 34–42

9. Klein, M., Konig-Ries, B.: Combining query and preference: An approach to fully automize dynamic service binding. In: Proc. of the IEEE Int'l. Conf. on Web Services. (2004) 788–791

10. Handorean, R., Sen, R., Hackmann, G., Roman, G.C.: Context aware session management for services in ad hoc networks. In: Proc. of the IEEE Int'l. Conf. on Services Comput. (2005) 113–120

11. Roman, G.C., Julien, C., Murphy, A.L.: A declarative approach to agent-centered context-aware computing in ad hoc wireless environments. In: Software Engineering for Large-Scale Multi-Agent Sys. Volume 2603 of LNCS. (2003) 94–109

12. Saif, U., Paluska, J.M.: Service-oriented network sockets. In: Proc. of the 1st Int'l. Conf. on Mobile Sys., Applications, and Services. (2003) 159–172

13. Bagrodia, R., Bhattacharyya, S., Cheng, F., Gerding, S., Glazer, G., Guy, R., Ji, Z., Lin, J., Phan, T., Skow, E., Varshney, M., Zorpas, G.: iMASH: Interactive mobile application session handoff. In: Proc. of the 1st Int'l. Conf. on Mobile Sys., Applications, and Services. (2003) 259–272

14. Cole, A., Duri, S., Munson, J., Murdock, J., Wood, D.: Adaptive service binding middleware to support mobility. In: Proc. of the 23rd Int'l. Conf. on Distributed Comput. Wkshps. (2003) 369–374

15. Abiteboul, S.: Querying semi-structured data. In: Proc. of the 6th Int'l. Conf. on Database Theory. (1997) 1–18

16. Berners-Lee, T., Hendler, J., Lassila, O.: The semantic web. Scientific American **284**(5) (2001) 34–43

17. Christensen, E., Curbera, F., Meredith, G., Weerawarana, S.: Web services description language (WSDL) 1.1 (2001) Current as of 2005.

18. Edwards, K.: Core Jini. Prentice Hall (1999)

19. Cabri, G., Leonardi, L., Zambonelli, F.: MARS: A programmable coordination architecture for mobile agents. IEEE Internet Comput. **4**(4) (2000) 26–35

20. Gelernter, D.: Generative communication in Linda. ACM Trans. on Programming Languages and Sys. **7**(1) (1985) 80–112

21. Andrews, G.: Foundations of Multithreaded, Parallel, and Distributed Programming. Addison Wesley (1999)

22. Back, R., Sere, K.: Stepwise refinement of parallel algorithms. Science of Computer Programming **13**(2-3) (1990) 133–180

23. Malan, D., Fulford-Jones, T., Welsh, M., Moulton, S.: CodeBlue: An ad hoc sensor network infrastructure for emergency medical care. In: Proc. of the Int'l. Wkshp. on Wearable and Implanted Body Sensor Networks. (2004)

24. Julien, C., Venkataraman, M.: Resource-directed discovery and routing in mobile ad hoc networks. Technical Report TR-UTEDGE-2005-01, Univ. of Texas (2005)

25. Johnson, D., Maltz, D., Broch, J.: DSR: The dynamic source routing protocol for multi-hop wireless ad hoc networks. Ad Hoc Networking (2001) 139–172

26. Julien, C., Roman, G.C.: Supporting context-aware interaction in dynamic multi-agent systems (invited paper). In: Environments for Multiagent Sys. Volume 3374 of LNCS. (2005) 168–189

A WSDL-Based Type System for WS-BPEL*

Alessandro Lapadula, Rosario Pugliese, and Francesco Tiezzi

Dipartimento di Sistemi e Informatica Università degli Studi di Firenze

Abstract. We tackle the problem of providing rigorous formal foundations to current software engineering technologies for web services. We focus on two of the most used XML-based languages for web services: WSDL and WS-BPEL. To this aim, first we select an expressive subset of WS-BPEL, with special concern for modeling the interactions among web service instances in a network context, and define its operational semantics. We call ws-calculus the resulting formalism. Then, we put forward a rigorous typing discipline that formalizes the relationship existing between ws-calculus terms and the associated WSDL documents and supports verification of their compliance. We prove that the type system and the operational semantics of ws-calculus are 'sound' and apply our approach to an example application involving three interacting web services.

1 Introduction

Service-Oriented Computing (SOC) has recently put forward as a promising computing paradigm for developing massively distributed, interoperable, evolvable systems and applications that exploit the pervasiveness of the Internet and its related technologies. The SOC paradigm advocates the use of 'services', to be understood as autonomous, platform-independent computational entities that can be described, published, discovered, and dynamically assembled, as the basic blocks for building applications. Web services (WS), along with grid computing, are the present most successful instantiation of the SOC paradigm, as it is demonstrated by the fact that companies like IBM, Microsoft and Sun invested a lot of efforts and resources to promote their deployment.

A *web service* is basically a set of operations that can be invoked through the Web via XML messages complying with given standard formats. To support the WS approach, many new languages, most of which based on XML, have been designed, like e.g. business coordination languages (such as WS-BPEL, WSFL, WSCI, and XLANG), contract languages (such as WSDL and SWS), and query languages (such as XPath and XQuery). However, current software engineering technologies for WS still lack rigorous formal foundations. The challenges come from the necessity of dealing at once with issues like communication, co-operation, resource usage, failures, security, etc. in a setting where demands and guarantees can be very different for the many components.

In this paper we focus on two of the most used XML-based languages for WS: *Web Services Description Language* (WSDL [CCMW01]) and *Web Services Business Process Execution Language* (WS-BPEL [BCG⁺05]). The former is a W3C standard

---

* Supported by EU within the FP6-2004-IST-FET Proactive project SENSORIA proposal contract number 016004.

P. Ciancarini and H. Wiklicky (Eds.): COORDINATION 2006, LNCS 4038, pp. 145–163, 2006.

that permits to express the functionalities offered and required by web services by defining, akin object interfaces in Object-Oriented Programming, the signatures of operations and the structure of the documents for invoking them and returned by them. The latter, currently under evaluation to become a standard by OASIS, permits to describe the activities to be executed for completing the service as a reaction to a service invocation. WSDL declarations can be exploited to verify the possibility of connecting different services, while WS-BPEL descriptions can be used to define new services by appropriately composing other existing ones.

We aim at formalizing the relationship existing between WS-BPEL processes and the associated WSDL documents by putting forward a rigorous typing discipline. In general, the WSDL document associated to a WS-BPEL process does not contain the declarations of all the operations provided and required by the process, together with the structure of the messages exchanged. In fact, some of these declarations usually are in the WSDL documents of the orchestrated services. Moreover, WSDL provides four different types of operations, but only two of them are really supported by WS-BPEL: (synchronous) request-response and one-way. There is another interaction pattern that is largely used in WS-BPEL (see, e.g., the example 16.1 in [BCG+05]) but it is not provided by WSDL: asynchronous request-response. This last pattern is implemented through a partner link connecting two one-way operations but no constraint is imposed on which process must declare the type of the operations. Finally, WS-BPEL provides many redundant programming constructs and suggest a quite liberal programming style. For example, it is possible for a programmer to write parallel activities that have strict implicit dependencies so that they are sequentially (rather than concurrently) executed.

To achieve our goal, we first define a semantic model for WS-BPEL because the semantics of the language, as presented in [BCG+05], is informal and, sometimes, ambiguous. Hence, as a first contribution of this paper, we introduce a process language, that we call ws-CALCULUS (*web services calculus*), that formalizes the semantics of an expressive subset of WS-BPEL, with special concern for modeling the interactions among web services, be them WS-BPEL processes or not, in a network context. This allows us to tackle those problems arising when executing WS-BPEL processes, such as multiple start activities, receive conflicts, routing of messages, while avoiding the intricacies of dealing with any, possibly redundant, WS-BPEL construct.

As a second contribution, we define a type system for ws-CALCULUS terms and show that the type system and the operational semantics are 'sound', in the sense that ws-CALCULUS terms reached along any reduction sequence starting from well-typed terms are still well-typed and, thus, do not generate runtime errors. The type system enforces many of the constraints imposed by WSDL/WS-BPEL, e.g. it prevents programs from passing links that have been implicitly initialized and from invoking callback operations that do not have previous triggering receive operations. However, in some cases it is even further restrictive so to enforce a more disciplined programming style. Thus, for example, the type system deems as ill-typed those programs containing flow activities that have strict implicit dependencies. Moreover, in case of asynchronous request-response, it forces the WSDL document associated to the process providing the service to contain the declaration of both the two operations, that for invoking the service and that for sending the reply back to the client. This last choice is dictated by the need to preserve two important properties of web services, namely compositionality and loose coupling. Indeed, should each client contain the declaration for the reply, then, if the service provider wants to modify such a declaration, all clients should be updated.

The rest of the paper is organized as follows. Syntax and operational semantics of ws-calculus are defined in Section 2, while the type system and the soundness results are presented in Section 3. Section 4 illustrates an application of our framework to modelling an example of web services composition. In Section 5 we touch upon directions for future work and comparisons with related work. We refer the interested reader to the full paper [LPT06] for a complete semantic account of WS-BPEL, for further examples and for the proofs of all results stated in this paper.

2   WS-CALCULUS

ws-calculus (*web services calculus*) permits to express web services in a primitive form with special concern for modeling the interactions among web service instances in a network context. Although ws-calculus can directly model the semantics of an expressive subset of WS-BPEL, we refer the interested reader to [LPT06] for a more complete account of this topic. Indeed, due to lack of space, here we do not deal with many features such as, e.g., flow graphs, timed activities, scopes and compensation handling, that should be considered for modeling the semantics of full-blown orchestration languages.

The *syntax* of ws-calculus, given in Table 1, is parameterized with respect to the following syntactic sets, which we assume to be countable and pairwise disjoint: *properties* (sorts of late bound constants storing some relevant values within service instances, ranged over by p), *basic values* (integers Int, strings Str, and booleans) and corresponding *variables* (ranged over by b), *addresses* (ranged over by a) and *partner links* (namely variables storing addresses used to identify service partners within an interaction, ranged over by l), and *service identifiers* (ranged over by A) each with a fixed nonnegative arity. The language is also parametric with respect to a set of *operations*, ranged over by o, which we do not specify, and *expressions*, ranged over by e, whose exact syntax is deliberately omitted; we just assume that expressions contain, at least, basic values and variables, partner links, addresses and properties. Notationally, we will use u to range over *values* (i.e. basic values and addresses), v to range over *variables* (i.e. basic variables and partner links), w to range over *operation parameters* (i.e. variables and properties), c to range over *correlation patterns* (i.e. values and properties), and r to range over addresses and partner links. Addresses may be *underlined* to denote that they cannot be transmitted as operation parameters, while partner links may be subject to the operator $\ulcorner \cdot \urcorner$ that forces them to be already initialized.

Notation $\tilde{\cdot}$ denotes tuples of objects. E.g. $\tilde{v}$ is a tuple of variables; this will sometimes be written as $\tilde{v}_{i \in I}$, for an appropriate index-set I, and v_i denotes the i-th element. We assume that variables in the same tuple are pairwise distinct. When convenient, we shall regard a tuple simply as a set writing e.g. $a \in \tilde{u}$ to mean that a is an element of $\tilde{u}$. All notations shall extend to tuples component-wise.

A ws-calculus *node* can be thought of as a WS-BPEL process web service. Nodes, written as $a ::^{Op,L} C$, are uniquely identified by an address a and have a declarative part

Table 1. ws-calculus syntax (The syntax of types Op, L is in Table 4)

$n ::= a ::^{Op,L} C$	(nodes)
$C ::= *s \mid m \gg s \mid \langle a, o, \bar{u} \rangle \mid C \mid C$	(components)
$m ::= \emptyset \mid \{p = u\} \mid m \cup m$	(correlation constraints)
$s ::=$	(services)
$\quad\quad \mathbf{0}$	(null)
$\quad\quad \mid \ \mathbf{exit}$	(exit)
$\quad\quad \mid \ \mathbf{ass}\,(\bar{w}, \bar{e})$	(assign)
$\quad\quad \mid \ \mathbf{inv}\,(r, o, \bar{w})$	(invoke)
$\quad\quad \mid \ \mathbf{rec}\,(r, o, \bar{w})$	(receive)
$\quad\quad \mid \ \mathbf{if}\,(e)\,\mathbf{then}\,\{s\}\,\mathbf{else}\,\{s\}$	(switch)
$\quad\quad \mid \ s; s$	(sequence)
$\quad\quad \mid \ s \mid s$	(flow)
$\quad\quad \mid \ \sum_{i \in I}\mathbf{rec}\,(r_i, o_i, \bar{w}_i)\,;\,s_i$	(pick)
$\quad\quad \mid \ A(\bar{w})$	(call)

Op, L, i.e. its *type*, and a behavioural part C. Finite sets of nodes are called *nets* and are ranged over by $N, N', N_1, \ldots$. The type of a node collects all the information about the format of the messages exchanged by the operations available at the node, Op, and the local declarations, L, like the WSDL document associated to the corresponding WS-BPEL process web service. Since we are interested in describing asynchronous interactions, we model each communication pattern by connecting one or more one-way operations. In the simplest interaction, a single one-way operation suffices; the service provider process, which is the one that performs the receive activity, holds the type definition of the requested operation. The more complex asynchronous request-response interaction pattern is expressed by connecting two one-way operations (request and callback); in this case, the provider holds the type definitions of both operations (the rationale for this choice has been explained in the Introduction). We defer syntax of types and comments on them to Section 3.

Components C may be service specifications, instances or requests. The behavioural specification of a service s is written $*s$, while $m \gg s'$ represents a service instance that behaves according to s' and whose properties evaluate according to the (possibly empty) set m of correlation constraints. A *correlation constraint* is a pair, written $p = u$, recording the value u assigned to the property p. Properties are used to store values that are important to identify service instances. For example, one might use a property named *purchase-order-id* to uniquely identify instances of a service that handles purchase orders. A service request $\langle a, o, \bar{u} \rangle$ represents an operation invocation that must still be processed and contains the invoker address a, the operation name o and the data $\bar{u}$ for operation execution. ws-calculus operation names represent WS-BPEL pairs 'partner link – operation' (instead, WS-BPEL partner links are not explicitly modeled), thus pairs '$a - o$', that are the first two components of service requests, represent endpoints between two interacting process web services.

Services are structured activities built from *basic activities*, i.e. instance forced termination **exit**, assignment **ass** $(\cdot, \cdot)$, service invocation **inv** $(\cdot, \cdot, \cdot)$ and service request processing **rec** $(\cdot, \cdot, \cdot)$, by exploiting operators for conditional choice **if** $(\cdot)$ **then** $\{\cdot\}$ **else** $\{\cdot\}$

(*switch*), sequential composition $\cdot;\cdot$ (*sequence*), parallel composition $\cdot \mid \cdot$ (*flow*), external choice[1] $\sum_{i \in I} \mathbf{rec}\,(\cdot, \cdot, \cdot)\,;\cdot$ (*pick*) and service call $A(w_1, \cdots, w_n)$ where n is the arity of A. Every service identifier A with arity n has a unique definition of the form $A(\bar{v}_{i \in \{1,..,n\}} : \bar{\tau}^{\star}_{i \in \{1,..,n\}}) \stackrel{def}{=} s$, where the v_i must be fresh and pairwise distinct. Notably, parameters of a service definition are typed (see the next section).

The WS-CALCULUS binding constructs are $\mathbf{ass}\,(\bar{w}, \bar{e})$ and $\mathbf{rec}\,(r, o, \bar{w})$ that bind the variables and the properties in $\bar{w}$. The latter also binds r if it is a partner link and is not subject to the operator $\ulcorner \cdot \urcorner$; we will say that r is *implicitly* initialized (conversely, we will say that a partner link is *explicitly* initialized in all other cases). This means that $\ulcorner l \urcorner$ represents a free occurrence of l (e.g. a callback address) that must have been bound previously. The scope of the bindings extends to the whole component where the binder occurs (namely, like in WS-BPEL, variables and properties are global to the instance). A variable occurrence is free if it is not under the scope of a binder. We assume that all bound partner links are pairwise distinct, but for those occurring within alternative branches of switch and pick constructs. Thus, the following fragment of service is well-defined:

$$\ldots \mathbf{if}\,(e)\,\mathbf{then}\,\{\ldots \mathbf{rec}\,(l, \ldots, \ldots)\ldots\}\,\mathbf{else}\,\{\ldots \mathbf{rec}\,(l, \ldots, \ldots)\ldots\}; \mathbf{inv}\,(l, \ldots, \ldots)\ldots$$

In general, we use $fv(s)$ (resp. $bv(s)$) to denote the set of variables which occur free (resp. bound) in s. In particular, variables of $\bar{w}$ are free in $A(\bar{w})$. In a definition $A(\bar{v} : \bar{\tau}^{\star}) \stackrel{def}{=} s$ we assume $fv(s) \subseteq \bar{v}$.

In the sequel we shall only consider nets that are *well-formed* in the sense that they comply with the following syntactic constraints. First, pairwise distinct nodes must have different addresses. Then, if we call *start activities* of a service s all those activities that are not syntactically preceded by other ones (as formalized by function $eR()$ whose inductive definition can be found in [LPT06]), then at least one start activity of $*s$ must be a $\mathbf{rec}\,(\cdot, \cdot, \cdot)$ and, if multiple $\mathbf{rec}\,(\cdot, \cdot, \cdot)$ are enabled concurrently, then they must use the same non-empty set of properties.

The *operational semantics* of WS-CALCULUS is given in terms of a structural congruence and of a reduction relation over nets. Due to space limitations, here we only present the major ingredients and refer the interested reader to [LPT06] for the details. For instance, we omit the rules for fault throwing and handling, and model taking place of errors (e.g. when the premises of reduction rules are not satisfied) simply as deadlock.

The semantics of nets will be defined over an enriched set of nets that also includes those auxiliary nets resulting from replacing (free occurrences of) variables with values in nets produced by the syntax of Table 1. Therefore, we will let free occurrences of v (and w) to also denote corresponding values.

The *structural congruence*, denoted by $\equiv$, identifies syntactically different terms which intuitively represent the same term. At the level of services, the structural congruence states that: the sequence operator is associative and has $\mathbf{0}$ as identity element (thus we have the law $\mathbf{0}; s \equiv s$, which is exploited to enable a new activity when a syntactically preceding one terminates); the flow operator is commutative, associative and has $\mathbf{0}$ as identity element; the pick operator enjoys the same properties and, additionally, is idempotent; services only differing for the bound variables are the same

---

[1] Whenever the external choice is between two activities, we shall simply write $s_1 + s_2$.

(*alpha-conversion*). The structural congruence is extended to components and nets in the obvious way. In particular, components composition is commutative and associative, and has $m \gg 0$ as identity element (i.e. instances of this form are terminated instances and, thus, can be removed).

The *reduction relation* over nets, written $\rightarrowtail$, relies on a labelled transition relation $\xrightarrow{\alpha}$ over service instances, where α is generated by the following production:

$$\alpha ::= \natural \mid \bar{w} := \bar{u} \mid i(a, o, \bar{u}) \mid r(r, o, \bar{w})$$

The meaning of labels is as follows: $\natural$ denotes forced termination of a service instance, $\bar{w} := \bar{u}$ denotes execution of a multiple assignment, $i(a, o, \bar{u})$ denotes invocation of operation o located at a with data $\bar{u}$ and $r(r, o, \bar{w})$ denotes launching of o with operation parameters $\bar{w}$ on request of a web service instance located at r.

To define the operational semantics, we exploit a few auxiliary functions. First, we define a function for evaluating expressions: it takes an expression and returns a basic value or an address. We write $m \triangleright e$ such a function, but we do not explicitly define it because the exact syntax of expressions is deliberately not specified (recall that ws-CALCULUS is parameterized wrt the syntax of expressions). Expressions to be evaluated can contain properties; thus, evaluation of e takes place wrt a set of correlation constraints m storing the values of the properties that may occur within e. On the contrary, expressions to be evaluated cannot contain (free) variables because these occurrences are replaced with the corresponding values as soon as the variables are bound. Indeed, execution of a binding construct generates a *substitution* (ranged over by σ), i.e. a map from basic variables to basic values and from partner links to addresses, that is applied to the whole instance where the binder occurs. A substitution σ will be sometimes written as $(\bar{v} \mapsto \sigma(\bar{v}))$ for $\bar{v} = dom(\sigma)$. Application of substitution σ to s is written $s \cdot \sigma$. The effect of $s \cdot \sigma$ is that, for each $x \in dom(\sigma)$, every free occurrence of x in s is replaced with $\sigma(x)$.

Another ingredient we need to define the semantics is a mechanism for checking if the assignments of u_i to w_i, for any index i in a given set I, comply with the correlation constraints in m. We will write $m \triangleright (\bar{w}_{i \in I} := \bar{u}_{i \in I})$ such a mechanism. In case the check succeeds, to take care of the effect of the assignments, a pair $\langle m', \sigma \rangle$ is returned where m' is the set of the correlation constraints for the properties in $\bar{w}_{i \in I}$ and σ is the substitution for the variables in $\bar{w}_{i \in I}$. The function is defined inductively on the syntax of $\bar{w}$ as follows:

$$m \triangleright (v := u) = \langle \emptyset, (v \mapsto u) \rangle$$

$$m \triangleright (p := u) = \begin{cases} \langle \emptyset, \emptyset \rangle & \text{if } p = u \in m \\ \langle \{p = u\}, \emptyset \rangle & \text{if it does not exists } u' \text{ s.t. } p = u' \in m \\ undef & \text{otherwise} \end{cases}$$

$$m \triangleright (w, \bar{w} := u, \bar{u}) = \langle m' \cup m'', \sigma \circ \sigma' \rangle \quad \begin{cases} \text{if } m \triangleright (w := u) = \langle m', \sigma \rangle \text{ and} \\ m \cup m' \triangleright (\bar{w} := \bar{u}) = \langle m'', \sigma' \rangle \end{cases}$$

Finally, the last two auxiliary functions we need are:

- $P(\bar{w})$ returns the set of properties contained in the set of operation parameters $\bar{w}$.
- $eR(C)$ returns the set of activities $\mathbf{rec}\,(\cdot, \cdot, \cdot)$ that are start activities of instances in C (it is defined inductively on the syntax of C, see [LPT06]).

Table 2. ws-calculus operational semantics: instances

$$m \vdash \textbf{exit} \xrightarrow{\natural} \mathbf{0} \quad (Exit) \qquad\qquad m \vdash \textbf{ass}\,(\bar{w}, \bar{e}) \xrightarrow{\bar{w}:=\,m \triangleright \bar{e}} \mathbf{0} \quad (Assign)$$

$$m \vdash \textbf{inv}\,(a, o, \bar{c}) \xrightarrow{i(a,o,m \triangleright \bar{c})} \mathbf{0} \quad (Invoke) \qquad\qquad \frac{r \neq \ulcorner l \urcorner}{m \vdash \textbf{rec}\,(r, o, \bar{w}) \xrightarrow{r(r,o,\bar{w})} \mathbf{0}} \quad (Receive)$$

$$\frac{m \triangleright e = \textbf{false} \quad m \vdash s_2 \xrightarrow{\alpha} s_2'}{m \vdash \textbf{if}\,(e)\,\textbf{then}\,\{s_1\}\,\textbf{else}\,\{s_2\} \xrightarrow{\alpha} s_2'} \quad (If_{\textup{ff}}) \qquad \frac{m \triangleright e = \textbf{true} \quad m \vdash s_1 \xrightarrow{\alpha} s_1'}{m \vdash \textbf{if}\,(e)\,\textbf{then}\,\{s_1\}\,\textbf{else}\,\{s_2\} \xrightarrow{\alpha} s_1'} \quad (If_{\textup{tt}})$$

$$\frac{m \vdash s_1 \xrightarrow{\alpha} s_1'}{m \vdash s_1; s_2 \xrightarrow{\alpha} s_1'; s_2} \quad (Sequence) \qquad \frac{m \vdash s_1 \xrightarrow{\alpha} s_1' \quad \alpha \neq r(\cdot, \cdot, \cdot)}{m \vdash s_1 \mid s_2 \xrightarrow{\alpha} s_1' \mid s_2} \quad (Flow)$$

$$\frac{m \vdash s_1 \xrightarrow{r(r,o,\bar{w})} s_1' \quad \nexists \, \textbf{rec}\,(r, o, \bar{w}') \in eR(s_2)\,.\,P(\bar{w}) = P(\bar{w}')}{m \vdash s_1 \mid s_2 \xrightarrow{r(r,o,\bar{w})} s_1' \mid s_2} \quad (Flow_{Rec})$$

$$\frac{m \vdash \textbf{rec}\,(r, o, \bar{w})\,;\,s \xrightarrow{r(r,o,\bar{w})} s' \quad \nexists \, i \in I\,.\,r_i = r \,\wedge\, o_i = o \,\wedge\, P(\bar{w}_i) = P(\bar{w})}{m \vdash \textbf{rec}\,(r, o, \bar{w})\,;\,s + \sum_{i \in I} \textbf{rec}\,(r_i, o_i, \bar{w}_i)\,;\,s_i \xrightarrow{r(r,o,\bar{w})} s'} \quad (Pick)$$

$$\frac{m \vdash s \cdot (\bar{v} \mapsto m \triangleright \bar{c}) \xrightarrow{\alpha} s'}{m \vdash A(\bar{c}) \xrightarrow{\alpha} s'} \; A(\bar{v} : \bar{\tau}^\star) \overset{def}{=} s \quad (Call)$$

The labelled transition $\xrightarrow{\alpha}$ is the least relation over service instances induced by the rules in Table 2. For the sake of simplicity, we explicitly write only those entities that are necessary for a transition to occur or are modified by it. For example, since correlation constraints are sometimes necessary but are never modified by a transition, we write the relation as $m \vdash s \xrightarrow{\alpha} s'$ instead of $m \gg s \xrightarrow{\alpha} m \gg s'$. The most of the rules are obvious, we only remark a few points. Rule (*Receive*) states that a **rec** $(\cdot, \cdot, \cdot)$ cannot be performed when the address of the sender of a request is unknown and cannot be learned (i.e. the first argument is neither an address nor a link). Rules (*Flow*) and (*Flow_Rec*) state that, in case no receive conflict occurs [2] (i.e. there aren't two or more receive activities simultaneously enabled for the same combination of partner link, operation and correlation

---

[2] Sets of correlation constraints are exploited precisely to deal with receive conflicts: they prevent loss of correlation information (which would be lost if properties are simply replaced by the corresponding values). For example, if properties are dealt with as basic variables, by applying the substitution $(p \mapsto 5)$ to the service instance $(\dots \textbf{rec}\,(r, o, \langle \ulcorner p \urcorner, v \rangle) \mid \textbf{rec}\,(r, o, \langle \ulcorner p \urcorner, v' \rangle) \dots)$ we would obtain $(\dots \textbf{rec}\,(r, o, \langle 5, v \rangle) \mid \textbf{rec}\,(r, o, \langle 5, v' \rangle) \dots)$ that does not permit to establish if the receive activities are in conflict. Indeed, we would obtain the same term by applying the substitution $(p \mapsto 5, v'' \mapsto 5)$ to $(\dots \textbf{rec}\,(r, o, \langle \ulcorner p \urcorner, v \rangle) \mid \textbf{rec}\,(r, o, \langle v'', v' \rangle) \dots)$, where no conflict occurs.

Table 3. ws-CALCULUS operational semantics: nets

$$\frac{m \vdash s \xrightarrow{\bar{w} := \bar{u}} s' \quad m \triangleright (\bar{w} := \bar{u}) = \langle m', \sigma \rangle}{\{a :: m \gg s \mid C\} \rightarrowtail \{a :: (m \cup m') \gg s' \cdot \sigma \mid C\}} \quad (Assign)$$

$$\frac{m \vdash s \xrightarrow{i(a_2, o, \bar{u})} s' \quad \underline{a'} \notin \bar{u}}{\{a_1 :: m \gg s \mid C_1, a_2 :: C_2\} \rightarrowtail \{a_1 :: m \gg s' \mid C_1, a_2 :: \langle a_1, o, \bar{u} \rangle \mid C_2\}} \quad (Invoke)$$

$$\frac{m \vdash s \xrightarrow{r(a', o, \bar{w})} s' \quad m \triangleright (\bar{w} := \bar{u}) = \langle m', \sigma \rangle \quad m \neq \emptyset}{\{a :: m \gg s \mid \langle a', o, \bar{u} \rangle \mid C\} \rightarrowtail \{a :: (m \cup m') \gg s' \cdot \sigma \mid C\}} \quad (Receive_{al})$$

$$\frac{m \vdash s \xrightarrow{r(l, o, \bar{w})} s' \quad m \triangleright (l, \bar{w} := \underline{a'}, \bar{u}) = \langle m', \sigma \rangle \quad m \neq \emptyset}{\{a :: m \gg s \mid \langle a', o, \bar{u} \rangle \mid C\} \rightarrowtail \{a :: (m \cup m') \gg s' \cdot \sigma \mid C\}} \quad (Receive_{ll})$$

$$\frac{\emptyset \vdash s \xrightarrow{r(a', o, \bar{w})} s' \quad \emptyset \triangleright (\bar{w} := \bar{u}) = \langle m, \sigma \rangle \quad rec(a', o, \bar{w}) \notin eR(C)}{\{a :: *s \mid \langle a', o, \bar{u} \rangle \mid C\} \rightarrowtail \{a :: *s \mid m \gg s' \cdot \sigma \mid C\}} \quad (Receive_{aS})$$

$$\frac{\emptyset \vdash s \xrightarrow{r(l, o, \bar{w})} s' \quad \emptyset \triangleright (l, \bar{w} := \underline{a'}, \bar{u}) = \langle m, \sigma \rangle \quad rec(l, o, \bar{w}) \notin eR(C)}{\{a :: *s \mid \langle a', o, \bar{u} \rangle \mid C\} \rightarrowtail \{a :: *s \mid m \gg s' \cdot \sigma \mid C\}} \quad (Receive_{lS})$$

$$\frac{m \vdash s \xrightarrow{\natural} s'}{\{a :: m \gg s \mid C\} \rightarrowtail \{a :: C\}} \quad (Terminate) \qquad \frac{N_1 \rightarrowtail N_1'}{N_1 \cup N_2 \rightarrowtail N_1' \cup N_2} \quad (Part)$$

$$\frac{N \equiv N_1 \quad N_1 \rightarrowtail N_2 \quad N_2 \equiv N'}{N \rightarrowtail N'} \quad (Cong)$$

set), executions of the two argument services are interleaved. Rule (*Pick*) states that, in case no receive conflict occurs, the pick activity can execute any of its receive activities and then proceed accordingly.

The reduction relation $\rightarrowtail$ is the least relation over nets induced by the rules in Table 3. Types of nodes are omitted because they play no role in the operational semantics of ws-CALCULUS. Let us now comment on the rules. Rule (*Assign*) states that the effect of an assignment is global wrt the instance and consists of replacing the free occurrences of the variables bound by the assignment with the corresponding values and of extending the set of correlation constraints identifying the instance with the pairs resulting from the assignment. Rule (*Invoke*) states that service invocation corresponds to adding a service request to the dataspace of the invoked service provided that no address implicitly received is exported as operation parameter. The request is a tuple, containing the address a_1 of the invoker, the name of the invoked operation o and the message $\bar{u}$ (i.e. the arguments to be passed to o). Hence, the invocation of a remote service is asynchronous because the invoker can proceed before its request is processed. WS-BPEL also provides a synchronous invocation that forces the invoker to wait for an answer by

Table 4. Type syntax

$$
\begin{array}{llll}
Op & ::= & \emptyset \mid \{o : \bar{\tau}\} \mid Op \cup Op & \text{(operation type sets)} \\
L & ::= & \emptyset \mid \{b : bt\} \mid \{p : bt\} \mid L \cup L & \text{(local declarations)} \\
bt & ::= & \text{INT} \mid \text{STR} \mid \text{BOOL} & \text{(basic types)} \\
\tau & ::= & bt \mid Op & \text{(message types)} \\
t & ::= & \bar{\tau} \mid \text{BNET} \mid \text{BSERV} & \text{(generic types)}
\end{array}
$$

the invoked service, which indeed performs a pair of activities *receive – reply*. In WS-CALCULUS, this behaviour is rendered as execution of a pair of activities *invoke – receive* by the invoker and of a pair of activities *receive – invoke* by the invoked service. Rule (*Receive$_{al}$*) states that activity receive cannot progress until a matching request has been received. Thus, differently from activity invoke, it is blocking. Requests are routed to the correct service instance by exploiting the partner link and the operation contained in the request, which must coincide with those in the label of the transition performed by the service instance, and the correlation constraints identifying the instance, which must enable the assignment of the values contained in the request to the parameters contained in the receive. The correlation set identifying the instance must not be empty otherwise it could not be possible to determine the correct instance to which the request must be delivered. When the reduction takes place, the matching request is consumed and the effect on the instance is the same as that of the corresponding assignment. Rule (*Receive$_{ll}$*) differs only because in this case the address of the invoker is not known in advance. After the reduction, the address contained in the request is marked as not further transmissible and is used to replace the partner link occurring in the receive. The last two rules for the activity receive, (*Receive$_{aS}$*) and (*Receive$_{lS}$*), permit to create a new service instance on receipt of a request that cannot be routed to an existing instance. The additional premise prevents interferences with the first two rules for receive in case of multiple start activities, as illustrated by the example

$$\{a :: *(\mathbf{rec}\,(l, o, \langle p \rangle) \mid \mathbf{rec}\,(l', o', \langle p \rangle)) \mid \{p = 10\} \gg \mathbf{rec}\,(l, o, \langle p \rangle) \mid \langle a', o, \langle 10 \rangle \rangle\}$$

where only the service instance can evolve. Rule (*Terminate*) states that the whole service instance performing a transition labelled ♮ immediately terminates. Rule (*Part*) states that if a part of a larger net evolves, the whole net evolves accordingly. Rule (*Cong*) is standard and states that structural congruent nets have the same reductions.

3   Types

The syntax of types is defined in Table 4. An *operation type set Op* is a collection of type definitions of operations $o : \bar{\tau}$, where $\bar{\tau}$ is a tuple of *message types* that characterizes the format of the arguments that an operation requires. We assume that the type definition of a given operation only occurs at a single node within a net. *Local declarations L* consist of type definitions of basic variables and properties, which have *basic types bt* (for simplicity sake, we only consider INT, STR and BOOL). Types BNET and BSERV are those of (well-typed) nets and services, respectively.

In the sequel, we will use the symbol $\star$ to type partner links that are implicitly initialized (i.e. they are bound as first argument of a **rec**$(,,)$). Notation $\tau^\star$, which is used to type the parameters of service definitions (see the previous section), stands for a message type τ or for $\star$. Typing a parameter with $\star$ means that it is a partner link that should have been bound implicitly by a receive activity that syntactically precedes the service call. Moreover, notation $\_s$ shall denote both service specifications $(*s)$ and service instances $(m \gg s)$.

Type inference. Type environments, ranged over by Γ, map addresses and partner links to sets of operation types Op or to $\star$, and service identifiers to BSERV. If $x \notin dom(\Gamma)$, we write $\Gamma, x : t$ for the type environment obtained by extending Γ with the binding of x to t (the notation generalizes to $\Gamma, \{x_i : t_i\}_{i \in I}$ with the obvious meaning). We write $\emptyset$ to denote the type environment with empty domain. Type environments are ordered by the standard preorder over functions, thus we write $\Gamma \leqslant \Gamma'$ when $dom(\Gamma) \supseteq dom(\Gamma')$ and $\Gamma(x) = \Gamma'(x)$ for each $x \in dom(\Gamma')$.

Type environments hold the types of nodes and of partner links. This information is exploited to properly deal with address passing (indeed, invoke and receive activities can use partner links as parameters to exchange node addresses). The type of a partner link is a set of operation types Op stating that the partner link can be bound only to addresses holding a type Op' such that $Op \subseteq Op'$. During the type checking wrt Γ, we can easily determine if a partner link l has been implicitly or explicitly initialized according to the fact that $\Gamma(l)$ is $\star$ or Op, respectively. When a partner link is implicitly initialized, the type system checks that the associated address is never transmitted (the example in Section 4 shows that this limitation does not affect the expressive power of the calculus), as required by WSDL / WS-BPEL. When a partner link is explicitly initialized, the type system checks that the link is not reassigned (in fact, this control is done implicitly because if $l \in dom(\Gamma)$ then $\Gamma, l : Op$ is undefined). Type environments also hold service identifiers: this information is exploited when typing recursive service definitions.

The judgment $\Gamma \vdash N :$ BNET, defined by the inference rules of Table 5, says that a net N is well-typed under the type environment Γ. The initial type environment used to typecheck a net does not contain type associations for partner links; this kind of associations may be added to the environment during the type checking of services, by means of the function $envExt_{..}(\cdot)$. Rule (*net*) says that a net is well-typed under a type environment, if each node is well-typed under the environment extended with type information extracted from all nodes. Rule (*netToServ*) says that a node is well-typed if its components are well-typed. Rule (*netWeak*) says that a type environment can be replaced with a stronger one (i.e. one making more assumptions).

The judgment $\Gamma \vdash_a^L S : t$, defined by the set of inference rules shown in Tables 6 and 7, says that S has type t, where S is a metavariable denoting values, variables, properties, requests and services, wrt a type environment Γ and a pair a–L made of the address of a node and a set of local declarations. The symbol $\sqsubseteq$ denotes the subtyping preorder over τ induced by letting $Op \sqsubseteq Op'$ if $Op \subseteq Op'$. The preorder extends to tuples of message types by letting $\langle \tau_1, \ldots, \tau_n \rangle \sqsubseteq \langle \tau'_1, \ldots, \tau'_n \rangle$ if $\tau_i \sqsubseteq \tau'_i$ for $i = 1..n$. To distinguish partner links within a tuple of variables and properties, we exploit the auxiliary function $pl(\cdot)$ that, given a tuple $\bar{w}_{i \in I}$, returns the set of indexes of the partner links therein. The function is defined inductively on the syntax of $\bar{w}_{i \in I}$ as follows:

Table 5. Inference rules for $\Gamma \vdash N : \text{BNET}$

$$\frac{\forall i \in I \qquad \Gamma, \{a_j : Op_j \mid j \in I\} \vdash a_i ::^{Op_i, L_i} C_i : \text{BNET}}{\Gamma \vdash \{a_i ::^{Op_i, L_i} C_i \mid i \in I\} : \text{BNET}} \quad (net)$$

$$\frac{\Gamma \vdash_a^L C : \text{BSERV}}{\Gamma \vdash a ::^{Op, L} C : \text{BNET}} \quad (netToServ) \qquad\qquad \frac{\Gamma' \vdash N : \text{BNET} \qquad \Gamma \leqslant \Gamma'}{\Gamma \vdash N : \text{BNET}} \quad (netWeak)$$

$$pl(b_i) = \emptyset \qquad pl(p_i) = \emptyset \qquad pl(l_i) = \{i\} \qquad pl(\bar{w}_{i \in I}) = \bigcup_{i \in I} pl(w_i)$$

We comment on the most significant rules in Table 7, since the rules in Table 6 are standard. Rule (inv) is applied when an invoke activity is performed by a client in a one-way interaction or to start a request-response interaction. In these cases, indeed, the address of the provider (holding the type definition of the operation) is given by r. Of course, the parameters of the invoked operation must conform to the corresponding operation type. In particular, when an invoke transmits an address, e.g. $\bar{w} = \bar{w}_{i \in I}$, $w_k = r'$ and $\tau_k = Op''$, then it must be that $Op'' \subseteq Op'$ where Op' is the operation type set associated to r' in Γ (i.e. $\Gamma \vdash_a^L r' : Op'$). This is indeed what the condition $\bar{\tau} \sqsubseteq \bar{\tau}'$ checks. Rule (inv_cb) is applied to an invoke activity performed as a callback in a request-response interaction. The local node is the operation provider. The only difference with the previous rule is that, in case the first argument of the activity is a partner link l, it is additionally checked that a triggering receive activity which initializes l logically precedes the invoke (this is expressed by the premise $\Gamma \vdash_a^L l : \star$). Rule ($rec\_cb$) is applied when a client performs a receive activity to obtain a callback in a request-response interaction. Similarly to rule (inv), the type of the operation must be retrieved from the provider node whose address is given by r. In case the first argument of the operation is a free occurrence of a link it is checked that the link is not transmitted. Rule (rec) is similar but is applied when the local node is the provider of the receive activity. Rule (seq) says that a sequence of services $s_1; s_2$ is well-typed under Γ if s_1 is well-typed under Γ and s_2 is well-typed under Γ extended with the type associations for the partner links bound by s_1 (notably, the extension is possible only if such partner links are not reassigned). The set of new associations is returned by the auxiliary function $envExt_{\cdot,\cdot}(\cdot)$, that can be defined inductively on the syntax of services. The most significant cases, i.e. those for the binding constructs, are defined as follows:

$$envExt_{\Gamma, a}(\mathbf{rec}\,(r, o, \bar{w})) =$$
$$\begin{cases} \{l : \tau_i \mid \exists i\,.\,w_i = l \wedge \tau_i \cap Op = \emptyset\} \cup \{l' : \star \mid r = l'\} & \text{if } \Gamma \vdash_a^0 a : Op \wedge o : \bar{\tau} \in Op \\[2mm] \{l : \tau_i \mid \exists i\,.\,w_i = l \wedge \Gamma \vdash_a^0 r : Op' \wedge o : \bar{\tau} \in Op' \wedge & \text{otherwise} \\ \qquad \Gamma \vdash_a^0 a : Op \wedge \tau_i \cap Op = \emptyset\} \end{cases}$$

$$envExt_{\Gamma, a}(\mathbf{ass}\,(\bar{w}, \bar{e})) = \{l : \tau_i \mid \exists i\,.\,w_i = l \wedge \Gamma \vdash_a^0 \bar{e} : \bar{\tau} \wedge \Gamma \vdash_a^0 a : Op \wedge \tau_i \cap Op = \emptyset\}$$

Condition $\tau_i \cap Op = \emptyset$ avoids that the service executing the activity can receive its same address as an argument. Finally, rule ($flow$) forces the two component services to

Table 6. Inference rules for $\Gamma \vdash_a^L S : t$

$$\frac{u \in \text{Int}}{\emptyset \vdash_a^L u : \text{INT}} \; (int) \qquad \frac{u \in \text{Str}}{\emptyset \vdash_a^L u : \text{STR}} \; (str) \qquad \frac{u \in \{\textbf{true}, \textbf{false}\}}{\emptyset \vdash_a^L u : \text{BOOL}} \; (bool)$$

$$r : Op \vdash_a^L r : Op \quad (ref) \qquad \frac{b : \tau \in L}{\emptyset \vdash_a^L b : \tau} \; (var) \qquad \frac{p : \tau \in L}{\emptyset \vdash_a^L p : \tau} \; (prop)$$

$$l : Op \vdash_a^L \ulcorner l \urcorner : Op \quad (ref_2) \qquad \frac{\Gamma \vdash_a^L w_1 : \tau_1 \quad \dots \quad \Gamma \vdash_a^L w_n : \tau_n}{\Gamma \vdash_a^L \langle w_1, \dots, w_n \rangle : \langle \tau_1, \dots, \tau_n \rangle} \; (\bar{w})$$

$$\frac{\Gamma' \vdash_a^L S : t \quad \Gamma \leqslant \Gamma'}{\Gamma \vdash_a^L S : t} \; (weak) \qquad \frac{\Gamma \vdash_a^L e_1 : \tau_1 \quad \dots \quad \Gamma \vdash_a^L e_n : \tau_n}{\Gamma \vdash_a^L \langle e_1, \dots, e_n \rangle : \langle \tau_1, \dots, \tau_n \rangle} \; (\bar{e})$$

type check in the same environment. This control prevents implicit flow of addresses from one component to the other (recall that partner link declarations are global to the instance) which would force a strict execution ordering of the components (thus, e.g., the service instance $\textbf{rec}\,(l, o, w) \mid \textbf{inv}\,(l, o', 5)$ does not type check).

Type soundness. The major property of our type system is that if a net typechecks then it does never generate runtime errors (Corollary 1). The proof proceeds in the style of [WF94] by first proving *subject reduction*, namely that nets well-typedness is an invariant of the reduction relation (Theorem 1), and then proving *type safety*, namely that well-typed nets do not immediately generate errors (Theorem 2). Due to lack of space, we omit the proofs of the results presented in this section (they are quite standard and can be found in [LPT06]).

First, we introduce some auxiliary definitions. A (generic) *context* C_g is a service with one subterm replaced by a hole, denoted $[\cdot]$. Formally, C_g is defined as follows:

$$C_g \; ::= \; [\cdot] \; \mid \; C_g \mid s \; \mid \; C_g; s \; \mid \; s; C_g \; \mid \; \textbf{rec}\,(r, o, \bar{w}); C_g + \sum_{i \in I} \textbf{rec}\,(r_i, o_i, \bar{w}_i); s_i$$
$$\mid \; \textbf{if}\,(e)\,\textbf{then}\,\{s\}\,\textbf{else}\,\{C_g\} \; \mid \; \textbf{if}\,(e)\,\textbf{then}\,\{C_g\}\,\textbf{else}\,\{s\} \; \mid \; A(\bar{c})$$

where the body of the service definition is a context, i.e. $A(\bar{v} : \bar{\tau}^\star) \stackrel{def}{=} C_g$. Notably, terms of the form $[\cdot]\,;\,s + \sum_{i \in I} \textbf{rec}\,(r_i, o_i, \bar{w}_i)\,;\,s_i$ are not considered (for the moment). Notation $C_g[s]$ denotes the service resulting from filling the hole of C_g with service s.

An *execution context* C is a context such that, once the hole is filled with a service s, the resulting service $C[s]$ is capable of immediately performing an activity of s. Formally, C is defined by the following grammar:

$$C \; ::= \; [\cdot] \; \mid \; C \mid s \; \mid \; C; s \; \mid \; \textbf{if}\,(e)\,\textbf{then}\,\{C\}\,\textbf{else}\,\{s\} \; \mid$$
$$\textbf{if}\,(e)\,\textbf{then}\,\{s\}\,\textbf{else}\,\{C\} \; \mid \; A(\bar{c})$$

where $A(\bar{v} : \bar{\tau}^\star) \stackrel{def}{=} C$. Whenever, we only consider basic receive activities, we can extend the set of possible execution contexts as follows:

$$C_r \; ::= \; C \; \mid \; [\cdot]\,;\,s + \sum_{i \in I} \textbf{rec}\,(r_i, o_i, \bar{w}_i)\,;\,s_i$$

Table 7. Inference rules for $\Gamma \vdash_a^L S : t$ (cont)

$$\frac{\Gamma \vdash_a^L C_1 : \text{BSERV} \qquad \Gamma \vdash_a^L C_2 : \text{BSERV}}{\Gamma \vdash_a^L C_1 \mid C_2 : \text{BSERV}} \; (par) \qquad\qquad \frac{\Gamma \vdash_a^L s : \text{BSERV}}{\Gamma \vdash_a^L \_s : \text{BSERV}} \; (serv)$$

$$\frac{\Gamma \vdash_a^L a : Op \qquad \Gamma \vdash_a^L a' : Op' \qquad o : \bar{\tau} \in Op \cup Op' \qquad \Gamma \vdash_a^L \bar{u} : \bar{\tau}' \qquad \bar{\tau} \sqsubseteq \bar{\tau}'}{\Gamma \vdash_a^L \langle a', o, \bar{u} \rangle : \text{BSERV}} \; (req)$$

$$\emptyset \vdash_a^L \mathbf{0} : \text{BSERV} \quad (nil) \qquad \emptyset \vdash_a^L \mathbf{exit} : \text{BSERV} \quad (exit) \qquad A : \text{BSERV} \vdash_a^L A : \text{BSERV} \quad (def_2)$$

$$\frac{\Gamma \vdash_a^L \bar{e}_{i \in I} : \bar{\tau}_{i \in I} \qquad \Gamma \vdash_a^L \bar{w}_{i \in (I \setminus J)} : \bar{\tau}_{i \in (I \setminus J)}}{\Gamma \vdash_a^L \mathbf{ass}\,(\bar{w}_{i \in I}, \bar{e}_{i \in I}) : \text{BSERV}} \; J = pl(\bar{w}_{i \in I}) \quad (ass)$$

$$\frac{\Gamma \vdash_a^L r : Op \qquad o : \bar{\tau} \in Op \qquad \Gamma \vdash_a^L \bar{w} : \bar{\tau}' \qquad \bar{\tau} \sqsubseteq \bar{\tau}'}{\Gamma \vdash_a^L \mathbf{inv}\,(r, o, \bar{w}) : \text{BSERV}} \; (inv)$$

$$\frac{\Gamma \vdash_a^L a : Op \qquad o : \bar{\tau} \in Op \qquad \Gamma \vdash_a^L \bar{w} : \bar{\tau}' \qquad \bar{\tau} \sqsubseteq \bar{\tau}' \qquad r = l \Rightarrow \Gamma \vdash_a^L l : \star}{\Gamma \vdash_a^L \mathbf{inv}\,(r, o, \bar{w}) : \text{BSERV}} \; (inv\_cb)$$

$$\frac{\Gamma \vdash_a^L r : Op \qquad o : \bar{\tau}_{i \in I} \in Op \qquad \Gamma \vdash_a^L \bar{w}_{j \in (I \setminus J)} : \bar{\tau}_{j \in (I \setminus J)}}{\Gamma \vdash_a^L \mathbf{rec}\,(r, o, \bar{w}_{i \in I}) : \text{BSERV}} \; J = pl(\bar{w}_{i \in I}) \quad (rec\_cb)$$

$$\frac{\Gamma \vdash_a^L a : Op \qquad o : \bar{\tau}_{i \in I} \in Op \qquad \Gamma \vdash_a^L \bar{w}_{j \in (I \setminus J)} : \bar{\tau}_{j \in (I \setminus J)}}{\Gamma \vdash_a^L \mathbf{rec}\,(r, o, \bar{w}_{i \in I}) : \text{BSERV}} \; J = pl(\bar{w}_{i \in I}) \quad (rec)$$

$$\frac{\Gamma \vdash_a^L e : \text{BOOL} \qquad \Gamma \vdash_a^L s_1 : \text{BSERV} \qquad \Gamma \vdash_a^L s_2 : \text{BSERV}}{\Gamma \vdash_a^L \mathbf{if}\,(e)\,\mathbf{then}\,\{s_1\}\,\mathbf{else}\,\{s_2\} : \text{BSERV}} \; (if)$$

$$\frac{\Gamma \vdash_a^L s_1 : \text{BSERV} \qquad \Gamma, envExt_{\Gamma,a}(s_1) \vdash_a^L s_2 : \text{BSERV}}{\Gamma \vdash_a^L s_1; s_2 : \text{BSERV}} \; (seq)$$

$$\frac{\Gamma \vdash_a^L s_1 : \text{BSERV} \qquad \Gamma \vdash_a^L s_2 : \text{BSERV}}{\Gamma \vdash_a^L s_1 \mid s_2 : \text{BSERV}} \; (flow) \qquad \frac{\forall i \in I \quad \Gamma \vdash_a^L \mathbf{rec}\,(r_i, o_i, \bar{w}_i)\,;\,s_i : \text{BSERV}}{\Gamma \vdash_a^L \sum_{i \in I} \mathbf{rec}\,(r_i, o_i, \bar{w}_i)\,;\,s_i : \text{BSERV}} \; (pick)$$

$$\frac{\Gamma \vdash_a^L A : \text{BSERV} \qquad \Gamma \vdash_a^L \bar{w} : \bar{\tau}_1^\star \qquad \bar{\tau}^\star \sqsubseteq \bar{\tau}_1^\star}{\Gamma \vdash_a^L A(\bar{w}) : \text{BSERV}} \; A(\bar{v} : \bar{\tau}^\star) \stackrel{def}{=} s \quad (call)$$

$$\frac{\Gamma, A : \text{BSERV}, \bar{v}_{j \in J} : \bar{\tau}_{j \in J}^\star \vdash_a^{L \cup \{\bar{v}_{i \in (I \setminus J)} : \bar{\tau}_{i \in (I \setminus J)}^\star\}} s : \text{BSERV}}{\Gamma \vdash_a^L A : \text{BSERV}} \; A(\bar{v}_{i \in I} : \bar{\tau}_{i \in I}^\star) \stackrel{def}{=} s, \; J = pl(\bar{v}_{i \in I}) \quad (def_1)$$

Table 8. Runtime errors (selected rules)

$$\frac{s \equiv C[\mathbf{inv}\,(a',o,\bar{w})] \quad o : \bar{\tau} \notin Op \quad o : \bar{\tau} \notin Op'}{\{a ::^{Op,L} \_s \mid C, a' ::^{Op',L'} C'\} \rightarrowtail^{err}} \quad (opDefError1)$$

$$\frac{s \equiv C_r[\mathbf{rec}\,(l,o,\bar{w})] \quad o : \bar{\tau} \notin Op}{\{a ::^{Op,L} \_s \mid C\} \rightarrowtail^{err}} \quad (opDefError2)$$

$$\frac{s \equiv C_r[\mathbf{rec}\,(a',o,\bar{w})] \quad o : \bar{\tau} \notin Op \quad o : \bar{\tau} \notin Op'}{\{a ::^{Op,L} \_s \mid C, a' ::^{Op',L'} C'\} \rightarrowtail^{err}} \quad (opDefError3)$$

$$\frac{s \equiv C_r[\mathbf{rec}\,(l,o,\bar{w})\,;C_g[\mathbf{inv}\,(l',o',\bar{w}')]] \quad \exists\,i \cdot w_i' = l}{\{a ::^{Op,L} \_s \mid C\} \rightarrowtail^{err}} \quad (linkError)$$

$$\frac{s \equiv C[\mathbf{inv}\,(l,o,\bar{w})] \quad o : \bar{\tau} \in Op}{\{a ::^{Op,L} \_s \mid C\} \rightarrowtail^{err}} \quad (rrError1)$$

$$\frac{s \equiv C[\mathbf{ass}\,(\bar{w},\bar{u})\,;C_g[\mathbf{inv}\,(l,o,\bar{w}')]] \quad o : \bar{\tau} \in Op \quad \exists\,i \cdot w_i = l}{\{a ::^{Op,L} \_s \mid C\} \rightarrowtail^{err}} \quad (rrError2)$$

The subject reduction theorem exploits the following two auxiliary lemmas. The former is the key for showing type preservation for reductions involving substitutions, the latter states that if a service is well-typed then its continuation after a transition is well-typed too.

Lemma 1. *Suppose* $\Gamma \vdash_a^L s :$ BSERV. *If* $\Gamma \vdash_a^L v : \tau$, $\Gamma \vdash_a^L u : \tau'$ *and* $\tau \sqsubseteq \tau'$, *then* $\Gamma \vdash_a^L s \cdot (v \mapsto u) :$ BSERV.

Lemma 2. *If* $\Gamma \vdash_a^L s :$ BSERV *and* $m \vdash s \xrightarrow{\alpha} s'$ *then* $\Gamma' \vdash_a^L s' :$ BSERV *with* Γ' *such that*[3]:

- $\Gamma' \leqslant \Gamma$ *in case of* $\alpha = \natural$, $i(a',o,\bar{u})$;
- $\Gamma' \leqslant \Gamma, envExt_{\Gamma,a}(\mathbf{rec}\,(r,o,\bar{w}))$ *in case of* $\alpha = r(r,o,\bar{w})$;
- $\Gamma' \leqslant \Gamma, envExt_{\Gamma,a}(\mathbf{ass}\,(\bar{w},\bar{e}))$ *in case of* $\alpha = (\bar{w} := \bar{u})$ *and* $s \equiv C[\mathbf{ass}\,(\bar{w},\bar{e})]$.

Theorem 1 (Subject Reduction). *If* $\Gamma \vdash N :$ BNET *and* $N \rightarrowtail N'$ *then* $\Gamma' \vdash N' :$ BNET *for some* Γ'.

The errors that our type system can capture, are characterized by predicate $\rightarrowtail^{err}$ that holds true when a net can immediately generate a runtime error. The most significant rules defining $\rightarrowtail^{err}$ are in Table 8 (the remaining rules can be found in [LPT06]).

Rule *(opDefError1)* raises an error when an operation is invoked whose type declaration is neither in the type of the caller nor in that of the callee. Rule *(opDefError2)* raises an error if the type declaration of the requested operation is not found in the type

---

[3] Notably, wrt the type environment on the right of $\leqslant$, Γ' can additionally contain further associations due to service calls. This explains the use of $\leqslant$ instead of $=$.

of the local node. Indeed, the service must be the provider since the activity first argument is a link. If the first argument of the activity is an address, there is no way to tell if the service is a client or a provider. Therefore, rule (*opDefError3*) raises an error only if the type declaration of the requested operation is neither in the type of the callee nor in that of the caller. Rule (*linkError*) raises an error when a partner link implicitly initialized is going to be passed in a communication. Rule (*rrError1*) raises an error if a callback invoke is going to be executed that does not have a previous triggering receive (indeed, its first argument is uninitialized). Finally, rule (*rrError2*) raises an error if the first argument of a callback invoke is initialized by an assignment rather than by a triggering receive.

Theorem 2 (Type Safety). $\Gamma \vdash N$: BNET *implies that* $N \rightarrowtail^{err}$ *holds false.*

To conclude, we have ($\rightarrowtail^*$ denotes the reflexive and transitive closure of $\rightarrowtail$).

Corollary 1 (Type Soundness). *Let* $\Gamma \vdash N$: BNET. *Then* $N' \rightarrowtail^{err}$ *holds false for every net* N' *such that* $N \rightarrowtail^* N'$.

4 A Brokerage Scenario

In this section we show an application of our framework. Suppose a client process invokes a process that acts as a broker for a third process. The latter process, once received a message with an integer value and the client address, increases the value by one (of course, this can be replaced with any complex operation) and sends the response back to the client by exploiting the received address. This scenario is modelled by the net (we write $Z \triangleq W$ to assign a symbolic name Z to the term W).

$$N \triangleq \{a_c ::^{Op_c, L_c} *s_c \mid \langle a_c, o_{init}, 10\rangle, a_b ::^{Op_b, L_b} *s_b, a_r ::^{Op_r, L_r} *s_r\} \quad (1)$$

where a_c, a_b and a_r are the addresses of client, broker and responder, respectively.

The client service is defined as follows:

$$s_c \triangleq \mathbf{rec}\,(l_{init}, o_{init}, p)\,;\mathbf{inv}\,(a_b, o, \langle p, a_c\rangle)\,;\mathbf{rec}\,(l_r, o_{cb}, \langle p, res\rangle)$$

The first receive creates a client instance by consuming the initialization tuple $\langle a_c, o_{init}, 10\rangle$. Since multiple client instances can wait a response along the same partner link and operation, we use a correlation set to route each incoming message to the correct instance. At instantiation time, a correlation set consisting of the property p is initialized. When the client process invokes the broker, it must send an integer value and its address to allow the responder process to send back the reply. After this invocation, the client waits the callback. The client type declarations are $Op_c = \{o_{init} : \langle \text{INT}\rangle, o_{cb} : \langle \text{INT}, \text{INT}\rangle\}$ and $L_c = \{p : \text{INT}, res : \text{INT}\}$. Notice that, in this communication pattern, differently from asynchronous request-response, the client has the provider role for the callback operation.

The broker service is defined as follows:

$$s_b \triangleq \mathbf{rec}\,(l, o, \langle b, l_c\rangle)\,;\mathbf{inv}\,(a_r, o', \langle b, l_c\rangle)$$

When invoked, the broker creates an instance (by using the receive activity) that will forward the client request to the responder and then terminate. Since no session with multiple interactions is started, the broker does not use a correlation mechanism. The broker type declarations are $Op_b = \{o : \bar{\tau}\}$ with $\bar{\tau} = \langle \text{INT}, \{o_{cb} : \langle \text{INT}, \text{INT} \rangle\} \rangle$ and $L_b = \{b : \text{INT}\}$. Of course, the broker has the provider role for the operation invoked by the client. In the message type of the operation, the second field is an operation type set and identifies the client operations that are visible to the broker.

Finally, the responder service is defined as follows:

$$s_r \triangleq \mathbf{rec}\,(l, o', \langle b, l_{cb} \rangle)\,;\,\mathbf{ass}\,(b', b + 1)\,;\,\mathbf{inv}\,(l_{cb}, o_{cb}, \langle b, b' \rangle)$$

When invoked, the responder creates an instance that will process the received value and send the response back to the client. Also this process does not need a correlation mechanism. The responder type declarations are $Op_r = \{o' : \bar{\tau}\}$ and $L_r = \{b : \text{INT}, b' : \text{INT}\}$. Notice that, since the responder receives the client address from the broker, its view of client operations along the partner link l_{cb} agrees with that of the broker.

According to our framework, to ensure that N will never generate errors, it suffices to prove that N is well-typed wrt the empty environment, i.e. $\emptyset \vdash N : \text{BNET}$. This, by rule (net), means that each node of N must be well-typed wrt the type environment $\Gamma = \{a_c : Op_c, a_b : Op_b, a_r : Op_r\}$. Now, by the rule (netToServ), (par) and (serv) this holds if all components $\langle a_c, o_{init}, 10 \rangle$, s_c, s_b and s_r are well-typed wrt Γ and appropriate local type declarations. Formally, we must check that judgements $\Gamma \vdash_{a_c}^{L_c} \langle a_c, o_{init}, 10 \rangle : \text{BSERV}$, $\Gamma \vdash_{a_c}^{L_c} s_c : \text{BSERV}$, $\Gamma \vdash_{a_b}^{L_b} s_b : \text{BSERV}$ and $\Gamma \vdash_{a_r}^{L_r} s_r : \text{BSERV}$ hold. The second inference is fully shown in Table 9 (the remaining inferences can be found in [LPT06]). For the sake of presentation, the inferences are split in a few parts with references between them.

Notably, for both receive activities we must apply rule (rec), because the type environment does not store type information for the partner links l_{init} and l_r. Indeed, the client has provider role for both the operations o_{init} and o_{cb} and we check if their type definitions are in the set of operation types of the client Op_c, which is obtained by inferring $\Gamma \vdash_{a_c}^{L_c} a_c : Op_c$. Instead, to check the invoke activity, we apply rule (inv), because in this case the service has client role. Op_b contains the type definition of the invoked operation o and is obtained by the inference of $\Gamma_c \vdash_{a_c}^{L_c} a_b : Op_b$, where a_b is the target of the invoke activity. Notice that the type associated to o is a subtype of the type associated to the operation parameters (i.e. $\bar{\tau} \sqsubseteq \langle \text{INT}, Op_c \rangle$), because $\{o_{cb} : \langle \text{INT}, \text{INT} \rangle\} \subseteq Op_c$.

We have thus proved that the net N defined in 1 behaves correctly. Now, we smoothly modify N so that its execution would eventually generate a runtime error and show that our type system can statically point out this situation. Indeed, suppose that $o_{cb} : \langle \text{INT}, \text{INT} \rangle \notin Op_c$. This could take place, for example, in case the client tries a request-response interaction with the broker (which would be the provider of both operations). The modified net N' would behave as follows (we omit the responder node because it plays no role):

$$
\begin{aligned}
N' \longmapsto\ & \{a_c ::^{Op_c, L_c} *s_c \mid \langle a_c, o_{init}, 10 \rangle\,,\,a_b ::^{Op_b, L_b} *s_b\} \\
\longmapsto\ & \{a_c ::^{Op_c, L_c} *s_c \mid \{p = 10\} \gg s'_c\,,\,a_b ::^{Op_b, L_b} *s_b\} \\
\longmapsto\ & \{a_c ::^{Op_c, L_c} *s_c \mid \{p = 10\} \gg \mathbf{rec}\,(l_r, o_{cb}, \langle p, res \rangle)\,,\,a_b ::^{Op_b, L_b} *s_b \mid \langle a_c, o, \langle 10, a_c \rangle \rangle\} \\
\longmapsto^{err}\ &
\end{aligned}
$$

Table 9. Type inference for the client service s_c (Γ_c is (Γ, l_{init} : $\star$))

$$\dfrac{res : \text{INT} \in L_c}{\dfrac{\emptyset \vdash_{a_c}^{L_c} res : \text{INT}}{\Gamma_c \vdash_{a_c}^{L_c} res : \text{INT}} \text{(weak)}} \text{(var)}$$

$$\dfrac{p : \text{INT} \in L_c}{\dfrac{\emptyset \vdash_{a_c}^{L_c} p : \text{INT}}{\Gamma_c \vdash_{a_c}^{L_c} p : \text{INT}} \text{(weak)}} \text{(prop)} \qquad \dfrac{\Gamma_c \vdash_{a_c}^{L_c} \langle p, res\rangle : \langle \text{INT}, \text{INT}\rangle}{} \text{(w)}$$

$$o_{cb} : \langle \text{INT}, \text{INT}\rangle \in Op_c \qquad (rec)$$

$$(2)\ \Gamma_c \vdash_{a_c}^{L_c} \mathbf{rec}(l_r, o_{cb}, \langle p, res\rangle) : \text{BSERV}$$

$$\dfrac{a_c : Op_c \vdash_{a_c}^{L_c} a_c : Op_c}{\Gamma_c \vdash_{a_c}^{L_c} a_c : Op_c} \text{(ref)}\big/\text{(weak)}$$

$$\dfrac{\Gamma_c \vdash_{a_c}^{L_c} \langle \text{INT}, Op_c\rangle}{} \text{(w)} \qquad \bar{\tau} \sqsubseteq \langle \text{INT}, Op_c\rangle \quad (inv)$$

$$\dfrac{p : \text{INT} \in L_c}{\dfrac{\emptyset \vdash_{a_c}^{L_c} p : \text{INT}}{\Gamma_c \vdash_{a_c}^{L_c} p : \text{INT}} \text{(weak)}} \text{(prop)} \qquad \dfrac{\Gamma_c \vdash_{a_c}^{L_c} \langle p, a_c\rangle : \langle \text{INT}, Op_c\rangle}{} \text{(rec)}$$

$$(1)\ \Gamma_c \vdash_{a_c}^{L_c} \mathbf{inv}(a_b, o, \langle p, a_c\rangle) : \text{BSERV}$$

$$\dfrac{a_b : Op_b \vdash_{a_c}^{L_c} a_b : Op_b}{\Gamma_c \vdash_{a_c}^{L_c} a_b : Op_b} \text{(ref)}\big/\text{(weak)}$$

$$o : \bar{\tau} \in Op_b$$

$$(1)\ \Gamma_c \vdash_{a_c}^{L_c} \mathbf{inv}(a_b, o, \langle p, a_c\rangle) : \text{BSERV} \qquad (2)\ \Gamma_c \vdash_{a_c}^{L_c} \mathbf{rec}(l_r, o_{cb}, \langle p, res\rangle) : \text{BSERV}$$

$$\dfrac{\Gamma_c \vdash_{a_c}^{L_c} \mathbf{inv}(a_b, o, \langle p, a_c\rangle)\,;\, \mathbf{rec}(l_r, o_{cb}, \langle p, res\rangle) : \text{BSERV}}{} \text{(seq)}$$

$$\dfrac{a_c : Op_c \vdash_{a_c}^{L_c} a_c : Op_c}{\Gamma \vdash_{a_c}^{L_c} a_c : Op_c} \text{(ref)}\big/\text{(weak)}$$

$$\dfrac{p : \text{INT} \in L_c}{\dfrac{\emptyset \vdash_{a_c}^{L_c} p : \text{INT}}{\Gamma \vdash_{a_c}^{L_c} p : \text{INT}} \text{(weak)}} \text{(prop)}$$

$$o_{init} : \langle \text{INT}\rangle \in Op_c \qquad (rec)$$

$$\dfrac{\Gamma \vdash_{a_c}^{L_c} \mathbf{rec}(l_{init}, o_{init}, p) : \text{BSERV}}{}$$

$$\Gamma \vdash_{a_c}^{L_c} \mathbf{rec}(l_{init}, o_{init}, p)\,;\, \mathbf{inv}(a_b, o, \langle p, a_c\rangle)\,;\, \mathbf{rec}(l_r, o_{cb}, \langle p, res\rangle) : \text{BSERV} \quad (seq)$$

where the runtime error is generated by rule *(opDefError2)*. This situation can be captured in advance, since N' is not well-typed because, in the inference for the client service, $\Gamma_c \vdash_{a_c}^{L_c} \mathbf{rec}\,(l_r, o_{cb}, \langle p, res \rangle)$: BSERV cannot be inferred.

5   Concluding Remarks

We have set a formal semantics framework for web services orchestration languages, and particularly for WS-BPEL. We have introduced WS-CALCULUS, a foundational language specifically designed for modelling interactions among web services, and a type system that permits to formalize the relationship between WS-BPEL processes and the associated WSDL documents. The type system forces a neat programming discipline for communicating processes. We have shown that the type system and the operational semantics of WS-CALCULUS are 'sound' and presented an illustrative example.

We are currently extending the typing system, and the related results, to the enriched language described in [LPT06]. We also plan to enrich the type system to enforce more rigorous type disciplines. For example, partner links could have assigned more sophisticated types that would correspond to complex interaction patterns, such as, e.g., 'one request – multiple responses' or 'one request – one of two possible responses'. Moreover, by exploiting some form of 'behavioural' types, such dynamic aspects of WS-CALCULUS processes could be captured as, e.g., 'an operation parameter may determine whether a callback uses operation A vs. operation B' or 'the invocation of a service of type X must be preceded by the invocation of a service of type Y'.

One major contribution of our work is the formal modelling of different aspects of WS-BPEL, such as multiple start activities, receive conflicts, routing of correlated messages, interactions among different web services, that have not been tackled at once in the literature. The mechanism of correlation sets was first investigated in [Vir04], that however only consider interaction of different instances of a single business process. Other works take the opposite route, and enrich some well-known process calculus with constructs inspired by those of WS-BPEL. The most of them deal with issues of web transactions such as interruptible processes, failure handlers and time. This is, for instance, the case of [LZ05a, LZ05b] that present a timed extension of the π-calculus, called webπ, tailored to study a simplified version of the scope construct of WS-BPEL. We have focused on service orchestration rather than on service choreography (that provides a means to describe service interactions in a top-view way) because we wanted to study those problems arising when executing WS-BPEL processes. In [BGG+05] both aspects are studied. Following [MB03], we have pushed forward the use of a type system to define basic contracts for web services. In [CL06, HSS05], alternative approaches are proposed that are based on the use of schema languages and Petri nets, respectively.

Acknowledgements. We thank the anonymous referees for their useful comments.

References

[BCG+05]   B. Bloch, F. Curbera, Y. Goland, N. Kartha, C. K. Liu, S. Thatte, P. Yendluri, and A. Yiu. Web services business process execution language version 2.0. TR, WS-BPEL TC OASIS, 2005. http://www.oasis-open.org/.

[BGG+05]   N. Busi, R. Gorrieri, C. Guidi, R. Lucchi, and G. Zavattaro. Choreography and orchestration: A synergic approach for system design. In *ICSOC 2005*, pages 228–240, 2005.

[CCMW01]   E. Christensen, F. Curbera, G. Meredith, and S. Weerawarana. Web services description language (wsdl) 1.1. TR, W3C, 2001. http://www.w3.org/TR/wsdl/.

[CL06]   S. Carpineti and C. Laneve. A basic contract language for web services. In *Proceedings of ESOP 06, LNCS*, 2006.

[HSS05]   S. Hinz, K. Schmidt, and C. Stahl. Transforming bpel to petri nets. In *Business Process Management*, pages 220–235, 2005.

[LPT06]   A. Lapadula, R. Pugliese, and F. Tiezzi. A WSDL-based type system for WS-BPEL. TR, Dipartimento di Sistemi e Informatica, Univ. Firenze, 2006. http://www.dsi.unifi.it/~pugliese/DOWNLOAD/wsc-full.ps.

[LZ05a]   C. Laneve and G. Zavattaro. Foundations of web transactions. *Fossacs'05*, LNCS(3441):282–298, 2005.

[LZ05b]   C. Laneve and G. Zavattaro. Webπ at work. In *TGC'05*, 2005.

[MB03]   L. G. Meredith and S. Bjorg. Contracts and types. *Comm. ACM*, 46(10):41–47, 2003.

[Vir04]   M. Viroli. Towards a formal foundational to orchestration languages. *Electronic Notes in Theoretical Computer Science*, 105:51–71, 2004.

[WF94]   A.K. Wright and M. Felleisen. A syntactic approach to type soundness. *Information and Computation*, 115(1):38–94, 1994.

Managing Ad-Hoc Networks Through the Formal Specification of Service Requirements*

Martín López-Nores, Jorge García-Duque, and José J. Pazos-Arias

Department of Telematics Engineering, University of Vigo. 36310, Vigo (Spain)
{mlnores, jgd, jose}@det.uvigo.es

Abstract. Mobile ad-hoc networks (MANETs) are dynamic computing environments where it is hard to make predictions about service provision. To ensure a level of predictability —and thus make the services more dependable—, it has been argued that the hosts must exchange information that allows guessing how the network is set up at a given moment, and how it will be in the near future. This paper introduces an approach to handling that information, which has been explicitly devised to deal with incomplete and changeable knowledge. As a contribution to the current state of the art, this approach enables a practical scheme where the different hosts in a MANET can collaborate to make up the network that best satisfies their service requirements.

1 Introduction

The past few years have witnessed a shift from traditional desktop machines reliant on fixed, wired networks to ubiquitous, wireless networks of mobile devices. At the head of this movement, mobile ad-hoc networks (MANETs) are computing environments supported collectively by the hosts they comprise, and where a small device can provide support for complex tasks by leaning on the services provided by the others [1]. This paradigm has a number of increasingly relevant real-world applications, from sensor networks [2] to peer-to-peer wireless computing [3].

MANETs are characterized by frequent changes in network topology. Small devices opportunistically arise and communicate with no reliance on any form of fixed infrastructure, and their physical mobility results in unpredictable connectivity. In turn, this volatility causes limited dependability at the level of service provision, as the applications may suffer disconnections at any time. To tackle this problem, several authors have argued that it is necessary to augment the predictability of the networks through *knowledge dissemination and exploitation*. The idea is to have the hosts expose and gather information that allows them to guess how the network is set up at a given moment and how it will be in the near future [4, 5]. Thus, it would be possible for the hosts to detect whether their *service requirements*[1] are likely to be satisfied, and react conveniently in case not (moving to specific locations, accomplishing service migrations, etc.).

---

* This work has been partially funded by the Xunta de Galicia Basic Research Project PGIDIT04PXIB32201PR.
[1] By *service requirements*, we mean indications that certain services should be available at specific times and places. Such indications can be issued by software applications or directly by human users.

P. Ciancarini and H. Wiklicky (Eds.): COORDINATION 2006, LNCS 4038, pp. 164–178, 2006.

The commented approach faces a fundamental problem: the knowledge available about a MANET is very likely to be imperfect. It is unrealistic to assume that the knowledge may be complete, because every host gathers information in a progressive way from the initial situation that it knows nothing about others. Also, it frequently happens that a host cannot even expose complete information about itself (for example, it may not be able to predict its future moves). Finally, the dynamism of the network worsens the problem, because the gathered information can easily become stale.

The works presented in [6, 7] evidence that there is still much research to do regarding what can be done when there are limitations in the knowledge available about a MANET. The authors in [6] proved the advantages of having the hosts gather and exploit knowledge about the network, but they left "*the partial observability of the domain*" as a crucial feature to consider in the future to attain much better results. On their part, the authors in [7] suggested that it could be a good starting point to assume *perfect knowledge*, and then examine the implications of gradually eliminating that assumption; this approach can certainly bring light from a theoretical point of view, but the initial assumption makes it inapplicable in practice.

In this paper, we introduce a practical approach to the management of knowledge about MANETs, leaning on a formal basis explicitly devised to handle imperfect and changeable knowledge. This solution has the following two major strengths:

- First, it endows mobile hosts with the ability to reason safely in the face of *uncertainty* (i.e. missing knowledge), allowing them to tune the amount of information they handle according to their memory and computing capabilities.
- Second, it provides efficient means to evolve a knowledge base in order to assimilate frequent updates/changes in the hosts' intents, as well as to analyze the service requirements and derive possibilities to increase the odds that they will be satisfied.

The next section presents a simplified scheme of our proposal, to motivate the formal basis we have adopted and explain its advantages. Section 3 shows the formal basis in action through an example that illustrates the building and maintenance of a knowledge base. Section 4 introduces the complete scheme of our proposal, describing the solutions it enables to improve the dependability of MANETs. The paper finishes with a discussion and the motivation of future work in Sect. 5 and Sect. 6, respectively.

2   The Core of the Scheme

The core of our proposal is the scheme shown in Fig. 1. Every host gathers information about the MANET from other hosts, and uses that information to automatically generate (*synthesize*) a formal model of the network. That model is later employed to check (*analyze*) whether it is possible to satisfy the host's service requirements, using a *model-checking* [8] algorithm.

For the time being, we will assume that the knowledge exchanged between the hosts is merely involved with i) the services they plan to make available for others to use, and ii) their intended/expected *motion profiles*[2]. Thereby, the formal model of the MANET can reflect the availability of the different services against time and space.

---

[2] A *motion profile* is any characterization of a host's spatial trajectory against time [4, 9].

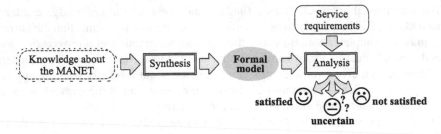

Fig. 1. The basic scheme: synthesis of formal models and analysis of service requirements

2.1 Capturing the Uncertainty of Having Incomplete Knowledge

Having generated a model that captures what is known about the network, a fundamental point to note about Fig. 1 is that the analysis of the service requirements can return three different results:

- **[satisfied]:** the service requirements can be satisfied in the envisaged network;
- **[not satisfied]:** the service requirements cannot be satisfied in the envisaged network;
- **[uncertain]:** the knowledge available does not suffice to conclude whether it is possible to satisfy the service requirements.

According to this fact, we cannot build up a solution to reason about MANETs over the classical Boolean logic, because it cannot reflect uncertainty (everything is either *true* or *false*, which leads to erroneous conclusions about the satisfiability of the service requirements).

To avoid taking for *false* what is indeed *unknown*, we advocate the use of modeling formalisms like *Partial Kripke Structures* (PKS [10]), *Modal Transition Systems* (MTS [11]) and *Models of Unspecified States* (MUS [12]), which lean on Kleene's three-valued semantics [13]. This semantics, depicted in Fig. 2, enables an explicit differentiation of what is known to be *true* (meaning 'allowed', 'possible', 'reachable' or 'available'), what is known to be *false* (meaning the opposite), and what is still *unknown* (represented by the symbol ⊥).

As shown in the diagram of Fig. 2, the logical value ⊥ lies halfway between the *truth levels* of the others (certainly, *unknown* is neither falser than *false*, nor truer than *true*); ⊥ is also placed in a *knowledge level* below *false* and *true*, thus capturing the point that learning new information can turn the *unknown* facts into known ones.

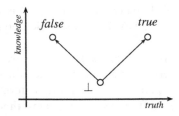

Fig. 2. The double Hasse diagram of Kleene's three-valued logic

2.2   Reacting to Updates/Changes in the Knowledge Base

The second crucial point about the scheme of Fig. 1 is that the knowledge available about a MANET can be highly changeable. Therefore, the utility of the whole approach depends on the ability to have the model of the network updated rapidly enough. The presumably-reduced power of a mobile device makes further claims for low computational cost.

Clearly, every piece of information received either provides new knowledge or contradicts part of what was known. So, the models must be readily capable of accomplishing two types of evolutions: *refinements* [14] and *retrenchments* [15]. As explained below, this requisite is catered for by the knowledge ordering of Kleene's logical values:

- The addition of new knowledge to a model is done by turning *unknown* elements into *true* or *false* ones, with no concern for whatever was already *false* or *true* (in other words, a model can be refined by keeping the previous synthesis efforts). Obviously, this *incremental synthesis* process has much lower computational cost than proceeding from scratch; in fact, as proved in [16], the complexity of the former is exponential with the amount of added knowledge, whereas it is exponential with the size of the knowledge base for the latter. Previous approaches to the synthesis problem using Boolean formalisms have only been able to reduce that high complexity by introducing human intervention [17, 18], which is pointless in our context.
- To alter a model in a way that it contradicts part of the knowledge it originally captured, it is first necessary to perform an *abstraction*, to turn into *unknown* the elements that were either *true* or *false* and have become obsolete; after that, the model is refined to incorporate the fresher information. Therefore, using a modeling formalism based on Kleene's semantics, the computational cost implied by a retrenchment is that of a refinement plus that of the preceding abstraction; the complexity of the latter is simply linear with the size of the model. Using Boolean formalisms, in contrast, it would even be questionable whether we could talk about abstractions, because *true* and *false* have the same knowledge level; anyway, since the transformation would consist of turning *true* elements into *false* ones or vice versa, it follows that it would have just the same complexity as the non-incremental synthesis.

The management of refinements and retrenchments has a greatly beneficial impact on the computational cost of verifying the service requirements, inasmuch as it helps identifying immediately the parts of a model that change in response to any new information. This way, the model-checking algorithm can revise the satisfiability of the service requirements by looking only at the updated parts of the model. This incremental approach has been successfully applied in software development (see [16, 19]) as a means to overcome the well-known problem of *state space explosion* [20], and so we adopt it in our approach to managing knowledge about MANETs.

2.3   Adopted Formalisms

From among the formalisms cited in Sect. 2.1, we have resorted to a variant of MUS conceived for the modeling of real-time systems, called MUS-T (*Timed Models of*

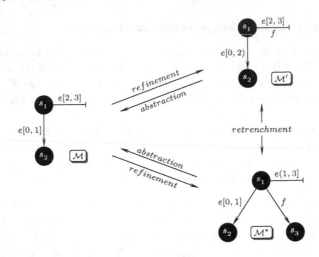

Fig. 3. Evolutions of MUS-T models

Unspecified States) [21]. This formalism is an extension of the classical *timed automaton* [22], the main difference being that it is based on Kleene's three-valued semantics instead of Boole's *true/false* interpretations.

To understand the MUS-T notation, consider the minimal MUS-T model $\mathcal{M}$ of Fig. 3. In this model, the event e is *true* (i.e. we know it can occur) in the time interval from $t = 0$ to $t = 1$, whereas it is *false* (we know it cannot occur) between $t = 2$ and $t = 3$. The rest of the time, we do not know whether event e can occur —this is not represented in the model, because $\perp$ is the default value.

Figure 3 also depicts the notions of refinement and retrenchment applied to MUS-T. The models $\mathcal{M}'$ and $\mathcal{M}^*$ are two refinements of $\mathcal{M}$, obtained by adding the knowledge that i) event e can/cannot occur between $t = 1$ and $t = 2$, and that ii) a new event, f, cannot/can occur at any time. Since the two knowledge additions are contradictory, it follows that $\mathcal{M}'$ and $\mathcal{M}^*$ are retrenchments of one another.

As a final remark, note that the scheme of Fig. 1 requires a suitable specification language, for a twofold purpose: first, to serve as the vehicle for exchanging knowledge between the hosts; and second, to express the service requirements that will be checked against the models. To this aim, we have opted for a temporal logic called SCTL-T (*Timed, Simple and Causal Temporal Logic*), which has been previously applied in conjunction with MUS-T —both in synthesis and analysis tasks— in the development of real-time systems (see [21]). Applied to the management of knowledge about MANETs, SCTL-T is flexible and powerful enough to express the phenomena on which we are interested: delays, dependencies between the requested services and spatial locations, usage times, etc.

3   Illustrating the Management of a Knowledge Base

In this section, we provide an example about managing a knowledge base in the simplified scheme of Sect. 2. We shall illustrate the evolutions of the MUS-T model of a

MANET in response to successive knowledge acquisitions, explaining the conclusions enabled at any time. For the sake of space, we will not indicate the SCTL-T expressions employed in the exchange of knowledge, but rather give textual explanations —readers interested on the details of the language should take a look at [21].

To start with, assume that we are running a host called h_1 that is continually offering the service a, and that this is indeed the only knowledge we have. The corresponding MUS-T model of the MANET is shown in Fig. 4, which must be interpreted according to the following general guidelines:

- The states of the model represent the overlaps between the communication ranges of the known hosts; these *zones* map to spatial locations where there is direct communication with the corresponding hosts. There always exists a zone z_0 where none of the known hosts is within range.
- For each state s_i, there are *true, false* or *unknown* events z_j depending on what we know about the possibility to move directly from zone z_i to zone z_j. The *true* z_j events take the model into the corresponding state s_j —a unit loop through event z_i indicates that it is possible to stay in the zone z_i.
- Also in each state s_i, there are *true, false* or *unknown* events representing the availability of the different services in the corresponding zone z_i —the available services are represented with unit loops, acting as state variables.
- Finally, for every host we know of, its being within communication range in a given zone is represented just the same way as the availability of the services.

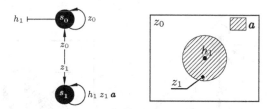

Fig. 4. Initial situation: the host h_1 only knows about itself

The model of Fig. 4 captures the fact that (obviously) the host h_1 delimits only one zone, z_1, where the service a is available at any time (a is a *true* event in state s_1). It is always possible to move from zone z_1 into z_0 (z_0 is a *true* event in s_1 at any time) and vice versa. We also know that h_1 is not within range in z_0 (event h_1 appears as a *false* event in s_0), but ignore whether the service a is available in that zone (event a is *unknown* in s_0); the reason for the latter is that some other host could be offering that service at some locations outside z_1.

Suppose that a new host h_2 appears, informing us about the existence of a third one, h_3. In addition, h_2 reports that it is continually offering the service b, whereas h_3 does the same with service c. The updated (refined) model of the network is that of Fig. 5.

Since h_1 has received the new information directly from h_2, it follows that the communication ranges of the two hosts do partially overlap. This fact has caused the appearance of the new state s_{12} representing the common zone z_{12}, where both the services a and b are available for use. The refinement has also implied the appearance of *true*

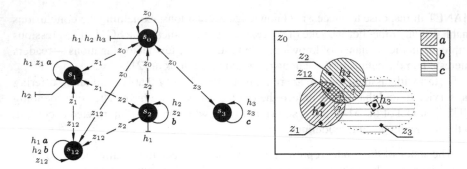

Fig. 5. Adding some knowledge about two new hosts, h_2 and h_3

events z_1, z_2 and z_{12} between s_1, s_2 and s_{12}, indicating the possibility to move directly between those zones. In contrast, the zone z_3 delimited by h_3 is only known to be reachable from z_0, because h_2 has not yet given us any information about where h_3 is located. Thanks to the three-valued semantics of MUS-T, this observation does not lead to concluding that h_3 cannot communicate directly with the other hosts; instead, as noted by the question marks in Fig. 5, we are uncertain about that possibility.

Assume that h_2 now says that the communication range of h_3 will never overlap the ranges of either h_1 and h_2. Having added this new knowledge, the model of the MANET becomes that of Fig. 6. This time, the events that have become *false* in states s_1, s_{12}, s_2 and s_3 do indicate that, for example, h_1 cannot communicate directly with h_3.

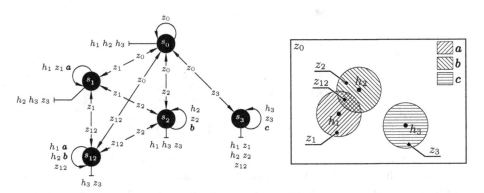

Fig. 6. Adding the knowledge that h_3 will never overlap h_1 or h_2

If, for whichever reason, we realized that the service **a** can only be provided by host h_1, the model of the network would be refined so as to remove the uncertainty about **a** in the zones not covered by h_1 (see Fig. 7).

To finish, suppose that h_2 now reports that (contrary to the previous expectations) h_3 will move so as to partially overlap the communication range of h_2 during the time interval (t_1, t_2). This information implies a retrenchment of the current model of the MANET, inasmuch as this model negates the possibility for h_2 to ever communicate directly with h_3 (in Fig. 7, h_3 is a *false* event all the time in the states where h_2 is *true*). The result of the retrenchment is depicted in Fig. 8.

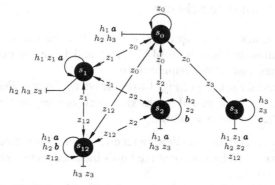

Fig. 7. Learning that the service a can only be provided by h_1

We see that a new zone z_{23} has appeared, covered by both h_2 and h_3, where it is possible to access the services b and c. This zone exists only between t_1 and t_2: as indicated by the temporal predicates linked to the *true* events z_{23} in s_0, s_2 and s_3, the new zone cannot be reached before t_1; on the other hand, z_{23} is a *false* event in s_{23} from t_2 onwards, indicating that it is not possible to stay in that zone any longer.

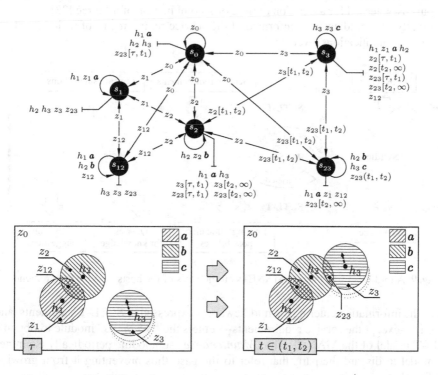

Fig. 8. Capturing a transient overlap between h_2 and h_3[†]

[†] The symbol 'τ' means "*now*".

4   A Taste of the Complete Scheme

Having explained the basics of our approach, we now describe the whole solution, which is intended to allow the hosts in a MANET to collaborate in making up the network that best satisfies their service requirements.

Our proposal augments the scheme of Fig. 1 to construct the layer of Fig. 9, which is to be placed between the applications and networking levels of every host in a MANET. The inputs to this middleware are as follows:

- From the applications level, the middleware receives information about its lodging host, indicating whatever is known about the host's intended motion profile and the services it plans to provide.
- From the networking level, the middleware receives analogous information about other hosts.
- From either level, the middleware can also receive information about the impossibility to take certain moves (e.g. due to the presence of walls), the fact that a given service can only be provided by certain hosts, etc. Moreover, as a remarkable addition with regard to the basic scheme we have been considering so far, it can receive information about the *elasticity properties* of the services, which indicate whether the services can be migrated from one host to another, cloned for hoarding purposes, leased for a duration of time or a combination of all three [23].
- Finally, the middleware is informed of the service requirements of its lodging host from the applications level.

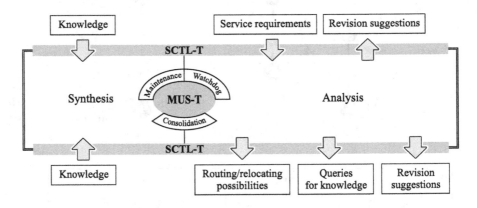

Fig. 9. A middleware to manage MANETs on the basis of the hosts' service requirements

All the information entering the middleware is expressed in SCTL-T statements, and all of it —except the service requirements— enters the *"Synthesis"* module to obtain a MUS-T model of the MANET. The *"Maintenance"* submodule periodically examines the model to discard the parts that refer to the past, thus preventing it from growing indefinitely.

The possibility to satisfy the service requirements of the host lodging the middleware is checked in the *"Analysis"* module using a model-checking algorithm. The *"Watchdog"* submodule is in charge of the incremental part (remember Sect. 2.2), supervising the updates of the MUS-T models to rapidly identify the service requirements affected and re-check their satisfiability.

Compared to other formal verification techniques, model-checking is advantageous for being fully systematic —even with multi-valued logics like Kleene's (see [24])— and not at all limited to finding YES/NO responses (in our case YES/NO/DON'T KNOW). Quite the opposite, as previously noticed in [25, 26], model-checking algorithms can explicitly record the *traces* (i.e. sequences of events and states) traversed over a model, helping to identify i) the reasons for a negative outcome, ii) the particular situations that yield a positive one, and iii) the missing knowledge that prevents from returning a conclusive response. This ability enables the main features of our middleware (the outputs in Fig. 9), which we describe and exemplify in the following subsections.

4.1 Routing/Relocating Possibilities

If the analysis finds that it is possible to satisfy the service requirements, the traces of the model-checking algorithm provide *routing possibilities* for the communication in the form of *direct, multihop* or *disconnected* routes [27, 28].

Example 1. Suppose that we are running host h_1 in the situation of Fig. 8. If we wanted to use the service c, we would be informed that there is no direct route to the zones where this service is available; instead of that, the analysis finds a multihop route to communicate with h_3 using h_2 as a relay.   □

Due to the exchange of knowledge about the elasticity of the services, the MUS-T model of the MANET does not only capture the kind of knowledge we illustrated in Sect. 3, but also the changes implied by events related to service migration, cloning, etc. Thereby, the analysis can find possibilities to satisfy the service requirements through certain relocations; in this case, the traces of the model-checking algorithm indicate the communications needed with the hosts involved in the relocations.

Example 2. Suppose that we are running host h_1 in the situation of Fig. 8. If we had received information indicating that it is possible to migrate the service c from h_3 to h_2, the model of the network would include a *true* event $migrate_{c,h_2}$ in state s_{23}; also, some new states would appear to reflect the fact that the occurrence of $migrate_{c,h_2}$ would make the service c available in the zones covered by h_2, leaving it *unknown* in the zone covered only by h_3.

Now, assume that we want to use the service c during the time period (t_{init}, t_{end}), with $t_{init} \in (t_1, t_2)$ and $t_{end} > t_2$. With the available knowledge, the analysis would find that the only possibility to satisfy this requirement implies migrating c from h_3 to h_2 at some time t between t_{init} and t_2. Remark that the model-checking algorithm is not only informing that there exists a possibility to satisfy the service requirement; in addition to that, its traces indicate that this possibility requires some collaboration from h_2 and h_3.   □

4.2 Queries for Knowledge

For the cases when there is not sufficient knowledge to conclude about the possibility to satisfy the service requirements, the traces of the model-checking algorithm allow identifying accurately what further information would be needed to provide a conclusive response. Thus, a host can inquire others just about the precise knowledge it needs.

Example 3. Suppose that we are running host h_1 in the situation of Fig. 5, and that we want to communicate with host h_3. The model-checking algorithm would find that there is uncertainty about this requirement, due to the fact that event z_3 is *unknown* in the states s_1, s_2 and s_{12}. So informed, h_1 would send a query to h_2 (the only host with which h_1 can surely communicate) asking for any details it might know about z_3, and h_2 would reply with the knowledge that takes from Fig. 5 to Fig. 6.   □

Generally, it is not necessary to know everything about the hosts and services involved to conclude about the possibility to satisfy a service requirement. An important feature of our middleware is that the conclusions obtained over partial knowledge are always *sound*, so that learning new information can never lead to contradicting previous analyses. This would not be true using a Boolean formal basis.

Example 4. In the same situation of Example 3, suppose that we require the service b to be available whenever we can communicate with host h_3. Any logic would find that this requirement can be satisfied even without having received information about the location of h_3, because service b is always available for h_1 to use.

However, if the service requirement merely indicated that we want to communicate with h_3 at some time in the future (just like in Example 3), a Boolean approach would mistakenly report that the requirement cannot be satisfied, assuming some information that h_1 has never received. The sound approach is to notify the uncertainty about the requirement.   □

The soundness property is important because it allows every host to tune the amount of information it handles according to its capabilities (memory, processor, etc.), with no risk of taking erroneous conclusions.

4.3   Revisions Suggestions

When the analysis finds that it is not possible to satisfy the service requirements, the middleware looks for ways to alter the planning of the network in quest for better expectations. To this aim, it can consider revisions of the intents announced by any host in the MANET (consisting of retrenchments of the SCTL-T statements used to construct the MUS-T model), as well as of the service requirements of the lodging host. Those revisions are derived directly from the traces of the model-checking algorithm —using *analysis-revision* mechanisms similar to the ones presented in [29, 30].

The revisions are provided as mere *suggestions*, and it depends on the applications to accept or reject the proposed solutions through whichever negotiation mechanisms. For instance, the applications could opt not to alter the service requirements unless it is absolutely necessary, and there may be cases in which the advertised motion profiles admit no variation (as when the hosts are attached to rails). The middleware limits itself to providing revision possibilities upon request, starting with the simplest solutions.

Example 5. Suppose that we are running host h_1 in the situation of Fig. 8, and that we want to use the service c during the time period (t_{init}, t_{end}), with $t_{init} < t_1$ and

$t_{end} \in (t_1, t_2)$. With the knowledge available, the analysis does not find a way to satisfy this requirement, because service c is only known to be accessible for h_1 from t_1 to t_2. In this case, the middleware would successively provide the following revision suggestions:

1. Change the service requirement, so that t_{init} is greater than t_1.
2. Tell h_1 to move so as to overlap the range of h_3 during a time period greater than (t_{init}, t_{end}).
3. Tell h_2 to move so that it starts overlapping the range of h_3 sooner, making t_1 lower than the requested t_{init}.
4. Tell h_3 to move faster, so that it starts overlapping the range of h_2 sooner, making t_1 lower than the requested t_{init}.

The latter suggestion would be passed to h_2 in a *best-effort* attempt, because h_1 does not know a way to communicate with h_3 —maybe h_2 knows a way, through other hosts which are currently unknown for us.   □

The acceptance of a revision suggestion implies that the hosts have agreed on a possibility to satisfy a given service requirement. With the aim of preserving that possibility, the host owning the requirement annotates the corresponding traces of the MUS-T model in the *"Consolidation"* submodule of the middleware (Figure 9), so that they are not considered as the subject for future revisions as far as possible.[†] The same submodule takes note of rejected suggestions, so that future ones do not insist on unwanted solutions unless all other alternatives have been discarded. This scheme allows implementing a range of policies at the applications level to support collaboration between multiple hosts, pursuing the global objective of building the network that best satisfies their service requirements.

5 Discussion

We have presented an approach to managing MANETs on the basis of the service requirements of their forming hosts, with the goal of achieving better dependability in terms of service provision. We have worked on the idea of *knowledge dissemination and exploitation*, paying special attention to the fact —only considered superficially in literature so far— that the knowledge that a host may gather about other hosts, about the services they provide and about their motion profiles is very likely to be partial and changeable.

Our solution takes the form of a middleware layer that provides the necessary modeling and reasoning mechanisms for the applications to check their service requirements. The middleware provides useful information (routing and relocating possibilities) if the service requirements can be satisfied, suggests re-arrangements of the MANET if they cannot, and guides the search for more information when there is uncertainty. It is not

---

[†] The *"Consolidation"* submodule also handles the cases commented in Sect. 4.1, storing the traces corresponding to service requirements which are found to be satisfiable with no need to revise the knowledge about the MANET.

involved with issues like the mapping of spatial locations to zones or the agreement on a time basis for the communications, which can be tackled with any of the solutions available in literature and practice.

At the core of our scheme, the modeling based on the MUS-T formalism provides two fundamental features for the practicality of the approach:

– On the one hand, by enabling sound reasoning over partial knowledge, we allow the hosts to tune the amount of information they handle according to their memory and computing power, without dooming themselves to providing erroneous analysis results. The missing knowledge that may prevent from drawing conclusions can be easily identified and requested from other hosts.

– On the other hand, the ability to identify the knowledge preserved or contradicted through any evolution of the knowledge base allows implementing efficient mechanisms for the synthesis, analysis and revision tasks. All of our algorithms proceed incrementally instead of from scratch.

6   Future Work

In this paper, we have addressed the changeability of the knowledge available about a MANET by implicitly assuming that the fresh information is always correct. This way, a retrenchment is immediately triggered whenever the middleware receives new information that conflicts with part of the knowledge it had previously gathered (as in the last step of the example in Sect. 3). Inspired by the works presented in [31, 32], we are currently considering the possibility to temporarily handle inconsistent knowledge, as it may be a better way to handle the changeability of the networks and to cope with malicious hosts publishing erroneous information. To this aim, we are resorting to previous works on inconsistencies in software development (see [33]) to make our middleware capable of i) interpreting the analysis results in the light of the agreement achievable between sources of conflicting information, and ii) guiding the search for information to support one of several conflicting stances.

Our current work also involves doing research to identify the best usage policies for our middleware, since there are many factors to be considered for optimal performance. From the networking point of view, we are mostly interested on characterizing the suitable balance between a *push* and a *pull* approach for knowledge dissemination. Our conjecture is that the best option depends mainly on the MANETs being sparsely-populated or densely-populated:

– In sparsely-populated networks, it is necessary to be aware of (and exploit) all the communication possibilities, because there may not be many. So, these networks seem good candidates for a *push* approach, in which the hosts exchange information proactively (i.e. in the background). This approach helps keeping the knowledge bases of the hosts fresh and complete, allowing fast reactions to the analysis results (it is rarely necessary to spend time querying information for other hosts). Moreover, since there are not many hosts, the overhead in the communications will be surely outweighed by the benefits achieved.

– In densely-populated networks, it seems wiser to opt for a predominantly *pull* approach, to have the hosts send information to others mainly (though not exclusively) upon request. In this kind of networks, there are generally many possibilities for the hosts to communicate, and so they can certainly tolerate a degree of staleness in the knowledge bases. Attempting to have complete and fresh knowledge bases in all of the hosts would imply an excessive (and unneeded) overhead, whereas the *pull* approach allows the hosts to handle little more than the information they need to check their service requirements.

From the software engineering point of view, our current work is devoted to studying the best policies to have the applications (or their human users, where applicable) negotiate re-arrangements of the network interpreting the revisions suggestions provided by our middleware. Here, we conjecture that the simplest policy (adopt the viable suggestions immediately, with no negotiation at all) may work well in densely-populated networks, with the advantage of incurring no overhead; in contrast, sparsely-populated networks should benefit from implementing policies that warn all the hosts affected by the re-arrangements.

References

1. Handorean, R., Roman, G.C.: Service provision in ad hoc networks. Lecture Notes in Computer Science **2315** (2002) 207–219
2. Akyildiz, I., Su, W., Sankarasubramaniam, Y., Cayirci, E.: A survey on sensor networks. IEEE Communications Magazine **40**(8) (2002) 102–114
3. Ghandeharizadeh, S., Krishnamachari, B., Song, S.: Placement of continuous media in wireless peer-to-peer networks. IEEE Transactions on Multimedia **6**(4) (2004) 335–342
4. Sen, R., Hackmann, G., Roman, G.C., Gill, C.: Towards predictable service provision in mobile ad-hoc networks. Technical Report WUCSE-04-60, Department of Computer Science and Engineering, Washington University (2004)
5. Dolev, S., Gilbert, S., Lynch, N., Schiller, E., Shvartsman, A., Welch, J.: Virtual mobile nodes for mobile ad hoc networks. Lecture Notes in Computer Science **3274** (2004) 230–244
6. Chang, Y.H., Ho, T., Pack Kaelbling, L.: Mobilized ad-hoc networks: A reinforcement learning approach. Technical Report AIM-2003-025, MIT (2003)
7. Sen, R., Hackmann, G., Roman, G.C., Gill, C.: Opportunistic exploitation of knowledge to increase predictability of agent interactions in MANETs. In: Proceedings of the 4th International Workshop on Software Engineering for Large-scale Multi-agent Systems. (2005)
8. Clarke, E., Grumberg, O., Peled, D.: Model checking. The MIT Press (2000)
9. Goldenberg, D.K., Lin, J., Morse, A.S., Rosen, B.E., Yang, Y.R.: Towards mobility as a network control primitive. In: Proceedings of the 5th ACM international Symposium on Mobile Ad-hoc Networking and Computing. (2004) 163–174
10. Bruns, G., Godefroid, P.: Model checking partial state spaces with 3-valued temporal logics. Lectures Notes in Computer Science **1633** (1999) 274–287
11. Larsen, K.G., Thomsen, B.: A modal process logic. In: Proceedings of the 3rd Annual Symposium on Logic in Computer Science, Edinburgh, United Kingdom (1988) 203–210
12. Pazos-Arias, J.J., García-Duque, J.: SCTL-MUS: A formal methodology for software development of distributed systems. A case study. Formal Aspects of Computing **13** (2001) 50–91
13. Kleene, S.C.: Introduction to Metamathematics. Volume 1 of Bibliotheca Mathematica. North-Holland (1952)

14. Huth, M.R.A., Jagadeesan, R., Schmidt, D.A.: A domain equation for refinement of partial systems. Mathematical Structures in Computer Science **14** (2004) 469–505
15. Banach, R., Poppleton, M.: Retrenching partial requirements into system definitions: A simple feature interaction case study. Requirements Engineering **8**(4) (2003) 266–288
16. Swamy, G.: Incremental methods for formal verification and logic synthesis. PhD thesis, University of California at Berkeley (1996) UMI publication 9723211.
17. Mäkinen, E., Systä, T.: MAS – an interactive synthesizer to support behavioral modelling in UML. In: Proceedings of the 23rd International Conference on Software Engineering, Toronto, Canada (2001) 15–24
18. Uchitel, S., Kramer, J.: A workbench for synthesising behaviour models from scenarios. In: Proceedings of the 23rd International Conference on Software Engineering, Toronto, Canada (2001) 188–197
19. Sokolsky, O.V., Smolka, S.A.: Incremental model checking in the modal μ-calculus. Lecture Notes in Computer Science **818** (1994) 351–363
20. Clarke, E.M., Grumberg, O., Jha, S., Lu, Y., Veith, H.: Progress on the state explosion problem in model checking. In: Informatics - 10 years back, 10 years ahead. Springer (2001) 176–194
21. Fernández-Vilas, A., Pazos-Arias, J.J., Gil-Solla, A., Díaz-Redondo, R.P., García-Duque, J., Barragáns-Martínez, B.: Incremental specification with SCTL/MUS-T: A case study. Journal of Systems and Software **70**(2) (2004) 189–208
22. Alur, R., Dill, D.L.: A theory of timed automata. Theoretical Computer Science **126**(2) (1994) 183–235
23. Braun, P., Rossak, W.: Mobile agents. Morgan Kaufmann (2005)
24. Easterbrook, S., Chechik, M.: A framework for multi-valued reasoning over inconsistent viewpoints. In: Proceedings of the 23rd International Conference on Software Engineering. (2001)
25. Ball, T., Naik, M., Rajamani, S.: From symptom to cause: Localizing errors in counterexample traces. In: Proceedings of the 30th Annual ACM Symposium on Principles of Programming Languages. (2003) 97–105
26. Gurfinkel, A., Chechik, M.: Generating counterexamples for multi-valued model-checking. In: Proceedings of the 12th International Symposium on Formal Methods, Pisa, Italy (2003) 503–521
27. Rappaport, T.: Wireless communications: Principles and practice. Prentice Hall (2002)
28. Zhao, W., Amma, M.: Message ferrying: proactive routing in highly-partitioned wireless ad hoc networks. In: Proceedings of the 9th IEEE Workshop on Future Trends of Distributed Computing Systems. (2003)
29. García-Duque, J., Pazos-Arias, J.J., Barragáns-Martínez, B.: An analysis-revision cycle to evolve requirements specifications by using the SCTL-MUS methodology. In: Proceedings of the 10th IEEE International Conference on Requirements Engineering, Essen, Germany (2002) 282–288
30. López-Nores, M., Pazos-Arias, J.J., García-Duque, J., Barragáns-Martínez, B.: An agile approach to support incremental development of requirements specifications. In: Proceedings of the IEEE Australian Software Engineering Conference, Sydney, Australia (2006)
31. Hunter, A.: Reasoning with contradictory information using quasi-classical logic. Journal of Logic and Computation **10**(5) (2000) 677–703
32. Nuseibeh, B., Easterbrook, S., Russo, A.: Making inconsistency respectable in software development. Journal of Systems and Software **58**(2) (2001) 171–180
33. Barragáns-Martínez, B., Pazos-Arias, J., Fernández-Vilas, A.: On measuring levels of inconsistency in multi-perspective requirements specifications. In: Proceedings of the 1st International Conference on the Principles of Software Engineering, Buenos Aires, Argentina (2004) 21–30

A Logical View of Choreography

Carlo Montangero and Laura Semini

Dipartimento di Informatica, Università di Pisa

Abstract. We present a model for choreography à la WS–CDL and formalize it in ΔDSTL(x), a spatio–temporal logic for the specification and verification of global computing systems. The approach builds on the formalization of an atomic interaction and defines composition rules to describe complex choreographies.

The logic permits to reason on the choreography formalization and to derive the properties of interest. A pleasant characteristics of the proposed approach is that the composition of formulae, corresponding to a choreography, results in a formula shaping as an atomic interaction formula. Therefore, the properties of complex choreographies can be uniformly described as interactions.

We demonstrate the approach using a business scenario already tackled in the literature.

1 Introduction

Service-oriented computing (SOC) is strongly influencing the way distributed software applications are designed and developed. Services are autonomous and heterogeneous computational entities that may be running on different platforms and/or owned by different organizations. Applications are built as networks of collaborating services distributed within and across organizational boundaries. The tenets of the SOC approach are the service description languages and the protocols for service publishing and discovering. Besides, the so–called *orchestrators* are used to coordinate the interaction among collaborating services. Finally, the global view of the interactions are described by the so–called *choreographies*. A thorough discussion of the differences between choreography and orchestration can be found in [4] and [14].

Much work has been carried out and much is still going on under the coordination of standard organizations like W3C and OASIS, to define a technological platform for SOC. The most important results are the orchestration language WS–BPEL [12] and the choreography language WS–CDL [15]. Both builds on the WebServices standard for service description WSDL [16].

WSDL defines the interface a Web service exhibits: other services can invoke it via this interface. An interface defines a set of *operations* by an XML schema. The most interesting kinds of operations are *one–way* and *request-response*. In the former only the incoming message is defined. In the latter both the incoming message and the response one are defined.

In WS–CDL a choreography is in essence a pair: a set of roles, describing the involved entities, and a set of interactions among the roles. The basic building

P. Ciancarini and H. Wiklicky (Eds.): COORDINATION 2006, LNCS 4038, pp. 179–193, 2006.

blocks are the primitives for expressing an interaction with a one–way operation or with a request–response operation. Then, interactions can be composed via sequence, parallel and choice operators to build full fledged choreographies. However, such proposals remain at the descriptive level, and do not provide any kind of reasoning mechanisms. There are a few formalization proposals that follow an operational approach, exploiting variations of process calculi [3, 11].

In this paper we present a first contribution towards a logical framework for SOC: we introduce a logical view of choreography, formalizing the WS–CDL approach. The final goal is to have also a formalization of the WS–BPEL approach to orchestration, and link the two by a refinement relationship, so that the behaviour of the peers and that of the overall system can be designed hand-in-hand, with the proof support offered by the logic. A similar approach is being pursued in an operational setting by [11], exploiting a bisimilarity notion to link orchestration and choreography.

In our approach, we characterize a choreography as a pair: a logical theory that expresses all the properties of the choreography, and a *black box view*, i.e. a formula holding in the theory which gives an abstract view of the behaviour of the choreography. More precisely, the black box view relates the conditions that enable the choreography in the initial state to the conditions holding in its final state. We call these pre– and post–conditions *triggers* and *consequences*, respectively. We exploit the spatial features of ΔDSTL(x) to specify triggers and consequences, and the temporal features to link triggers and consequences. The shape of the black box view is the same for elementary interactions and for complex choreographies. Indeed, thanks to the expressiveness of the spatial facet of ΔDSTL(x), it is natural to express conditions in the initial and final states, even if these states are distributed and pertain to different roles. We start by characterizing the elementary interactions (one–way and request– response) as choreographies, and then we provide rules to compose choreographies in sequence, parallel and choice. We also show how to exploit variables to deal with dynamic channel passing.

Compositions are monotonic, in the sense that all the properties holding for the composing choreographies also hold (modulo a sistematic transformation in the case of choice) in the composed one: in particular all the black box views of the components express properties of the composed choreography.

2   The Logic

Our long term research goal is logical reasoning on systems based on asynchronous communication [8, 7]. We defined a Distributed States Temporal Logic (ΔDSTL(x)), whose pragmatic aim is to ease the expression of properties in a setting of growing interest. The logic permits to name system components and to causally relate properties which might hold in distinguished components, in an asynchronous setting. A typical formula is $m\,p$ LEADS_TO $n\,q \wedge m\,w$ where the operator LEADS_TO is similar to Unity's $\mapsto$ (leads to) [5], and m, n express locality. The formula says that a property p holding in component m, causes properties

q and w to hold in future states of components n and m, respectively. Future has to be intended as the partial order relationship defined by state transitions and communications. An example model is the computation in Figure 1.

For reasons of space, we present here only a fragment of the logic. Full presentation and discussion are given in [9, 10].

2.1 Syntax

We assume a denumerable set of component names $\{m, n, m_1, m_2, \ldots\}$, and a denumerable set of variables, which includes the set of component variables, $\{M, N, M_1, M_2, \ldots\}$.

We introduce location modalities for each component in a system: we use component names, with a different font. For instance, $\mathsf{m_1}$ is the location modality corresponding to component m_1, and $\mathsf{m_1} Iam(m_1)$ stands for "in component m_1, $Iam(m_1)$ holds". We let quantifiers range over modalities, and M , N , M_i ... are location modality variables. Binding between location variables and regular variables is possible. For example, saying that for all M, $M Iam(M)$ holds, means that for all components m_i, $\mathsf{m_i} Iam(m_i)$ holds. Quantification over modality variables is done in a standard way, following, for instance [6].

$$F ::= A \mid \perp \mid \sim F \mid F \wedge F' \mid \mathsf{M_i} F$$
$$\psi ::= F \mid F \text{ leads\_to } F' \mid F \text{ because } F'$$

The first equation defines distributed state formulae, which are used to build $\Delta\text{DSTL(x)}$ formulae: A is an atom, $\perp$ is the propositional constant *false*. With $\bar{\mathsf{M}}_i$ we denote the dual of $\mathsf{M_i}$, i.e., $\bar{\mathsf{M}}_i F \equiv \sim \mathsf{M_i} \sim F$. With $\top$ we denote *true*, i.e. $\top \equiv \sim \perp$.

The second equation defines $\Delta\text{DSTL(x)}$ formulae. They are implicitly universally quantified, and all variables appearing in the consequences of a formula must be bound by the formula premises. For instance, $\mathsf{m}\, p(x, S)$ leads_to $S\, q(x)$, is implicitly prefixed by $\forall S, x$. The domain over which a variable is quantified (i.e. its sort) can be understood from the context or explicitly defined. We assume that these domains are invariant during time and in space.

The following sections informally present the semantics of the logic. The formal definitions are in [9, 10].

2.2 Models

The key characteristic of the logic is a novel semantic domain: the Kripke models are built on worlds that are arbitrary sets of computation states, rather than single states or tuples of them (one for each component), as it is normally proposed.

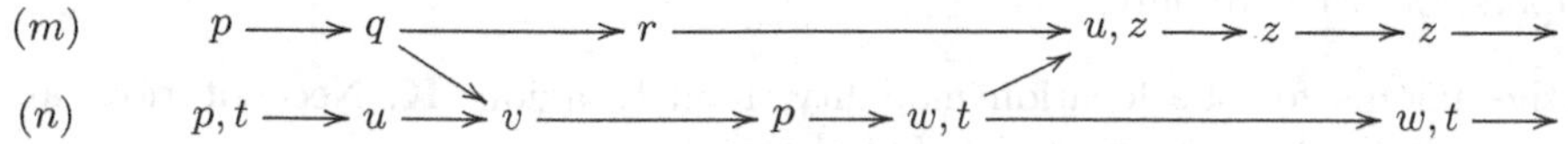

Fig. 1. An example model for $\Delta\text{DSTL(x)}$ formulae

A computation is an n–partite directed acyclic graphs like the one in Figure 1, which describes the computation of a system with two components. Here, p, q, ... are the properties holding in the states, arrows from a component to another denote communications, and arrows in one component denote local state transitions, as the computation progresses locally.

We call S_i the set of states of component m_i, and S the set of all the states of the computation. A *distributed state* is any subset ds of S, i.e. any set of states, and ds^0 is the set of the initial states. We say that ds *follows* ds' if and only if each state in ds' is followed by a state in ds, and each state in ds is preceded by a state in ds', where a state s follows s' if and only if there is a path in the model graph from s to s'. Symmetrically, we define ds *precedes* ds'.

2.3 Semantics by Examples

F a distributed state formula is also a $\Delta DSTL(x)$ formula, with the meaning of being an invariant: all distributed states (in particular all the singletons, i.e. all the computation states) must satisfy the formula.

For instance, $\bar{o}v \vee \bar{o} \sim v$ means that, chosen an arbitrary distributed state ds either all the states in ds belonging to component o satisfy v or they satisfy $\sim v$. A particular distributed state is S_o, the set of states of component o. Hence either v or $\sim v$ are invariants of o.

A distributed state ds satisfies the distributed state formula mF iff ds contains a singleton state of component m satisfying F. Consider, in figure 1, the distributed state ds composed of the first two states of m: ds satisfies mp, mq, and $mp \wedge mq$. On the contrary, ds does not satisfy $m(p \wedge q)$: no singleton state satisfies the conjunction.

F LEADS_TO F' means that F is always followed by F': each distributed state satisfying F is followed by a distributed state satisfying F'. Operator LEADS_TO expresses a liveness condition, and is similar to Unity's $\mapsto$ (leads to).

F BECAUSE F' says that F must be preceded by F': BECAUSE is a safety operator, used to express "only if" temporal conditions. Formally, a system satisfies F BECAUSE F' if and only if each distributed state that satisfies F is preceded by a distributed state satisfying F'.

2.4 Design Methodology and Tools

Our design methodology is based on refinements [2], and the refinement relation between two logical theories corresponds to logical deduction. MaRK, our proof assistant [7] that partially automates the verification process, is a valuable tool supporting the refinement process, making it feasible to avoid error prone "by hand" arguments. Axioms and rules of the logic were presented in our previous papers, we list here only:

– the axioms for the location modality, namely axiom **K**, Necessitation, and three axioms characterizing distributed states:

DSL1 : $\bar{\mathsf{M}}(\bar{\mathsf{M}}F \leftrightarrow F)$ **DSL2** : $\mathsf{M} \neq \mathsf{N} \rightarrow \bar{\mathsf{M}}\bar{\mathsf{N}}\bot$ **DSL3** : $(\forall M\, \bar{\mathsf{M}}p) \; \leftrightarrow \; p$

– the axioms and rules of LEADS_TO relevant for this paper. Corresponding rules hold for BECAUSE, just replace LEADS_TO with BECAUSE.

$$\frac{F \text{ LEADS\_TO } F' \quad F' \text{ LEADS\_TO } G}{F \text{ LEADS\_TO } G} \; LTR \qquad \frac{G \rightarrow F \quad F \text{ LEADS\_TO } F' \quad F' \rightarrow G'}{G \text{ LEADS\_TO } G'} \; LSW$$

$$\frac{F \text{ LEADS\_TO } G \quad F' \text{ LEADS\_TO } G}{F \vee F' \text{ LEADS\_TO } G} \; LPD \qquad \frac{G \text{ LEADS\_TO } F \quad G \text{ LEADS\_TO } F'}{G \text{ LEADS\_TO } F \wedge F'} \; LCC$$

2.5   OLTO

It is useful in this paper to express liveness and safety conditions paired, i.e. to say that in a model both F LEADS_TO G and G BECAUSE F hold. To this purpose, we introduce operator OLTO , which reads *only leads to*. The following rules hold:

$$\frac{F \text{ LEADS\_TO } G \quad G \text{ BECAUSE } F}{F \text{ OLTO } G} \; \text{OLTO\_I}$$

$$\frac{F \text{ OLTO } G}{F \text{ LEADS\_TO } G} \; \text{OLTO\_E1} \qquad \frac{F \text{ OLTO } G}{G \text{ BECAUSE } F} \; \text{OLTO\_E2}$$

$$\frac{F \text{ OLTO } G \quad G \text{ OLTO } H}{F \text{ OLTO } H} \; \text{OLTO\_TR}$$

$$\frac{F \text{ OLTO } F' \quad G \text{ OLTO } G'}{F \wedge G \text{ OLTO } F' \wedge G'} \; \text{OLTO\_}\wedge \qquad \frac{F \text{ OLTO } F' \quad G \text{ OLTO } G'}{F \vee G \text{ OLTO } F' \vee G'} \; \text{OLTO\_}\vee$$

3   The Logical View

Definition 1. *We say that a formula is in canonical form if it shapes*

$$F \text{ OLTO } F'$$

Definition 2. *Let C be a choreography, T a logical theory, and ϕ a formula in canonical form. By*

$$C : T \vdash \phi$$

we mean $T \vdash \phi$ is the logical view of C. We also say that C is described by T and it is abstracted by its black box view ϕ. As the notation suggests, we require that ϕ can be derived from T.

The idea is that any choreography has a trigger state, and a consequence. Formula ϕ abstracting a choreography, relates trigger and consequence. This holds for the single interactions, as well as for complex choreographies. Using a UML like notation, we draw:

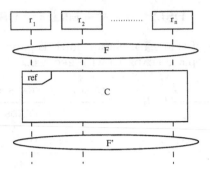

to say that F is the trigger of C, and F' are the consequences. Using the logic, we say that F OLTO F' is the formula abstracting C.

An interaction is the exchange of messages between roles, and represent the basic building block of any choreography. An interaction can be one–way interaction (the sending of single message) or a request–response:

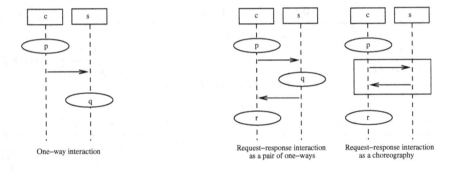

One–way interaction   Request–response interaction   Request–response interaction
                             as a pair of one–ways   as a choreography

We build on the logical view of a one–way interaction to define a describing theory and a black box view for request–response, i.e. its logical view. Then, recursively, we can build the logical view of any choreography.

Let p be a property holding in role c, acting as a trigger for the one–way interaction, and let q be a property of s, consequence of the interaction. Then we say:

$$\mathcal{ONE-WAY} : \{ \text{c } p \text{ OLTO s } q \} \vdash \text{c } p \text{ OLTO s } q$$

Remark 3. In the very basic case the describing theory coincides with its black box view. From now on, to enhance readability of the basic interactions, not to repeat the formula twice, we simply write $C : \phi$.

Now consider request–response as a pair of interactions, where the receipt of the request acts as trigger for the response. We have:

$$\mathcal{REQUEST} : \text{c } p \text{ OLTO s } q$$
$$\mathcal{RESPONSE} : \text{s } q \text{ OLTO c } r$$
$$\mathcal{REQ-RESP} : \{ \text{c } p \text{ OLTO s } q, \text{ s } q \text{ OLTO c } r \} \vdash \text{c } p \text{ OLTO c } r$$

Following CL [4], we depart from WS–CDL with respect to the request-response operations, and we consider as primitives the single interactions, i.e the request and the response. In this way it is easier to express how a choreography can implement a service, enhancing the support for the definition of complex services out of simpler ones. Obviously, the choreographer can restrict himself, and always use request-response pairs in a strict sequence à la WS–CDL.

As an example, consider the case of two nested request–response: a client c invoking a service s, which in turn invokes s' to build the response. The choreography, call it $\mathcal{NESTED}$, can be illustrated as follows:

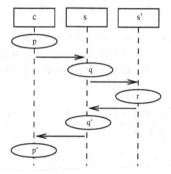

and has the following logical view:

$$\mathcal{NESTED}: \left\{ \begin{array}{l} c\ p\ \text{OLTO}\ s\ q,\ s\ q\ \text{OLTO}\ s'\ r \\ s'\ r\ \text{OLTO}\ s\ q',\ s\ q\ \text{OLTO}\ c\ p' \end{array} \right\} \vdash c\ p\ \text{OLTO}\ c\ p'$$

We can now show how model the WS–CDL composition operators, i.e. how to build the logical view of any choreography. We do it in a recursive manner, building on the logical view of the basic interaction, and defining sequence, choice, parallel, and dynamic passing of channel values.

In the following paragraphs we will compose pairs of choreographies. These can involve disjoint, overlapping, or coincident sets of roles as in the figures below.

The rules to compose logical views are independent of the various cases. For simplicity, in the next paragraphs, we will only exhibit pictures for overlapping roles.

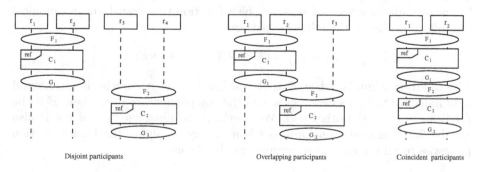

Disjoint participants   Overlapping participants   Coincident participants

Interaction. In the general case, an interaction can be triggered by a distributed formula, and have distributed consequences, hence:

$$\mathcal{INTERACTION} : \ F \ \text{OLTO} \ F'$$

where F and F' are distributed state formulae.

Sequence. Let $\mathcal{C}_1$ and $\mathcal{C}_2$ be choreographies, with logical views:

$$\mathcal{C}_1 : \ T_1 \vdash F_1 \ \text{OLTO} \ G_1$$
$$\mathcal{C}_2 : \ T_2 \vdash F_2 \ \text{OLTO} \ G_2$$

The sequencing of $\mathcal{C}_1$ and $\mathcal{C}_2$ is possible if the consequences of $\mathcal{C}_1$ coincide with the trigger of $\mathcal{C}_2$ as in the request–response, or more in general if an OLTO relation holds between them. Hence the new formula in the describing theory. The rule is sound by transitivity.

$$\frac{\mathcal{C}_1 : \ T_1 \vdash F_1 \ \text{OLTO} \ G_1 \qquad \mathcal{C}_2 : \ T_2 \vdash F_2 \ \text{OLTO} \ G_2}{(\mathcal{C}_1; \ \mathcal{C}_2) : \ T_1 \cup T_2 \cup \{G_1 \ \text{OLTO} \ F_2\} \vdash F_1 \ \text{OLTO} \ G_2}$$

The union of theories does not lead to inconsistencies, as discussed in Section 3.1.

Parallel. Let $\mathcal{C}_1$ and $\mathcal{C}_2$ be choreographies. Their parallel composition is described by the union of the theories, and abstracted by a formula where the trigger is the conjunction of the triggers, and the consequence the conjunction of the consequences. The rule is sound thanks to OLTO $\_\wedge$.

$$\frac{\mathcal{C}_1 : \ T_1 \vdash F_1 \ \text{OLTO} \ G_1 \qquad \mathcal{C}_2 : \ T_2 \vdash F_2 \ \text{OLTO} \ G_2}{(\mathcal{C}_1 \parallel \mathcal{C}_2) : \ T_1 \cup T_2 \vdash (F_1 \wedge F_2) \ \text{OLTO} \ (G_1 \wedge G_2)}$$

Choice. Let $\mathcal{C}_1$ and $\mathcal{C}_2$ be choreographies. We want to derive the logical view of the choice between them. Choice is intended to be exclusive, which, in a logical perspective means that either the trigger of $\mathcal{C}_1$ or the trigger of $\mathcal{C}_2$ hold, but not both of them. To the purpose, we introduce a discriminating oracle, i.e. a component (belonging to the roles of the two choreographies or not) where a given predicate, say v is always true or always false. The oracle o is described by the formula $\bar{o}v \vee \bar{o}{\sim}v$. Now, let t_E^o be a function that transforms a canonical formula according to the following pattern:

$$t_E^o(F \ \text{OLTO} \ F') = (F \wedge \bar{o}E) \ \text{OLTO} \ (F' \wedge \bar{o}E)$$

The resulting formula, when E is the predicate v of an oracle, is meaningful only in half of the possible models, and the complementary one, where E is the predicate $\sim v$, in the other half. We overload the notation t_E^o and use it also for the function that transforms a whole theory, applying the transformation piecewise to all the canonical formulae in the theory.

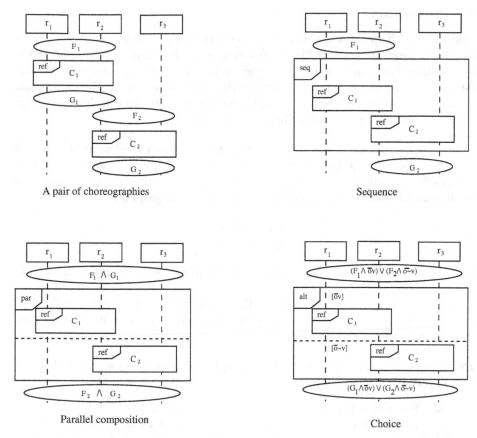

A pair of choreographies Sequence

Parallel composition Choice

Fig. 2. Sequence, parallel composition, and choice between two choreographies

Assume again C_1 and C_2 as above. The following rule is sound thanks to OLTO $\_\vee$.

$$\frac{C_1 : T_1 \vdash F_1 \text{ OLTO } G_1 \qquad C_2 : T_2 \vdash F_2 \text{ OLTO } G_2}{\begin{array}{c}(C_1 + C_2) : t_v^o(T_1) \cup t_{\sim v}^o(T_2) \cup \{\bar{o}v \vee \bar{o} \sim v\} \vdash \\ [(F_1 \wedge \bar{o}v) \vee (F_2 \wedge \bar{o} \sim v)] \text{ OLTO } [(G_1 \wedge \bar{o}v) \vee (G_2 \wedge \bar{o} \sim v)]\end{array}}$$

The use of eclusive "or" might apparently look like a simpler solution. However, to preserve the correctness of the canonical formula, one need to relate F_1 with G_1 and F_2 with G_2. The indexing that is needed is a mechanism equivalent to the oracle, and would only add complexity to the logic.

Dynamic passing of channel values. We can model dynamic passing of channel values, by letting the recipient of an interaction to be a variable name. To this purpose, we use the location variables. The binding between normal variables and location variables permits to communicate recipient names with any interaction.

$$\mathcal{DYNAMIC} : \{c\ p(S) \text{ OLTO } S\ q\} \vdash c\ p(S) \text{ OLTO } S\ q$$

3.1   Discussion

Consistency. Note that the union of two overlapping theories could lead to ill-formed choreographies, for which there are no possible executions. E.g., the union of two formulae with overlapping triggers and contradictory consequences, like for instance $\bar{o}v$ and $\bar{o} \sim v$. It is obvious that the constraint in the choice rule does not lead to inconsistency. We note that there is the need to have different v for different choices, to make them independent.

Monotonicity. Choreography composition has a property of monotonicity, of a sort: essentially, the black box views ϕ_1 and ϕ_2 of the choreographies under composition still hold in the composed choreography, modulo the transformation in the case of choice. More precisely, given two choreographies

$$\mathcal{C}_1 : T_1 \vdash \phi_1$$
$$\mathcal{C}_2 : T_2 \vdash \phi_2$$

let T be the theory of $(\mathcal{C}_1 \text{ OP } \mathcal{C}_2)$, where OP is either ; or $\|$. We have $T \vdash \phi_1$ and $T \vdash \phi_2$.

Besides, if T is the theory of $(\mathcal{C}_1 + \mathcal{C}_2)$, we have $T \vdash t_v^o(\phi_1)$ and $T \vdash t_{\sim v}^o(\phi_2)$. That is, the properties of the composing choreographies still hold, once they have been tagged with the oracle.

Properties. The composition of choreographies enjoys some associativity and commutativity properties, namely:

$$\mathcal{C}_1; (\mathcal{C}_2; \mathcal{C}_3) \equiv (\mathcal{C}_1; \mathcal{C}_2); \mathcal{C}_3 \qquad \mathcal{C}_1 \| (\mathcal{C}_2 \| \mathcal{C}_3) \equiv (\mathcal{C}_1 \| \mathcal{C}_2) \| \mathcal{C}_3$$
$$\mathcal{C}_1 \| \mathcal{C}_2 \equiv \mathcal{C}_2 \| \mathcal{C}_1 \qquad \mathcal{C}_1 + \mathcal{C}_2 \equiv \mathcal{C}_2 + \mathcal{C}_1$$

Equivalence means that the sets of models are the same. The last equivalence holds modulo isomorphisms.

4   Example

We consider the example in [11], and derive the choreography's logical view. The example consists in a business scenario where a customer invokes a store service in order to buy a good and where, depending on the customer's credit card type (Visa or American Express), the store service invokes the respective payment service. After the payment is performed, the store service can send the response to the customer. At the end, the receipt from the credit card agency can be sent to the customer.

We first follow the formalization of [11], then, in Section 4.2 exploit the logical view of dynamic passing of channel names.

4.1   Modeling with Choice

The formal model for representing choreography in [11] consists of a declaration of roles and variables, and the formal description of the *conversation* between the roles, where a conversation is a message or a sequence, choice, or parallel composition of conversations.

Choreography is defined by introducing four roles: the customer c, the store service s, the Visa and American Express payment services v and ae, respectively, communicating as illustrated by the sequence diagram in the figure below.

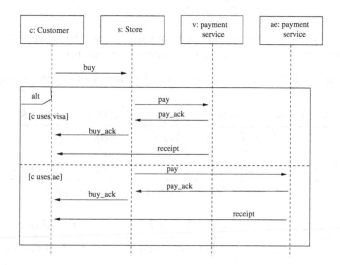

The basic interactions shown in the figure above are the following:

$$\mathcal{C}_1 : \quad c \; want\_to\_buy \; \text{OLTO} \; s \; buy$$
$$\mathcal{C}_2 : \quad s \; buy \; \text{OLTO} \; v \; pay$$
$$\mathcal{C}_3 : \quad v \; pay \; \text{OLTO} \; s \; pay\_ack$$
$$\mathcal{C}_4 : \quad s \; pay\_ack \; \text{OLTO} \; c \; buy\_ack$$
$$\mathcal{C}_5 : \quad v \; paid \; \text{OLTO} \; c \; receipt$$
$$\mathcal{C}_6 : \quad s \; buy \; \text{OLTO} \; ae \; pay$$
$$\mathcal{C}_7 : \quad ae \; pay \; \text{OLTO} \; s \; pay\_ack$$
$$\mathcal{C}_8 : \quad ae \; paid \; \text{OLTO} \; c \; receipt$$

Note that we systematically use the name of the message in the sequence diagram as the predicate for the consequence of the corresponding interaction. With respect to triggers, we use the consequences of an interaction as triggers for the next one, whenever they are in immediate sequence in the diagram, as in the case of the messages pay and pay_ack, and of pay_ack and buy_ack. Instead, we need to introduce an explicit trigger when there is not an incoming message that immediately precedes an outgoing one, as it happens for the first interaction of the customer, where we introduce $want\_to\_buy$, and for the $receipt$ message of the payment services, where we introduce $paid$.

The complete choreography for the business service is

$$\mathcal{C}_{bs} = \mathcal{C}_1 ; (\mathcal{C}_{visa} + \mathcal{C}_{ae})$$

where

$$\mathcal{C}_{visa} = (\mathcal{C}_2 ; \mathcal{C}_3 ; \mathcal{C}_4 ; \mathcal{C}_5)$$
$$\mathcal{C}_{ae} = (\mathcal{C}_6 ; \mathcal{C}_7 ; \mathcal{C}_4 ; \mathcal{C}_8)$$

and the choice is controlled by the customer c with oracle $\bar{c}\,visa \vee \bar{c} \sim visa$.

To compute the black box view, we proceed bottom–up.

Remark 4. In the following we write T_i for the theory of choreography $\mathcal{C}_i$.

$$\frac{\mathcal{C}_2 : \text{s } buy \text{ OLTO v } pay \qquad \mathcal{C}_3 : \text{v } pay \text{ OLTO s } pay\_ack}{\mathcal{C}_{23} : T_2 \cup T_3 \vdash \text{s } buy \text{ OLTO s } pay\_ack}$$

$$\frac{\mathcal{C}_{23} : T_2 \cup T_3 \vdash \text{s } buy \text{ OLTO s } pay\_ack \qquad \mathcal{C}_4 : \text{s } pay\_ack \text{ OLTO c } buy\_ack}{\mathcal{C}_{234} : T_2 \cup T_3 \cup T_4 \vdash \text{s } buy \text{ OLTO c } buy\_ack}$$

$$\frac{\mathcal{C}_{234} : T_2 \cup T_3 \cup T_4 \vdash \text{s } buy \text{ OLTO c } buy\_ack \qquad \mathcal{C}_5 : \text{v } paid \text{ OLTO c } receipt}{\mathcal{C}_{visa} : T_2 \cup T_3 \cup T_4 \cup T_5 \cup \{\text{c } buy\_ack \text{ OLTO v } paid\} \vdash \text{s } buy \text{ OLTO c } receipt}$$

Similarly we obtain

$$\mathcal{C}_{ae} : T_6 \cup T_7 \cup T_4 \cup T_8 \cup \{\text{c } buy\_ack \text{ OLTO ae } paid\} \vdash \text{s } buy \text{ OLTO c } receipt$$

We can now choose between the two payment services, with $\bar{c}\,visa \vee \bar{c} \sim visa$:

$$\frac{\mathcal{C}_{visa} : T_{visa} \vdash \text{s } buy \text{ OLTO c } receipt \qquad \mathcal{C}_{ae} : T_{ae} \vdash \text{s } buy \text{ OLTO c } receipt}{\begin{array}{l} \mathcal{C}_{ps} : t_{visa}^c(T_{visa}) \cup t_{\sim visa}^c(T_{ae}) \cup \{\bar{c}\,visa \vee \bar{c} \sim visa\} \vdash \\ \qquad [(\text{s } buy \wedge \bar{c}\,visa) \vee (\text{s } buy \wedge \bar{c} \sim visa)] \text{ OLTO} \\ \qquad [(\text{c } receipt \wedge \bar{c}\,visa) \vee (\text{c } receipt \wedge \bar{c} \sim visa)] \end{array}}$$

The logical view of $\mathcal{C}_{ps}$ can be simplified by propositional calculuss. Thus the last step:

$$\frac{\mathcal{C}_1 : \text{c } want\_to\_buy \text{ OLTO s } buy \qquad \mathcal{C}_{ps} : T_{ps} \vdash \text{s } buy \text{ OLTO c } receipt}{\mathcal{C}_{bs} : T_1 \cup T_{ps} \vdash \text{c } want\_to\_buy \text{ OLTO c } receipt}$$

We can exploit monotonicity to derive a property of example choreography, which has been discussed at some length in [11]: the customer receives both a confirmation from the payment service and a receipt. By monotonicity, the black box view of $\mathcal{C}_{234}$, s *buy* OLTO c *buy_ack*, also holds in the theory describing $\mathcal{C}_{visa}$. Hence we can derive that $\mathcal{C}_{visa}$ satisfies s *buy* OLTO (c *buy_ack* $\wedge$ c *receipt*).

Finally the sequencing of $\mathcal{C}_4$ and $\mathcal{C}_5$ ($\mathcal{C}_4$ and $\mathcal{C}_8$) entails c *buy_ack* OLTO c *receipt*, i.e. that the acknowledgment preceded the receipt.

4.2   Modeling with Dynamic Binding

Consider the following interactions

$$\mathcal{C}_1 : \text{c } want\_to\_buy(PS) \text{ olto s } buy(PS)$$
$$\mathcal{C}_2 : \text{s } buy(PS) \text{ olto PS } pay$$
$$\mathcal{C}_3 : \text{PS } pay \text{ olto s } pay\_ack(PS)$$
$$\mathcal{C}_4 : \text{s } pay\_ack(PS) \text{ olto c } buy\_ack(PS)$$
$$\mathcal{C}_5 : \text{PS } paid \text{ olto c } receipt(PS)$$

where the customer expresses his choice of payment service assigning a value to variable PS ($\mathcal{C}_1$), and the store uses this value to select the appropriate service ($\mathcal{C}_2$). $\mathcal{C}_3$ subsumes the payment interactions of the two services of the example in the previous section (there known as $\mathcal{C}_3$ and $\mathcal{C}_7$). The variable PS in the consequence of the black box view of $\mathcal{C}_3$ and in $\mathcal{C}_4$ keeps track of the payment service in use (visa or ae). Finally, $\mathcal{C}_5$ subsumes the receipt interactions $\mathcal{C}_5$ and $\mathcal{C}_8$ of the previous version, always keeping track of the payment service in use.

It is easy to verify that the black box view of $\mathcal{C}_1$; $\mathcal{C}_2$; $\mathcal{C}_3$; $\mathcal{C}_4$; $\mathcal{C}_5$ is

$$\text{c } want\_to\_buy(PS) \text{ olto c } receipt(PS)$$

its theory being

$$T_1 \cup T_2 \cup T_3 \cup T_4 \cup T_5 \cup \{\text{c } buy\_ack(PS) \text{ olto PS } paid\}$$

By monotonicity, also the following property holds:

$$\text{c } want\_to\_buy(PS) \text{ olto c } buy\_ack(PS) \wedge \text{c } receipt(PS)$$

5   Conclusions

The technological platform which is being developed for SOC includes a language (WS–CDL) to describe choreographies. However, these proposals remain at the descriptive level, and do not provide any kind of reasoning mechanisms.

In this paper we present a first contribution towards a declarative framework for SOC: we introduce a logical view of choreography, formalizing the WS–CDL approach. We start by formalizing the elementary interactions as choreographies, in terms of properties of their initial and final states. Then, we provide rules to compose choreographies in sequence, parallel and choice. Finally, we show how to deal with dynamic channel passing.

We characterize a choreography as a pair: a logical theory that keeps track of all the interactions, and a formula that gives an abstract view. The logic, $\Delta DSTL(x)$, shows spatial and temporal features. The formers permit to express conditions of the initial and final states of a choreography even if they are distributed (e.g. pertaining to different roles), the temporal features permit to temporally relate them.

Our final goal is to have also a formalization of the WS–BPEL approach to orchestration, and to assess the conformance by providing a refinement relation between the theories for choreography and orchestration, with the tool support offered by MaRK [7].

We used, in this paper a fragment of the logic. The full logic ΔDSTL(x) includes an *event* operator Δ [10]. We say that ds satisfies ΔF iff ds is a model for F, and the state ds' immediately preceding ds does not satisfy F. The use of a mix of events and conditions as in $m(\Delta F \wedge G)$, offers a straightforward way to express the premises of event–condition rules.

The ability to deal with events explicitly, and to use pairs event–condition as triggers, may enhance the expressivity and simplicity of logical specifications, and actually the interest for event–condition description is growing in the SOC community [1, 13].

Acknowledgments

The work was supported by the Software Engineering for Service-Oriented Overlay Computers (SENSORIA) project, an IST project funded by the European Union as an integrated project in the FP6 GC initiative.

References

1. J.J. Alferes, R. Amador, and W. May. A general language for evolution and reactivity in the semantic web. In *Principles and Practice of Semantic Web Reasoning (PPSWR'04)*, volume 3703 of *Lecture Notes in Computer Science*, pages 101–115, 2005.
2. R.J.R. Back and J. von Wright. *Refinement Calculus. A Systematic Introduction.* Graduate texts in computer science. Springer-Verlag, 1998.
3. A. Brogi, C. Canal, E. Pimentel, and A. Vallecillo. Formalizing Web Service Choreographies. In *First International Workshop on Web Services and Formal Methods (WSFM 2004)*, volume 105 of *ENTSC*. Elsevier, 2004.
4. N. Busi, R. Gorrieri, C. Guidi, R. Lucchi, and G. Zavattaro. Towards a formal framework for Choreography. In *International Workshop on Distributed and Mobile Collaboration (DMC 2005)*. IEEE Computer Society Press.
5. K.M. Chandy and J. Misra. *Parallel Program Design: A Foundation.* Addison-Wesley, Reading Mass., 1988.
6. T. Costello and A. Patterson. Quantifiers and operations on modalities and contexts. In A.G. Cohn, L. Schubert, and S.C. Shapiro, editors, *KR'98: Principles of Knowledge Representation and Reasoning*, pages 270–281. Morgan Kaufmann, San Francisco, 1998.
7. G. Ferrari, C. Montangero, L. Semini, and S. Semprini. Mark, a reasoning kit for mobility. *Automated Software Engineering*, 9(2):137–150, Apr 2002.
8. C. Montangero and L. Semini. Composing Specifications for Coordination. In P. Ciancarini and A. Wolf, editors, *Proc. 3nd Int. Conf. on Coordination Models and Languages*, volume 1594 of *Lecture Notes in Computer Science*, pages 118–133, Amsterdam, April 1999. Springer-Verlag.

9. C. Montangero and L. Semini. Distributed states logic. In 9th International Symposium on Temporal Representation and Reasoning (TIME'02), Manchester, UK, July 2002. IEEE CS Press.

10. C. Montangero, L. Semini, and S. Semprini. Logic Based Coordination for Event–Driven Self–Healing Distributed Systems. In R.De Nicola, G.Ferrari, and G. Meredith, editors, Proc. 6th Int. Conf. on Coordination Models and Languages, COORDINATION'04, volume 2949 of Lecture Notes in Computer Science, pages 248–262, Pisa, Italy, Feb. 2004. Springer-Verlag.

11. N.Busi, R.Gorrieri, C.Guidi, R. Lucchi, and G.Zavattaro. Choreography and Orchestration: A Synergic Approach for System Design. In ICSOC, volume 3826 of Lecture Notes in Computer Science, pages 228–240, Amsterdam, Dec 2005. Springer-Verlag.

12. OASIS. Web Services Business Process Execution Language Version 2.0. www.oasis-open.org/committees/download.php/16024/wsbpel-specification-draft-Dec-22-2005.htm.

13. G. Papamarkos, A. Poulovassilis, and P. T. Wood. Event–Condition–Action Rules on RDF Metadata in P2P Environments. In 2nd Workshop on Metadata Management in Grid and P2P Systems (MMGPS): Models, Services and Architectures, Dec. 2004. To be published in Elsevier Computer Networks journal, (October 2006).

14. Chris Peltz. Web services orchestration and choreography. IEEE Computer, 36(10): 46–52, 2003.

15. W3C. Web Services Choreography Description Language Version 1.0. www.w3.org/TR/ws-cdl-10/.

16. W3C. Web Services Description Language (WSDL) 1.1. www.w3.org/TR/wsdl.

Using LIME to Support Replication for Availability in Mobile Ad Hoc Networks

Amy L. Murphy[1] and Gian Pietro Picco[2]

[1] Faculty of Informatics, University of Lugano, Switzerland
amy.murphy@unisi.ch
[2] Dipartimento di Elettronica e Informazione, Politecnico di Milano, Italy
picco@elet.polimi.it

Abstract. Mobile ad hoc networks (MANETs) define a challenging computing scenario where access to resources is restrained by connectivity among hosts. Replication offers an opportunity to increase data availability beyond the span of transient connections. Unfortunately, standard replication techniques for wired environments mostly target improvements to fault-tolerance and access time, and in general are not well-suited to the dynamic environment defined by MANETs.

In this paper we explore replication for mobility in the context of a veneer for LIME, a Linda-based middleware for MANETs. This veneer puts into the hands of the application programmer control over what to replicate as well as a set of novel replication and consistency modes meaningful in mobile ad hoc networks. The entire replication veneer is built on top of the existing LIME model and implementation, confirming their versatility.

1 Introduction

Mobile ad hoc networks (MANETs) recently emerged as a technology enabling distributed computing in untethered scenarios. Typical applications exhibiting novel coordination patterns range from collaborative work in impromptu meetings to coordination of rescue teams in a disaster recovery setting. As MANETs are characterized by fluid topology and transient connectivity, they undermine the assumptions traditionally made by established distributed computing methods, algorithms, and technologies, and in many cases demand new solutions taking into account the *opportunistic* nature of communication in the mobile ad hoc environment.

In this paper we focus on the issue of data replication. In traditional distributed systems, replication is usually employed for fault tolerance or performance by exploiting, respectively, the redundancy and the locality of data copies. In a mobile environment, and especially in MANETs, replication achieves data availability by enabling access to the data beyond the span of a transient connection. Moreover, traditional replication schemes usually aim at providing a high degree of consistency in the way clients perceive access to replicas. Consistency protocols introduce synchronization and therefore communication and computational

P. Ciancarini and H. Wiklicky (Eds.): COORDINATION 2006, LNCS 4038, pp. 194–211, 2006.
© Springer-Verlag Berlin Heidelberg 2006

overhead, often make assumptions about the placement of replicas, and usually assume stable connectivity—characteristics that often clash with the requirements of MANET applications.

The work we present here tackles replication from a different angle. To begin with, the data we replicate are tuples belonging to a distributed tuple space system. More specifically, we developed our replication strategy as a veneer on top of the federated tuple space provided by LIME [18, 14, 21], a middleware we developed expressly for the MANET environment. In LIME, each mobile host[1] carries a local tuple space; an agent running on a given host is given access to a global, federated tuple space constituted by the "fusion" of all the tuple spaces belonging to the hosts in range. Therefore, in a mobile setting the content of this global tuple space changes dynamically based on the current connectivity.

In LIME, a tuple exists at a single location, and becomes available only for the time span during which the host carrying it is transiently connected to the rest of the system. Following what has been done in related work targeted to improving fault tolerance or access performance, one could support replication by copying tuples across machines and providing transparent, consistent access to them (e.g., by properly serializing read and write operations). As we mentioned, however, the available techniques need substantial adaptation to become usable in the MANET environment. Replicating the whole tuple space is likely to generate too much overhead, and keeping the tuple space consistent is hard if not impossible in the presence of hosts that can disconnect arbitrarily and possibly never reconnect.

Instead, our focus here is a simple and yet effective mechanism to increase data availability. We achieve this by providing the programmer with the ability to specify *replication profiles*, denoting the tuples of interest for the application. The underlying replication system exploits these profiles to opportunistically and automatically create a local replica whenever a matching tuple is encountered in the system. Differently from traditional replication systems, where replication is entirely transparent to the programmer, in our model the programmer is aware of whether a tuple is the original copy or a replica, as in the uncertain environment we target this information is often key in determining the confidence to be placed in the data being communicated. We do, however, provide guarantees about when a tuple is updated to a newer version, and provide options for specifying constraints on how this update is performed (e.g., only from the master copy or from any replica). Notably, replicating from replicated data instead of only from original data enables transitive models of coordination where replicas epidemically spread in the system, even if the master copy is not available.

In the work we present here, all these aspects are folded into the LIME application programming interface (API). This provides the programmer with the ability to query for and react to conventional tuples as well as replicas—and to do this in a distributed fashion regardless of connectivity, by exploiting the LIME federated tuple space. Moreover, our replication veneer is entirely built on top of

---

[1] LIME actually provides support for *both* mobile agents and hosts, therefore encompassing both logical and physical mobility.

the original LIME middleware, exploiting in particular its reactive features, and therefore providing additional evidence of LIME's versatility and expressiveness.

The paper is structured as follows. Section 2 provides the reader with the necessary background, by surveying related work and concisely illustrating the features of the LIME middleware. Section 3 illustrates the motivations behind our approach by leveraging our previously reported experience [13] in developing context-aware applications with LIME. Section 4 presents the replication model we define, together with the API provided to the programmer. Section 5 reports about the design and implementation of our replication veneer. Section 6 elaborates on the previous sections and highlights opportunities for alternative designs. Section 7 contains brief concluding remarks.

2   Background

In this section we first survey related work concerning replication applied to tuple space systems or in the mobile environment, and then provide a concise overview of the LIME model and middleware.

2.1   Related Work

With the growing interest in MANETs, strategies have been investigated for hoarding data and keeping it accessible when hosts are disconnected from data servers. Coda [12] was among the first hoarding systems, using user profiles to decide what to hoard and requiring user intervention for conflict resolution. Bayou [22] and IceCube [11] maintain consistency by logging changes and ensuring log serializability. Similarly, [2] proposes a middleware service for increasing data availability among groups of users according to user-specified profiles. It applies a conservative coherence protocol to ensure data is accessed consistently among group members in the presence of data updates and allows any member to update data as long as the object's unique consistency token is available. Instead, the work presented here is based on less constraining assumptions about the connectivity among hosts and thus their ability to reconcile inconsistent data. This choice simplifies the model, yet still addresses the needs of a wide range of applications where data availability is necessary even during disconnection.

In fixed networks, some distributed implementations of Linda investigated replication for fault tolerance [23, 1, 19] and strategies have been proposed for maintaining consistency among the distributed data [5]. All of these approaches assume that disconnection of a host is a failure and require extensive network communication to maintain data consistency. Both of these assumptions are fundamentally challenged by the MANET environment in which disconnection is an expected event and wireless communication is more constrained than wired communication.

Two interesting alternatives are GSpace [20] and PeerSpaces [3]. GSpace proposes a system-level framework for managing the trade-offs between replication for availability versus performance. PeerSpaces supports shared data spaces in the peer-to-peer environment and introduces replication for availability, but only for read-only data. Nonetheless, both systems target large scale networks, and are not applicable in MANET environments.

MobiSpaces [9] targets replication of tuple spaces among mobile devices and shares many goals with the work presented here. It allows replication from non-primary sources and accepts *interest profiles* from mobile users to control what data is replicated. However, The MobiSpaces assumes a single, master tuple space that serves as the primary holder of the data and determines the legal sequence of access to tuples based on a form of causal ordering. In contrast, our work assumes each mobile device can be the primary holder data and we do not assume any causal ordering semantics among access to tuples, keeping our semantics closer to the original Linda.

2.2   LIME: Linda in a Mobile Environment

The LIME model [18] defines a coordination layer for applications that exhibit logical and/or physical mobility, and has been embodied in a middleware [14] available as open source at http://lime.sourceforge.net. LIME borrows and adapts the communication model made popular by Linda [10].

In Linda, processes communicate through a shared *tuple space*, a multiset of tuples accessed concurrently by several processes. Each tuple is a sequence of typed parameters, such as <"foo",9,27.5>, and contains the actual information being communicated. Tuples are added to a tuple space by performing an **out**(t) operation. Tuples are anonymous, thus their removal by **in**(p), or read by **rd**(p), takes place through pattern matching on the tuple content. The argument p is often called a *template*, and its fields contain either *actuals* or *formals*. Actuals are values; the parameters of the previous tuple are all actuals, while the last two parameters of <"foo",?integer,?float> are formals. Formals act like "wild cards" and are matched against actuals when selecting a tuple from the tuple space. For instance, the template above matches the tuple defined earlier. If multiple tuples match a template, selection is non-deterministic.

Linda characteristics resonate with the mobile setting. Communication is implicit, and decoupled in *time* and *space*. This decoupling is of paramount importance in a mobile setting, where the parties involved in communication change dynamically due to migration, and hence the global context for operations is continuously redefined. LIME accomplishes the shift from a fixed context to a dynamically changing one by breaking up the Linda tuple space into many tuple spaces, each permanently associated to a mobile unit, and by introducing rules for transient sharing of the individual tuple spaces based on connectivity.

Transiently shared tuple spaces. In LIME, a mobile unit accesses the global data context only through a so-called *interface tuple space* (ITS), permanently and exclusively attached to the unit itself. The ITS, accessed using Linda primitives, contains tuples that are physically co-located with the unit and defines the only data available to a lone unit. Nevertheless, this tuple space is also *transiently shared* with the ITSs belonging to the mobile units currently accessible. Upon arrival of a new unit, the tuples in its ITS are logically merged with those already shared, belonging to the other mobile units, and the result is made accessible

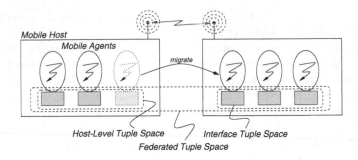

Fig. 1. Transiently shared tuple spaces encompass physical and logical mobility

through the ITS of each of the units. This sequence of operations, called *engagement*, is performed as a single atomic operation. Similarly, the departure of a mobile unit results in the *disengagement* of the corresponding tuple space, whose tuples are no longer available through the ITS of the other units.

Transient sharing of the ITS is a very powerful abstraction, providing a mobile unit with the illusion of a local tuple space containing tuples coming from all the units currently accessible, without any need to know them explicitly. Moreover, the content perceived through this tuple space changes dynamically according to changes in the system configuration.

The LIME notion of a transiently shared tuple space is applicable to a mobile unit regardless of its nature, as long as a notion of connectivity ruling engagement and disengagement is properly defined. Figure 1 shows how transient sharing may take place among mobile agents co-located on a given host, and among hosts in communication range. Mobile agents are the only active components, and the ones carrying a "concrete" tuple space; mobile hosts are just roaming containers providing connectivity and execution support for agents.

Operations on the transiently shared tuple space of LIME include those already mentioned for Linda, namely **out**, **rd**, and **in**, as well as the probing operations **rdp** and **inp** whose semantics is to return a matching tuple or return `null` if no matching tuple exists at the time the query is issued. For convenience LIME also provides the bulk operations **rdg** and **ing** that return a set of tuples that match the given pattern. If no matching tuples exist, the set is empty.

Restricting Operation Scope. The concept of transiently shared tuple space reduces the details of distribution and mobility to changes in what is perceived as a local tuple space. This view is powerful as it relieves the designer from specifically addressing configuration changes, but sometimes applications may need to address explicitly the distributed nature of data for performance or optimization reasons. For this reason, LIME extends Linda operations with scoping parameters, expressed in terms of agent or host identifiers, that restrict operations to a given projection of the transiently shared tuple space. For instance, $\mathbf{rd}[\omega, \lambda](p)$ looks for tuples matching p that are currently located at ω but destined to λ. LIME allows ω to be either a host or an agent, enabling queries over the entire host-level tuple space or only over the subset pertaining to a specific agent.

Reacting to changes. In the dynamic environment defined by mobility, reacting to changes constitutes a large fraction of application design. Therefore, LIME extends the basic Linda tuple space with a notion of *reaction*. A reaction $\mathcal{R}(s, p)$ is defined by a code fragment s specifying the actions to be performed when a tuple matching the pattern p is found in the tuple space. A notion of *mode* is also provided to control the extent to which a reaction is allowed to execute. A reaction registered with mode ONCE is allowed to fire only one time, i.e., it becomes automatically deregistered after its execution. Instead, a reaction registered with mode ONCEPERTUPLE is allowed to fire an arbitrary number of times, but never twice for the same tuple. Details about the semantics of reactions can be found in [15]. Here, it is sufficient to note that two kinds of reactions are provided. *Strong reactions* couple in a single atomic step the detection of a tuple matching p and the execution of s. Instead, *weak reactions* decouple the two by allowing execution to take place eventually after detection. Strong reactions are useful to react locally to a host, while weak reactions are suitable for use across hosts, and hence on the entire transiently shared tuple space.

LIME provides a number of additional features, including the ability to output a tuple into the tuple space of a different agent with the **out**$[\lambda](t)$ operation, and to obtain information about the host, agents, and tuple spaces currently present in the system through a specialized LimeSystem tuple space. However, as these and other features are not central to the work described here, we redirect the reader interested in a comprehensive description to [15], which also includes a formal semantics of the LIME model.

3   A Motivating Example

In this section we discuss the motivation behind our particular approach to improving data availability through replication by leveraging off our previously reported experience [13] with the LIME tuple space primitives to develop context-aware applications.

In [13] we discussed the design of TULING, a location-aware application supporting collaborative exploration of geographical areas, e.g., to coordinate the help in a disaster recovery scenario. Users are equipped with portable computing devices and a localization system (e.g., GPS), are freely mobile, and are transiently connected through ad hoc wireless links. The key functionality provided is the ability for a user to request the visualization of the current location and/or trajectory of any other user, provided wireless connectivity is available towards her. Additionally, applicative data (e.g., images or notes) can be annotated with location information before being stored in the tuple space, and therefore searched based on context. The implementation exploits tuple spaces as repositories for context information—i.e., location data in this case. The LIME primitives are used to seamlessly perform queries not only on a local tuple space, but on all the spaces in range. For instance, a user's location can be determined by performing a **rdp** operation for the location tuple associated to the given user identifier. Similarly, reactions can be used to trigger some behavior when a user changes her location.

The thesis of the paper was simple and yet relevant: tuple spaces can be successfully exploited to store not only the application data needed for coordination, but also data representing the *physical context*. The advantage is the provision of a single, unified programming interface—the LIME coordination primitives—for accessing both forms of data, therefore simplifying the programmer's chore.

Nevertheless, the paper also elicited a number of shortcomings in the primitives and mechanisms traditionally provided by tuple space systems in general, and by LIME in particular. For instance, it evidenced how the matching by equality traditionally provided by Linda is not sufficiently expressive for context-aware applications. This observation provided the main motivation for a recent extension [17] to the LIGHTS tuple space engine [16] at the core of LIME.

Similarly, the motivation for the particular flavor of replication presented here can be found among the "lessons learned" we reported after developing TULING, as evident in the following excerpt (see [13], p. 276):

> Another feature to consider adding to LIME is replication. In TULING, the previous locations of the other components are effectively replicated at the application level, to enable their visualization. Location information, however, is not duplicated within the tuple space. Therefore, if A copies B's history, and then later meets C, the information about B is outside the tuple space and therefore not accessible to C. Several efforts in the mobile ad hoc community have looked at the issue of replication [...], but none of the solutions is immediately applicable to the tuple space environment.

This excerpt captures the essence of the problem. The reactive primitives provided by LIME can be used effectively to copy location information as soon as it becomes available through the federated space and carry on the associated behavior, but replication occurs *at the application level* and therefore does not enable further sharing of the information acquired. The desired scenario is instead the one shown in Figure 2.

Clearly, one could write a reaction reinserting the location tuple in the local tuple space, but care must be taken in "tagging" this copy so that it does not get reacted again, locally or remotely. Therefore, rather than simply build this behavior into TULING, we created an application-independent middleware layer on top of LIME to support this kind of replication. As we detail in the next section, the goal is to give users the ability to declare the patterns of tuples to be replicated, when and how to replicate, and whether and how the replica should be updated in the presence of new values.

Obviously, location is only one of the many kinds of data that is meaningful to replicate. Besides other contextual data (e.g., energy level, temperature, light, and so on), replication of application data is useful as well. For instance, TULING users can share images, e.g., pictures useful for a damage assessment of buildings in an earthquake scenario.

By using the features of our middleware, programmers can leverage replication in many ways. Not only can the programmer specify replication profiles such as *"replicate all pictures of buildings between the 5th and 7th avenue"*,

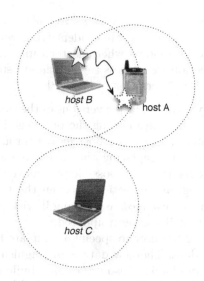 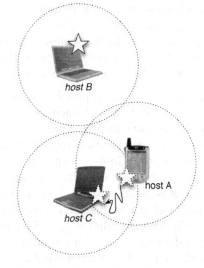

(a) A and B engage: B's tuple is replicated in A's tuple space.

(b) A disengages from B and engages with C: the replica of B's tuple is copied in C's tuple space.

Fig. 2. A motivating scenario. Dashed outlines indicate replicated data.

but she can also choose whether such pictures should be downloaded only from the user that took them or from anyone. The implications of what looks like a trivial choice are amplified by the integration of replication with the transiently shared tuple space abstraction provided by LIME. Indeed, in the first case our system implicitly supports a sort of "hoarding" [12] from information producers, which materializes the requested information in the tuple space of a potential consumer tuple space as soon as it becomes available in the system. In the second case, by allowing duplication from any replica, information can flow even in the absence of a connected path between its producer and its consumers, by "hopping" opportunistically from one machine to another whenever connectivity becomes available. This pattern of information dissemination, somewhat reminiscent of epidemic protocols [7], is more closely related to the disconnected transitive communication model explored in [4] and, more recently, by the networking community under the notion of *delay tolerant network* [8].

Therefore, besides enhancing data availability, our replication layer can be regarded (and exploited) as a building block for a different form of coordination that extends the transient communication enabled by LIME by removing the need for interacting parties to be present at the same time.

4   Replication Model and API

Throughout the development of the model and implementation, our goal was to put control over replication in the hands of the programmer while keeping the interface straightforward and easy to use. The primary issues to address are updating tuple contents to allow tuples to evolve over time, identifying what to replicate based on user input, and updating replicas when master tuples are updated and connectivity allows. In this section we address each of these issues as they relate to the model, concluding with a description of the API.

Updating tuples. Some applications logically create multiple versions of the same piece of information with each successive version invalidating the previous. For example, location data in TULING constantly changes as a host moves through space. Each new location represents an update, replacing the now-irrelevant previous location. In most tuple space systems, it is only possible to remove the old data and insert new data, losing any logical connection between the two. Instead, it is meaningful to allow the data to be *changed*, associating it with the old data and at the same time identifying that it has been updated.

This is precisely what we provide, allowing the user to specify a template for the old data together with the actual new data. The new data is distinguished from the old with a version number. This mechanism also serves as a building block upon which consistency between master and replicas is managed.

Identifying what to replicate. As our goal is to improve availability of data for users rather than to improve the performance of the system, our replication mechanism is driven by user input in the form of replication profiles. These are composed of the template specifying the tuples to be replicated, together with the replication and consistency modes controlling the replica creation and update.

As we discussed in Section 2.2, the scope of LIME operations can be restricted to the tuple space associated to a single host or agent, by properly setting the current and destination location of matching tuples. We provide a similar feature for replication, therefore enabling the programmer to to replicate matching data only if it belongs to the specified tuple space projection, e.g., tuples belonging to a given host. Alternately, this tuple location information can be left unspecified in the template, therefore enabling replication of tuples from any connected host. One notable exception, however, is that replication of local tuples is suppressed because it does not improve information availability.

Another dimension of the replication profiles is whether replicas should be made only from original data or also from replicas held by other users. Because no single policy holds for all applications, we place this decision in the hands of the programmer in the form of a *replication mode* as shown in Figure 3. Replication mode MASTER makes replicas *only* from the original data while mode ANY allows a replica to be made indifferently from the original or a replica.

To make this more concrete, consider an extension of the case outlined in Section 3 in which host A replicates B's location information and then later meets C. Without replication inside the tuple space information about B is not available to C, as in TULING. However, with the mechanism described here and replication mode ANY, this information is available as replica tuples carried inside A's tuple space. This enables transitive communication of data as shown in Figure 2(b) even though B and C have never been in communication range.

Updating replicas. When a tuple is updated, a new version is created that makes any replicas of this tuple out of date. If connectivity exists between the holder of the master tuple and the holder of the replica it is possible to update the replica to the new version, however this comes at the cost of the data transfer. Depending on the type of data, it is reasonable to keep the replica out of date or to update it. Location information, for example, is typically small and most useful if kept up to date. Large documents, instead, may remain useful even if they are slightly out of date. Therefore, our model allows the user to specify the policy for keeping replicated data consistent with the original. As shown in Figure 3, three possibilities are provided: NEVER, which never updates a replica, MASTER, which updates only from the master version of the tuple, and ANY, which updates from master or replica versions. If a replica is updated, its previous copy is deleted from the system.

To continue with the location example, by using replication mode ANY and consistency mode ANY at host A, when it engages with C as in Figure 2(b), C will have access to the most recently known location of B from when A and B were last connected. Although this is likely to be out of date with respect to the actual, current location of B, is it the best that can be done in the mobile environment with transient connections.

Replication API. For the programmer familiar with LIME, using replication requires minor changes to deal with extensions of tuple and template formats and new operations for dealing with replication profiles. The primary access to the tuple space is through an instance of the `ReplicableLimeTupleSpace`, as shown in Figure 4. The operations here retain the same meaning as in the original `LimeTupleSpace`, however the parameters are changed to deal with the additional information maintained for replication. Specifically, tuples, templates, and reactions have been replaced with their "replicable" counterparts, as seen in the figure.

For space reasons, we do not show the interfaces of all public classes here, however it is worth noting that the `ReplicableTemplate` allows the user to specify whether the tuple returned should be a MASTER, REPLICA, or ANY. Furthermore, `ReplicableTuple` exposes the `isMaster` method to allow the user to distinguish if the tuple returned from the tuple space is a master or not.

Reactions are also extended with respect to what available in LIME. Namely, when specifying a `ReplicableReaction` and a `ReplicableLocalizedReaction`, the user must identify the reaction mode. In addition to the ONCE mode which

Replication Mode	MASTER	The first replica must be made from the master
	ANY	The first replica can be made from any tuple
Consistency Mode	NEVER	Replicas must never be updated
	MASTER	Replicas must only be updated from their master
	ANY	Replicas can be updated from any newer version

Fig. 3. Replication and consistency modes

```
public class ReplicableLimeTupleSpace {
  public ReplicableLimeTupleSpace(String name);
  public boolean          setShared(boolean isShared);
  public ReplicableTuple  out(ITuple t);
  public ReplicableTuple  out(AgentLocation destination, ITuple t);
  public ReplicableTuple  in(ReplicableTemplate p);
  public ReplicableTuple  inp(ReplicableTemplate p);
  public ReplicableTuple[] ing(ReplicableTemplate p);
  public ReplicableTuple  rd(ReplicableTemplate p);
  public ReplicableTuple  rdp(ReplicableTemplate p);
  public ReplicableTuple[] rdg(ReplicableTemplate p);
  public ReplicableRegisteredReaction[] addStrongReaction(ReplicableLocalizedReaction[] rlr);
  public ReplicableRegisteredReaction[] addWeakReaction(ReplicableReaction[] rr);
  public void removeStrongReaction(ReplicableRegisteredReaction[] rrr);
  public void removeWeakReaction(ReplicableRegisteredReaction[] rrr);
  // REPLICATION-SPECIFIC OPERATIONS
  public ReplicableTuple        change(ReplicableTemplate p, ITuple t);
  public RegisteredReplicaRequest addReplicaRequest(LimeTemplate p,
                                                    int replicationMode,
                                                    int consistencyMode);
  public void                   removeReplicaRequest(RegisteredReplicaRequest r);
}
```

Fig. 4. The class `ReplicableLimeTupleSpace`

reacts one time before deregistering, we provide ONCEPERREPLICA and ON-CEPERCHANGE. The former allows the user to react one time for each tuple, but not for each version of that tuple. The latter reacts also to each version.

The `ReplicableLimeTupleSpace` offers three new methods not present in the `LimeTupleSpace` to support tuple updating and replication. The `change` method accepts as parameters the template of the tuple to change and the contents of the new tuple. If no tuple matches the template, no change is made to the tuple space. Similar to the `out` operation, `change` operates only on the *local* tuples contained in the tuple space of the agent issuing the operation. Moreover, only master tuples can be selected and changed. The last two methods, `addReplicaRequest` and `removeReplicaRequest` allow the user to activate replication for the specified replication profile (template, replication mode, and consistency mode), and stop it, respectively.

5   Design and Implementation

Implementing the replication model just described was accomplished as a combination of two application-level packages above LIME, requiring no changes to LIME itself. The two layers support tuple versioning and tuple replication, respectively. Internally, each layer is implemented as a wrapper around the lower layer. Specifically, the `VersionedLimeTupleSpace` wraps an instance of `LimeTupleSpace` and the `ReplicableLimeTupleSpace` of Figure 4 wraps a `VersionedLimeTupleSpace`. Each layer implements the operations visible to the user by adapting and delegating them to the layer below. It should be noted that in a federated system, all tuple spaces must be of the same type, e.g., it is not possible to federate a `LimeTupleSpace` with a `VersionedLimeTupleSpace`.

In this section we describe the key components of each layer, focusing primarily on the replication layer.

5.1 Versioning

The primary functionality of the versioning layer is to support the **change** operation, allowing tuples to be updated instead of replaced. This requires changes both to the tuple format and to the primary tuple space operations.

Tuple format. Versioning of tuples requires that the new version both be associated with the old and distinguished as newer. The former is accomplished by assigning a tuple identifier to each newly created tuple. This identifier is simply prepended to the user data before the tuple is passed to LIME. When a tuple is updated, the new version uses the same tuple identifier. To identify the relative newness of a tuple, we also insert a version number, incremented each time the tuple is changed. To clarify, if the user requests insertion of the tuple ⟨*data*⟩, the versioning layer creates the following and passes it to LIME:

$$\langle data \rangle \rightarrow \langle tupleID, versNum, data \rangle$$

Operations. To support updating tuples, the API is extended with the **change** operation, similar to that shown in Figure 4, accepting the template and new data as parameters. Internally, **change** is implemented by performing an **inp** on the embedded `LimeTupleSpace` to remove a tuple matching the pattern. If a tuple is returned, the versioning layer extracts the tuple identifier and version number, increments the version number, prepends both to the tuple, and issues an **out** to insert the new tuple.

Similar to `ReplicableLimeTupleSpace`, the `VersionedLimeTupleSpace` operations have been modified to accept "versioned" tuples and templates to address the tuple identifier and version number. Reactions have also been modified to use two new modes in addition to ONCE, namely ONCEPERID and ONCEPERVERSION to react only one time per tuple identifier, or one time to each version of each tuple. These reactions, with their enhanced modes, are actually the main building block for implementing replication, as described next.

5.2 Replication

Building replication on top of the versioning layer involved much the same process as implementing the versioning layer on top of LIME. It requires fields to be added to tuples and new operations to accept and implement replication profiles. The new operations, however, have already been described in Section 4: here, we describe their implementation.

Tuple format. The first design decision we faced was whether to keep the replica tuples in the same tuple space as the master tuples or to divide the two explicitly. We chose the former, opting to tag each tuple with a new field (*isReplica*) to distinguish whether it is a master or a replica. A nice side effect of this choice is that a query for a tuple without explicitly specifying replica or master requires only one operation, with the aforementioned field set to formal. Dividing the tuples would require issuing operations on both spaces.

In addition to the *isReplica* field, tuples are also extended with two fields representing the current and destination locations of the master tuple. To understand the need for these new fields, it is important to remember that LIME uses current and destination fields to identify the *current* location of a tuple and whether it should be migrated into the tuple space of a different, remote agent upon engagement. Because replica tuples are normal LIME tuples, location information is also maintained for all replica tuples internally to LIME. However, this information reflects the current and destination of the replica tuples, namely the agent that requested the replication, not the original location of the master tuple. Because the user may need to know this original location, we provide accessor methods on `ReplicableTuple` and append fields to all user tuples to represent the original current and destination locations of the master tuple as in the following:

$$\langle data \rangle \rightarrow \langle origCur, origDest, isReplica, data \rangle$$

Note how the tuple we obtain is then passed as a "data" tuple to the versioning layer where it gets extended with other fields, as described in Section 5.1.

Implementing replication. The core of the implementation is the internal mechanism used for replication. Our model requires creation and updating of replicas. Both operations occur in reaction to the appearance, in the federated tuple space, of new tuples matching the specified pattern and conforming to the replication and consistency modes. Therefore, implementing reaction with a set of (versioning-layer) reactions over master and replica tuples is a natural approach.

Implementing a replication request for a given profile involves installing a reaction watching for master tuples and, depending on the replication and consistency modes, possibly one for replica tuples as well. When the reaction fires with a new tuple, the listener for that reaction must take the appropriate action to keep the replicas inside the tuple space in line with the replication profile.

Consider, for instance, a case where the programmer requests a replication profile with a MASTER replication mode and a NEVER consistency mode. In this case, only the reaction watching for master tuples is needed, as subsequent versions are uninteresting. For the same reason, the corresponding listener needs to react each time a new master tuple is inserted, but not when it is updated. Therefore, the reaction (with the semantics defined in Section 5.1 for the versioning layer), must be installed with a ONCEPERID reaction mode. The reaction takes care of sending matching tuples from their owner to the requesting host when connectivity is available. However, LIME ensures also, through its engagement protocol, that the reaction is installed when hosts initially come into contact and that it remains enabled while the hosts are connected. Therefore, because LIME deals with the distribution and installation of listeners as connectivity changes, the replication layer can simply use this functionality, significantly reducing its own complexity.

To round out the other actions that must be taken to effect the various replication profiles, Figure 5 shows all combinations of the replication and consistency

Replication Mode	Consistency Mode	Master listener	Replica listener
MASTER	NEVER	*Keep*	—
MASTER	MASTER	Keep or update	—
MASTER	ANY	Keep or update	Discard if first, else update
ANY	NEVER	*Keep*	*Keep*
ANY	MASTER	Keep or update	Keep
ANY	ANY	Keep or update	Keep or update

Fig. 5. Implementing replication using reactions belonging to the versioning layer. For all combinations of replication and consistency mode, the listeners describe the actions performed when the reaction fires with a tuple on either a master or replica tuple. Italicized listeners are mode ONCEPERID, all others are ONCEPERVERSION.

modes and the actions of all listeners for master and replica tuples. The other listeners for master tuples differ from the one we just described because they must also update the replica if it already exists. Therefore, the listener "Keep or update" updates the replica tuple if it already exists, or creates one if not. The combination MASTER/ANY utilizes a third type of listener that does not allow creation of the first replica from another one, but instead uses replicas only to update existing ones. Finally, all the combinations requiring updates upon a change in version number utilize ONCEPERVERSION reactions in order to capture all updates.

6 Discussion

Our current implementation, albeit fully working according to the design just described, must be considered as a proof-of-concept prototype demonstrating the feasibility of our ideas. A number of improvements and additional features can be introduced, some of which are discussed in the following.

Communication overhead. The current implementation just described may generate unnecessary overhead when the network is dense and stable and many nodes requested the replication mode ANY. Consider a host joining the system with replication mode ANY. By virtue of engagement its replication reactions are propagated to the other hosts, where they are immediately evaluated and return any matching replicas the hosts possess. However, if in turn the replication mode on the other hosts is ANY as well, the same process unfolds in the opposite direction. This causes not only new replicas brought by the joining host to be communicated to the other hosts, but also the newly inserted replica to follow the same destiny. This last replica is most likely discarded, because it carries information already present in the network. In the scenarios mentioned above, this unnecessary extra step my cause a significant contribution to overhead.

A couple of points are worth making, however. First of all, in scenarios where the system contains many hosts enjoying rather stable connectivity, the replication mode ANY is bound to generate a lot of traffic anyway, since everybody is likely to be up-to-date with respect to the system. Consider an impromptu meeting: a replication mode MASTER is probably the best choice, allowing each meeting attendees to obtain a copy of the document as soon as the latter is published by its owner. Instead, the mode ANY is well-suited to address the sparse scenarios typical of many MANET applications, where very few nodes are connected at any given time but over time overall system connectivity is provided as a consequence of movement and opportunistic interaction. For instance, in a disaster recovery scenario the members of the exploration team may be connected only transiently and unpredictably, and yet be able to get the images and notes posted by fellow members without ever being connected with them, thanks to transitive replication of replicas of the original documents. As we pointed out in Section 3, these scenarios are similar to those targeted, at the network layer, by disconnected transitive communication [4] and delay tolerant networks [8].

From an implementation standpoint, it is worth saying that there are ways to remove the aforementioned extra communication. A quick-and-dirty solution is simply to timestamp replicas upon their insertion in the tuple space, and use this time information to defer its propagation by a time T, under the assumption that the rest of the system (from where it came in the first place) is already aware of it. The question is clearly how to set the deferring time T: values too small reduce the benefit of the optimization if the network is stable, while in dynamic scenarios values too high may prevent propagation of the replica to hosts that recently joined the system. More sophisticated mechanisms (e.g., piggybacking lists of reacted-upon replicas) can be implemented, but at the cost of building replication management directly into the LIME system. Indeed, our mechanism is based on LIME's ONCEPERTUPLE reactions, which are not aware of replication and simply react to the presence of a new tuple. In our current prototype we aimed instead at preserving the independence of the replication layer from the base middleware, in an effort to foster separation of concerns and modularity.

Ultimately, the need for more optimized communication must be weighed against the deployment scenario and the way applications use replication. We contend that the design and implementation we chose is appropriate for the assumptions made by the deployment scenario and application examples motivating this work, as well as for the "exploratory" goals of the research we report. Its exploitation in scenarios characterized by different assumptions may obviously require significant adaptation.

Automatic purging of local replicas. In the current implementation, replicated tuples are automatically inserted in the local tuple space, where they remain until the programmer expressly decides to remove them. This policy constitutes the most basic solution and meets the needs of simple applications. Nevertheless, in the presence of several replicas that need different treatment, their management may place considerable bookkeeping burden on the programmer.

Automatic purging can be easily defined by modifying `addReplicaRequest` to accept, in addition to replication and consistency mode, a "purge mode". For instance, the purge mode can be one of the values MANUAL, NUMBER, TIME.

MANUAL corresponds to the current strategy, while the other two modes allow purging of the tuple space based on an additional parameter, i.e., either the maximum number of replicas for the specified template or their maximum permanence time in the tuple space. The implementation of this additional functionality is straightforward, and consists of either modifying the replication listeners to keep track of a counter (NUMBER) or associating a timer to the replica (TIME).

Removal of the master copy. As we discussed in Section 3, our motivation for tackling replication was provided by applications where the data being replicated is continuously updated (e.g., location). As such, we did not include mechanisms for dealing with the removal of a master tuple, and accordingly remove the replicas in the system. Moreover, in a true MANET scenario no assumption can be made about the movement of hosts, which therefore can remain out for range after the tuple withdrawal has been performed, complicating—or completely preventing—the reconciliation of the distributed tuple space.

One way to achieve this functionality is through the notion of a "death certificate" [6] associated to the tuple. A simple implementation of this notion is to update the master tuple by nullifying the application data, while retaining the version identifier. Hosts becoming connected with the master's host would get a copy of the master tuple, but its nullified content would signal that the master has actually been withdrawn from the tuple space, and therefore the replica must be withdrawn as well.

In a MANET environment, however, there is no guarantee that all the hosts owning a replica eventually become again part of the system, thus receiving the death certificate. Interestingly, a replication mode ANY somewhat helps in this respect, as its ability to epidemically spread information may bypass disconnections. At the same time, however, it complicates matters since the master host has absolutely no control over the replication of its tuple, which can be duplicated from a different replica. Therefore, the master faces the option of either keeping the death certificate *ad infinitum*, or removing it after a given time but potentially leaving some hosts with an inconsistent view of the tuple space.

Future work will investigate more sophisticated schemes able to strike better tradeoffs by making different assumptions about the movement of hosts.

7   Conclusions

Replication is a well-studied topic in distributed system, often applied also in the case of coordination languages exploiting tuple spaces. Nevertheless, the motivations for exploiting replication are typically to improve fault-tolerance or access time to tuples, while preserving a consistent view of the tuple space.

In this work, we took a different angle motivated by the desire to exploit coordination in the highly dynamic and disconnected environment characterizing MANETs, where the preeminent reason for replication is to ensure availability of the replicated data in the face of disconnection. Consistency is less important, as it may be difficult if not impossible to provide if no assumption about the movement of hosts is made. This particular flavor of replication may also be effectively exploited as a new form of coordination, based on interactions that occur without the coordination parties ever being connected at the same time.

We made these observations concrete by describing how they can be incorporated in LIME, an existing coordination middleware for MANETs. We defined an appropriate replication model, extended the LIME API with replication primitives, and built replication mechanisms as a veneer on top of LIME.

Acknowledgments. The work described in this paper was partially supported by the Italian Ministry of Education, University, and Research (MIUR) under the VICOM project, by the National Research Council (CNR) under the IS-MANET project, and by the European Community under the IST-004536 RUNES project. The authors wish to thank Francesco Merlo and Massimo Montani for their implementation of the work described here.

References

1. D.E. Bakken and R. Schlichting. Supporting fault-tolerant parallel programming in Linda. *IEEE Transactions on Parallel and Distributed Systems*, 1994.
2. M. Boulkenafed and V. Issarny. A middleware service for mobile ad hoc data sharing, enhancing data availability. In *Proc. of the Int. Middleware Conf.*, 2003.
3. N. Busi, C. Manfredini, A. Montresor, and G. Zavattaro. PeerSpaces: Data-driven coordination in peer-to-peer networks. In *Proc. of ACM Symposium on Applied Computing (SAC)*. ACM Press, 2003.
4. X. Chen and A.L. Murphy. Enabling disconnected transitive communication in mobile ad hoc networks. In *Proc. of the Workshop on Principles of Mobile Computing (POMC)*, pages 21–27, Newport (RI, USA), August 2001.
5. A. Corradi, L. Leonardi, and F. Zambonelli. Strategies and protocols for highly parallel Linda servers. *Software: Practice and Experience*, 28(14):1493–1517, 1998.
6. A. Demers et al. Epidemic algorithms for replicated data management. In *Proc. of the 6th Symp. on Principles of Distributed Computing*, pages 1–12, 1987.
7. P. Eugster, R. Guerraoui, A.-M. Kermarrec, and L. Massoulié. From epidemics to distributed computing. *IEEE Computer*, 37(5):60–67, May 2004.
8. K. Fall. A delay-tolerant network architecture for challenged internets. In *Proc. of ACM SIGCOMM*, pages 27–34. ACM Press, 2003.
9. A. Fongen and S. J. E Taylor. MobiSpace: A Distributed Tuplespace for J2ME Environments. In 14th *IASTED Int. Conf. on Parallel and Distributed Computing and Systems*, Arizona, USA, 2005.
10. D. Gelernter. Generative Communication in Linda. *ACM Computing Surveys*, 7(1):80–112, Jan. 1985.
11. A.-M. Kermarrec, A. Rowstron, M.Shapiro, and P. Druschel. The IceCube approach to the reconciliation of divergent replicas. In 20th *Symp. on Principles of Distributed Computing (PODC)*, August 2001.
12. J.J. Kistler and M. Satyanarayanan. Disconnected Operation in the Coda File System. *ACM Trans. on Computer Systems*, 10(1):3–25, 1992.
13. A.L. Murphy and G.P. Picco. Using coordination middleware for location-aware computing: A LIME case study. In *Proc. of the 6th Int. Conf. on Coordination Models and Languages*, LNCS 2949, pages 263–278. Springer, February 2004.

14. A.L. Murphy, G.P. Picco, and G.-C. Roman. LIME: A Middleware for Physical and Logical Mobility. In *Proc. of the 21st Int. Conf. on Distributed Computing Systems (ICDCS-21)*, pages 524–533, May 2001.
15. A.L. Murphy, G.P. Picco, and G.-C. Roman. LIME: A coordination middleware supporting mobility of hosts and agents. *ACM Trans. on Software Engineering and Methodology (TOSEM)*, 2006. To appear. Available at www.elet.polimi.it/upload/picco.
16. G.P. Picco. LIGHTS Web page. lights.sourceforge.net.
17. G.P. Picco, D. Balzarotti, and P. Costa. LIGHTS: A Lightweight, Customizable Tuple Space Supporting Context-Aware Applications. In *Proc. of the 20th ACM Symposium on Applied Computing (SAC05)—Special Track on Coordination Models, Languages and Applications*, pages 1134–1140, March 2005. Extended version to appear in the *Int. J. on Web Intelligence and Agent Systems (WAIS)*.
18. G.P. Picco, A.L. Murphy, and G.-C. Roman. LIME: Linda Meets Mobility. In *Proc. of the 21st Int. Conf. on Software Engineering*, pages 368–377, May 1999.
19. J. Pinakis. *Using Linda as the Basis of an Operating System Microkernel*. PhD thesis, University of Western Australia, Australia, August 1993.
20. G. Russello, M. Chaudron, and M. van Steen. Dynamically adapting tuple replication for managing availability in a shared data space. In *Proc. of the 7th Int. Conf. on Coordination Models and Languages*, LNCS 3454. Springer, April 2005.
21. Lime Team. LIME Web page. lime.sourceforge.net.
22. D. Terry, M. Theimer, K. Petersen, A. Demers, M. Spreitzer, and C. Hauser. Managing Update Conflicts in Bayou, a Weakly Connected Replicated Storage System. *Operating Systems Review*, 29(5):172–183, 1995.
23. A. Xu and B. Liskov. A design for a fault-tolerant, distributed implementation of Linda. In *Digest of Papers of the 19th Int. Symp. on Fault-Tolerant Computing*, pages 199–206, June 1989.

Coordinating Computation with Communication

Thomas Nitsche

Research Institute for Communication, Information Processing and Ergonomics
(FGAN/FKIE)
nitsche@fgan.de

Abstract. While in the sequential world the programmer can concentrate on the algorithmic solution to his given problem, in parallel and distributed systems he also has to consider aspects of communication, synchronization and data movement. In this paper we describe a prototypical middleware solution that enables the clear separation of these aspects. We combine algorithmic skeletons describing the computational aspects with overlapping data distributions describing the communication and synchronization. Both are expressed in a high-level manner. The system automatically coordinates the different activities and allows the programmer to easily change the underlying communication topology.

1 Introduction

Programming of massive parallel systems is much more complex than in the sequential case. This is due to the fact, that in addition to the problems occurring in the sequential case, the programmer must coordinate different parallel activities, which means that synchronization and communication issues have to be taken into account [13]. The programmer thus has to consider the distribution of the work respectively data onto the different processors, as well as synchronization and data exchange between them.

The decision of which data will be communicated and when depends largely on the characteristics of the parallel computer such as its network topology, bandwidth, etc. To achieve maximum efficiency, many low-level machine- and algorithm-specific details have to be considered. The resulting parallel program is highly problem- and machine-specific, which makes it difficult to port to another parallel machine or to reuse the code for another program. Since one of the ideas behind grid computing is to make parallel computing power as easily available on the market as today's electricity or telephony services [14], parallel programs should not be written for a specific parallel machine but rather parameterized using certain architectural parameters. The number of available processors is one such architectural parameter; others are the computing power of each processor, its memory, the network parameter, etc.

For the communication among different processors there have emerged standardized message passing libraries like MPI [31, 19] or PVM [15]. However, their use is relatively low-level as the whole responsibility for a correct communication is left to the user. This is quite error-prone and may easily result in deadlocks.

P. Ciancarini and H. Wiklicky (Eds.): COORDINATION 2006, LNCS 4038, pp. 212–227, 2006.

The use of low-level message passing primitives like send and receive is sometimes seen as assembler-level programming [17].

A second observation is that although low-level message-passing routines appear to be the most efficient way of communicating, this is not always the case. Since different messages may interfere with each other owing to network contention, the local view may hinder optimal performance results. BSPLIB [21], for instance, achieves performance improvements as large as a factor of two over MPI if an overall knowledge of all message sizes and a randomized communication schedule is used [11].

To achieve a higher level of programming effectiveness and coordination of parallel activities, we can use *algorithmic skeletons* [7].

The remainder of this paper is organized as follows. In order to make this paper self-contained, Sect. 2 describes the use of algorithmic skeletons for parallel coordination. Sect. 3 introduces the notion of data distributions as an abstract means to specify communication operations, while Sect. 4 describes the extension of the usual skeleton approach with data distributions and our prototypical middleware system that automatically coordinates both computational and communicational aspects of the program. We use a PDE solver as a case study to illustrate the benefits of our approach and compare the run-time results of our middleware solution with that of a hand-coded, low-level program. Finally, Sect. 5 concludes.

2 Algorithmic Skeletons as Parallel Coordination Framework

Using algorithmic skeletons as a kind of collective operation instead of directly using low-level (point-to-point) communication operations not only avoids programming errors such as deadlocks but also enables better cost predictions, program optimizations and, in some cases, better performance because global knowledge about the program allows optimized communication schedules.

2.1 Parallel Coordination

Algorithmic skeletons are abstractions of certain algorithmic aspects which are to be executed in parallel. The idea behind using them is to encapsulate parallelism within the skeletons which are supposed to be the only parallel algorithmic operations within the program. This creates a coordination language in which the skeletons describe the parallel behavior of the overall program, while the parameter functions of the skeletons describe the sequential parts that have to be executed locally on each processor.

Algorithmic skeletons can be seen as patterns for parallel and distributed computing [30]. More formally, they can be specified as higher-order functions with an efficient implementation on different parallel systems [9].

2.2 Standard Skeletons

Examples of standard skeletons are given in Figures 1 and 2.

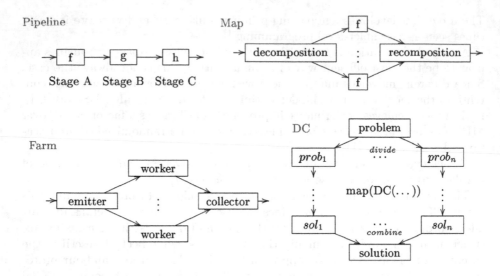

Fig. 1. Some standard skeletons

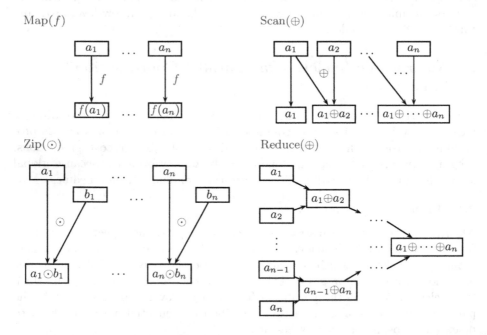

Fig. 2. Some standard data-parallel skeletons

Pipeline: The *pipe* skeleton combines a sequence of functions which are applied in different stages one after the other.

Map: Here, a function f is applied to all data elements of a data structure. This generally requires the decomposition or traversal of the data structure down to the data elements, applying the function and recomposing the data structure with the updated elements.

Farm: The *farm* skeleton applies a worker function to a set of tasks. These tasks can be distributed among the available processors either statically or dynamically according to the manager-worker model.

DC: The *DC* or *divide-and-conquer* skeleton recursively divides a given problem into a list of subproblems until the problems are simple enough to be solved directly. Then, the partial solutions are combined to form the solution to the main problem.

This skeleton is quite flexible because it allows us to express other skeletons as well as numerous algorithms which give rise to a hierarchy of DC skeleton variants [20]. The *broadcast* skeleton, which sends a value from a root processor to all processors, and the quick-sort function are examples for possible divide-and-conquer instantiations, where the work is mainly done in the dividing phase. On the other hand, *reducing* a set of values to a single one or the merge-sort function mainly involve work in the combine phase.[1] Even `map` can be expressed as a special case of divide-and-conquer, dividing and combining corresponding to decomposing and recomposing the data structure and the function application to the data elements corresponding to the solution of the trivial cases. However, in most cases it is advisable to use the specialized skeletons like map or reduce instead of the general DC because they are more appropriate to the special problem and can also achieve better performance.

Zip: It combines the elements of two data structures of the same size using an arbitrary binary operator. We can extend the `zip` skeleton such that it combines k data structure elementwise using an operator $\odot : t_1 \times \cdots \times t_k \to t$. Moreover, the data structures itself can even have different shape, as long as their size is the same.

Reduce: The *reduce* skeleton, sometimes also called *fold*, combines all elements of a data structure using some binary operator.

It allows us, for instance, to summarize or multiply all elements or to compute the maximum or minimum over all values. If the binary operator $\oplus$ is associative, the `reduce` skeleton can calculate the result in parallel using a tree-like algorithm (see Figure 2) in $O(\log N)$ time steps. Since `reduce` is otherwise a sequential operation, associativity of $\oplus$ is often required.

Scan: If we are not only interested in the accumulated value of all data elements but also in partial results, we can use the *scan* skeleton. It computes all partial sums $a_1 \oplus \cdots \oplus a_i$.

Their behavior can formally be specified as follows:

$$map(f)([a_1, \ldots, a_N]) \overset{\text{def}}{=} [f(a_1), \ldots, f(a_N)] \tag{1}$$

$$zip(\odot)([a_1, \ldots, a_N], [b_1, \ldots, b_N]) \overset{\text{def}}{=} [a_1 \odot b_1, \ldots, a_N \odot b_N] \tag{2}$$

---

[1] The former correspond to recursion schemes where the values are propagated downwards the tree structure, while the latter correspond to upward recursion schemes.

$$reduce, e(\oplus)([a_1, \ldots, a_N]) \overset{\text{def}}{=} ((e \oplus a_1) \oplus \cdots) \oplus a_N \qquad (3)$$

$$scan(\oplus)([a_1, a_2, \ldots, a_N]) \overset{\text{def}}{=} [a_1, a_1 \oplus a_2, \ldots, a_1 \oplus \cdots \oplus a_N] \quad (4)$$

2.3 Communication Handling in Skeletal Systems

Parallel programming with algorithmic skeletons has been an active field of research for the last few years starting with the work of Cole [7]. See [30, 8] for more recent surveys.

To handle communication and data movement, skeleton systems try to fully hide these aspects from the user, or offer some specific skeletons for explicit communication operations.

Examples for the first approach are Skil (Skeleton Imperative Language) [5] and eSkel (Edinburgh Skeleton Library) [2]. Skil offers a library of skeletons for the efficient solution of numerical problems. However, much of these skeletons are domain specific and to extend the library one has to explicitly code the low-level communication details within the new skeletons by hand. eSkel, on the other hand, is explicitly designed as an extension of MPI's collective operations suite, so to use the (currently five) skeletons the user has to program (a small portion of his program) in a MPI style.

In the second approach systems like the structured coordination language SCL[2] [9] or the Münster skeleton library Muesli [24] have some explicit communication skeletons. These include **rotate**, **brdcast** and even explicit **send/fetch** operations in case of SCL, or **broadcast**, **gather** and **allToAll** communication primitives in Muesli. Thus the programmer has to call the corresponding communication functions explicitly. Computation and communication are hence mixed with each other. However, if both aspects were separated more explicitly, the resulting program could become even easier.

3 Data Distributions as Abstractions for Communication Operations

In our approach, we extend the skeletons by data distributions [32, 25]. The main idea behind this concept is overlapping data structures. A data structure is split into overlapping subobjects, which are distributed among different processors. Fig. 3 shows, by way of an example, the splitting of a matrix into overlapping submatrices. This approach allows us to express both local computations as well as communication on a high, abstract level. Computations on subobjects correspond to local computations (see Eq. (6) in Sect. 4.1 below), while accesses to overlapping data elements induces communication (cf. Fig. 5).

3.1 Covers

Conceptually, a *cover* C of an object O is simply a set $C = \{S_i | i \in I\}$ of subobjects $S_i \subseteq O$. Each of the subobjects is partitioned into an *own* part

---

[2] SCL embeds a skeletal coordination language into a sequential host language like Fortran or C.

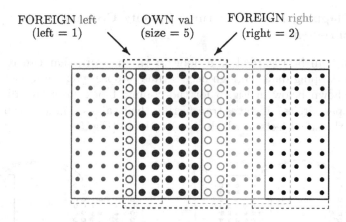

Fig. 3. An overlapping column-block cover with p = 4 subobjects with one column overlapping to the left and two columns overlapping to the right

```
COVER ColumnBlock[α, p, left, right]    --cover−specific parameter
   SORT α   --type of data elements
   FUN p : nat   --number of processors
   FUN left, right : nat   --number of overlapping columns on each side

   TYPE obj[α]      == matrix[α]   --whole object
        subobj[α] == matrix[α]   --local subobjects
        cover[α]   == vector[subobj[α]]   --topology of local subobjects

   FUN split : obj[α] → cover[subobj[α]]   --matrix [α] → vector [matrix [α]]
   FUN glue : cover[subobj[α]] → obj[α]   --vector [matrix [α]] → matrix [α]
   AXM glue ∘ split = Id
```

Fig. 4. Definition of the column-block cover

and a *foreign* part. The own parts of all subobjects have to be a partition of the object, i.e., the disjoint union of the own parts restores the whole object: $\biguplus_{i \in I} own(S_i) = O$. Thus, each data-element belongs to the own part of exactly one particular subobject. The idea is that the own part specifies local data, while the foreign part can be regarded as a reference to the data of another processor.

Consider, for example, the division of a matrix into a vector of column blocks (Fig. 3). Formally, each cover can be described in terms of splitting an object into subobjects and a corresponding gluing function, together with corresponding type definitions for object, subobject and cover structure (Fig. 4). Note, that we make also the topology, i.e. the structure of the the neighborhood-relation of the subobjects, explicit by a corresponding cover structure.[3] In the case of the column-block cover this is merely a one-dimensional vector of submatrices.

---

[3] Here, code[subobj[α]] means that the type cover[β] is parameterized with β = subobj[α].

3.2   Overlapping Data Structures Specify Communication Requirements

A subobject can be regarded as a node in the network that can request and provide overlapping data. Foreign access thus imposes communication requirements, as shown below in Fig. 5 for the column-block cover. Reading foreign elements (open circles) involves transferring their values from the own part (full circles) of the subobjects in which they originate (Fig. 5).

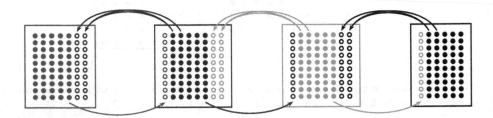

Fig. 5. Communication through foreign accesses (column-block cover with **p** = 4 subobjects and overlapping sizes `left` = 1 and `right` = 2)

Note, however, that there is not necessarily a one-to-one correspondence between subobjects and processors. If the object is split into more subobjects than the number of processors available, multiple subobjects are mapped to one processor. In this case, the computation on a subobject corresponds to a thread, so the subobject can still be regarded conceptually as an independent processing unit.

Covers can be defined not only for matrices but for arbitrary container types as well, i.e., arbitrary algebraic data types, arrays and nested combinations of these [25]. Fig. 6 shows some example covers on different data types. We define container types $t \in C(V, B)$ over sets of base types B and type variables V^4 formally as follows:

$$
\begin{aligned}
C(V, B) \longrightarrow\ & B & & \text{base type} \\
\mid\ & V & & \text{type variable} \\
\mid\ & C(V, B) \times C(V, B) & & \text{product} \qquad\qquad (5) \\
\mid\ & C(V, B) + C(V, B) & & \text{sum} \\
\mid\ & C(V, B)^n & & \text{array}
\end{aligned}
$$

They are used to formalize the notion of shape, i.e. the structure of a data type, and hence to separate the shape from the actual data elements which are to be distributed onto the different processors [25, 22]. Abbot et al. [1] give a more general, categorical definition of containers. In the case of locally cartesian closed categories,[5] this is equivalent to the notion of shapely types [23].

---

[4] Base types and arguments for the type parameter variables can be arbitrary types including function types.

[5] Note, that cartesian closed categories can be used to model the λ-calculus.

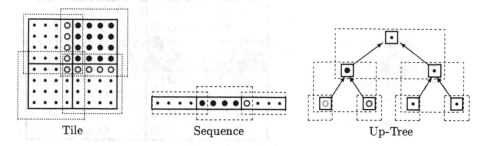

Tile   Sequence   Up-Tree

Fig. 6. Examples for overlapping covers

4 Combining Algorithmic Skeletons with Data Distributions — Coordinating Computation with Communication

4.1 Parameterizing Skeletons with Overlapping Covers

Now we extend the usual notion of algorithmic skeletons (abstracting parallel computations) with data distributions (specifying communication). A skeleton is, in our system, parameterized by a – possibly overlapping – data distribution (cover).

Formally, this can be expressed by defining a skeleton operation in such a way that it operates on a cover, i.e., an overlapping data structure. If C is a cover, we can lift a function $f : \text{subobj}_C[\alpha] \rightarrow \text{subobj}_C[\beta]$ on subobjects onto the original object $\text{Obj} \in \text{obj}_C[\alpha]$. For example, the map skeleton can be defined as follows:

$$
\begin{aligned}
\text{FUN Map}: \text{COVER} \;&\rightarrow\; (\text{subobj}_C[\alpha] \rightarrow \text{subobj}_C[\beta]) \rightarrow \text{obj}_C[\alpha] \rightarrow \text{obj}_C[\beta] \\
\text{DEF Map}(C)(f)(\text{Obj}) \;&=\; (\text{glue}_C \circ \text{map}(f) \circ \text{split}_C)(\text{Obj})
\end{aligned}
\tag{6}
$$

The object is thus split into subobjects, which are then transformed by the parameter function f (cf. the definition of $\text{map}(f)$ in (1)). If we have, for instance, a function **stencil** that (sequentially) applies a stencil to a matrix block, we can obtain a function $\text{Map}(\text{ColumnBlock}[\text{real}, p, 1, 1])(\text{stencil})$ that operates on each submatrix in parallel. Note that we have here a single overlapping column to both the left and right neighbors. Its semantics is – according to Eq. 6 – such that the whole matrix is split into overlapping submatrices with the overlapping columns being duplicated, the function **stencil** is then applied to each submatrix independently from the others, and, finally, the resulting submatrices are glued together to a new matrix. In the implementation proper, however, we do not exchange full subobjects between processors in each skeleton application. Instead, we keep the subobjects distributed over the different processors. Thus we merely communicate the referenced overlapping elements to the neighbor processors in order to update their current values (cf. Fig. 5), and then continue with the local computation.

More generally, we can even allow the map skeleton to be applied to different covers C_1 and C_2. Analogously, we can define other skeletons operating on covers.

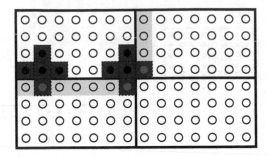

(a) stencil definition   (b) application to a tiling-block distribution

Fig. 7. 5-point stencil

4.2 Case Study: PDE Solver

To demonstrate the benefits of our approach, we consider as a case study the solution of the Poisson equation $\frac{\delta^2 u(x,y)}{\delta x^2} + \frac{\delta^2 u(x,y)}{\delta y^2} = g(x,y)$ with Dirichlet boundary condition as a simple example of partial differential equations (PDEs). To solve this equation in the domain $[0,1] \times [0,1]$, we use a discretization with a grid of $N \times N$ grid points, i.e., a step width of $h = \frac{1}{N-1}$ leading to a two-dimensional matrix U of grid points $U_{i,j}$. The value of each grid point of iteration $t+1$ can be computed by using the values of the four neighboring grid points of the previous iteration t (Jacobi–Method):

$$U_{i,j}^{t+1} = \frac{1}{4} \left(U_{i,j-1}^t + U_{i-1,j}^t + U_{i+1,j}^t + U_{i,j+1}^t - h^2 g(i,j) \right) \tag{7}$$

These neighboring values are given by the usual Laplacian finite-difference 5-point stencil (Fig. 7-(a)). Distributing the matrix U onto multiple processors leads to overlapping data at the border (cf., e.g., Fig. 7-(b)).

By using algorithmic skeletons and covers, the programmer is not bothered by low-level communication details and can concentrate on the algorithmic solution to the problem. Fig. 8 shows the Jacobi algorithm in skeletal form based on data distributions. The function `solve` gets a distributed matrix (type `objectInfo[matrix]` in line 2)[6] as a parameter and computes the new matrix with the map skeleton on an overlapping cover

$$C_1 \stackrel{\text{def}}{=} \texttt{coverEnv(p, foreign(1), foreign(1))},$$

which corresponds to `ColumnBlock[real, p, 1, 1]` (lines 4,10). To compute the residuum as the termination criteria we first calculate the absolute difference between the old and new matrix using the skeleton `zip` (line 5). Then we can calculate the residuum as the maximal difference value of the matrix using `reduce` (line 6). Note that the later two skeleton applications operate on a non-overlapping cover $C_0 ==$ `ColumnBlock[real, p, 0, 0]` (line 9).

Not only is this an elegant solution, we can now very easily change the data distribution used. Another distribution of the matrix can be specified simply

---

[6] The communication side effects of the function are denoted by the monad type `com[α]`.

```
IMPORT ColumnBlock SkelMapCE SkelZipCE SkelReduceCE ...                                    1

FUN solve: objectInfo[matrix[real]] × real → com[objectInfo[matrix[real]]]                 2
DEF solve(A, ε) =                                                                          3
        newA    = Map(C₁)(stencil)(A) ;        //Map(ColumnBlock[real,p,0,0])(stencil)(A)  4
        Diff    = Zip(C₀,C₀)(abs ∘ −)(A, newA) ;                                            5
        residuum = Reduce(C₀)(max)(Diff) ;                                                  6
        IF residuum < ε THEN newA                                                          7
                        ELSE solve(newA, ε) FI                                             8
        WHERE C₀ = coverEnv(p, foreign(0), foreign(0)) //ColumnBlock[real,p,0,0]           9
              C₁ = coverEnv(p, foreign(1), foreign(1)) //overlapping columns(l=r=1)       10
```

Fig. 8. Jacobi iterative PDE solver (version with skeletons over covers)

by using another cover while the rest of the program remains unchanged. This is a significant advantage compared to other implementations like, e.g., a low-level MPI implementation, because the parallel program remains readable and maintainable. A tiling-block distribution with one line and column overlapping on each side can be achieved simply by importing the `TilingBlock` cover and defining the corresponding cover environment

$$C_1 = \text{coverEnv}(\sqrt{p}, \sqrt{p}, \text{foreign}(1), \text{foreign}(1), \text{foreign}(1), \text{foreign}(1))$$

to specify the overlapping. The new communication pattern is then automatically derived by the system. The Map skeleton is thus applied to the two-dimensional tiling-block cover and we can benefit from its better computation-to-communication ratio.

In an MPI implementation, this is much harder to achieve. Here the user code is three to five times larger than our high-level solution because all communication operations have to be programmed explicitly. In the resulting program computational aspects dealing with the algorithmic solution and communication aspects are intermixed with each other. This not only complicates programming but also makes it harder to change the data distribution and its resulting communication structure. Moreover, the user explicitly has to match all send operations with their matching receive operations in order to avoid deadlocks. Even for the simple one-dimensional column-block distribution we have to distinguish between groups with odd or even processor number and need four communication phases, while for a two-dimensional (tiling-block) or three-dimensional cover as many as four or eight versions necessary, respectively. So not only increases the code size, and therefore the probability of errors in it, but the actual algorithmic part of the program also becomes hidden by the large overhead for the parallelization.

In our system, however, programmers do not have to take care of such low-level details as shown before. It enables a clean separation of computational operations and communication aspects, where both parts can be combined (and hence changed) easily. The necessary communication is than managed automatically by the middleware system (see [26] for a more detailed description). Despite the high-level of programming abstraction in our system, the performance results are comparable to that of a low-level hand-coded MPI implementation (Fig. 9).

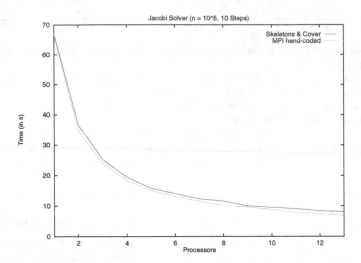

Fig. 9. Runtime of the PDE solver, (skeletons with cover vs. MPI)

4.3   Implementation

To achieve such a high-level programming style, the application programmer can use a library of predefined skeletons and data distributions. Extensions to this library can be made in a high-level, purely functional manner without having to deal with explicit communication operations. The different layers of the implementation (see [25] for details) are shown in Fig. 10.

The underlying basis is a *communication library*, which could be MPI, BSP, a (distributed) shared-memory system, etc. In our current implementation, we use MPI. Since the MPI standard only defines the message passing operations for standard languages like C and Fortran, we have to lift the corresponding communication functions to our implementation language OPAL [10, 27].

On top of this communication layer, we have implemented a *generic cover* that handles all the communication necessary for foreign data access and data distributions in a generalized way. It provides a common interface for parallel operations, based on `getSubobj` and `storeSubobj` to access the *local* subobjects on each processor. The generic cover encapsulates all communication operations for the upper layers (skeletons and specific data distributions). It is generic because it allows all specific covers over arbitrary data types to be built on it.

Specific data distributions (covers) over arbitrary data types are then defined by parameter functions to specify overlappings and traversing the cover structure. Overlappings are specified by types for requesting foreign data and the corresponding answers as well as functions for extracting and inserting foreign values from and into subobjects, respectively.

Algorithmic skeletons can be defined based on the operations of the generic cover. This leads to generic skeletons that operate with arbitrary data distributions over any types. It allows the easy combination and replacement of skeletons and data distributions as shown in Sect. 4.2. In the implementation proper, we internally operate on the set of subobjects rather than the whole object itself.

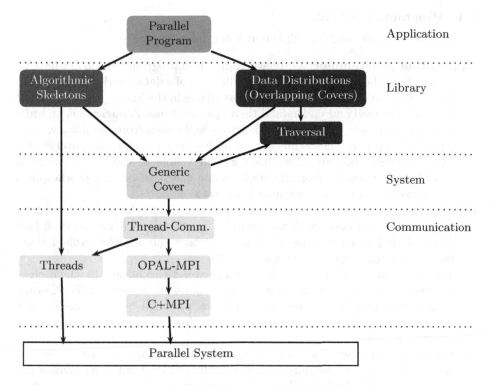

Fig. 10. System architecture

That means that we regard the cover as a distributed object whose subobjects are distributed among the available computers. Algorithmic skeletons now operate in a collective manner on the locally available subobjects of each computer. The skeletons are hence independent of the cover type because only the local subobjects are relevant. Thus we can, for instance, combine different data structures with the `zip` skeleton, provided the number and mapping of subobjects are the same.

In order to respect the semantics of the parallel program, we have to update the overlapping foreign parts of the subobjects within each skeleton execution. This is done automatically, since the access function `getSubobject` from the underlying generic cover always yields subobjects whose foreign parts have been updated already. If an algorithmic skeleton is used for the first time, a function is called that computes the necessary communication schedule. The resulting communication operations are specific for each subobject and depend on the overlapping specification of the corresponding cover. The corresponding (neighbor) communication scheme may look as in Fig. 5.

In the parallel *program*, we now merely have to select the proper algorithmic skeletons and data distributions and combine them.

4.4 Programming Model

In our programming model we distinguish the following roles:

Application programmer: Ordinary application programmers do not have to worry about the complexity of the specification of a data distribution or skeleton. They merely have to know what is available in the library without having to be able to read and understand their specifications. A novice, i.e. an ordinary user, has only to import the skeletons and covers from the library.

Application programmers thus have a high-level view onto the parallel system. However, the parallelism itself is still visible to them. The skeleton describe the parallel algorithm itself, while the (size of the) overlappings give a prediction of the communication costs.

Library programmer: An experienced user can extend the library. New data distributions (covers) are defined purely functionally within the base language. This is done in a high-level style without the need for explicit (low-level) communication operations.

Thus even application programmers can extend the library by themselves because no explicit message passing operations are necessary. The library programmer only has to use the operations provided by the generic cover which serve as the underlying middleware. However, further optimizations are still possible.

System programmer: The system programmer that implemented the underlying middleware is the only person that has to deal with communication operations explicitly. In this layer the necessary communication is generated, thus encapsulating all the lower-level details of data management, communication and synchronization from the upper layers and their users.

5 Conclusion

In this paper we described a system that allows the programming of parallel systems on a high, abstract level using algorithmic skeletons. In contrast to coordination languages like Linda [16], that also abstract MIMD parallel computations but (like the Linda tuple space) interact via shared memory, we explicitly target at distributed memory systems. These systems can consists of thousands of machines, so data distribution and communication issues are crucial for an efficient program execution.

We extend the skeleton approach by a notion of (overlapping) data distributions which are thus under explicit control of the programmer. However, we do not complicate the problem solution by technicalities of communication and synchronization details. These are handled implicitly on the application level, where overlapping parts specify communication requirements. The underlying middleware system then derives and schedules the necessary communication automatically. Note that, for reasons of efficiency, we try to exchange only the overlapping data elements and not full subobjects.[7] In contrast to common

---

[7] Which can be done in the case of shapely covers [25, 23].

data-parallel languages like HPF [12], Nesl/Nepal [3, 6] or SAC [18] we do not restrict ourself to certain data types like arrays or nested vectors, but allow arbitrary container types, i.e. combinations or algebraic types and arrays, to be used.

The separation of concerns allows skeletons and data distributions to be defined and used independently from each other. The skeletons encapsulate the algorithmic aspects of the (parallel) behavior, while the data distributions (covers) encapsulate the aspects of the distribution and the (overlapping neighboring) communication. Both aspects can be defined independently from each other, while their combined use within the program is coordinated by the underlying generic cover system (cf. Fig. 10).

Obviously we cannot completely eliminate the inherent complexity of the parallel program, but we can reduce it. Since algorithmic aspects and distribution/communication aspects are clearly separated, it is easier to write programs that are correct than when using lower-level approaches where these aspects are intermixed and confuse the programmer.

Our approach can be classified as an endogenous, data-driven coordination model according to [28]. The description of the data distribution defines the communication and synchronization requirements. Unlike [4], where the shared data is duplicated among the different processors and write operations correspond to broadcasting of data, we explicitly distribute the subobjects onto the different processors. The list of local subobjects can thus be seen as a kind of local data space, with the subobjects being the data stored. In this sense we have some similarities with the TuCSoN model [28], which enhances the ordinary, global Linda tuple space with behavior specifications and a notion of local tuple-based interaction spaces, called tuple centers. A control-oriented coordination language is, e.g., Manifold [29]. Here the processes are separated into computation and coordination processes, allowing event-driven control-structure to be described independently of the actual data elements. In our system, the communication structure is also independent of the data elements themselves, provided the data distribution is shapely, but, obviously, depends on the shape of the data structure.

As future work we plan to re-implement our prototypical system in an object-oriented language like Java (or C++) to make it usable for real-world applications and the Grid. The libraries of the generic cover and the skeletons built on top of it can be carried over to any other implementation language.

In this context we also want to examine how we can define skeletons that operate on covers that are not distributed onto different machines but whose subobjects are all locally on the same machine. From the semantical definition of overlapping data distributions (covers) this is possible, which allows algorithms to be expressed very concisely. We can, e.g., change the Jacobi algorithm to a Gauß-Seidel like methods merely by using an overlapping data distributions with FUTURE synchronization.

Acknowledgments. I would like to thank the anonymous reviewers for their helpful comments, and Phil Bacon for improving the English presentation.

References

[1] M. Abbott, T. Altenkirch, and N. Ghani. Categories of containers. In A. D. Gordon, editor, *FOSSACS'03*, volume 2620 of *LNCS*, pages 23–38. Springer, 2003.

[2] A. Benoit, M. Cole, S. Gilmore, and J. Hillston. Flexible skeletal programming with eSkel. In *Euro-Par'05*, volume 3648 of *LNCS*, pages 761–770. Springer, 2005.

[3] G. E. Blelloch. *Vector Models for Data-Parallel Computing*. MIT Press, 1990.

[4] M. M. Bonsangue, J. N. Kok, and G. Zavattaro. Comparing software architectures for coordination languages. In P. Ciancarini and A. L. Wolf, editors, *COORDINATION'99*, volume 1594 of *LNCS*, pages 150–165. Springer, Apr. 1999.

[5] G.H. Botorog and H. Kuchen. Efficient high-level parallel programming. *Theoretical Computer Science, Special Issue on Parallel Computing*, 1998.

[6] M. M. T. Chakravarty, G. Keller, R. Leshchinskiy, and W. Pfannenstiel. Nepal - nested data parallelism in Haskell. In *Euro-Par'01 Parallel Processing*, volume 2150 of *LNCS*, pages 524–534. Springer, 2001.

[7] M. I. Cole. *Algorithmic Skeletons: Structured Management of Parallel Computation*. MIT Press, 1989.

[8] M. I. Cole. Bringing skeletons out of the closet: a pragmatic manifesto for skeletal parallel programming. *Parallel Computing*, 30(3):389–406, 2004.

[9] J. Darlington, Y. Guo, H.W. To, and J. Yang. Functional skeletons for parallel coordination. In S. Haridi, K. Ali, and P. Magnusson, editors, *Euro-Par'95 Parallel Processing*, volume 966 of *LNCS*, pages 55–69. Springer, Aug. 1995.

[10] K. Didrich, A. Fett, C. Gerke, W. Grieskamp, and P. Pepper. OPAL: Design and Implementation of an Algebraic Programming Language. In J. Gutknecht, editor, *Programming Languages and System Architectures (PLSA'94)*, volume 782 of *LNCS*, pages 228–244. Springer, 1994.

[11] S. R. Donaldson, J. M. D. Hill, and D. B. Skillicorn. Predictable performance on unpredictable networks: Implementing BSP over TCP/IP. In *Euro-Par'98 Parallel Processing*, volume 1470 of *LNCS*, pages 970–980. Springer, 1998.

[12] High Performance Fortran Forum. High Performance Fortran — language specification. *Scientific Programming*, 2(1), Jun. 1993.

[13] I. Foster. *Designing and Building Parallel Programs: Concepts and Tools for Parallel Software Engineering*. Addison-Wesley, 1995.

[14] I. Foster and C. Kesselmann. *The Grid: Blueprint for a New Computing Infrastructure*. Morgan Kaufmann Publishers, 1999.

[15] G. A. Geist, A. Beguelin, J. Dongarra, W. Jiang, R. Mancheck, and V. S. Sunderam. *PVM: Parallel Virtual Machine - A Users' Guide and Tutorial for Networked Parallel Computing*. MIT Press, 1994.

[16] D. Gelernter and N. Carriero. Coordination languages and their significance. *Commun. ACM*, 35(2):97–107, Feb. 1992.

[17] S. Gorlatch. Send-receive considered harmful: Myths and realities of message passing. *ACM Transactions on Programming Languages and Systems (TOPLAS)*, 26(1):47–56, Jan. 2004.

[18] C. Grelck and S.-B. Scholz. Generic array programming in SAC. In W. Goerigk, editor, *Programmiersprachen und Rechenkonzepte. 21. GI-Workshop, 2004*, pages 43–53, Jan. 2005.

[19] W. Gropp. Learning from the success of MPI. In *High Performance Computing - HiPC 2001*, volume 2228 of *LNCS*, pages 81–92, 2001.

[20] C. Herrmann and C. Lengauer. Parallelization of divide-and-conquer by translation to nested loops. *Journal of Functional Programming*, 9(3):279–310, 1999.

[21] J. M. D. Hill, B. McColl, D. C. Stefanescu, M. W. Goudreau, K. Lang, S. B. Rao, T. Suel, T. Tsantilas, and R. H. Bisseling. BSPlib: The BSP programming library. *Parallel Computing*, 24(14):1947–1980, 1998.

[22] C. B. Jay. Separating shape from data. In *Category Theory and Computer Science (CTCS'97)*, volume 1290 of *LNCS*, pages 47–48. Springer, 1997.

[23] C.B. Jay. A semantics for shape. *Sci. Comput. Program.*, 25(2-3):251–283, 1995.

[24] H. Kuchen. A skeleton library. In B. Monien and R. Feldmann, editors, *Euro-Par'02 Parallel Processing*, volume 2400 of *LNCS*, pages 620–629. Springer, 2002.

[25] T. Nitsche. *Data Distribution and Communication Management for Parallel Systems*. PhD thesis, Technical Univ. of Berlin, Dept. of Comp. Sci. and Electr. Eng., 2005.

[26] T. Nitsche. Deriving and scheduling communication operations for generic skeleton implementations. *Parallel Processing Letters*, 15(3):337–352, Sep. 2005.

[27] T. Nitsche and W. Webers. Functional message passing with OPAL-MPI. In *Proc. EuroPVM/MPI'98*, volume 1497 of *LNCS*, pages 281–288. Springer, 1998.

[28] A. Omicini and F. Zambonelli. Coordination of mobile agents in TuSCoN. *Internet Research*, 8(5), 1998.

[29] G. A. Papadopoulos and F. Arbab. Coordination models and languages. *Advances in Computers*, 46, 1998.

[30] F. A. Rabhi and S. Gorlatch, editors. *Patterns and Skeletons for Parallel and Distributed Computing*. Springer, 2003.

[31] M. Snir, S. W. Otto, S. Huss-Ledermann, D. W. Walker, and J. Dongarra. *MPI — The Complete Reference: Volume 1, The MPI Core*. MIT Press, 1998.

[32] M. Südholt. *The Transformational Derivation of Parallel Programs using Data Distribution Algebras and Skeletons*. PhD thesis, Technical Univ. of Berlin, 1997.

Distributed Workflow
upon Linkable Coordination Artifacts

Andrea Omicini, Alessandro Ricci, and Nicola Zaghini

DEIS, Alma Mater Studiorum—Università di Bologna
via Venezia 52, 47023 Cesena, Italy
{andrea.omicini, a.ricci, nicola.zaghini}@unibo.it

Abstract. Coordination infrastructures can be used for the general-purpose support of WfMSs (workflow management systems). Suitably-expressive coordination artifacts can be specialised as workflow engines, encapsulating workflow rules expressed in terms of coordination laws.

In this paper, we focus on the issue of inter-organisational workflow (IOW), and show how the issue of multiple, interdependent, distributed workflows requires coordination artifacts to be *linkable*, so as to create a network of inter-connected coordination flows.

After discussing a model of workflow engine based on ReSpecT tuple centres, we introduce a distributed workflow architecture based on TuCSoN, exploiting a logic-based workflow language. In particular, we focus on the definition of a scoping mechanism, and show how this enable workflows to be dynamically governed and distributed upon a coordination infrastructure based on artifact linkability. An example of a VE (virtual enterprise) workflow is finally discussed.

1 Introduction

The ever-increasing requirements of today distributed scenarios are making many results of the research in the field of coordination models and languages become of interest for real-world applications and systems. WfMSs (workflow management systems), for their very nature, apparently represent one of the most natural applications for coordination models and languages. As discussed in [1], agent-based coordination infrastructures are seemingly well-suited to support workflow management—especially in the case of VEs (virtual enterprises) and inter-organisational workflows [2], where decoupling and autonomy of execution are essential features. In particular, the notion of *coordination artifact*, introduced in the field of MASs (multiagent systems) as a generalisation of coordination media [3, 4, 5], is in principle expressive enough to fully capture the structure and function of workflow engines, by encapsulating workflow rules in terms of coordination laws.

In this paper, we focus on the issue of inter-organisational workflow, where multiple, interdependent, distributed workflows have to be synchronised and co-ordinated across different participant organisations. To this end, in Sect. 2 we introduce a model of workflow engine based on ReSpecT tuple centres, which

P. Ciancarini and H. Wiklicky (Eds.): COORDINATION 2006, LNCS 4038, pp. 228–246, 2006.
© Springer-Verlag Berlin Heidelberg 2006

are programmed as general-purpose interpreters for workflow specifications expressed in terms of a logic-based workflow language. Then, in Sect. 3 we motivate the issue of distributed workflow, and elicit requirements: accordingly, we define a scoping mechanism enabling workflows to be dynamically distributed. Such a mechanism requires coordination artifacts to be *linkable*—that is, able to be composed and interact with each other—so as to create a network of inter-connected coordination flows: this allows distributed workflow engines to synchronise, and workflow activities to be coordinated across the network. In order to give a better intuition of our approach, in Sect. 4 we present an example of a VE (virtual enterprise) based on inter-organisational workflow (IOW). Finally, Sect. 5 reports on related works, and concludes.

2   Workflow Engines Upon ReSpecT

2.1   Workflow Engines as Coordination Artifacts

In the context of WfMSs, *workflow engines* play a fundamental role as the components in charge of the coordination of the workflow activities, encapsulating the execution of *workflow specifications*, encoded in some workflow language (examples are BPEL [6], XPDL [7]). When a WfMS is to be built upon a coordination infrastructure, workflow engines are to be modelled and engineered as coordination artifacts, encapsulating the workflow specification in terms of their coordinating behaviour.

As discussed in [1], on the one hand agents can be used to encapsulate the execution of tasks and individual activities, aimed at the achievement of some kind of goal, possibly requiring different levels of skills and reasoning capabilities. Agents can either play the role of artificial workflow participants—responsible of the automated execution of some tasks—, or work as personal assistants of humans—as intelligent interfaces with respect to the workflow system. On the other hand, artifacts can be used either as the target of the agents activities—as computational objects being constructed, manipulated, evolved—, or the tools that agents use either individually or collectively to support their work toward goal achievement.

In the context of WfMSs two basic kinds of artifacts can be considered as useful: *(i)* artifacts supporting awareness, as means to improve mutual knowledge and reuse by agents (and humans) [3]; *(ii)* artifacts supporting coordination, i.e., artifacts specialised to manage dependencies and interactions occurring among agents (and humans) involved in the same activities [8]. Workflow engines can then be naturally modelled as coordination artifacts, embedding the (workflow) rules that define the coordination among the tasks executed by the workflow participants (agents).

The basic properties defined in general for the coordination artifact abstraction—inspectability, controllability, malleability, predictability, formalisability, linkability, distribution [4]—can be suitably exploited to create flexible, dynamic and scalable workflow management architectures. First of all, malleability allows the coordinating behaviour of workflow engines to be forged and tuned dynamically. Then, inspectability makes it possible to design workflow engines whose coordinating state and behaviour are fully observable, thus providing a straightforward support for management activities, in particular for automated forms of on-line analysis of workflow data. Finally, linkability can be suitably exploited for enabling the distribution of the workflow activities and scaling with their complexity, by allowing multiple workflow engines (built as coordination artifacts) to be linked together, carrying on parts of the same (distributed) workflow within different execution contexts.

2.2   ReSpecT Tuple Centres as Coordination Artifacts

As a concrete technology for implementing coordination artifacts, we adopt ReSpecT tuple centres [9]. Generally speaking, features provided by the tuple centre model make it an effective model for designing and implementing flexible agent-based WfMSs [1].

Tuple centres are programmable tuple spaces: while the behaviour of a tuple space in response to communication events is fixed, the behaviour of a tuple centre can be in fact programmed through the ReSpecT language [10]. ReSpecT *specification tuples* define the behaviour of a tuple centre in terms of *reactions* to interaction, by determining how a tuple centre should react to incoming/outgoing communication events—such as Linda-like operations like *out*, *rd*, *in*. In short, ReSpecT primitives make it possible to catch and observe interaction events involving the tuple centre, to manipulate tuples inside the tuple centre, and also to interact with other tuple centres, for instance making it possible to insert tuples in other tuple centres [11]. Since ReSpecT is Turing-equivalent, any kind of computable coordination law can be in principle embedded in a ReSpecT tuple centre. Also, two basic operations, set_spec and get_spec, are provided to support run-time inspection and modification of the specification tuples of a tuple centre. In the overall, then, tuple centres can be framed as general-purpose coordination artifacts that can be dynamically customised (programmed) to provide specific coordination functionalities.

The kind of communication featured in general by tuple-based models [12] provides for time, space, and name uncoupling, by making tuple spaces (tuple centres in ReSpecT) mediate all interactions. Agent interacting via tuple spaces (and tuple centres, as well) need not to coexist in time and / or space, nor are they required to know each other or to share a common implementation / architecture. This is a desirable property of any open workflow system indeed, where agents behaviour cannot be predicted, and also eases interoperability among a set of agents that could be heterogeneous under many aspects. Moreover, associative access to information represented in form of tuples makes it easier for agents acting in an open and heterogeneous environments to work with incomplete knowledge, whether in task description or in workflow documents. So, facing heterogeneity of information is made easy by the possibility of accessing information only on the basis of partial / incomplete knowledge. As a further benefit of tuple-based coordination, synchronisation based on information availability is well-suited to represent task-based or document-based synchronisation of most workflow processes.

The very notion of coordination artifacts represented by tuple centres is the most important feature with respect to workflow management. By enabling the representation of workflow rules in terms of coordination rules programmed into tuple centres, tuple centres can work as workflow engines, encapsulating the set of rules constituting the workflow. Inspectability and malleability are supported by the possibility respectively to read and change dynamically both the content (logic tuples) of the tuple centres and their behaviour (specification tuples). Linkability is supported by the possibility of exchanging tuples with other tuple centres directly from the execution of reactions inside a tuple centre itself [11].

2.3   A General-Purpose Workflow Engine upon ReSpecT

By exploiting the expressive power of the Turing-equivalent ReSpecT language, it is possible to design and develop a *general purpose* workflow engine on top of a ReSpecT tuple centre. Accordingly, a ReSpecT tuple centre is programmed so as to enact workflow specification encoded in terms of a set of logic tuples, stored dynamically inside the tuple centre. So, on the one side ReSpecT specification tuples define the behaviour of the tuple centre as an interpreter of the workflow specification; on the other side, logic tuples dynamically stored inside the tuple centre are used to represent both the state of a workflow in execution, and the description of the workflow to be executed or in execution.

The model described here is intentionally kept simple, by omitting some details that are not strictly needed to understand the essential features of the approach. In the following, we sketch the model, by articulating the fundamental aspects that typically concern the design of a workflow engine.

Basic Ontology. The elementary unit of work inside a workflow is the *task*: a workflow *schema* is then a collection of tasks that collectively achieve the goal(s) of a process. Tasks are interrelated into a flow structure via *connectors*, such as split and join elements, which define the execution dependencies among tasks— that is, the order in which tasks should be executed. A (workflow) *case* is an execution of a workflow schema, i.e. an instance of the corresponding business process. A case is composed by a collection of *task instances*, as instances of the task specified in the corresponding workflow schema. Each workflow schema has a meaningful name used as an identifier, and so does each task inside a workflow. Analogously, runtime cases and task instances are denoted by a unique identifier—automatically generated by the workflow engines.[1]

In order to better support workflow (de)composition—and distribution, as discussed in the next section—the notion of *scope* is introduced, as a way to identify the context where a part of a case should be executed [14]. A workflow schema can then be partitioned by identifying a set of scopes and specifying

---

[1] We deviate from WfMC terminology just to be clear and avoid ambiguities [13]: the interested reader could easily find the straightforward mapping between the two syntaxes.

which part of the workflow—i.e. which tasks—is to be executed in which scope. Scopes can be naturally organised in hierarchies, with child scopes defined as linked to a parent scope. The *main scope* is the root of the hierarchy, and defines the scope for the global workflow.

Scopes are used to specify the granularity of the mapping between workflows and their execution engines—tuple centres in our case. One or multiple scopes can be executed by a single workflow engine, and the execution of each individual scope is associated to exactly one workflow engine. As detailed in next section, different scopes of the same workflow schema can be executed on top of different workflow engines, linked together.

The design of a general purpose workflow engine on top of ReSpecT tuple centres concerns three main aspects:

- the *agent interaction protocol*, which specifies the actions that agents can perform on the workflow engines;
- the *event model*, defining which kind of *internal* and *external* events should be accounted for;
- the *process model*, describing the behavioural aspects of a workflow specification, from its initial state to (one of) its final states.

The Agent Interaction Protocol. This protocol specifies which actions can be performed by agents on the workflow engine, and how they should be expressed. Agent actions typically concern task allocation and task completion. As usual in tuple-based models, actions are manifested in our model by requiring that agents deliberately insert in the tuple centre a tuple to express their activity: such a tuple is said to *reify* the agent's action, and may cause events inside the workflow engine.

Here we assume that an agent willing to take charge of a given task does so by removing from the workflow engine tuple centre the corresponding `task_todo` tuple, performing a `inp` operation[2] of the form

$$inp(task\_todo(\textit{?TaskName},\textit{?CaseID},\textit{-TaskID}))^3$$

where *TaskName* identifies the type of tasks the agent wants to take charge of, *CaseID* the specific case that the agent is considering, and *TaskID* is the identifier of the specific task instance, returned by the engine. The operation is issued on the tuple centre where the case is running. Information possibly required for task execution is meant to be stored in tuples apart, readable by the agent after taking in charge the task.

---

[2] The `inp` primitive removes a tuple matching the template specified as argument, and returns a success / failure condition: the operation succeeds if a matching tuple is found, or immediately fails otherwise, yet without blocking the agent activity.

[3] Following Prolog convention for parameter passing, the + sign means that it is an input parameter (can be also not specified: _), the - sign means that it is an output parameter (variable), the ? sign means that it can be both input and output, the @ sign means that it is an input parameter and must be specified (it cannot be _).

Analogously, agents manifest the successful completion of the task *TaskID* that they were charged of by inserting in the tuple centre a suitable `task_success` tuple by performing an **out** invocation:

`out(task_success(@TaskID))`

Analogously to information required by task execution, also information eventually provided with task execution is meant to be stored in tuples apart, inserted by the agent before signalling task completion.

The Event Model. As for agent actions above, also the occurrence of events is represented here through reifying tuples. According to [15], events can be either *internal* or *external*.

Internal events define the normal flow of activities within the workflow (such as temporal events related to the beginning and the termination of a task): tuples reifying these events are not inserted by agents, but are generated by the workflow engine itself as a result of its coordination activity. Such tuples take the form `event(`*Desc, Time*`)`, where *Desc* is a description of the event, *Time* is a timestamp indicating when the event occurred (taking the local time of the tuple centre as a reference).

- the *start of a new task*, represented by a `task_started(`*TaskID, ExecutorID*`)` tuple—where *TaskID* is the identifier of the task, and *ExecutorID* is the identifier of the agent responsible for this task;
- the *termination of a task*, represented by a `task_finished(`*TaskID,Result*`)` tuple—where *TaskID* is the identifier of the task, and *Result* is the information about the success / failure of the task;
- the *start of a case*, represented by a `case_started(`*CaseID,ExecutorID*`)` tuple—where *CaseID* is the identifier of the case, and *ExecutorID* is the identifier of the agent initiator of the case;
- the *termination of a case*, represented by a `case_finished(`*CaseID,Result*`)` tuple—where *CaseID* is the identifier of the case, and *Result* is the information about the success / failure of the case.

External events are instead outside the control of the WfMS, and typically represent error conditions: examples are asynchronous external events (such as task cancellation), changes in the process organisation (such as the sudden unavailability of an agent), or the violation of constraints either on the workflow data or on the workflow timing. In state-of-the-art workflow systems, exception management usually requires the definition of a set of triggers (rules) which specify the asynchronous actions (typically notifications) to be taken when the conditions defining exceptions occur. Analogously, workflow exceptions are managed in tuple centres by reactions triggered by the interaction events related to the exception conditions: exception events, too, are reified as tuples inserted in the tuple centre.

Since these issues are not essential for the focus of the paper, we forward the interested readers to other articles [1] where the problems of exception handling and workflow dynamic change are considered.

The Process Model. Typically, a WfMS describes control flow structures by means of either flow diagrams (Petri-nets and similar) or special-purpose languages designed for workflow management, such as XPDL [7] or BPEL [6]. In our approach such information is described declaratively, as a logic theory about the coordination enacted by the workflow. Basically, the theory is composed by *(i)* a set of assertion describing the tasks involved in the workflow, *(ii)* a set of assertions describing the workflow rules which define task coordination, and *(iii)* a set of assertions that define the scopes on which the workflow is structured.

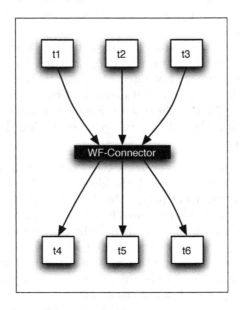

Fig. 1. A generic workflow connector

By using the ReSpecT tuple centre model, such theory is encoded as a set of logic tuples of the following kind:

`task_def(`*TaskName,WfName,TaskDesc,ScopeName*`)` defines a task, characterised by a name *TaskName*, the name *WfName* of the workflow schema where it is defined, a task description *TaskDesc*, and the scope *ScopeName* where the task is supposed to be executed. For each task defined in a schema, a tuple of this kind must be specified;

`wf_def(`*WfName,InTasks,OutTasks,Pattern*`)` defines a workflow rule belonging to the workflow schema *WfName*, linking together two sets of tasks—listed in *InTasks* and *OutTasks*—, according to a specific semantics. The two sets of tasks can be thought as the input and the output tasks of a workflow connector as typically presented in workflow diagrams (see Fig. 1), coordinating the completion of input tasks and the triggering of output tasks. The semantics of the connector is defined by specifying *Pattern*, which represents the type of connection among the tasks. *Pattern* can be either a *PatternName*—that is, a term denoting one of the basic types of connection such as sequence, and_split, and_join, or_join— or a *CondList*—that is, a list of logic terms denoting the conditions that must dynamically hold to trigger the execution of the output tasks (*activating condition*), defined through cond/3 clauses. While the former syntax is maybe the most natural for the straightforward representation of workflow schema, the latter is the most general (including the former as a subcase), and can supposedly express most (if not all) of the patterns listed in [14].

scope_def(*ScopeName,WfName,ParentScopeName*) defines a scope, belonging to workflow schema *WfName*, identified by the term *ScopeName* and whose parent scope is *ParentScopeName*.

Tuple centres acting as workflow engines are programmed so as to dynamically react to the communication events that characterise agent interaction during the workflow, and to update the state of the coordination activity—by consuming, transforming, producing set of tuples. Such updates trigger new tasks to be executed as well as agent activities according to the theory defined in wf_def, task_def and scope_def tuples.

In short, here is how a tuple centre behaves as a workflow engine:[4] A workflow case starts when a tuple case_tostart(*WfName,ScopeName*) is inserted in the workflow engine tuple centre. This event triggers a set of reactions, which sets the basic data structures (in form of logic tuples) required for the execution of a new case, and collects the names of all the tasks that should be triggered to start the workflow. In particular, this is achieved by reading all the wf_def tuples that have the task case_start among the input tasks.

The conditions specified in wf_def are dynamically evaluated, and only the output tasks for which the related condition holds are triggered, by generating a tuple task_todo(*TaskName,CaseID,TaskID*). Actually, this tuple is generated only if the scope specified for the task in the tuple task_def is mapped on the tuple centre executing the reaction: otherwise, as described in the next section, the task execution is exported to the tuple centre where such a scope is mapped.

When an agent retrieves a task_todo—preparing for the execution of a task—, the tuple centre reacts and updates the tuples carrying the state of the workflow accordingly. The core of the coordinating activity of the tuple centre takes place when agents insert task_finished tuples, to manifest the completion of tasks. This event triggers a set of reactions, which find out the next tasks to do by evaluating the content of the wf_def tuples that have the task completed among the input tasks. The coordinating activity goes on as long as case_end is specified as the task to be triggered.

---

[4] ReSpecT reactions defining the tuple centre behaviour are here omitted for the lack of space: the interested reader can find all the code at http://www.alice.unibo.it/download/workflow/coord06.zip.

3 Distributing Workflows with Linkability

3.1 Distributed Workflow: Motivations and Requirements

Whereas exploiting a single coordination artifact as a workflow engine for complex workflows is technically feasible, e.g. by using the approach discussed in previous section, this is seemingly not an sensible solution under many respects.

The ability to distribute a workflow among different engines is first of all required for reasons of *expressiveness*. Distribution, in fact, may be inherent to the application scenario, where agents, services and resources could be intrinsically distributed in space. So, simple principles of locality and encapsulation would require the corresponding activities to be distributed as well, along with the workflow engines. Also, distribution may in principle improve *efficiency*, in particular when independent activities can be carried on concurrently by distinct workflow nodes. Finally, distribution may also have a favourable impact on *robustness*, since the failure of a workflow node does not necessarily lead to the global workflow failure.

This holds in particular in the case of inter-organisational workflow (IOW) [2]. There, portions of multiple distributed workflows have typically to be combined and aggregated into complex workflow structures, constituting for instance the backbone of a VE. So, the problem is not to distribute a workflow, rather the other way round: that is, to aggregate some inherently distributed activities in a higher-level workflow. Distribution is no longer an option, then—just a matter of fact.

The first point here is then *composability* of workflows, in general, and in particular of workflow engines. How to share information among several independent activities, and how to coordinate them over a distributed, asynchronous scenario, are the central issues here.

The second point is *ownership*: stakeholders of independent activities within an IOW may not be willing to share everything, and to open up completely to the other participants. It is quite often the case, for instance, that VEs are made up of competitors, typically fighting each other in the local market, but willing to cooperate to win some share on a larger setting. In this scenario, most of the workflow activities should remain under the control of each participant, which should then be allowed to carry on its portions of workflow locally and in autonomy.

The third and final point is *alterity*: IOW does not belong in principle to any of the participant organisations—at least, not necessarily. So, it is typically required that the main workflow is hosted by a third-party (an external host, a provider, a shared space) that is not directly owned / controlled by any of the workflow participants—and so, that an external infrastructure of some sort supports the main workflow engine.

In next subsection, we take the above requirements for IOW as driving principles for distributed workflow in general, and show how an architecture for distributed workflow can be accordingly defined based on a distributed coordination infrastructure.

3.2   A Coordination Architecture for Distributed Workflows

Based on the remarks in previous subsection, it is now quite straightforward to devise out an abstract architecture for distributed workflow based on a coordination infrastructure.

First of all, ownership implies that portions of the supporting infrastructure should be owned by each of the participants, and autonomously governed by them. Of course, this also means that such an infrastructure does not need to be pervasive, but should only affect those processes that need to be shared in the workflow. So, each of the workflow nodes may contain one or more workflow engines, built as suitably-specialised coordination artifacts, as discussed in the previous section. The engines represent in principle the only things that each node (for instance, a participant to an IOW) is required to open and share with other nodes (other participant organisations) to function as a part of the distributed workflow. Local activities can then be carried on autonomously by local agents, with no need for unnecessary disclosures. The main consequence, then, is that the supporting coordination infrastructure needs to be distributed, and owned by each of the workflow participants in terms of one or more workflow nodes, connected to each other through the network.

Then, composability of workflow engines is a fundamental pre-condition to distribute workflow activities. In fact, while interoperability of nodes is an obvious feature for any distributed infrastructure, the same does not hold for distributed coordination artifacts, at least for Linda-based models: interaction between tuple spaces, for instance, is not a typical features of Linda-like models. Instead, the ability to link different stages of separate but related workflows is essential to synchronise and coordinate the activities of multiple autonomous agents in a distributed workflow. This obviously mandates for the ability to exchange information among the coordination artifacts working as workflow engines: to set when a task can be started, when another task has been completed, when a problem arises. Linkability of artifacts is then another essential feature for a coordination infrastructure to support distribution of workflow.

Finally, alterity means that a distributed workflow may in principle be hosted by a workflow node (call it the *main workflow node*, implicitly defining the main scope of the workflow) which is not required to belong to one of the workflow participants—in IOW, it might be required *not* to.

In all, a simple abstract architecture for distributed workflow could be envisioned as follows: *(i)* a main workflow node, containing the general specification of the distributed workflow, *(ii)* a number of workflow nodes distributed across workflow participants (one or more node for each participant), in charge of their own portions of the workflow, *(iii)* a network of workflow events exchanged among the workflow engines, in order to maintain global consistency of the distributed workflow activities. In terms of the supporting coordination architecture, this essentially means that coordination artifacts should be *(i)* programmable—working as general-purpose workflow engines—, *(ii)* distributable—so they can be located *chez* each workflow node, and *(iii)* linkable—to reify workflow events, so that distributed workflow engines can synchronise and coordinate across the network.

3.3 Distributing Workflows Via Artifact Linkability

All the above requires also some suitable abstractions with the expressive power to encapsulate workflow portions (simple tasks, more articulated workflow branches) so as to preserve consistency while distributing them. The notion of *scope* can be used to this purpose. In short, a scope is an independent workflow process generated by a parent process, and represents a sort of container for workflow activities. To us, here, it works as a sort of local environment for workflow activities, and as such can be conceived as the basic abstraction to encapsulate and distribute workflows.

As shown in the previous section, a scope is defined among the three main entities of our basic approach (workflow schema, task structures, scopes) through the `scope_def/3` predicate. Beyond these three predicates, a fourth predicate `scope_location/3` is then used to structure the "workflow environment" by associating each node of the scope hierarchy to a workflow engine belonging to a given workflow node. Since workflow engines are here mapped upon coordination artifacts, a clause `scope_location(`*ScopeName,WfName,ArtID*`)` associates scope *WfName:ScopeName* to the workflow engine built upon coordination artifact *ArtID*. The portion of the workflow associated to scope *WfName:ScopeName* by clauses of the form `task_def(`*TaskName,WfName,...,ScopeName*`)` has to be then executed on the workflow engine running over artifact *ArtID*.

Of course, artifact denotation should include the syntax for distribution. For instance, in our reference architecture, TuCSoN, artifacts are tuple centres denoted by a *TupleCentreID* composed as *TupleCentreName@HostID*, where *TupleCentreName* is just the local tuple centre name, and *HostID* is the DNS identifier of the TuCSoN node hosting the tuple centre.[5] As a result, a clause of the form `scope_location(`*ScopeName, TupleCentreID*`)` makes a given number of workflow tasks associated to scope *ScopeName* be executed by the workflow engine built on tuple centre *TupleCentreID*.

Distributing a workflow is now a matter of when, what and how. Whereas the when and the what are soon solved, the how is precisely when linkability of artifacts comes in. Distribution of a workflow starts as soon as a task is activated whose execution should happen elsewhere: that is, when its scope is associated to an artifact that is not the engine where the workflow is currently being executed. Since scopes are defined hierarchically, all the subsequent tasks defined in the same scope and in all the subscopes should be moved along with the corresponding ontology definitions: workflow schema, tasks, scope definitions and locations are what should be moved across workflow engines.

How this should happen—it is on the one hand a quite simple issue, on the other hand the core point of this paper. Two things in fact need to be transferred:

---

[5] According to the TuCSoN syntax, when *TupleCentreID* is simply *TupleCentreName*, it means that the tuple centre is hosted locally in the same TuCSoN node.

information and control. Information needs to flow among engines in order to allow the execution of workflow (sub-)processes to move along while maintaining structural consistency. Then, control needs to be exchanged among workflow engines so as to allow for synchronisation and coordination of distributed and interdependent activities.

To this end, coordination artifacts should be linkable, by allowing information to be exchanged, events to be notified, and exchanges to be captured across different artifacts. So, first of all, a mechanism to send information to another coordination artifact is required to distribute scopes—along with the corresponding workflow, task and subscope information. Then, a way to ask for information when available is needed, in order to synchronise and coordinate distributed workflows: for instance, to be notified of the end of a task, of a milestone reached, of a task failure. Finally, a way to capture information coming from another artifact—either solicited or not—and to associate it to computational activities, is mandatory to ensure timeliness of workflow activities, such as distributed task selection and activation.

In the case of the TuCSoN coordination infrastructure, the last requirement is straightforwardly met by the reaction model: the ReSpecT language, in fact, not only enables programmability of the tuple centres, but also allows any event traversing the tuple centre's boundaries to be captured, associated to a specific computation (a reaction) and there fully observed so as to catch and exploit any relevant related information [9]. The other two aspects, instead, clearly need tuples to be sent from a tuple centre to another, and to be required for delivery when available by a tuple centre to another: this means that tuple centres have to be able to perform *in*s, *rd*s and *out*s one another.

Even though linkability is not a property of the original ReSpecT model [9], it has been added later to deal with multiple coordination flows [11]. So, ReSpecT reactions can contain `out_tc`, `in_tc`, `rd_tc`, `inp_tc`, `rdp_tc` primitives, which allow tuples to flow bi-directionally between tuple centres, and distributed tuple centres to synchronise and coordinate their activities. The semantics of such operations is exactly what anyone would expect by any Linda-like set of primitives—on the side of the receiving tuple centre, so for instance an `in_tc` waits for a suitable tuple, then consumes it and returns it to the caller tuple centre. By contrast, on the side of the requesting tuple centre, the properties of ReSpecT are maintained, while the expected Linda ones are not—so, for instance, *in*s and *rd*s are asynchronous: their execution is triggered only at the end of a successful reaction invoking them, reactions do not wait for them to complete, and the completions of the operations (when an answer is returned) is handled through further specialised reactions.

In all, linkability of tuple centres is exploited by the WfMS essentially in two fundamental phases: *(i)* when a workflow portion, defined by a scope, has to be moved from a workflow node to another, *(ii)* when any activity requires a form of distributed notification to be started. ReSpecT *setter* (`out_tc`) and *getter* primitives (`in_tc`, `rd_tc`, `inp_tc`, `rdp_tc`), respectively, are used for this.

While the general distributed implementation of the WfMS is relatively simple, it is anyway too large for this paper to be presented in detail. To this end, next section discusses a workflow example, allowing us to illustrate many of the issues raised till now.

4 A Case Study: The Simple-Goods-Seller over the Internet Virtual Enterprise

As our (toy) case study, here we consider the design and development of a WfMS for a virtual organisation called SGSI (Simple-Goods-Seller over the Internet), and its engineering upon the TuCSoN coordination infrastructure. The goal of this example is mainly to provide the reader with some glimpses of the actual implementation of a WfMS upon TuCSoN according to the approach presented in this paper—in particular, how scopes implemented on top of artifact linkability can be used to have multiple, interdependent, distributed workflows, and to create a network of inter-connected coordination flows. The case study does not pretend to cover in detail all the complex issue of real-world scenarios: however, it should be useful to understand how these issues could be further addressed by adopting the logic-based workflow language and the distributed workflow architecture discussed in previous sections.

4.1 SGSI Distributed Workflow General Description

The aim of the SGSI virtual enterprise is to expand a real shop marketplace to the Internet virtual market, by exploiting the competences of several collaborating enterprises. We assume that four companies participate to the VE:

Web Portal company which manages the web interface and collects the online client orders;

Financial company which manages all the financial and administrative details about money transactions;

Goods company which manages all the process concerning the development and wherehousing of assets;

Delivery company which manages the delivery of the acquired goods.

The VE business process starts when the Web Portal receives an order by customer. The process goes on enabling and validating payment and collecting all the assets required, in parallel. When payment is received, the invoice can be generated; when the assets are collected, goods can be delivered. Finally, the client can be informed that shipment has been executed.

4.2 SGSI Distributed Workflow Specification

The behaviour of the SGSI VE can be modelled by assuming that all the participants have agreed on a business workflow schema representing the VE workflow, like the one in Fig. 2. We consider two description levels. At the first level, the

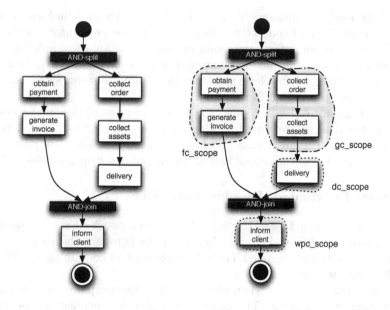

```
wf_def(sgsiWf, [case_start], [obtain_payment,collect_order], and_split).
wf_def(sgsiWf, [obtain_payment], [generate_invoice], sequence).
wf_def(sgsiWf, [collect_order], [collect_assets], sequence).
wf_def(sgsiWf, [collect_assets], [delivery], sequence).
wf_def(sgsiWf, [generate_invoice,delivery], [inform_client], and_join).
wf_def(sgsiWf, [inform_client], [case_end], sequence).
```

```
task_def(obtain_payment, sgsiWf, ..., fc_scope).
task_def(generate_invoice, sgsiWf, ..., fc_scope).
task_def(collect_order, sgsiWf, ..., gc_scope).
task_def(collect_assets, sgsiWf, ..., gc_scope).
task_def(delivery, sgsiWf, ..., dc_scope).
task_def(inform_client, sgsiWf, ..., wpc_scope).

scope_def(main_scope, sgsiWf, root).
scope_def(fcscope, sgsiWf, main_scope).
scope_def(gcscope, sgsiWf, main_scope).
scope_def(dcscope, sgsiWf, main_scope).
scope_def(wpcscope, sgsiWf, main_scope).

scope_location(main_scope, sgsi@web_portal_node).
scope_location(fc_scope, fc@financial_node).
scope_location(gc_scope, gc@goods_node).
scope_location(dc_scope, dc@delivery_node).
scope_location(wp_cscope, wpc@webportal_node).
```

Fig. 2. *(Top)* Workflow schema of the selling business process for SGSI VE (left), with tasks allocated to scopes (right). *(Bottom)* Sketch of the workflow schema specification using our logic-based approach.

focus of the workflow manager/designer is related to the real business, abstracting away from the real context in which tasks will be performed. At this level, abstract tasks are identified, encapsulating the execution of complex activities, and dependencies among such tasks are defined (top of Fig. 2, left). At a second level, the content of the first level is refined by defining the scopes and associating tasks to scopes (top of Fig. 2, right).

The bottom part of Fig. 2 reports the logic-based description of the workflow, where the two distinct parts are in evidence—corresponding to the two levels: the description of the overall process—and of the task dependencies in particular—, and the description of the scopes and of the mapping between scopes and tasks.

4.3   SGSI Distributed Workflow Behaviour

Given the simple structure of the SGSI VE, we can assume here the main scope of the workflow is handled by the Web Provider company, hosting a workflow engine (a suitably-programmed TuCSoN tuple centre) containing the SGSI VE workflow specification.

The worklow case starts when the Web Provider company receives an order confirmation from a client. The `case_start` clause is evaluated, and the two out-tasks `obtain_payment` and `collect_order` are activated. Since they both are associated to external scopes (`fc_scope` and `gc_scope`), two scope-export processes are activated, copying all the clauses defining such scopes (as well as the other tasks belonging to them, such as `collect_assets` for `gc_scope`) to the workflow engines / tuple centres specified by `scope_location/2` clauses. Then, the two corresponding sub-cases are activated by the main workflow engine (the Web Portal one), which also manages synchronisation by waiting for `task_finished` tuples from the `fc_scope` and `gc_scope` tuple centres, manifesting the end of the two sub-cases. The rest of the workflow follows as intuitive, and ends when also the last `inform_client` task has been successfully completed.

5   Related Work and Conclusion

With respect to our previous work on the subject of workflow management and coordination infrastructures, in this paper we explicitly face for the first time the issue of workflow distribution through linkability of coordination artifacts, based on TuCSoN tuple centres programmed in ReSpecT. After discussing a model of workflow engine based on ReSpecT tuple centres, in this paper we introduce a distributed workflow architecture based on TuCSoN, exploiting a logic-based workflow language, capable of capturing all the known workflow patterns [14]. The issue of workflow distribution is addressed through the definition of an explicit scoping mechanism, enabling workflows to be dynamically governed and distributed upon a coordination infrastructure based on linkability of coordination artifacts.

Linkability in its most general acceptation is not strictly a new idea in the field of coordination models and languages. The most prominent example is Reo

[16], where channel composition is one of the most important and relevant features. Also, Reo has been recently experimented explicitly in the MAS field [17]. However, Linda-based approaches better cope with agent autonomy, since coordination is not forced upon the agents participating to the workflow, but is instead provided them as a service [18]. Also, the properties of generative communication and associative access of Linda-like models, along with the use of logic tuples, are essential for our declarative approach to agent-based workflow. Even more, programmability of tuple centres in TuCSoN enables coordination artifacts to be suitably modelled as workflow engines with the fundamental properties of inspectability and malleability.

In the context of Linda-based models, to the best of our knowledge, only Lime [19] could exhibit some sort of mechanism for tuple space composition. However, such a mechanism is essentially implicit, and does not allow for the explicit control required in WfMSs—and allowed instead by ReSpecT linkability primitives.

In the area of (research and industrial) WfMSs, currently available approaches are mainly extensions of DBMS. Notable examples are WIDE [20], Regatta [21], APM [22], MILANO [23], TriGS [24], and the commercial systems ATI Action Workflow, XSoft InConcert, and TeamWARE Flow. The above systems face the requirements for classic WfMS, but are not especially suited to support Inter-Organisational and Web-based WfMS [2].

Indeed, this scenario requires the ability to cope with the openness and distribution of the Web environment, the capability to face heterogeneity at different levels (information models, resources, processes), to support the dynamic modification of workflow rules, and to adapt the evolution of business processes so as to easily face changes and exceptions, which frequently occur in an open environment. However, approaches based on agents and coordination infrastructures are now emerging. The METEOR$_2$ system [25], for instance, goes beyond the classic workflow systems, addressing issues such as Web-based workflow, workflow adaptation and integral support for collaboration. In [26], the researchers involved in the METEOR project asserted that *"Coordination (as supported by current generation of workflow technology), collaboration (as supported by CSCW and work group systems) and information management will increasingly together merge into a higher level form of middleware"*. OrbWork and WebWork, which are two implementations of the METEOR$_2$ model, make a meaningful step toward coordination and collaboration, even though they might not be expressive enough to provide the required general-purpose coordination middleware. On the other hand, TuCSoN provides a general-purpose, distributed coordination infrastructure, which seems to be expressive enough to support distributed workflow management, as well as coordination and collaboration among heterogeneous agents.

In [27], [28], and [29], mobile and intelligent agent technologies are used for VE management, yet without providing an explicit model for WfMS. In [30] and [31], VEs are represented using MASs, with an explicit model of WfMS. Basically, all these approaches support business processes execution with subjective coordination, encapsulating the social rules directly within agents. As discussed in [1], we found that objective coordination, provided by TuCSoN and by most approaches from the field of coordination models and languages [32], is better suited to the context of VE than subjective coordination, since it provides a more effective support for dynamics, heterogeneity, and process traceability.

The Workspaces coordination technology [33], specifically developed for distributed workflow management, provides one further way of developing a Web-based WfMS making explicit use of a coordination infrastructure for agent-based systems. Basically, its architecture is based on coordinated transformation of XML documents by means of distributed XSL (workflow) engines: the work-flow rules are expressed via an XML-based Workspaces Coordination Language, and then compiled into a set of XSL rules to specify the engine behaviour. Our TuCSoN-based approach uses logic tuples for both communication and coordination, instead of XML: however, as far as any XML fragment can be expressed in terms of first-order logic, an analogous approach could in principle be adopted by TuCSoN, too. Also, Workspaces apparently does not faces explicitly the issue of workflow distribution—which was instead the main motivation behind this work.

References

1. Ricci, A., Omicini, A., Denti, E.: Virtual enterprises and workflow management as agent coordination issues. International Journal of Cooperative Information Systems **11**(3/4) (2002) 355–379 Special Issue: Cooperative Information Agents – Best Papers of CIA 2001.
2. Divitini, M., Hanachi, C., Sibertin-Blanc, C.: Inter–organizational workflows for enterprise coordination. In Omicini, A., Zambonelli, F., Klusch, M., Tolksdorf, R., eds.: Coordination of Internet Agents: Models, Technologies, and Applications. Springer-Verlag (2001) 369–398
3. Omicini, A., Ricci, A., Viroli, M., Castelfranchi, C., Tummolini, L.: Coordination artifacts: Environment-based coordination for intelligent agents. In Jennings, N.R., Sierra, C., Sonenberg, L., Tambe, M., eds.: 3rd international Joint Conference on Autonomous Agents and Multiagent Systems (AAMAS 2004). Volume 1. ACM, New York, USA (2004) 286–293
4. Omicini, A., Ricci, A., Viroli, M.: *Agens Faber*: Toward a theory of artefacts for MAS. Electronic Notes in Theoretical Computer Sciences (2006) 1st International Workshop "Coordination and Organization" (CoOrg 2005), COORDINATION 2005, Namur, Belgium, 22 April 2005. Post-proceedings.
5. Ricci, A., Viroli, M., Omicini, A.: Programming MAS with artifacts. In Bordini, R.P., Dastani, M., Dix, J., El Fallah Seghrouchni, A., eds.: Programming Multi-Agent Systems III. Volume 3862 of LNAI. Springer (2006) 206–221 3rd International Workshop (PROMAS 2005), AAMAS 2005, Utrecht, The Netherlands, 26 July 2005. Revised and Selected Papers.
6. OASIS Consortium: Business Process Execution Language. http://www.oasis-open.org/committees/ tc_home.php?wg_abbrev=wsbpel (2005)
7. Workflow Management Coalition Group: XML Process Definition Language. http://www.wfmc.org/standards/XPDL.htm (2003)

8. Malone, T., Crowstone, K.: The interdisciplinary study of coordination. ACM Computing Surveys **26**(1) (1994) 87–119
9. Omicini, A., Denti, E.: From tuple spaces to tuple centres. Science of Computer Programming **41**(3) (2001) 277–294
10. Omicini, A., Denti, E.: Formal ReSpecT. In Dovier, A., Meo, M.C., Omicini, A., eds.: Declarative Programming – Selected Papers from AGP'00. Volume 48 of Electronic Notes in Theoretical Computer Science. Elsevier Science B. V. (2001) 179–196
11. Ricci, A., Omicini, A., Viroli, M.: Extending ReSpecT for multiple coordination flows. In Arabnia, H.R., ed.: International Conference on Parallel and Distributed Processing Techniques and Applications (PDPTA'02). Volume III. CSREA Press, Las Vegas, NV, USA (2002) 1407–1413
12. Gelernter, D.: Generative communication in Linda. ACM Transactions on Programming Languages and Systems **7**(1) (1985) 80–112
13. Workflow Management Coalition: Home page. http://www.wfmc.org/ (2006)
14. van der Aalst, W.M.P., ter Hofstede, A.H.M., Kiepuszewski, B., Barros, A.P.: Workflow patterns. Distributed and Parallel Databases **14**(1) (2003) 5–51
15. Casati, F., Castano, S., Fugini, M., Mirabel, I., Pernici, B.: Using patterns to design rules in workflows. IEEE Transactions on Software Engineering **26**(8) (2000) 760–785
16. Arbab, F.: Reo: A channel-based coordination model for component composition. Mathematical Structures in Computer Science **14** (2004) 329–366
17. Dastani, M.: Coordination and Composition of Multi-Agent Systems. Invited talk, 1st International Workshop on Coordination and Organisation (CoOrg 2005), COORDINATION 2005, Namur, Belgium (2005)
18. Viroli, M., Omicini, A.: Coordination as a service. Fundamenta Informaticae **71**(4) (2006)
19. Picco, G.P., Murphy, A.L., Roman, G.C.: LIME: Linda Meets Mobility. In Garlan, D., ed.: 21st International Conference on Software Engineering (ICSE'99), Los Angeles, CA, USA, ACM Press (1999) 368–377
20. Grefen, P., Pernici, B., Sanchez, G., eds.: Database support for Workflow Management – The WIDE Project. Kluwer Academic Publishers (1999)
21. Swenson, K.D., Maxwell, R.J., Matsumoto, T., Saghari, B., Irwin, K.: A Business Process Environment Supporting Collaborative Planning. Collaborative Computing **1**(1) (1994) 15–34
22. Carlsen, S.: Action port model: A mixed paradigm conceptual workflow modeling language. In Halper, M., ed.: 3rd IFCIS International Conference on Cooperative Information Systems, IEEE Computer Society (1998) 300–309
23. Agostini, A., De Michelis, G., Grasso, M.A.: Rethinking CSCW systems: The architecture of MILANO. In Hughes, J.A., Prinz, W., Rodden, T., Schmidt, K., eds.: 5th European Conference on Computer Supported Cooperative Work (ECSCW'97), Kluwer Academic Publishers (1997) 33–48
24. Kappel, G., Rausch-Scott, S., Retschitzegger, W.: A framework for workflow management systems based on objects, rules and roles. ACM Computing Surveys **32**(1es) (2000) Article no. 27.
25. Miller, J.A., Palaniswami, D., Sheth, K.J., Singh, H.: Webwork: METEOR$_2$'s web-based workflow management system. Journal of Intelligent Information Systems **10**(2) (1998) 185–215
26. Sheth, A.P., Kochut, K.J.: Workflow applications to research agenda: Scalable and dynamic work co-ordination and collaborative systems. In Dogaç, A., Kalinichenko,

L., Tamer Özsu, M., Sheth, A.P., eds.: Advances in Workflow Management Systems and Interoperability, Istanbul (Turkey) (1997)

27. Fischer, K., Muller, J., Heimig, I., Scheer, A.W.: Intelligent agents in virtual enterprises. In: Practical Application of Intelligent Agents and Multi-Agent Technology (PAAM 96). (1996)

28. Shen, W., Norrie, D.H.: Implementing internet enabled virtual enterprises using collaborative agents. In: Infrastructures for Virtual Enterprises, Kluwer Academic Publisher (1999) 343–352

29. Aerts, A., Szirbik, N., Hammer, D., Goossenaerts, J., Wortmann, H.: On the design of a mobile agent web for supporting virtual enterprises. In: IEEE 9th International Workshops on Enabling Technologies: Infrastructure for Collaborative Enterprises "Web-based Infrastructures and Coordination Architectures for Collaborative Enterprises" (WET ICE 2000), Gaithersburg (MD), IEEE CS (2000) 236–241

30. Chrysanthis, P.K., Znati, T., Banerjee, S., Chang, S.K.: Establishing virtual enterprises by means of mobile agents. In: Workshop on Research Issues in Data Engineering (RIDE 1999), IEEE CS (1999) 116–125

31. Merz, M., Liberman, B., Lamersdorf, W.: Using mobile agents to support interorganizational workflow-management. Applied Artificial Intelligence **6**(11) (1997) 551–572

32. Tolksdorf, R.: Models of coordination. In Omicini, A., Tolksdorf, R., Zambonelli, F., eds.: Engineering Societies in the Agents World. Volume 1972 of LNAI., Springer-Verlag (2000) 78–92

33. Tolksdorf, R.: Coordinating work on the Web with Workspaces. In: IEEE 9th International Workshops on Enabling Technologies: Infrastructure for Collaborative Enterprises "Web-based Infrastructures and Coordination Architectures for Collaborative Enterprises" (WET ICE 2000), Gaithersburg (MD), IEEE CS (2000) 248–253

Actors, Roles and Coordinators — A Coordination Model for Open Distributed and Embedded Systems*

Shangping Ren, Yue Yu, Nianen Chen,
Kevin Marth, Pierre-Etienne Poirot, Limin Shen

Computer Science Department
Illinois Institute of Technology
Chicago, IL 60616
{ren,yyu8,nchen3,marth,poirpie,shenl}@iit.edu

Abstract. This paper presents a coordination model, the Actor, Role and Coordinator (ARC) model, to address three main concerns inherent in a pervasive Open Distributed and Embedded (ODE) system: dynamicity, scalability, and stringent QoS requirements. The model treats a pervasive ODE system as a composition of concurrent computation and coerced coordination. In particular, concurrent computation is modeled as Actors, while coerced coordination specifies the system's QoS requirements by mapping them to coordination constraints. The coordination constraints are transparently imposed on actors through message manipulations, which are carried out by the roles and coordinators. The coordinators are responsible for the coordination among roles, while the roles in our model provide abstractions for coordinated behaviors that may be shared by multiple actors and further assume local coordination responsibilities for the actors playing the roles. The role's behavior abstraction decouples the syntactic dependencies between the coordinators and the actors, thus shielding the coordinator layer from the dynamicity of underlying actors inherent in ODE systems. This paper also formally defines the role and coordinator behaviors and the composition of the actor computation model with the proposed coerced coordination model. Our formal study has shown that the ARC system is closed under composition and recursion.

1 Introduction

As smart devices and communication schemes advance, embedded computer systems and their applications are emerging from closed and centralized domains into a more open and distributed environment. Open, distributed, and embedded (ODE) software systems must be concerned with the environment in which they are executed. One aspect of the environment is its extent. Computational entities may join or leave at any time, introducing dynamicity into the system. This openness also implies that the number of entities entering the system is not bounded, so the system could be arbitrarily large. A second aspect is the quality of service (QoS) requirements. An embedded application by nature has rigid requirements not only on the accuracy of the delivered

---

* This research is supported by NSF under grant CNS 0431832.

P. Ciancarini and H. Wiklicky (Eds.): COORDINATION 2006, LNCS 4038, pp. 247–265, 2006.

functionality, but also on the quality of the delivery, which is usually manifested through real-time constraints, reliability, fault-tolerance, and other QoS requirements. The dynamicity, scalability, and QoS concerns therefore distinguish ODE systems.

To accomplish the desirable delivery of certain functionalities, special policies — such as real-time constraints, adaptation strategies, security, reliability and fault-tolerance — must be integrated into the systems so that the autonomous and often asynchronous embedded software entities are forced to coordinate with each other and to respect the QoS requirements.

Concurrent and distributed computation models have been well studied over the past decades. CSP [1], π-calculus [2], and the Actor model [3, 4] are good examples. These models are well-defined mathematical abstractions for concurrent computation in a distributed environment. To meet the QoS demands in embedded applications, a separate coordination model needs to be composed with the concurrent computation model, coercing asynchronous entities to coordinate.

In this paper, we present a group-based and distributed coordination model, the Actor, Role and Coordinator (ARC) model. The focus of the ARC model is to better address the dynamicity and scalability issues inherent in pervasive ODE systems while fulfilling the system's QoS requirements. The ARC model has the following characteristics:

1. The Actor model is used to model the concurrent computational part of an ODE system, while an independent coordination model is developed to address the system's QoS requirements.
2. The concept of role is introduced into the coordination model. The role provides an abstraction for coordinated behaviors that may be shared by multiple actors and also provides localized coordination among its players.
3. Coordination in our model is divided into *inter-role* and *intra-role* coordination to ensure clearer separation of responsibilities, reduce the complexity of individual coordination entities, and enable distributed coordination among active roles and coordinators.
4. QoS requirements are mapped to coordination constraints and are transparently imposed on actors through message manipulations carried out by roles and coordinators.

The rest of the paper is organized as follows: Section 2 discusses related work. Section 3 presents the design considerations of the ARC model. Section 4 formally defines the ARC model and the composition between the computational subsystem (actors) and coordination subsystem (roles and coordinators). The section further uses an example to illustrate the composition scheme and show the soundness of the model. Section 5 draws conclusion and discusses future work.

2 Related Work

There are a number of proposals to capture QoS requirements as first class aspects in open distributed software, such as [5, 6, 7, 8]. However, few proposals have considered interpreting QoS requirements as coordination constraints so that qualitative demands can be specified and realized by utilizing the power of coordination models.

Recent research has yielded significant contributions on coordination models and languages. In their landmark survey [9], Papadopoulos et. al. conclude that coordination models can be classified into two categories, i.e., data-driven and control-driven. The tuple space [10] model and their extensions represent the data-driven category; while the IWIM and Manifold [11] present a control-driven or "exogenous" category. Recently, tuple center and ReSpecT [12, 13] provide a hybrid view.

Control-driven models, such as ABT [14], LGI [15], ROAD [16], IWIM [11] and CoLaS [17] isolate coordination by considering functional entities as black boxes. For example, the ABT model and its language Reo [14, 18] extend the IWIM by treating both computation and coordination components as composable Abstract Behavior Types (ABT). Similarly to IWIM, ABT is a two-level control-driven coordination model where computation and coordination concerns are achieved in separate and independent levels.

Other control-driven models, such as ROAD, CoLaS, TuCSoN with ACC [19] and Finesse [20] target the scalability issues of open distributed systems through group-based coordination models. In these group-based coordination models, roles are often treated as organizational concepts abstracting coordination behaviors among participants who play them. The ARC model differs from this increasing body of work by treating roles as proactive, stateful and first class entities. A survey of existing role-based coordination models is presented by Cabri and colleagues in [21].

Additionally, quite a few coordination models take decentralization into account. TuCSoN [12] distributes communication abstractions (tuple centers) to the Internet nodes. Every tuple center produces and maintains its own local coordination rules. CoLaS divides the whole distributed system into multiple coordination groups. Each coordination group takes care of an independent set of coordination policies. ROAD provides a recursive structure that composes fine-grained, small coordination groups into coarse-grained, large ones. LGI follows a controller metaphor and provides a controller for every object in the system, and hence implements a full-fledged decentralization. The ARC model differs from these models by separating inter-role coordination and intra-role coordination and distributing the coordination among coordinators and roles. The distribution of coordination responsibility is based on the functionalities of roles and is therefore more logical and customizable.

A set of coordination models have been proposed to address the coordination issues involving autonomous, asynchronous and active actors. In particular, Frølund [22] proposed a set of declarative linguistic constructs (*Synchronizers*) to specify two types of synchronization among actors: atomic dispatch of messages among a group of actors and synchronization constraints local to an actor that selectively disable message processing. *Synchronizers* are closed in the sense that all participant actors must be individually specified when a synchronizer is instantiated, whereas the role-based coordination in the ARC model is open and collectively based on actor behaviors. Furthermore, the ARC model directly addresses the potential behavioral volatility of coordinated actors, while the dynamicity was not a main concern for *synchronizers*. Ren [28] further extended Frølund's work to support quantitative synchronizations, such as real-time constraints, among actors. The coordination objects in both Frølund and Ren's work can be treated as meta-actors that are capable of intercepting actor messages and enforcing certain temporal and timing constraints upon message dispatches. Venkatasubramaniam's [23] two-level actor model further separates actor messages from the communications among coordinators (meta-message). However, the emphasis on role-based coordination distinguishes the ARC model from previous multi-level meta architectures.

Instead of treating coordination objects or communications as meta-level entities, Varela [24] has introduced the concept of hierarchal *directors* which encapsulate coordination among a cast of actors. However, the cast is not based on roles or behaviors. The directors are regular actors in the sense that the directors do not have the capability of intercepting messages. Nevertheless, a director represents a group of actors when the group interfaces with other groups. In particular, when a message is targeted to an actor within a group, the message must first be routed to the director of the group, and then routed to the director's director, and so forth. The message is dispatched to the target actor only after all directors on the hierarchical path have approved. As the author noted in [24], such a hierarchical model avoids the special runtime support required by a meta-level approach; however, the price paid for such simplicity is the coordination transparency. Furthermore, as the hierarchical model does not put a limit on the depth of a director tree, it is possible for a simple message dispatch to require many levels of potentially expensive routing and approval.

3   The Actor, Role, and Coordinator (ARC) Model

In this section, we first give a high level description of the ARC model, and then the explanations of the main concepts associated with the model and the intuitions behind them.

3.1   The ARC Model

The ARC model may be conceptualized as the composition of three layers, with each of the three components associated with a dedicated layer, as illustrated in Figure 1. The separation of concerns is apparent in the relationships involving the layers. The actor layer is dedicated to functional behavior and is oblivious to the coordination enacted in the role and coordinator layers. The roles and coordinators form a disjoint coordination layer responsible for imposing coordination and QoS constraints among the actors. The coordinator layer is oblivious to the actor layer and is reserved to inter-role coordination. The role layer bridges the actor layer and the coordinator layer and may therefore be viewed from two perspectives. From the perspective of a coordinator, a role enables the coordination of a set of actors that share the static description of abstract behavior associated with the role without requiring the coordinator to have fine-grained knowledge of the individual actors that play the role. From the perspective of an actor, a role is an active coordinator that transparently manipulates the messages sent and received by the actor.

The roles in the role layer and the coordinators in the coordinator layer are meta-actors. Role meta-actors are able to observe and manipulate messages in the actor layer. The role and coordinator meta-actors react to events that are communicated via special meta-messages. All events and message manipulation associated with an initial triggering event appear to be indivisible and atomic, with no intermediate states visible across or within the three layers. Since the role and coordinator meta-actors are state-based objects, the coordination policies within an application may adapt over time.

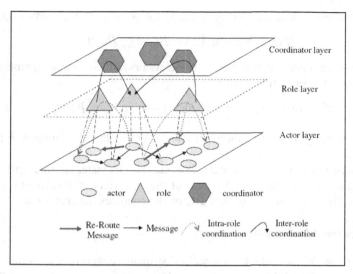

Fig. 1. ARC Model

3.2 Roles, Coordinators and Their Responsibilities

Because of the intrinsic dynamicity and extent of an ODE environment, the underlying actors could be both very dynamic and very extensive in number. The stability and scalability of coordination policies is difficult to maintain if coordination is based on these numerous and highly dynamic actors. However, the numerous actors in an ODE system have a limited set of well-defined behaviors. Hence, the concept of roles that represent abstractions for system behaviors/functionalities is introduced as a remedy to conceal the dynamicity and extent of an ODE environment from the coordinators.

Roles serve two purposes. First, roles provide static abstractions (declarative properties) for functional behaviors that must be realized by actors. Coordination based on roles is therefore relatively stable, even though the underlying actors may be numerous and dynamic. In addition, roles actively coordinate the actors playing the roles to satisfy QoS requirements. The intra-role coordination coerced by roles complements the inter-role coordination enacted by coordinators.

Each role has a distinct purpose. This assumption disallows overlapping roles, eliminating the possibility that a role may be replaced by a set of other roles and eliminating the possibility that conflicting constraints will be imposed on an actor. This assumption also has its basis in the underlying actor model: each actor has only a single thread of control and therefore may play only one role at any given time. More precisely, let $B(\gamma)$ denote the actor functional behaviors declared by role γ, $B(\alpha)$ denote the functional behaviors provided by actor α, Γ and A denote the set of roles and actors in the system, respectively, and $F : A \rightarrow \Gamma$ is the actor to role assignment function. At any given time, well-defined roles and actors in a system must satisfy the following requirements:

Roles are exclusive: role declared behaviors do not overlap, i.e.,

$$\forall i \neq j, B(\gamma_i) \cap B(\gamma_j) = \varnothing$$

1▷   Roles are exhaustive: every actor belongs to one of the roles, i.e.,

$$\forall \alpha \in A, \exists \gamma \in \Gamma, s.t.\ B(\alpha) \subseteq B(\gamma)$$

2.   Roles are repetitive: repeated actor behaviors replicate the assignment of the actor to the same role, i.e.,

$$\forall \alpha_i, \alpha_j \in A, B(\alpha_i) = B(\alpha_j) \rightarrow F(\alpha_i) = F(\alpha_j) \qquad \qquad \Box$$

It is worth pointing out that requirement 1 and 2 ensure that the function $F: A \rightarrow \Gamma$ is well-defined.

As an active object, a role has state, and based on its state, the role actively coordinates the actors sharing the role. Because of the involvement of roles in the coordination process, the coordination in the ARC model becomes decentralized.

3.3   Concurrent Constraints

In the ARC model, we adopt Saraswat's distributed concurrent constraint programming (CCP) model [25] to propagate constraints from coordinators to roles. In the CCP model, there are two principal operations: ask and tell. The tell operation posts constraints to a constraint store and will succeed if the constraint to be told is logically consistent with the current contents of the store. The ask operation will block until it is decidable whether the constraint being asked is consistent or inconsistent with the constraint store. Once the ask operation is decidable, the operation will succeed or fail, respectively. By using the constraint store and the tell and ask primitives, a coordinator propagates role-based constraints to the corresponding roles. Based on the consistency of the constraint store, the role decides whether to reject or accept the constraints and further propagated the constraints to the underlying actors.

3.4   Coerce Coordination Through Message Manipulation

In the ARC model, the underlying computation of an ODE system is modeled by message-based actors. Messages exist in time and space. Our preliminary study has shown that most of the QoS requirements can be realized through message time-space manipulations. For instance, real-time related QoS constraints, such as deadlines, earliest invocation time, frequencies, jitters, etc. can be mapped to message constraints on the time-axis [26, 27, 28]. On the other hand, requirements for reliability, security, fault-tolerance, etc. can be mapped to message management in the actor space domain [29]. For example, based on QoS requirements and the current environment, a message may be rerouted to another destination for security, reliability or adaptation purposes or may be broadcast to a group for reliability and fault-tolerance purposes. In the ARC model, coordination among actors is coerced through message time-space manipulations, and QoS requirements are fulfilled by the coerced coordination that is transparent to the actors. On the time-axis, coordination operators give high level instructions for schedulers as to when a message must be moved to the beginning of a job queue, blocked, or postponed to a later time. In the space domain, the coordination operators manipulate messages in the actor space to satisfy the coordination requirements.

4 Composition of Concurrent Computation and Coerced Coordination

In this section, we formally define the three different entities that constitute the ARC model and focus our study on the composition of concurrent computation (actor system) with coerced coordination (role-coordinator system).

4.1 Actor Behavior

In the ARC model, actors are independent from the roles and coordinators. The coordination among actors is imposed on actors through message manipulations that are transparent to the actors, thus preserving the semantics of the original actor model [3, 4]. For completeness, we quote key results that are related to our work here.

Definition 4.1 (Actor Behavior): An actor behavior is a mapping which specifies the set of operations an actor may perform upon receiving a message.

Upon receiving a message (*rcv*), an actor may send (*send*) messages, create (*new*) actors, initialize (*init*) the behaviors of the created actors, and change its own behavior (*bec*). Primitives *in* and *out* specify inter-configuration communication. The operational semantics of actor primitives, i.e. *fun*, *rcv*, *send*, *new*, *init*, *bec*, *in* and *out* are defined in terms of transitions between actor configurations.

Definition 4.2 (Actor Configuration): An actor configuration contains an actor map α, multi-set of messages, μ, receptionists, ρ, and external actors, χ:

$$\langle\langle \alpha | \mu \rangle\rangle_{\chi}^{\rho} \qquad \Box$$

The set of receptionists are names of actors within the configuration that are externally visible. External actors are names of actors that are outside this configuration but to which messages may be sent.

4.2 Role Behaviors

The role behavior has both group and coordination aspects: membership management behavior (which presents an abstraction for actors' behavior to the coordinators) and coordination behavior.

For completeness of the roles in our system, we introduce a default role γ_0. Let $B(\gamma)$ denote the functional behaviors declared by role γ, and $B(\alpha)$ denote the functional behaviors provided by actors, we have:

$$B(\gamma_0) = \bigcup_{i=1}^{n} B(\alpha_i) - \bigcup_{i=1}^{m} B(\gamma_i)$$

where, γ_i are the roles defined in the system. The behavior declared by the default role γ_0 covers the behaviors provided by actors, but not claimed by existing roles in the system. Hence, by introducing the default role and the restrictions discussed in section 3.2, the roles partition the underlying actor system into disjoint actor subsystems and every actor plays a role. To formally define the role's behavior, we first define role configurations.

Definition 4.3 (Role configuration): A role configuration contains a set of actors playing the role, α_γ, the role itself, γ, a multi-set of messages stored in the mailboxes of the actors playing the role, μ_γ, a set of events that the role observes, ε_γ, receptionists, ρ, and external actors, χ. It is denoted as:

$$\langle\langle \alpha_\gamma, \gamma | \mu_\gamma, \varepsilon_\gamma \rangle\rangle_\chi^\rho \qquad \square$$

It should be noted that an actor configuration is equivalent to a default role configuration with empty observable event set, i.e.

$$\langle\langle \alpha | \mu \rangle\rangle_\chi^\rho \equiv \langle\langle \alpha, \gamma_0 | \mu, \varnothing \rangle\rangle_\chi^\rho \qquad \square$$

4.2.1 Membership Management Behavior

A role's membership management behavior is reflected by the membership changes within the role. When a role observes an *actor init* event or an *actor become* event, the potential new actor behavior is tested against the role membership criteria to determine whether the actor should join or leave the role. More precisely, a role's management behavior is a mapping from a set of actor events to role configurations defined in Definition 4.3.

Definition 4.4 (Membership Management Behavior):

$$B_{\gamma-management} : E_\alpha \rightarrow C_\gamma$$

where E_α is the set of actor events, and C_γ is the set of role configurations. $\square$

The set of actor events includes observable actor behaviors, namely: ε_{fun}, ε_{rcv}, ε_{send}, ε_{new}, ε_{init}, ε_{bec}, ε_{in} and ε_{out}, which correspond to reduction rules given in [4]. For a role's management behavior, we restrict observable actor events to be ε_{init} and ε_{bec} which corresponds to the two actor primitives that result in new actor behaviors. The membership management behavior of a role can be defined using the primitives *join* and *leave* operations.

Definition 4.5 (join): Given an actor subsystem α with configuration $\langle\langle \alpha | \mu_a \rangle\rangle_{\chi_\alpha}^{\rho_\alpha}$, the actor subsystem can join a role γ with configuration $\langle\langle \alpha_\gamma, \gamma | \mu_\gamma, \varepsilon_\gamma \rangle\rangle_\chi^\rho$ if:

(1)   the domains of actor maps α and α_γ (i.e. the set of internal actor addresses) are disjoint, which entails that the receptionists of α and γ are disjoint:

$$\left(Dom(\alpha_\gamma) \cap Dom(\alpha) = \varnothing \right) \Rightarrow \left(\rho \cap \rho_a = \varnothing \right)$$

(2)   α should not know the addresses of the actors within γ other than its declared receptionists and vice versa:

$$\left(\chi_a \cap Dom(\alpha_\gamma) \subseteq \rho \right) \wedge \left(\chi \cap Dom(\alpha) \subseteq \rho_a \right)$$

The primitive *join* is given as $[\varepsilon_{init/bec}] < join : \alpha >$

$$\left\langle\!\left\langle \alpha_\gamma, [R[\varepsilon_{init/bec} : join(\alpha)]]_\gamma \, \middle| \, \mu_\gamma, \varepsilon_\gamma \uplus < \varepsilon_{init/bec} > \right\rangle\!\right\rangle_\chi^\rho$$

$$\mapsto \left\langle\!\left\langle \alpha_\gamma \cup \alpha, [R[nil]]_\gamma \, \middle| \, \mu_\gamma \uplus \mu_\alpha, \varepsilon_\gamma \right\rangle\!\right\rangle_{(\chi \cup \chi_\alpha)-(\rho \cup \rho_\alpha)}^{\rho \cup \rho_\alpha}$$

The two sufficient conditions for an actor to join a role are adopted from the definition of composability of actor configurations in [4]. The first condition immediately follows from the restrictions mentioned in section 3.2. Similar to *join*, we define the primitive *leave* as follows:

Definition 4.6 (leave): $[\varepsilon_{init/bec}] < leave : \alpha >$

$$\left\langle\!\left\langle \alpha_\gamma \cup \alpha, [R[\varepsilon_{init/bec} : leave(\alpha)]]_\gamma \, \middle| \, \mu_\gamma \uplus \mu_\alpha, \varepsilon_\gamma \uplus < \varepsilon_{init/bec} > \right\rangle\!\right\rangle_{(\chi \cup \chi_\alpha)-(\rho \cup \rho_\alpha)}^{\rho \cup \rho_\alpha}$$

$$\mapsto \left\langle\!\left\langle \alpha_\gamma, [R[nil]]_\gamma \, \middle| \, \mu_\gamma, \varepsilon_\gamma \right\rangle\!\right\rangle_\chi^\rho$$

4.2.2 Coordination Behavior
A role's coordination behavior propagates intra-role coordination constrains to actors by manipulating messages in the underlying actor model and is defined by the following mapping:

Definition 4.7 (Coordination Behavior):

$$B_{\gamma-coordination} : E_\alpha \uplus E_\theta \to M \times F_s(E_\gamma) \times R$$

where $E_\alpha, E_\theta, E_\gamma$ are a set of actor events, coordinator events, and role events, respectively, R is a set of role states, and M is multiple sets of messages.

The coordination behavior of a role can be given the following interpretation. Upon observing an event from either an actor or a coordinator, based on its current state, the role may manipulate messages, generate events (which are observable by coordinators) and change its state. As we discussed, coordination constraints are mapped to manipulation of messages in the time and space dimensions, so here we provide a primitive *reroute*, which manipulates messages in the space dimension, and a *timed sink actor*, which is used to buffer messages for a specific period of time to achieve control in the time dimension.

Definition 4.8 (reroute): $[\varepsilon] < reroute : cv, a_1, a_2 >$

$$\left\langle\!\left\langle \alpha_\gamma, [R[\varepsilon : reroute(cv, a_1, a_2)]]_\gamma \, \middle| \, \mu_\gamma \uplus < a_1 \Leftarrow cv >, \varepsilon_\gamma \uplus < \varepsilon > \right\rangle\!\right\rangle_\chi^\rho$$

$$\mapsto \left\langle\!\left\langle \alpha_\gamma, [R[nil]]_\gamma \, \middle| \, \mu_\gamma \uplus < a_2 \Leftarrow cv >, \varepsilon_\gamma \right\rangle\!\right\rangle_\chi^\rho$$

Our intuition is that *reroute* is functionally complete for most of the coordination behaviors. For example:

(1) Broadcast a message $< a \Leftarrow cv >$ to all actors performing the role:

$$< replicate: cv, a >= \bigcup_{a_i \in \gamma} < reroute: cv, a, a_i >$$

(2) Permanently block (delete) a message $< a \Leftarrow cv >$:

$$< delete : cv, a >=< reroute : cv, a, a_\perp >$$

where $a_\perp$ **is a sink actor with** $behavior_{a_\perp} = rec(\lambda b.\lambda m.become(b))$

(3) Temporarily block (delay) a message $< a \Leftarrow cv >$:

$$< delay : cv, a, t >=< reroute : cv, a, a_\perp (t) >$$

where $a_\perp (t)$ **is a timed sink actor with**

$$behavior_{a_\perp (t)} = rec(\lambda b.\lambda m.\lambda t.\lambda self$$
$$seq(become(b(t, self)),$$
$$if (Zero(t))$$
$$send(cust(m), m)$$
$$seq(t--, send(self, m)))$$

(4) Serialize the delivery of two messages $< a_1 \Leftarrow cv_1 >, < a_2 \Leftarrow cv_2 >$:

$$< serialize : cv_1, a_1; cv_2, a_2 >=$$
$$< reroute : cv_2, a_2, a_\perp (\infty) > [\varepsilon_{rcv<a_1, cv_1>}] < reroute : cv_2, a_\perp (\infty), a_2 > \qquad \square$$

The "targeted send and receive" (TSR) intrinsic in the actor model has been criticized by the coordination community ([11, 14]). However, a role's transparent *reroute* functionality avoids the shortcoming of the TSR model and achieves the same effect as connecting components by channels.

As meta-actors, roles are also active and may change their states upon observing an event. The *become* primitive is defined to represent the transition of role state change.

Definition 4.9 (become): $[\varepsilon] < become : v >$

$$\left\langle\left\langle \alpha_\gamma, [R[\varepsilon : become(v)]]_\gamma \middle| \mu_\gamma, \varepsilon_\gamma \uplus < \varepsilon > \right\rangle\right\rangle_\chi^\rho \mapsto \left\langle\left\langle \alpha_\gamma, (v)_\gamma \middle| \mu_\gamma, \varepsilon_\gamma \right\rangle\right\rangle_\chi^\rho \qquad \square$$

Moreover, roles also support two primitives, i.e., *tell* and *ask* that are adopted from CCP to maintain the constraint consistencies. The detailed semantics of *tell* and *ask* is introduced in [25].

These primitives permit the roles to impose coordination constraints on actors.

4.3 Coordinator Behavior

Coordinators are responsible for coordinating system-wide QoS requirements among different roles. Coordinators are meta-actors and are able to observe events. Based on observed events, the coordinators may change their states and enact different coordination constraints on coordinated roles. The behavior of a coordinator is defined by the following mapping.

Definition 4.10 (Coordinator Behavior): The coordination behavior is a mapping from a set of role events and a constraint store to a set of coordinator events and a new constraint store.

$$B_\theta : E_\gamma \rightarrow F_s(E_\theta) \times C \qquad \square$$

The observable role events are ε_{tell}, ε_{ask}, which correspond to the two role primitives, and the observable coordinator events are ε_{fail} and $\varepsilon_{success}$, which indicate the results of *tell* and *ask*. The Concurrent Constraint Programming semantics enable a coordinator to refine the constraint store and propagate constraints to the coordinated roles.

4.4 System Behavior

Our last conclusion is to recall a principle that has been so often fruitful in computer science and that is central to Scott's theory of computation:

A good concept is one that is closed
1. under arbitrary composition,
2. under recursion

-Gilles Kahn (1974)

In this section, we discuss system behavior in terms of the actor, role and coordinator discussed in previous sections.

Definition 4.11 (System Configuration): An ARC system configuration is a set of actor subsystems categorized by roles, Γ, a set of coordinators, θ, a multi-set of messages stored in the mailboxes of the actors in the system, μ_θ, a set of observable events, $\mathcal{E}_\theta$, receptionists, ρ, and external actors, χ. It is represented as:

$$\langle\langle \Gamma, \theta \,|\, \mu_\theta, \mathcal{E}_\theta \rangle\rangle_\chi^\rho \qquad \square$$

4.4.1 Subsystem Composition
Despite the fact that actors are dynamic, at the role level, coordination is relatively stable because the actor behavior changes are transparent to the coordinators. For example, consider a system within which an actor changes its behavior by executing a *bec* primitive. Because of the behavior change from α to α', the actor leaves its original role (γ_1) and join a new role (γ_2), i.e.,

$$< bec : \alpha, \alpha' > \text{ where } B(\alpha) \subseteq B(\gamma_1) \text{ and } B(\alpha') \subseteq B(\gamma_2)$$

This will trigger an event ε_{bec} that is observable by both γ_1 and γ_2. The management behaviors of γ_1 and γ_2 guarantee the following system configuration transition:

$$\left\langle\!\!\left\langle \gamma_1\{\alpha_{\gamma_1} \cup \alpha\}, \gamma_2\{\alpha_{\gamma_2}\}, \theta \middle| \mu_\theta \uplus (\mu_1 \uplus \mu_\alpha) \uplus \mu_2, \varepsilon_\theta \uplus \varepsilon_{bec(\alpha,\alpha')} \right\rangle\!\!\right\rangle_\chi^\rho \mapsto {}_{\gamma_1.[\varepsilon_{bec}]<leave:\alpha>}^{\gamma_2.[\varepsilon_{bec}]<join:\alpha'>}$$

$$\left\langle\!\!\left\langle \gamma_1\{\alpha_{\gamma_1}\}, \gamma_2\{\alpha_{\gamma_2} \cup \alpha'\}, \theta \middle| \mu_\theta \uplus \mu_1 \uplus (\mu_2 \uplus \mu_\alpha), \varepsilon_\theta \right\rangle\!\!\right\rangle_\chi^\rho$$

where

α *behavior* : $\dfrac{<bec:\alpha,\alpha'>}{\left\langle\!\!\left\langle \alpha \middle| \mu_\alpha \right\rangle\!\!\right\rangle_{\chi_\alpha}^{\rho_\alpha} \mapsto \left\langle\!\!\left\langle \alpha' \middle| \mu_\alpha \right\rangle\!\!\right\rangle_{\chi_\alpha}^{\rho_\alpha}}$

γ_1 *behavior* : $\dfrac{[\varepsilon_{bec}]<leave:\alpha>}{\left\langle\!\!\left\langle \alpha_{\gamma_1} \cup \alpha, \gamma_1 \middle| \mu_1 \uplus \mu_\alpha, \varepsilon_1 \uplus<\varepsilon_{bec}> \right\rangle\!\!\right\rangle_{(\chi_1 \cup \chi_\alpha)-(\rho_1 \cup \rho_\alpha)}^{\rho_1 \cup \rho_\alpha} \mapsto \left\langle\!\!\left\langle \alpha_\gamma, \gamma_1 \middle| \mu_1, \varepsilon_1 \right\rangle\!\!\right\rangle_{\chi_1}^{\rho_1}}$

γ_2 *behavior* : $\dfrac{[\varepsilon_{bec}]<join:\alpha'>}{\left\langle\!\!\left\langle \alpha_{\gamma_2}, \gamma_2 \middle| \mu_2, \varepsilon_2 \uplus<\varepsilon_{bec}> \right\rangle\!\!\right\rangle_{\chi_2}^{\rho_2} \mapsto \left\langle\!\!\left\langle \alpha_{\gamma_2} \cup \alpha', \gamma_2 \middle| \mu_2 \uplus \mu_\alpha, \varepsilon_2 \right\rangle\!\!\right\rangle_{(\chi_2 \cup \chi_\alpha)-(\rho_2 \cup \rho_\alpha)}^{\rho_2 \cup \rho_\alpha}}$

For simplicity, the redexes in actor and role configurations are ignored. As we can see from the above reduction, by partitioning the actor subsystem into equivalence classes based on their behavior abstractions, the crucial compositional closure property advocated by Kahn is guaranteed by the roles.

4.4.2 Composed System Behavior

An ARC system can also be recursively viewed as an actor system.

Definition 4.12 (ARC System Behavior): The ARC system behavior defines the set of actions an actor can take upon receiving a message in M :

$$B_\alpha : M \to F_s(M) \times F_s(A) \times A \qquad\qquad \square$$

For example, consider an ARC system $\left\langle\!\!\left\langle \Gamma \cup \gamma_0\{\alpha_{car}\}, \theta | \varnothing \right\rangle\!\!\right\rangle_{\{\alpha\}}^{\{\alpha_{car}\}}$, where α_{car} is a car actor and α is an external actor. The system can be viewed as an actor system which has the following behavior $B_{ARC}(< \alpha_{car} \Leftarrow car >) = (\{< \alpha \Leftarrow car >\}, \varnothing, self)$. Based on the ARC system behavior definition, the processing of the 'produce a car' message by the ARC system will result in the following reduction

$$\left\langle\!\!\left\langle \Gamma \cup \gamma_0\{\alpha_{car}\}, \theta \middle| \{<\alpha_{car} \Leftarrow car>\}_\mu \right\rangle\!\!\right\rangle_\chi^{\{\alpha_{car}\}}, \left\langle\!\!\left\langle \alpha \middle| \{\}_\mu \right\rangle\!\!\right\rangle_{\{\alpha_{car}\}}^{\{\alpha\}} \mapsto \left\langle\!\!\left\langle \Gamma \cup \gamma_0\{\alpha_{car}\}, \theta \middle| \{\}_\mu \right\rangle\!\!\right\rangle_\chi^{\{\alpha_{car}\}}, \left\langle\!\!\left\langle \alpha \middle| \{<\alpha \Leftarrow car>\}_\mu \right\rangle\!\!\right\rangle_{\{\alpha_{car}\}}^{\{\alpha\}}$$

As will be seen in the following example, the ARC system reduces to an actor system from computation perspective in which the actor semantics remains intact.

4.5 Case Study

In this section, we present an extension of the car manufacturer example first introduced in [30] to illustrate the transition rules and the closure properties of the ARC model. In this example, the cars are simplified as having only 4 wheels and 1 chassis. The manufacturer produces cars on several production lines. Two assumptions are made: (1) the product lines are heterogeneous; and (2) the manufactory system is dynamic in that a product line may freely go on/off line. Further, it is possible for a line to produce both wheels and chassis, but only one type at any given time. In addition, we have the following coordination requirements:

- Requirement 1: the ratio of wheels and chassis must be 4:1.
- Requirement 2: atomicity of wheel and chassis delivery.
- Requirement 3: even distribution of wheel production on the product lines.

Coordination requirements 1 and 2 are global (inter-role) because they involve relationships between different roles; coordination requirement 1 defines a quantitative relationship and coordination requirement 2 defines a temporal relationship. Coordination requirement 3 is local (intra-role) because it only specifies distinct policies within roles.

4.5.1 Role and Coordinator Behaviors

Role wheel γ_w with state variable $x = 0$ can be written as:

$$\gamma_w(x = 0):$$

$$P_1 : [\varepsilon_{init(\alpha)}] if (\mathrm{B}(\alpha) \subseteq \mathrm{B}(\gamma_w)) join(\alpha);$$

$$P_2 : [\varepsilon_{\alpha'.send(\alpha,m)}] if (\alpha \notin \gamma_w \wedge \alpha' \in \gamma_w)\{$$

$$if (\alpha' \neq \alpha_{w\perp}(t))\{become(\gamma_w(x = x++))\}$$

$$tell(X = x) \rightarrow \alpha'.out(m)\Box ask(X \neq x) \rightarrow reroute(m, \alpha, \alpha_{w\perp}(t))\}$$

$$P_3 : [\varepsilon_{\alpha_{car}.send(\alpha,car)}] become(\gamma_w(x = 0));$$

$$P_4 : [\varepsilon_{\alpha.in(m)}] if (\exists \alpha' \in \gamma_w \ s.t. |\mu_{\alpha'}| < |\mu_\alpha|) reroute(<\alpha \Leftarrow m >, \alpha, \alpha');$$

The four behaviors (P_1, P_2, P_3, and P_4) are interpreted respectively as follows:

- Actor behavior change triggers role membership change.
- Each time an actor within the role sends a message to an actor outside the role, the role increments its state variable (except for the case the sending actor is a sink) and makes a consistency check. If the check succeeds, the message is allowed to continue to the receiver; otherwise, the message is delayed. (The disjunctive operator "$\Box$" in CCP means the corresponding actions will be taken if either $tell(X=x)$ or $ask(X\neq x)$ succeeds.)
- After a car actor assembles the parts (the four wheels and one chassis) and sends the result back to its customer, reset the state variable.
- When a message comes into the role subsystem, reroute the message to the actor under the role with a smaller number of unprocessed messages (load balancing).

$\gamma_c(y)$ is similar to $\gamma_w(x)$ except that it does not support the load balancing.

The coordinator θ state variable $X:Y=4:1$ is in fact a constraint store. We implicitly add a constraint $X \in \mathrm{N} \wedge Y \in \mathrm{N}$, that is, the domain of X and Y are natural numbers so that $tell(X=1)$ will not succeed because it would entail that $Y=0.25$, which is not a natural number. The behavior is defined as:

$$\theta(X:Y=4:1):[\varepsilon_{\gamma_w.become(\gamma_w(x=0))}\cup\varepsilon_{\gamma_c.become(\gamma_c(y=0))}]become(\theta(X:Y=4:1))$$

The behavior states that after the car actor assembles the car, the coordinator will reset its constraint store (since roles will modify the store during the course). The atomicity constraint (requirement 2) is accomplished as follows:

Given the original constraint store $X:Y=4:1$, if a wheel actor completes a wheel and tell($X=1$), this tell will not succeed and the message will be temporarily blocked. Only when the number of wheel is four and tell($X=4$) succeeds that all four wheels are delivered atomically. All subsequent wheel deliveries will again be delayed before the delivery of one chassis since tell($X=5$) is not entailed by the current store $X:Y=4:1 \wedge X=4$. Therefore, the atomicity constraint is guaranteed by the constraint store in the coordinator as well as the message manipulation (delay) in the role. For details of how this works, please refer to the reductions in the appendix.

4.5.2 Composed System Behavior

The following configuration transition shows the reduction of the ARC system upon receiving a message from an external actor α:

$$\left\langle\langle\gamma_0\{\alpha_{car}\},\gamma_w(x)\{\alpha_1,\alpha_{w\perp}(t)\},\gamma_c(y)\{\alpha_{c\perp}(t)\},\theta(X:Y=4:1)\big|\{<\alpha_{car}\Leftarrow car>\}_\mu,\{\}_\varepsilon\rangle\rangle_\chi^{\{\alpha_{car}\}},\left\langle\langle\alpha\big|\{\}_\mu\rangle\rangle_{\{\alpha_{car}\}}^{\{\alpha\}}\mapsto^*$$

$$\left\langle\langle\gamma_0\{\alpha_{car}\},\gamma_w(x)\{\alpha_1,\alpha_2,\alpha_{w\perp}(t)\},\gamma_c(y)\{\alpha_3,\alpha_{c\perp}(t)\},\theta(X:Y=4:1)\big|\{\}_\mu,\{\}_\varepsilon\rangle\rangle_\chi^{\{\alpha_{car}\}},\left\langle\langle\alpha\big|\{<\alpha\Leftarrow car>\}_{\mu'}\rangle\rangle_{\{\alpha_{car}\}}^{\{\alpha\}}$$

One possible reduction path based on the pseudo code described is given in the appendix. As the example shows, the composed system fulfills the coordination constraints while preserving the actor semantics.

5 Conclusion and Future Work

In this paper, we have presented the ARC model, a role-based decentralized coordination model for open distributed and embedded systems. In the ARC model, we map system's QoS requirements to coordination concerns and separate these concerns from concurrent computation logic. The coordination constraints are imposed on computations through message manipulations that are transparent to the computation itself. Furthermore, to address the dynamicity and the openness inherent in an ODE system, we introduced active roles that not only provide abstractions for actor functional behaviors, but also take part in the coordination activities. Hence, the coordination subsystem itself becomes distributed and thus inherits all the benefits a distributed system may offer. Our formal study on the role and coordinator's behavior and their composition with the actor model shows that the composed system is closed under composition and recursion.

The ARC model presently employs the concurrent constraint programming model for the satisfaction and communication of coordination constraints among the active and concurrent ARC coordinator objects. The shared constraint store in CCP may only be monotonically refined, and constraints are either satisfied or violated in an absolute sense. The ARC model disallows overlapping roles to avoid conflicting constraints to be applied on the computation subsystem, i.e., the actors. However, at the coordinator level, multiple coordinators may impose constraints upon a single role, which implies the possibility of conflicting constraints and the requirement to resolve the conflicts. We plan to investigate the soft CCP model [31] as an alternative, since the ability to express preferences and priorities among constraints during constraint satisfaction is inherent to the soft CCP model.

The other aspect of future work is to study if a general scheme can be defined to map other QoS related constraints, such as adaptability constraints, security constraints, etc., to message manipulations on time-space axis.

Acknowledgements

We would like to thank those anonymous reviewers for their valuable comments on this work.

References

1. Hoare, C. A. R.: Communicating Sequential Processes. Prentice Hall International Series in Computer Science (1985)
2. Milner, R.: The Pi Calculus and its Applications (keynote address). In IJCSL (1998)
3. Agha, G.: Actors: A Model of Concurrent Computation in Distributed Systems. MIT Press (1986)
4. Agha, G., Mason, I., Smith, S., Talcott, C.: Towards a Theory of Actor Computation. In Third International Conference on Concurrency Theory. Lecture Notes in Computer Science, Springer-Verlag (1992) 565-579
5. Siqueira, F., Cahill, V.: Quartz: A QoS architecture for Open Systems. In Proceedings of International Conference on Distributed Computing Systems (2000) 197-204
6. Becker, C., Geihs, K.: MAQS: management for adaptive QoS-enabled services. In Proceedings of the IEEE Workshop on Middleware for Distributed Real-Time Systems and Services. (1997)
7. Nahrstedt, K., Wichadakul, D., and Xu, D.: Distributed QoS Compilation and Runtime Instantiation. In Proceedings of IEEE/IFIP International Workshop on QoS (2000)
8. Halteren, A. T.: A reflective QoS provisioning service for object middleware. Position paper for the Workshop on Reflective Middleware (2000)
9. Papadopoulos, G. A., Arbab, F.: Coordination models and languages. Advances in Computer. (1998) 329-400
10. Carriero, N., Gelernter, D.: Linda in context. Communications of the ACM (1989) 444-458
11. Arbab, F.: IWIM: A communication model for cooperative systems. In Proceedings of the 2nd International Conference on the Design of Cooperative Systems, Juanle-Pins, France (1996) 567-585
12. Omicini, A., Zambonelli, F.: Tuple Centres for the Coordination of Internet Agents. In Proceedings of the ACM Symposium on Applied Computing (1999)
13. Omicini, A., Denti, E.: Formal ReSpecT. Electronic Notes in Theoretical Computer Science. (2001)
14. Arbab, F.: Abstract behavior types: A foundation model for components and their composition. Technical report, CWI, Amsterdam, Netherlands (2004)
15. Minsky, N. H., Ungureanu, V.: Law-governed interaction: a coordination and control mechanism for heterogeneous distributed systems. ACM Trans. (2000) 273-305

16. Colman, A., Han, J.: Coordination Systems in Role-based Software. In Proceedings of 7th International Conference on Coordination Models and Languages (2005)

17. Cruz, J. C., Ducasse, S.: A Group Based Approach for Coordinating Active Objects. In Proceedings of 2nd International Conference on Coordination Models and Languages (1999)

18. Arbab, F.: Reo: A Channel-based Coordination Model for Component Composition. Mathematical Structures in Computer Science, Vol. 14, No. 3, (2004) 329–366

19. Omicini, A., Ricci, A., Viroli, M.: Formal Specification and Enactment of Security Policies through Agent Coordination Contexts. Electronic Notes in Theoretical Computer Science, Elsevier Science B.V. (2003)

20. Berry, A. and Kaplan, S.: Open, Distributed Coordination with Finesse. Technical Report, School of Information Technology. The University of Queensland, Australia (1999)

21. Cabri, G., Ferrari, L., Leonardi, L.: Agent role-based collaboration and coordination: a survey about existing approaches. In International Conference on Systems, Man and Cybernetics (2004) 5473–5478

22. Frølund, S.: Coordinating Distributed Objects: An Actor-Based Approach for Synchronization. MIT Press (1996).

23. Venkatasubramanian, N., Agha, G., Talcott, C.: A MetaObject Framework for QoS-Based Distributed Resource Management. In Proceedings of the Third International Symposium on Computing in Object-Oriented Parallel Environments (ISCOPE '99) (1999).

24. Varela, C. A.., Agha, G.: A Hierarchical Model for Coordination of Concurrent Activities, International Conference on Coordination (COORDINATION '99), LNCS 1594 (1999)

25. Saraswat, V. A.: Concurrent Constraint Programming. The MIT Press. (1993).

26. Jamali, N., Ren, S.: A layered architecture for real-time open distributed systems. In Proceedings of the 4th International Workshop on Software Engineering for Large-Scale Multi-Agent Systems (2005)

27. Ren, S., Shen L., Tsai, J.: Reconfigurable coordination model for dynamic autonomous real-time systems. In The IEEE International Conference on Sensor Networks, Ubiquitous, and Trustworthy Computing (2006)

28. Ren, S., Venkatasubramanian, N., Agha, G. A.: Formalizing qos constraints using actors. In Proceedings of Second IFIP International Conference on Formal Methods for Open Object Based Distributed Systems (1997)

29. Kwiat, K. and Ren, S.: A coordination model for improving software system attack tolerance and survivability in open hostile environments. In The IEEE International Conference on Sensor Networks, Ubiquitous, and Trustworthy Computing (2006)

30. Callsen, C. J., Agha, G.: Open Heterogeneous Computing in Actor Space. Journal of Parallel Distributed Computing (1994) 289–300

31. Bistarelli, S., Montanari, U., Rossi, F.: Soft Concurrent Constraint Programming. European Symposium on Programming (2002) 53–67

Appendix: ARC System Reduction for the Car Manufacturer Example (Section 4.5)

$$\left\langle\left\langle \gamma_0\{\alpha_{car}\}, \gamma_w(x=0)\{\alpha_1, \alpha_{w\perp}(t)\}, \gamma_c(y=0)\{\alpha_{c\perp}(t)\}, \theta(X:Y=4:1) \right.\right.$$

$$\left.\left. \left|\{<a_{car} \Leftarrow car>\}_\mu, \{\}_\varepsilon\right\rangle\right\rangle_{\chi}^{\{\alpha_{car}\}}$$

$$\mapsto \quad \begin{array}{l} \alpha_{car}.init(\alpha_2) \\ \alpha_{car}.init(\alpha_3) \end{array}$$

$$\Big\langle\!\Big\langle \gamma_0\{\alpha_{car},\alpha_2,\alpha_3\}, \gamma_w(x=0)\{\alpha_1,\alpha_{w\perp}(t)\}, \gamma_c(y=0)\{\alpha_{c\perp}(t)\}, \theta(X:Y=4:1)$$
$$\Big|\{\}_\mu, \{\varepsilon_{init}(\alpha_2),\varepsilon_{init}(\alpha_3)\}_\varepsilon \Big\rangle\!\Big\rangle_\chi^{\{\alpha_{car}\}}$$

$$\mapsto \quad \begin{array}{l} [\varepsilon_{init}(\alpha_2)]\gamma_w.join(\alpha_2) \\ [\varepsilon_{init}(\alpha_3)]\gamma_c.join(\alpha_3) \\ \alpha_{car}.send(\alpha_2,w)\times 4 \\ \alpha_{car}.send(\alpha_3,c) \end{array}$$

$$\Big\langle\!\Big\langle \gamma_0\{\alpha_{car}\}, \gamma_w(x=0)\{\alpha_1,\alpha_2,\alpha_{w\perp}(t)\}, \gamma_c(y=0)\{\alpha_3,\alpha_{c\perp}(t)\}, \theta(X:Y=4:1)$$
$$\Big|\{<\alpha_2\Leftarrow w>\times 4, <\alpha_3\Leftarrow c>\}_\mu, \{\varepsilon_{\alpha_2.in(m)}\times 4, \varepsilon_{\alpha_3.in(m)}\}_\varepsilon \Big\rangle\!\Big\rangle_\chi^{\{\alpha_{car}\}}$$

$$\mapsto \quad \begin{array}{l} [\varepsilon_{\alpha_2}.in(m)]\gamma_w.reroute(<\alpha_2\Leftarrow w>,\alpha_2,\alpha_1) \\ [\varepsilon_{\alpha_2}.in(m)]\gamma_w.reroute(<\alpha_2\Leftarrow w>,\alpha_2,\alpha_1) \end{array}$$

$$\Big\langle\!\Big\langle \gamma_0\{\alpha_{car}\}, \gamma_w(x=0)\{\alpha_1,\alpha_2,\alpha_{w\perp}(t)\}, \gamma_c(y=0)\{\alpha_3,\alpha_{c\perp}(t)\}, \theta(X:Y=4:1)$$
$$\Big|\{<\alpha_1\Leftarrow w>\times 2, <\alpha_2\Leftarrow w>\times 2, <\alpha_3\Leftarrow c>\}_\mu, \{\}_\varepsilon \Big\rangle\!\Big\rangle_\chi^{\{\alpha_{car}\}}$$

$$\mapsto \quad \begin{array}{l} \alpha_2.rcv(\alpha_2,w) \\ \alpha_2.send(\alpha_{car},w) \end{array}$$

$$\Big\langle\!\Big\langle \gamma_0\{\alpha_{car}\}, \gamma_w(x=0)\{\alpha_1,\alpha_2,\alpha_{w\perp}(t)\}, \gamma_c(y=0)\{\alpha_3,\alpha_{c\perp}(t)\}, \theta(X:Y=4:1)$$
$$\Big|\{<\alpha_1\Leftarrow w>\times 2, <\alpha_2\Leftarrow w>, <\alpha_{car}\Leftarrow w>, <\alpha_3\Leftarrow c>\}_\mu, \{\varepsilon_{\alpha_2.send(\alpha_{car},w)}\}_\varepsilon \Big\rangle\!\Big\rangle_\chi^{\{\alpha_{car}\}}$$

$$\mapsto \quad \begin{array}{l} [\varepsilon_{\alpha_2}.send(\alpha_{car},w)]\{ \\ \quad \gamma_w.become(\gamma_w(x=1)); \\ \quad \gamma_w.tell(X=1)(tell\ fail) \\ \quad \gamma_w.reroute(w,\alpha_{car},\alpha_{w\perp}(t))\} \end{array}$$

$$\Big\langle\!\Big\langle \gamma_0\{\alpha_{car}\}, \gamma_w(x=1)\{\alpha_1,\alpha_2,\alpha_{w\perp}(t)\}, \gamma_c(y=0)\{\alpha_3,\alpha_{c\perp}(t)\}, \theta(X:Y=4:1)$$
$$\Big|\{<\alpha_1\Leftarrow w>\times 2, <\alpha_2\Leftarrow w>, <\alpha_{w\perp}(t)\Leftarrow w>, <\alpha_3\Leftarrow c>\}_\mu, \{\}_\varepsilon \Big\rangle\!\Big\rangle_\chi^{\{\alpha_{car}\}}$$

$$\mapsto \quad \begin{array}{l} \alpha_3.rcv(\alpha_3,c) \\ \alpha_3.send(\alpha_{car},c) \end{array}$$

$$\langle\langle \gamma_0\{\alpha_{car}\}, \gamma_w(x=1)\{\alpha_1,\alpha_2,\alpha_{w\perp}(t)\}, \gamma_c(y=0)\{\alpha_3,\alpha_{c\perp}(t)\}, \theta(X:Y=4:1)$$

$$\left| \{<\alpha_1 \Leftarrow w>\times 2, <\alpha_2 \Leftarrow w>, <\alpha_{w\perp}(t) \Leftarrow w>, <\alpha_{car} \Leftarrow c>\}_\mu, \{\varepsilon_{\alpha_3.send(\alpha_{car},c)}\}_\varepsilon\rangle\rangle_\chi^{\{\alpha_{car}\}}$$

$$\longmapsto$$

$$[\varepsilon_{\alpha_3}.send(\alpha_{car},c)]\{$$
$$\gamma_c.become(\gamma_c(y=1));$$
$$\gamma_c.tell(Y=1)(tell\ succeed)$$
$$\alpha_3.out(\alpha_{car},c);\}$$

$\longmapsto$ *two more messages under γ_w get delayed

since $tell(X=2)$ and $tell(X=3)$ will also fail

$$\langle\langle \gamma_0\{\alpha_{car}\}, \gamma_w(x=3)\{\alpha_1,\alpha_2,\alpha_{w\perp}(t)\}, \gamma_c(y=1)\{\alpha_3,\alpha_{c\perp}(t)\}, \theta(X:Y=4:1\wedge Y=1)$$

$$\left| \{<\alpha_1 \Leftarrow w>, <\alpha_{w\perp}(t) \Leftarrow w>\times 3, <\alpha_{car} \Leftarrow c>\}_\mu, \{\}_\varepsilon\rangle\rangle_\chi^{\{\alpha_{car}\}}$$

$$\longmapsto$$
$$\alpha_1.rcv(\alpha_1,w)$$
$$\alpha_1.send(\alpha_{car},w)$$

$$\langle\langle \gamma_0\{\alpha_{car}\}, \gamma_w(x=3)\{\alpha_1,\alpha_2,\alpha_{w\perp}(t)\}, \gamma_c(y=1)\{\alpha_3,\alpha_{c\perp}(t)\}, \theta(X:Y=4:1\wedge Y=1)$$

$$\left| \{<\alpha_{car} \Leftarrow w>, <\alpha_{w\perp}(t) \Leftarrow w>\times 3, <\alpha_{car} \Leftarrow c>\}_\mu, \{\varepsilon_{\alpha_1.send(\alpha_{car},w)}\}_\varepsilon\rangle\rangle_\chi^{\{\alpha_{car}\}}$$

$$\longmapsto$$

$$[\varepsilon_{\alpha_1}.send(\alpha_{car},w)]\{$$
$$\gamma_w.become(\gamma_w(x=4));$$
$$\gamma_w.tell(X=4)(tell\ succeed)$$
$$\alpha_1.out(\alpha_{car},w);\}$$

$$\langle\langle \gamma_0\{\alpha_{car}\}, \gamma_w(x=4)\{\alpha_1,\alpha_2,\alpha_{w\perp}(t)\}, \gamma_c(y=1)\{\alpha_3,\alpha_{c\perp}(t)\}, \theta(X:Y=4:1\wedge Y=1\wedge X=4)$$

$$\left| \{<\alpha_{w\perp}(t) \Leftarrow w>\times 3, <\alpha_{car} \Leftarrow c>, <\alpha_{car} \Leftarrow w>\}_\mu, \{\}_\varepsilon\rangle\rangle_\chi^{\{\alpha_{car}\}}$$

$$\longmapsto$$
$$\{$$
$$\alpha_{w\perp}(t)\ timeup$$
$$\alpha_{w\perp}(t).send(\alpha_{car},w)$$
$$[\varepsilon_{snd}(\alpha_{w\perp}(t)\rightarrow\alpha_{car})]\{$$
$$\gamma_w.tell(X=4)(tell\ succeed)$$
$$\alpha_{w\perp}(t).out(\alpha_{car},w);\}$$
$$\}\times 3$$

$$\langle\langle \gamma_0\{\alpha_{car}\}, \gamma_w(x=4)\{\alpha_1,\alpha_2,\alpha_{w\perp}(t)\}, \gamma_c(y=1)\{\alpha_3,\alpha_{c\perp}(t)\}, \theta(X:Y=4:1\wedge Y=1\wedge X=4)$$

$$\left| \{<\alpha_{car} \Leftarrow c>, <\alpha_{car} \Leftarrow w>\times 4\}_\mu, \{\}_\varepsilon\rangle\rangle_\chi^{\{\alpha_{car}\}}$$

$$\longmapsto$$
$$\alpha_{car}.rcv(\alpha_{car},c)$$
$$\alpha_{car}.rcv(\alpha_{car},w)\times 4$$
$$\alpha_{car}.send(\alpha,car)$$

$$\langle\langle \gamma_0\{\alpha_{car}\}, \gamma_w(x=4)\{\alpha_1, \alpha_2, \alpha_{w\perp}(t)\}, \gamma_c(y=1)\{\alpha_3, \alpha_{c\perp}(t)\}, \theta(X:Y=4:1 \wedge Y=1 \wedge X=4)$$

$$\left| \{<\alpha \Leftarrow car>\}_\mu, \{\varepsilon_{\alpha_{car}.send(\alpha,car)}\}_\varepsilon \rangle\rangle_\chi^{\{\alpha_{car}\}}$$

$$\longmapsto$$

$$[\varepsilon_{\alpha_{car}.send(\alpha,car)}]\gamma_w.become(\gamma_w(x=0))$$
$$[\varepsilon_{\alpha_{car}.send(\alpha,car)}]\gamma_c.become(\gamma_c(y=0))$$
$$[\varepsilon_{\gamma_w.become(\gamma_w(x=0))} \cup \varepsilon_{\gamma_c.become(\gamma_c(y=0))}]\theta.become(\theta(X:Y=4:1))$$
$$\alpha_{car}.out(\alpha,car)$$

$$\langle\langle \gamma_0\{\alpha_{car}\}, \gamma_w(x=0)\{\alpha_1, \alpha_2, \alpha_{w\perp}(t)\}, \gamma_c(y=0)\{\alpha_3, \alpha_{c\perp}(t)\}, \theta(X:Y=4:1) \left| \{\}_\mu, \{\}_\varepsilon \rangle\rangle_\chi^{\{\alpha_{car}\}}$$

Tuple Space Coordination Across Space and Time

Gruia-Catalin Roman[1], Radu Handorean[2], and Rohan Sen[1]

[1] Department of Computer Science and Engineering
Washington University in St. Louis
Campus Box 1045, One Brookings Drive
St. Louis, MO 63130-4899, USA
[2] Qualcomm Inc.
6180 Spine Road, Boulder, CO 80301

Abstract. CAST is a coordination model designed to support interactions among agents executing on hosts that make up a mobile ad hoc network (MANET). From an application programmer's point of view, CAST makes it possible for operations to be executed at arbitrary locations in space, at prescribed times which may be in the future, and on remote hosts even when no end-to-end connected route exists between the initiator and target(s) of the operation. To accomplish this, CAST assumes that each host moves in space in accordance with a motion profile which is accurate but which at any given time extends into the future for a limited duration. These motion profiles are freely exchanged among hosts in the network through a gossiping protocol. Knowledge about the motion profiles of the other hosts in the network allows for source routing of operation requests and replies over disconnected routes. In this paper, we present the CAST model and its formalization. We also discuss the feasibility of realizing this model.

1 Introduction

Mobile Ad hoc Networks (MANETs) are a special class of wireless networks, which do not rely on any external infrastructure and are formed opportunistically among physically mobile hosts. By definition, a MANET is an open, dynamic environment where hosts may join or leave the network of their own volition and connectivity between host pairs is transient, requiring a decoupled style of computing. Developing applications for MANETs is especially challenging because peer-to-peer interactions between hosts can be short lived and the hosts participating in the computation change often and in an unpredictable fashion.

Coordination middleware is a software solution that has been proven to be able to handle the open environment and decoupled interactions as evidenced by systems such as MARS [1] and KLAIM [2], designed for wired settings, and systems such as LIME [3], Limone [4] and Ara [5] which are targeted to mobile settings. However, mobile settings, and MANETs in particular impose additional challenges which cannot be handled by the current generation of coordination

P. Ciancarini and H. Wiklicky (Eds.): COORDINATION 2006, LNCS 4038, pp. 266–280, 2006.
© Springer-Verlag Berlin Heidelberg 2006

models. The key problem is that current technology has a very restricted definition of *reachability* in the dimensions of *space* (hosts must be strategically located in space so as to have access to a route to the destination) as well as *time* (the routes are only valid at the current instant). Handling more sophisticated applications requires us to develop models that expand the present narrow interpretation of reachability, allowing more predictable interactions with larger numbers of participants in a MANET.

CAST (Coordination Across Space and Time) is a new kind of coordination model that extends the reach of coordination activities across space and time by addressing restrictions imposed by current models. In the spatial domain, we use disconnected routing, a type of routing algorithm which does not enforce end-to-end connectivity between the source and destination of a message. This type of routing algorithm is similar to source routing in that the complete sequence of intermediary hosts is specified in the message header. The difference lies in the manner in which the hosts that form the route are selected. We use information about the motion of hosts (exchanged among hosts using a gossiping protocol) to compute intervals of pairwise connectivity among hosts extending from the present moment for a fixed amount of time into the future. The hosts forming the route are selected such that the sequence of intervals of pairwise connectivity between them will be sufficient to deliver a message from the source to the destination. The message is temporarily buffered on each host when the incoming communication window and outgoing communication window do not coincide, allowing coordination among hosts that are never in direct pairwise contact.

CAST also addresses the temporal domain by offering operations that have an explicit space and time value associated with it. The operations are moved to the required location using the mechanism described above and held in an inactive status until the activation time is reached. If there is no route which can get the operation to the required location by the specified time, the middleware can immediately raise an exception and reject the operation. Spatiotemporal operations allow coordination to occur across the reaches of space and time, thereby expanding the reach of the model.

In this paper, we describe the CAST model and its operation. The model assumes the use of a gossiping protocol to discover knowledge about the motion of other hosts which is stored in a local knowledge base and used to compute disconnected routes. Atop this, we offer Linda-like coordination operations via a simple API. The remainder of the paper is organized as follows. Section 2 provides background and a motivating example. Section 3 formally describes the key concept of reachability upon which disconnected routes are built, while Section 4 describes the semantics of the operations we support. Section 5 covers related work in coordination models before we conclude in Section 6.

2 Background and Motivation

Typically, a coordination model is characterized by its use of a shared dataspace that offers the following operations: (1) out, which places data in the shared space, (2) in which removes data from the shared space, and (3) rd which creates a local copy of some data in the shared space. An agent that wishes to interact with another agent places data in the shared space which is subsequently retrieved by the target agent, thereby completing the interaction. This basic functionality, while sufficient for supporting applications that need simple message passing, is not suited to more sophisticated scenarios, specifically those where space and time are an inherent facet of the application.

Consider the example of a construction site where many people work in a highly dynamic environment. Each person carries a PDA that serves as a multipurpose mobile computing platform. No fixed computing resources are available since there is no safe, suitable location for them. SynchroTask is an application that is used by construction supervisors on-site to manage day to day issues. SynchroTask allows supervisors and workers to manage and exchange project activities through opportunistic sharing of information.

Take for instance, the case of two shift supervisors needing to pass on lists of outstanding concerns. The problem is that shifts seldom overlap due to lunch breaks, etc. However, the construction site does have a rudimentary ready room which is used by the crew to rest and almost always has someone occupying it. The configuration is shown pictorially in Figure 1.

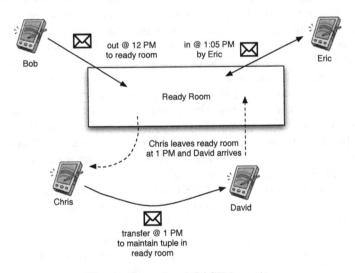

Fig. 1. Example of CAST in action

Towards the end of the shift, Bob uses SynchroTask to make notes on his PDA which lists the tasks requiring attention on a priority basis by the supervisor of the afternoon shift. As he leaves at 12 PM, he asks SynchroTask to forward the list to the afternoon supervisor. Since the afternoon supervisor has not yet arrived, SynchroTask requests that CAST, the middleware atop which it is executing, to store the information in a location where the incoming supervisor can easily retrieve it. The information is stored in the ready room. When

Eric arrives to supervise the next shift at 1:10 PM, he retrieves the information from the ready room. Supporting such interactions requires features not available in current coordination technology. The next two sections describe the CAST model that is designed to support applications such as SynchroTask.

3   A Model for Disconnected Coordination

The notion of coordinating across time and space is the distinguishing feature of CAST. By coordination we mean the execution of Linda-like operations on tuple spaces that may be either local or remote. For simplicity, we will assume that each tuple space is uniquely associated with a particular mobile host; this allows us to talk about coordination among hosts while ignoring the structural aspects of the host software. The scope of the coordination is controlled by which remote hosts can be reached at any given time. CAST assumes that hosts move according to some locally controlled plan called a motion profile, i.e., for a finite duration of time the host knows where it is heading and will not change its mind mid course. At first glance, the concept of using motion profiles might appear restrictive and impractical. However, motion profiles can be built automatically from individual schedules, thus avoiding the need for additional input by the user. Additionally, motion profiles are not practical only when the motion of hosts is completely random. When motion has even a simple pattern, motion profiles can be effectively exploited. Information about motion profiles is shared freely among hosts thus allowing them to build an egocentric view of where hosts might be in the future. Each host maintains such information in a *knowledge base*, which is a collection of the motion profiles of other hosts that the reference host is aware of. It is this information that makes it possible to identify disconnected routes which are used to transfer data and operation requests to a wider set of hosts than otherwise might be possible.

By exploiting disconnected routes, CAST makes it possible to reach out into the future and to coordinate across expanses of space. Coordination across time is associated with the ability to specify a lifetime for both data and operations in terms of a starting and an ending point. Coordination across space relates to the ability to identify a specific location or area in which the operation or the data is to exist, either initially or throughout its lifetime; the latter situation is complicated by the mobility of hosts in and out of the area of interest.

At this point it is reasonable to ponder whether the central enabling notion of computing and disseminating motion profile is reasonable. There exist some situations in which hosts follow prescribed patterns over extended periods of time because the application itself demands it: explorers follow a certain plan for safety and in order to accomplish their daily tasks; unmanned vehicles are restricted to a specific mission plan; robots are engaged in repetitive and redefined activities; office workers make their calendars public, etc. Despite these considerations, we must acknowledge that a study of coordination under uncertainty of motion profiles is intellectually exciting, but is out of the scope of this paper.

The remainder of this section is dedicated to a formal abstract description of the CAST model. We present the formalization initially from a global oracular point of view, where all available knowledge in the system is known to us. We show how the system evolves from this perspective. We then examine the model from an egocentric host perspective, where the available knowledge is a subset of the knowledge that exists in the system as a whole. A discussion of how to extend this formalization to cover the set of operations available in CAST is postponed to Section 4.

3.1   Underlying Computational Model

The core concept in our definition of the CAST model is the notion of motion profile. At the most basic level it is simply a function from time to space denoting the expected location of a particular host at some time in the future. Because it is mathematically convenient to work with total functions, we augment the space domain with the symbol $\perp$ (unknown location) and allow the motion profile to be a function from time to the augmented space:

$$\mu : T \rightarrow S^+$$

where
T denotes the time domain
S denotes the space domain
$\perp$ signifies an unknown location
S^+ is defined as $S \cup \{\perp\}$

We consider both time and space to be discrete. The time domain is modeled as the set of natural numbers and space is defined as the Cartesian product of two integer domains. Since we assume a global notion of time, we model the current time simply as an integer variable τ. The current location of a host is given by evaluating the motion profile at time τ. In general, we assume that motion profiles associated with specific hosts are defined starting from the current time up to some point in the future and nowhere else:

$$\langle \exists t_e : \tau \leq t_e :: \langle \forall t :: t \in [\tau, t_e] \Leftrightarrow \mu(t) \neq \perp \rangle \rangle$$

We abuse language by referring to points in time when the motion profile takes the value $\perp$ as being "undefined" from an application point of view, even though mathematically speaking the function is defined for all values in T.

As a first approximation, we define a system of coordinating hosts as a set of hosts H and their respective motion profiles. The state of the system is formally characterized by its *configuration* C, a function that maps hosts to their respective motion profiles

$$C : H \rightarrow (T \rightarrow S^+)$$

The system configuration evolves in response to two different kinds of actions. First, hosts may explicitly update their motion profiles by extending them into the future as in

$$C := C[i/\mu] \text{ where } C(i) \ll \mu$$

The condition captures the fact that the new motion profile μ for host i is defined everywhere the old motion profile $C(i)$ is defined. Formally, the relation $\ll$ is expressed as

$$\mu_1 \ll \mu_2 \equiv \langle \forall t :: \mu_1(t) \neq \bot \Longrightarrow \mu_2(t) \neq \bot \rangle$$

Second, time may advance affecting the value of the variable τ

$$\tau := \tau + 1$$

Time advance has an implicit global impact on the system configuration because all host motion profiles that are older must become undefined.

$$C := C[i/C(i)[(\tau - 1)/\bot]] \ \forall i \in H$$
$$\text{where } \tau - 1 \text{ refers to the old value of } \tau$$

3.2   Disconnected Routes

Given a configuration C, one could (in principle) determine whether it is possible to transfer data from host i_1 to host i_2. The first step involves identifying when hosts are close enough and, therefore, able to communicate. We assume that communication is possible whenever the distance between two hosts is less than the communication range of the wireless transmitters, some constant δ. In reality, transmission distances vary a great deal and rarely conform to an idealized circular pattern. Nevertheless, it is always possible to select a conservative value for δ, one that offers a high probability for successful communication between any two hosts. The time intervals during which hosts can exchange data are called *communication windows* and are formally captured in the definition of the relation w below:

$$i_1 \ w[t_1, t_2] \ i_2 = \langle \forall t : t \in [t_1, t_2] ::$$
$$C(i_1, t) \neq \bot \wedge C(i_2, t) \neq \bot \wedge |C(i_1, t) - C(i_2, t)| < \delta \rangle$$

Disconnected communication is established by having data move from one host to another during such periods of communication. Since we do not expect all hosts to be end-to-end connected, the data is temporarily buffered on an intermediate host until a communication window to the next host is available. In this manner a route is established between a source and a destination. It is called disconnected because the hosts along the route may never be simultaneously connected. A host along the route may obtain data from a peer and then become completely isolated for an extended period of time before handing off the same data to another peer. A disconnected route is said to exist between two hosts i_1 to i_n from time t_1 to t_n if there exists a set of hosts (i_2 to i_{n-1}) and communication windows between them such that data can travel from the origin to the destination as described above. Formally, a disconnected route r is a temporally ordered sequence of communication windows:

$$r = (i_1, i_2, t_1, t_{1'}), ..., (i_{n-1}, i_n, t_{n-1}, t_{n'-1})$$

subject to the constraint

$$t_i < t_{i'} < t_{i+1} \wedge i_i \ w[t_i, t_{i'}] \ i_{i+1} \text{ for i} = 1, ..., \text{n - 1}$$

The corresponding disconnected path is defined as the sequence of hosts involved in defining the route. In this case, the hosts involved in the disconnected route above define the disconnected path

$$(i_1, i_2, ... i_{n-1}, i_n)$$

Computing disconnected routes from locally available knowledge about the system configuration is central to our model. The brute force approach to accomplishing this entails building a directed graph which includes a vertex for each host/time pair denoting the start and the end of a communication window and an edge between any two vertices whose corresponding hosts can communicate in the respective time interval, i.e., two vertices (i_1, t_1) and (i_2, t_2) are connected by an edge only if $i_1 \ w[t_1, t_2] \ i_2$. Once the graph is constructed, finding a disconnected route is simply a matter of identifying a path in the graph between the source and the destination vertices. However, the algorithms involved in accomplishing this are outside the scope of this paper. For now, all we need to consider is the fact that a disconnected route can be computed, if one exists, given the current knowledge of the motion profiles of hosts in the system. Post facto one may discover that many more routes were actually established but planning can use only what is known at the time some coordination action is initiated.

3.3   Reachability

In the most abstract sense, disconnected routes expand the definition of reachability, which has been used in the past to determine the maximal set of hosts with which a reference host can coordinate. We introduce a relation ρ to formally capture this notion of reachability that is based on successive communication windows. The definition is recursive with the base case being reachability within a communication window, which includes the default case of a host being able to "communicate with itself" across any interval of time by holding the data for future delivery:

$$i_1 \rho[t_1, t_2] i_2 \equiv i_1 w[t_1, t_2] i_2 \vee \langle \exists i, t : t_1 \leq t \leq t_2 :: \\ i_1 \rho[t_1, t] i \wedge i \rho[t, t_2] i_2 \rangle$$

It should be immediately obvious that prior forms of reachability differ from this definition in two fundamental ways. First and foremost, earlier definitions of reachability are not parametrized with respect to a time interval; they can be seen as having an implicit time parameter defined by a single point in time. Second, in such definitions w holds true if the hosts are collocated, form a connected group, or are subject to other similar restrictions.

The other distinctive feature of CAST is the ability to coordinate across the spatial domain without explicit knowledge of the other participating hosts. A new notion of reachability needs to be introduced in order to accommodate this capability, one that captures the idea that a specific point or region is reachable within the constraints of a particular time interval. Clearly, the presence of some host operating in that space is implicit and the extensions we are introducing below make this fact evident in their respective formalizations. The simplest extension considers a point $p \in S$ to be reachable from some reference host in a specific time interval whenever a reachable host exists at that point in space. The new relation is called σ and it is defined as follows:

$$ i_1 \; \sigma[t_1, t_2] \; p \equiv \langle \exists i : C(i, t_2) = p :: i_1 \; \rho[t_1, t_2] \; i \rangle $$

Similarly, a region $r \subseteq S$ is considered reachable if it contains a point that is reachable:

$$ i_1 \; \sigma[t_1, t_2] \; r \equiv \langle \exists p : p \in r :: i_1 \; \sigma[t_1, t_2] \; p \rangle $$

Still other notions of reachability can be introduced to capture more subtle aspects of the semantics of coordination across space. We conclude this section with one such example. In some situations we may need to assert that data can be disseminated to any host entering a specific region throughout a particular interval in time. A region is said to be *continuously covered* with respect to some host i holding the critical data at the start if all the hosts in the required area are reachable from it during the specified time interval

$$ i_1 \; \nu[t_1, t_2] \; r \equiv C(i_1, t_1) \in r \; \wedge $$
$$ \langle \forall i, t : t \in [t_1, t_2] \wedge C(i, t) \in r :: i_1 \; \rho[t_1, t_2] \; i \rangle $$

The presentation thus far has focused on considering reachability given global knowledge. Such a view, while helpful for illustration purposes, does not mirror the reality of a MANET where hosts have egocentric perspectives. Hosts in the MANET have access only to a subset of the motion profiles that make up the global knowledge. The difference between the local and global knowledge determines how effective a host is at coordinating with other hosts in the MANET over disconnected routes. Since disconnected routes are calculated from motion profiles, a dearth of motion profiles on a given host results in it having access to fewer disconnected routes, which translates into fewer opportunities for disconnected coordination. In such a situation, a host is stymied with respect to operations that it wants to carry out in the future and at locations other than its own location. This is why the knowledge base on each individual host becomes critical to its functionality. The closer the host's local knowledge is to the global knowledge, the more effective the host is, the caveat being that in some situations, even global knowledge may not be sufficient. For instance, if all global knowledge only looks 1 second into the future, there are no opportunities for disconnected coordination beyond that time. Motion profiles that extend reasonably far into the future allow for timely dissemination and better planning.

3.4   The Egocentric Perspective

In this section we make the transition from unattainable global knowledge to maintainable local knowledge bases. Formally, the kind of information being held locally is of the same type as the global configuration described earlier, but what is known locally is only an approximation of the instantaneous global configuration of the system. The fact that the formalization is identical is helpful in system analysis. Properties of the system can be stated in terms of global configurations and proven using local knowledge. During this transition we make one fundamental change in the characterization of the individual hosts. Recall that so far a host i has been characterized by its unique identifier and a motion profile μ. The change consists of replacing the local motion profile with a more general knowledge base $M(i)$ of the same type as the system configuration C but which is always a subset thereof.

As expected, the motion profile of i in the global view C is identical to the motion profile in its own knowledge base $M(i)$. In other words, a host i always knows its own motion profile fully, which is proper as i establishes its own motion profile:

$$M(i,i) = C(i)$$

The situation changes when we consider the knowledge that host i has regarding the motion profile of some other host j:

$$\langle \forall j :: M(i,j) \ll C(j) \rangle$$

We use a gossiping protocol to exchange motion knowledge among hosts. Whenever two hosts encounter each other, i.e., they are directly connected, they exchange the contents of their knowledge bases (their own motion profile and the motion profiles collected through previous encounters). Hence, it is always the case that the motion profile of a reference host as known at another host is most often less defined than on the reference host; updates could have occurred on the reference host after the motion profile was given away.

The system now evolves in three different ways: (1) implicitly through the passage of time, (2) explicitly due to a change in a host's own motion profile where we define change to be an extension to the existing motion profile rather than a complete replacement, and (3) by acquisition of knowledge about other hosts as shown below:

$$M(i) := M(i) \cup M(j) \text{ where}$$
$$\langle \forall l, MM : MM = M(i) \cup M(j) :: M(i,l) \ll MM(i,l) \wedge M(j,l) \ll$$
$$MM(j,l) \wedge (M(i,l) = MM(i,l) \vee M(j,l) = MM(j,l)) \rangle$$

When two hosts exchange knowledge bases, the motion profile for a particular host as known by host i is compared against the motion profile for the *same* host as known by host j. The profile that extends farthest into the future is adopted as the "new" motion profile. In this way, two hosts synchronize their knowledge bases thus improving the quality of the information each holds. Even though this may seem to lead to unbounded growth in terms of storage requirements, the progression of time eliminates data that is older than a predefined limit.

4   Operations

Given the central role motion profiles play in planning interactions among mobile hosts in our model, it is natural to employ a similar formalization for the operations which execute across disconnected routes. The approach is attractive because it provides the opportunity to employ a unified knowledge-based treatment to describe all aspects of the coordination model. Take for instance an out operation. A reference host issues the operation, specifying a target for the operation. The target can be a remote host as in traditional distributed systems, or simply a set of spatiotemporal constraints that define a place and time where the operation must execute. Allowing hosts to perform remote operations can be complicated since it requires synchronized access to the data state on the target host. Thus, any operation that has a remote target is converted to an operation request which is routed to the target host which queues requests and sequentially performs the operations locally on behalf of the originator of the operation.

At this point we must consider how the operation is routed to its target. In CAST, the system formulates a plan for moving the operation request to the target. A plan is simply a motion profile that the operation request must follow to reach its target. This motion profile can be easily derived from the reachability information that is contained in the knowledge base of the originating host as described in Section 3. However, using the same type of motion profile for operations as is used for hosts is not possible. This is because the motion profile of a host can be arbitrary whereas the motion profile of an operation must always map to a location where a host is present. To remedy this, we use an *allocation profile* which is similar to a motion profile but returns the host on which the operation is to be located at a particular time rather than a physical location. This motivates the need for a separate knowledge base that contains all operations which are transferred between hosts at the same time they are gossiping to exchange host motion profiles.

The final issue we must consider is the actual insertion of the tuple in the target tuple space. At a basic level, we can build this action into the system itself. However, we can gain much more expressive power by allowing actions to be customized according to the task at hand. Consider an out operation to a physical space. The semantics of this operation call for each host in the physical area to receive a copy of the tuple associated with the out operation. However, the allocation profile yields a path to only one host among those present in the target area. The built-in action would simply place the tuple in the tuple space of that one host. To overcome this, we introduced the concept of an *operation function*, which operates on the data state of all target hosts. This concept is especially important as it allows a great deal of flexibility when specifying the effects of coordination operations. In the case of the out operation, operation function places the tuple in the tuple space of the host that is reachable via the allocation profile. After this, the function uses the knowledge base on the host to compute which other hosts are in the target area and sends them copies of the tuple using out operations to those specific hosts. Thus, the operation function encapsulates the basic operation and the maintenance of the operation in its target scope.

An **in** operation is a three phase operation that requires three paths between the originator and the target. During the first phase, the **in** operation can be routed to its target destination in the same manner as the **out** operation. The only difference between the two is the operation function which determines what action must be taken at the target. Here again, we emphasize the importance of the operation function which helps separate the concerns related to routing of the operation to its target from the actual effect of the operation. This allows CAST to treat all operations uniformly during the routing phase, with the actual effect of the operation being hidden until the target is reached, which is the only time that it is relevant. The **in** operation is a more complex operation than the **out** because an **in** request to multiple hosts could result in multiple tuples being removed which is inconsistent with the semantics of the operation. Thus, once an **in** request reaches its target, it searches for tuples that match the required *template*, which specifies the data being searched for. Every tuple that matches the template, is removed from the main data tuple space to a temporary tuple space by the operation function of **in**. The function then formulates, for each tuple, an **out** operation targeted towards the originator of the **in** function containing copies of the matching tuples. These **out** operations are routed to the originator in the standard way. Upon arrival, the operation function in the **out** operation places the copies in temporary storage on the originator since placing them in the main tuple space would indicate that this data is available for use. The system then chooses one of the copies returned non-deterministically. This completes the second phase of the operation. During the last phase, the host that owns the original of the copy selected is sent yet another operation request which destroys the original tuple in the temporary storage of that host. All others are sent a different operation that restores the original to the main data space. The copies of the tuples that were not chosen during the second phase are destroyed. Thus at the end of the **in** operation, only one tuple is removed from the system. The system registers a reaction on behalf of the calling application on the temporary storage space of the originator to return the result of the **in** to the caller.

We have seen how a knowledge base consisting solely of motion profiles is not sufficient since it does not account for the operational and data aspects of the coordination model. Thus, we split $K(i)$ as follows:

$M(i)$ - the set of motion profiles known to the local host (Section 3)
$O(i)$ - the set of operation requests that are on the local host
$D(i)$ - the data state of the local host
$T(i)$ - temporary storage space (not accessible to applications)

$M(i)$ holds tuples that contain motion profiles, $O(i)$ holds tuples that contain operation requests while $D(i)$ and $T(i)$ can hold any type of data tuple. The separation of these knowledge bases is key since $M(i)$ is modified using a gossiping protocol, $D(i)$ and $T(i)$ are modified only locally by operation requests, and O(i) is modified by either 1) operations requests moving from one host to another, 2) operation requests being serviced, or 3) operation requests expiring. We have already described the nature of the contents of M(i), while D(i) and T(i) contain generic data tuples. O(i) contains operation requests that are generated by hosts to have an operation execute on their behalf. To summarize the presentation above, each generic operation request is formulated as a 6-tuple as follows:

a unique identifier for the request
the allocation profile of the operation
the time at which the operation becomes active
the time at which the operation becomes inactive
the operation function
the originator of the operation request

The unique identifier is required to distinguish requests for similar operations by different hosts, and more importantly, to distinguish the results so that a host does not mistakenly collect the results of a similar operation issued by another host. The allocation profile describes the hosts on which the operation is resident at a given time. The time of activation and deactivation indicate the time interval for which the operation is valid and able to be executed. There are two points of note: (1) in most cases, there is an implicit dependency between activation time and the allocation profile since the activation time cannot precede the time at which the operation reaches the target host as given by the allocation profile and (2) a bounded deactivation time in effect makes every operation in CAST a polling operation because the system waits for the result of an operation only for the duration that it is active. If the current time exceeds the time at which the operation becomes inactive, the system unblocks and lets the execution continue. The operation function is a constant function that encodes the effect of the operation on the knowledge state of the target host and may also manage adequate coverage of the operation in a physical space. Examples of operation functions for out and in have already been described.

Before concluding, we return to SynchroTrack, presented in Section 2. SynchroTask uses various facilities provided by CAST to deliver the intended functionality. Consider the time when Bob placed the message in the ready room. CAST's spatial out operation was used to deliver the tuple to the ready room. The CAST system's knowledge base on Bob's PDA was used to determine that Chris will be in the ready room from 12 PM to 1 PM and David from 1 PM to 2 PM. This information resulted in the message being moved from Bob to Chris at 12 PM and from Chris to David at 1 PM, allowing a message to be associated with a physical area rather than be associated with any particular host. SynchroTask on Eric's PDA used a spatially targeted in operation to retrieve the information when he came in. The entire structure allowed the person that fulfilled the role of the afternoon supervisor to retrieve the information. If an operation was targeted specifically to Alice (the expected afternoon supervisor), then Eric would have not gotten the message.

5   Related Work

Since the work presented in this paper is a new approach to coordination built on top of a novel MANET routing protocol, we address related work in two areas–coordination models and MANET routing protocols.

The first example of a coordination model was Linda [6]. In Linda, coordination is characterized by a centralized coordination mechanism while the application that uses it may be distributed. In modern implementations of the coordination concept, such as JavaSpaces [7] and TSpaces [8], various parts of the application coordinate with each other by means of a tuple space maintained at a central location.

Coordination models have also found favor in agent-based systems. TuCSoN [9] introduced multiple tuple spaces called tuple centers while in MARS [10], mobile agents are provided upon arrival on a particular host with a handle to the local tuple space, which is shared among all agents present on the same host. Ara [11] introduced a constrained rendezvous type of coordination: some agents assume the role of coordination servers and represent meeting points where agents can ask for services.

More recently, coordination models have been adapted to novel computational environments [12], [13], [14], and [15], which highlights their versatility. One such environment where coordination models were introduced in support of new classes of applications was MANETs. LIME [3] proposed the idea of multiple (local) tuple spaces that were transiently shared to form a federated shared dataspace when hosts are in communication range. Limone [4] is a lightweight alternative to LIME implemented to offer fewer guarantees. TOTA [16] uses spatially distributed tuples, injected in the networks and propagated according to applications specific patterns.

Coordination models adapted for MANETs often support only peer-to-peer connections. To support multihop connections, they need to be combined with MANET routing protocols which fall into four broad categories: (1) proactive protocols such as DSDV[17], WRP[18], CSGR[19], which constantly maintain and update routes using routing tables at the cost of high bandwidth usage; (2) reactive protocols such as AODV[20], TORA[21], ABR[22], DSR[23], which only search for routes when they are required at the cost of low responsiveness; and (3) disconnected routing such as Epidemic[24], Message Relay[25], which allow messages to be sent via a gossiping protocol.

Most of the protocols mentioned above use broadcasts for route discovery and maintenance. Recent developments have targeted the use of location information to reduce the overhead required to discover and maintain routes. This has resulted in a new family of routing protocols called geographic routing protocols [26], [27]. The basic idea is to greedily forward the message to the next hop neighbor physically the closest to the destination. The greedy approach fails often in local optima that become dead-ends before the target is reached. This problem has multiple solutions in the form of the GPSR protocol [28], terminode routing [29], among others. Our work is different from geographic routing protocols in that (1) we do not use location information to optimize routing tasks, (2) we do not enforce an end-to-end route, and (3) common problems with geographic routing such as topology holes and local minima do not affect our approach. Location information is important to us for the purpose of determining when hosts are going to be connected with each other and are an integral part of the model (along with time).

6   Conclusions

In this paper, we have presented Coordination Across Space and Time (CAST), a new coordination model tailored for MANETs that enables coordination across the reaches of space and time. CAST achieves this functionality by its use of 1) disconnected routing, which allows two hosts that are not in direct contact to coordinate with each other, 2) spatiotemporal operations that enable operations to execute at specific locations in space and at any point in time, and 3) a knowledge driven architecture that unifies the treatment of motion of hosts, operations, and data state. The next steps in our investigation are a formal examination of the model's expressive power and an engineering effort to deliver the model's functionality in the form of an operational middleware.

Acknowledgments. This research was supported in part by ONR-MURI research contract N00014-02-1-0715. Any opinions, findings, and conclusions expressed in this paper are those of the authors and do not necessarily represent the views of the sponsors.

References

1. Cabri, G., Leonardi, L., Zambonelli, F.: MARS: A programmable coordination architecture for mobile agents. IEEE Internet Computing **4** (2000) 26–35
2. de Nicola, R., Ferrari, G.L., Pugliese, R.: klaim: a kernel language for agents interaction and mobility. IEEE Transactions on Software Engineering (Special Issue on Mobility and Network Aware Computing) (1998)
3. Murphy, A., Picco, G., Roman, G.C.: LIME: A middleware for physical and logical mobility. In: Proc. of the 21st Int'l Conf. on Distributed Computing Systems. (2001) 524–533
4. Fok, C.L., Roman, G.-C., Hackmann, G.: A lightweight coordination middleware for mobile computing. In: Proceedings of COORDINATION 2004. Volume 2949 of LNCS., Springer Verlag (2004) 135–151
5. Peine, H., Stolpmann, T.: The architecture of the Ara platform for mobile agents. In Popescu-Zeletin, R., Rothermel, K., eds.: First International Workshop on Mobile Agents MA'97. Volume 1219 of Lecture Notes in Computer Science., Berlin, Germany, Springer Verlag (1997) 50
6. Gerlenter, D.: Generative communication in Linda. ACM Computing Surveys **7** (1985) 80–112
7. Microsystems, S.: Javaspace specification. (http://java.sun.com/products/jini/specs)
8. Wyckoff, P.: Tspaces. IBM System Journal **37** (1998) 454–474

9. Omicini, A., Zambonelli, F.: The TuCSoN coordination model for mobile information agents. In: Proceedings of the 1st Workshop on Innovative Internet Information Systems, Pisa, Italy (1998)
10. Cabri, G., Leonardi, L., Zambonelli, F.: MARS: A programmable coordination architecture for mobile agents. IEEE Internet Computing 4 (2000) 26–35
11. Peine, H., Stolpmann, T.: The architecture of the Ara platform for mobile agents. In Popescu-Zeletin, R., Rothermel, K., eds.: First International Workshop on Mobile Agents MA'97. Volume 1219 of Lecture Notes in Computer Science., Berlin, Germany, Springer Verlag (1997) 50–61
12. Papadopoulos, G.A., Arbab, F.: Coordination models and languages. In: 761. Centrum voor Wiskunde en Informatica (CWI) (1998) 55
13. Papadopoulos, G.: Models and technologies for the coordination of internet agents: A survey (2000)
14. Cabri, G., Leonardi, L., Zambonelli, F.: The impact of the coordination model in the design of mobile agent applications. In: Proceedings of the 22nd International Computer Software and Application Conference. (1998) 436–442
15. Fok, C.L., Roman, G.C., Lu, C.: Software support for application development in wireless sensor network. In: Mobile Middleware. CRC Press (2005)
16. Mamei, M., Zambonelli, F., Leonardi, L.: Tuples on the air: a middleware for context-aware computing in dynamic networks. In: Proceedings of the 2nd International Workshop on Mobile Computing Middleware at the 23rd International Conference on Distributed Computing Systems (ICDCS). (2003) 342–347
17. Perkins, C., Bhagwat, P.: Highly dynamic destination-sequenced distance-vector routing (DSDV) for mobile computers. In: ACM SIGCOMM'94 Conference on Communications Architectures, Protocols and Applications. (1994)
18. Murthy, S., Garcia-Luna-Aceves, J.J.: An efficient routing protocol for wireless networks. Mobile Networks and Applications 1 (1996) 183–197
19. Chiang, C., Wu, H., Liu, W., Gerla, M.: Routing in clustered multihop, mobile wireless networks. In: IEEE Singapore International Conference on Networks. (1997) 197–211
20. Perkins, C.: Ad-hoc on-demand distance vector routing. In: MILCOM '97 panel on Ad Hoc Networks. (1997)
21. Park, V.D., Corson, M.S.: A highly adaptive distributed routing algorithm for mobile wireless networks. In: Proceedings of INFOCOM'97. (1997) 1405–1413
22. Toh, C.K.: A novel distributed routing protocol to support ad-hoc mobile computing. In: Fifteenth Annual International Phoenix Conference on Computers and Communications. (1996) 480–486
23. Johnson, D.B., Maltz, D.A.: Dynamic source routing in ad hoc wireless networks. Mobile Computing 353 (1996)
24. Vahdat, A., Becker, D.: Epidemic routing for partially connected ad hoc networks. Technical Report CS-200006, Duke University (2000)
25. Li, Q., Rus, D.: Communication in disconnected ad hoc networks using message relay. Parallel and Distributed Computing 63 (2003) 75–86
26. Imielinski, T., Navas, J.: Rfc 2009 - gps-based addressing and routing. http://rfc2009.x42.com/ (1996)
27. Navas, J.C., Imielinski, T.: GeoCast – geographic addressing and routing. In: Mobile Computing and Networking. (1997) 66–76
28. Karp, B., Kung, H.T.: GPSR: greedy perimeter stateless routing for wireless networks. In: Mobile Computing and Networking. (2000) 243–254
29. Blazevic, L., Boudec, J.Y.L., Giordano, S.: A location-based routing method for mobile ad hoc networks. IEEE Transactions on Mobile Computing 4 (2005) 97–110

Compositional Semantics of an Actor-Based Language Using Constraint Automata

Marjan Sirjani[1,2], Mohammad Mahdi Jaghoori[2],
Christel Baier[3], and Farhad Arbab[4,5]

[1] University of Tehran, Tehran, Iran
[2] IPM School of Computer Science, Tehran, Iran
[3] University of Bonn, Bonn, Germany
[4] CWI, Amsterdam, Netherlands
[5] Leiden University, Leiden, Netherlands
msirjani@ut.ac.ir, jaghoori@mehr.sharif.edu, baier@cs.uni-bonn.de
farhad@cwi.nl

Abstract. Rebeca is an actor-based language which has been success-fully applied to model concurrent and distributed systems. The seman-tics of Rebeca in labeled transition system is not compositional. In this paper, we investigate the possibility of mapping Rebeca models into a coordination language, Reo, and present a natural mapping that pro-vides a compositional semantics of Rebeca. To this end, we consider reactive objects in Rebeca as components in Reo, and specify their be-havior using constraint automata as black-box components within Reo circuits. Modeling coordination and communication among reactive ob-jects as Reo circuits, and the behavior of reactive objects as constraint automata, provides a compositional semantics for Rebeca. Although the result is a compositional model, its visual representation in Reo shows very well that it still reflects the tight coupling inherent in the commu-nication mechanism of object-based paradigms, whereby the real control and coordination is built into the code of the reactive objects themselves. We describe an alternative design that overcomes this deficiency. This illustrates the differences between objects and components, and the chal-lenges in moving from object-based to component-based designs.

Keywords: actor model, Compositional semantics, Rebeca, Reo, Con-straint Automata.

1 Introduction

Managing large and complex systems requires techniques that support reusabil-ity and modifiability [1]. In general, compositionality allows one to master both the complexity of the design and verification of software models. Having a com-positional semantics for a modeling language allows us to construct a model from its sub-models and reuse the already derived semantics of the sub-models. Com-positional construction and verification can be exploited effectively only when the model is naturally decomposable [2], and there is no general approach for

P. Ciancarini and H. Wiklicky (Eds.): COORDINATION 2006, LNCS 4038, pp. 281–297, 2006.
© Springer-Verlag Berlin Heidelberg 2006

decomposing a system into components [3]. Different researchers have worked on composing specifications and verifying their properties [4, 5, 6]. In this paper, we build up a compositional semantics for an actor-based language, using a component-based language and taking advantage of its compositional semantics. In this way we can use our object-based Java-like modeling language which is familiar for software engineers, while benefitting from the component-based paradigm to build models from their sub-models.

Rebeca (*Reactive Objects Language*) is an actor-based language with a formal foundation, presented in [7, 8, 9]. A model in Rebeca consists of a set of reactive objects (called *rebecs*) which are concurrently executing and asynchronously communicating. Rebeca can be considered as a reference model for concurrent computation, based on an operational interpretation of the actor model [10, 11]. It is also a platform for developing object-based concurrent systems in practice. Formal verification approaches are used to ensure correctness of concurrent and distributed systems. The Rebeca Verifier tool, as a front-end tool, translates Rebeca code into languages of existing model-checkers, allowing verification of their properties [12, 13]. There is also an ongoing project on developing a direct model checker for Rebeca using state space reduction techniques [14, 15].

The Rebeca semantics, expressed in LTS (Labeled Transition System) [7, 8] is not compositional. We cannot construct the semantics of the total model by composing the semantics of each rebec used to construct the model. The compositional verification approach proposed in [7, 9] is based on decomposing a closed Rebeca model and not composing the rebecs as the components of a model.

Reo [16, 17] is an exogenous coordination model wherein complex coordinators, called connectors are compositionally built out of simpler ones. The atomic connectors are a set of user-defined point-to-point *channels*. Reo is based on the foundation model of Abstract Behavior Types (ABT), as a higher level alternative to Abstract Data Types (ADT), which serve as the foundation of object oriented languages [18]. Reo can be used as a *glue language* for compositional construction of connectors that orchestrate component instances in a component based system.

In this paper, we investigate the possibility of mapping Rebeca models into Reo and propose a natural mapping that provides a compositional semantics of Rebeca. As reactive objects (rebecs) are encapsulated and loosely coupled modules in Rebeca, we consider them as components in a coordination language. Modeling the coordination and communication mechanisms between rebecs can be done by Reo circuits, and the behavior of each rebec is specified by constraint automata [19] as a black-box component within the Reo circuit.

In [20] and [21] a component-based version of Rebeca is proposed where the components act as wrappers that provide higher level of abstraction and encapsulation. The main problem in constructing a component in this object-based configuration is the rebec-to-rebec communication and the need to know the receiver names. In [20] and [21] components are sets of rebecs and the communication between components is via broadcasting anonymous and asynchronous messages. In this paper, we use the coordination language Reo and model each rebec as a component. The rebec-to-rebec communication remains the main problem in exploiting the reusability provided by our compositional semantics. The semantics of Rebeca in Reo demonstrates this problem very well. We propose a solution based on the behavior of synchronous channels in Reo, the interleaving nature of concurrency in Rebeca models, and the fact that, in this case, there is only one message sent in an atomic step. Hence, the work in this paper is our first successful attempt to build-up components out of reactive objects without changing the semantics of Rebeca.

Another interesting outcome of our mapping is to clearly show the problems in moving from an object-based model to a component-based model of the kind proposed by Reo. The components that we construct out of reactive objects are not really amenable to external coordination control provided by the glue code. We cannot simply change the coordination glue code and expect another execution pattern independent from the behavior of the rebecs. The coupling inherent in the message passing mechanism will also be reflected in the Reo circuitry representing their communication. We show that in this case the glue code will grow in size and complexity as the system evolves. We then propose a solution for the special case of Rebeca.

Organization of the Paper. In Section 2, we provide a brief overview of Rebeca and a Rebeca model as an example which we also use in Section 7. Reo is described in Section 3, and our mapping of Rebeca to Reo is explained in Section 4. Constraint automata are used to build the compositional semantics of Reo. In Section 5 we describe their extended form of parameterized constraint automata which we use in this paper. In Section 6 we describe our algorithm for generating parameterized constraint automata out of Rebeca code. Section 7 shows a case study. Section 8 is a short conclusion and a view of our future work.

2   Rebeca: An Actor-Based Language

Rebeca models consist of concurrently executing _reactive objects_, called rebecs. Rebecs are encapsulated objects, with no shared variables, which can communicate only by asynchronous message passing. Each rebec is instantiated from a _reactive class_ and has a single thread of execution; it also has an unbounded buffer, called a queue, for arriving messages. Computation takes place by message passing and execution of the corresponding methods of messages. Each message specifies a unique method to be invoked when the message is serviced. In this paper we abstract from dynamic object creation and dynamic topology, both of which are present in Rebeca models.

The operational semantics of Rebeca is defined using as a labeled transition system, a quadruple of a set of states (S), a set of labels (L), a transition relation on states (T), and a set of initial states of the system (s_0), $M = (S, L, T, s_0)$, where we have the followings (for a more detailed formal definition refer to [7]): The state space of the model is $\prod_{i=1}^{n}(S_i \times q_i)$, where each S_i denotes the local state of rebec r_i consisting of a valuation that maps each local field variable to a value of the appropriate type; and the inbox q_i, an *unbounded* buffer that stores all incoming messages for rebec r_i in a FIFO manner.

The set of action labels L is the set of all possible message calls in the given model; such calls cause the processing of those messages that are part of the target rebec (if it provides the corresponding message server).

A triple $(s, l, s') \in S \times L \times S$ is an element of the transition relation T iff

- in state s there is some r_i such that l is the first message in the inbox q_i, l is of the form $\langle sender, receiver, msg \rangle$, where *sender* is the rebec identifier of the requester (implicitly known by the receiver), *receiver* is the rebec identifier of r_i (receiver rebec), and *msg* is the name of the method m of r_i which is invoked;
- state s' results from state s through the atomic execution of two activities: first, rebec r_i deletes the first message l from its inbox q_i, second, method m is executed in state s. The latter may add requests to rebecs' inboxes (by sending messages), change the local state (by assignments), and/or create new rebecs;
- if new rebecs are created in the invocation of m, then the state space S *expands dynamically*, which is out of the scope of this paper.

Clearly, the execution of the above methods relies implicitly on a standard semantic for the imperative code in the body of method m. Regarding the *infinite* behavior of our semantics, communication is assumed to be fair [11]: all the sent messages eventually reach their respective inboxes and will eventually be serviced by the corresponding rebec. The initial state s_0 is the one where each rebec has its `initial` message as the sole element in its inbox.

We use a simple example of trains and a controller to show a Rebeca model and also the mapping algorithm further in Section 7. Consider a bridge with a track where only one train can pass at a time. There are two trains, entering the bridge in opposite directions. A bridge controller uses red lights to prevent any possible collision of trains, and guarantees that each train will finally enter the bridge assuming that the trains pass the bridge after entering it.

Figure 1 shows the Rebeca code for the bridge controller example. There are two reactive classes, one for the bridge controller and one for the trains. The numbers in front of each reactive class name show the length of the queue of the rebecs instantiated from that class. For model checking purposes we need a bound on the queue lengths. The bridge controller uses its state variables to keep the value of the red lights on each side, and has flags to know whether or not a train is waiting on each side of the bridge. In the initial state, rebecs have their initial messages as the only message in their queues.

3   Reo: A Coordination Language

Reo is a model for building component connectors in a compositional manner [16, 17]. Reo offers a compositional approach to defining component connectors. Reo *connectors* (also called *circuits*) are constructed in the same spirit

```
reactiveclass BridgeController(5) {          reactiveclass Train(3) {
  knownobjects{Train t1; Train t2;}             knownobjects{BridgeController controller;}
  statevars {                                   statevars { boolean onTheBridge; }
    boolean isWaiting1; boolean isWaiting2;     msgsrv initial() {
    boolean signal1;    boolean signal2;            onTheBridge = false;
  }                                                 self.Passed();
  msgsrv initial() {                            }
    signal1 = false; isWaiting1 = false;        msgsrv YouMayPass() {
    signal2 = false; isWaiting2 = false;            onTheBridge = true;
  }                                                 self.Passed();
  msgsrv Arrive() {                             }
    if (sender == t1) {                         msgsrv Passed() {
      if (signal2 == false) {                       onTheBridge = false;
        signal1 = true;                             controller.Leave();
        t1.YouMayPass();                            self.ReachBridge();
      } else { isWaiting1 = true; }             }
    } else {                                    msgsrv ReachBridge() {
      if (signal1 == false) {                       controller.Arrive();
        signal2 = true;                         }
        t2.YouMayPass();                      }
      } else { isWaiting2 = true; } }         main {
  }                                               Train train1(theController);
  msgsrv Leave() {                                Train train2(theController);
    if (sender == t1) {                           BridgeController theController
      signal1 = false;                                        (train1, train2);
      if (isWaiting2) {                           }
        signal2 = true;
        t2.YouMayPass();
        isWaiting2 = false; }
    } else {
      signal2 = false;
      if (isWaiting1) {
        signal1 = true;
        t1.YouMayPass();
        isWaiting1 = false; } }
  }
}
```

Fig. 1. Rebeca Model for a Bridge Controller

as logic and electronics circuits: take basic elements and connect them. Basic connectors in Reo are *channels*. Each channel has exactly two ends, which can be a *sink* end or a *source* end. A *sink* end is where data flows out of a channel, and a *source* end is where data flows into a channel. It is possible for the ends of a channel to be both sinks or both sources. Reo places no restriction on the behavior of a channel. This allows an open-ended set of different channel types to be used simultaneously together in Reo, each with its own policy for synchronization, buffering, ordering, computation, data retention/loss, etc. For our purpose to model Rebeca models, we need a small set of basic channels, which we define later (in Figure 5).

Channels are connected to make a circuit. Connecting (or *joining*) channels is putting channel ends together in a *node*. So, a *node* is a set of coincident channel ends. The semantics of a node is as follows.

A component can write data items to a source node that it is connected to. The write operation succeeds only if all (source) channel ends coincident on the node accept the data item, in which case the data item is transparently written to every source end coincident on the node. A source node, thus, acts as a *replicator*. A component can obtain data items, by an input operation, from a sink node that it is connected to. A take operation succeeds only if at least one of the (sink) channel ends coincident on the node offers a suitable data item; if more than one coincident channel end offers suitable data items, one is selected nondeterministically. A sink node, thus, acts as a nondeterministic *merger*. A mixed node nondeterministically selects and takes a suitable data item offered by one of its coincident sink channel ends and replicates it into all of its coincident source channel ends.

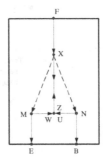

Fig. 2. Exclusive Router in Reo

Figure 2 shows a Reo connector, an exclusive router, which we call *Xrouter*. Here, we use it to show the visual syntax for presenting Reo connector graphs and some frequently useful channel types. This circuit is also used to model Rebeca in Reo. The enclosing thick box in this figure represents *hiding*: the topologies of the nodes (and their edges) inside the box are hidden and cannot be modified. It yields a connector with a number of input/output *ports*, represented as nodes on the border of the bounding box, which can be used by other entities outside the box to interact with and through the connector.

The simplest channels used in these connectors are synchronous (*Sync*) channels, represented as simple solid arrows (like edges FX and MW in Figure 2). A Sync channel has a source and a sink end, and no buffer. It accepts a data item through its source end iff it can simultaneously dispense it through its sink. A lossy synchronous (*LossySync*) channel is similar to a Sync channel, except that it always accepts all data items through its source end. If it is possible for it to simultaneously dispense the data item through its sink (e.g., there is a take operation pending on its sink) the channel transfers the data item; otherwise the data item is lost. LossySync channels are depicted as dashed arrows, e.g., XM and XN in Figure 2. Another channel is the synchronous drain channel (*SyncDrain*), whose visual symbol appears as the edge XZ in Figure 2. A *SyncDrain* channel has two source ends. Because it has no sink end, no data value can ever be obtained from this channel. It accepts a data item through one of its ends iff a data item is also available for it to simultaneously accept through its other end as well. All data accepted by this channel are lost.

Two channels that are used in modeling Rebeca but are not included in the *Xrouter* circuit, are *FIFO* and *Filter* channels. We define *FIFO* as an unbounded asynchronous channel where data can flow in unboundedly from its source and flow out of its sink, if its buffer is not empty; input and output cannot take place simultaneously when the buffer is empty. Figure 5.a in Section 5 shows the Reo notation (and the constraint automaton) for a 1-bounded *FIFO* channel. *Filter* is a channel with a corresponding data pattern. It lets the data that match with the pattern pass and loses all other data. A *Filter* channel and its constraint automaton are shown in Figure 5.b.

4   Rebecs as Components in Reo

To model Rebeca using Reo, we can consider each rebec as a black-box component, and model the coordination and communication among the rebecs as Reo circuits. To model this coordination, we use an *Xrouter* which passes the control to each rebec nondeterministically. Communication takes place by asynchronous message passing which is modeled by FIFO and filter channels in Reo.

Each rebec starts its execution by receiving a *start* signal, and sends an *end* signal at its end. The behavior of a rebec as a component is to take a message from its message queue upon receiving the *start* signal through its start port, execute the corresponding message server, and send an *end* signal through its end port. The coordination, which is modeled by interleaved execution of rebecs, is handled by an *Xrouter* which passes the *start* signal to one and only one rebec, waits until it receives an *end* signal, and passes the *start* signal again, guaranteeing the atomic execution of each method according to the semantics of Rebeca in [7]. This loop is repeated by *Xrouter*, and sending the signals is done by a nondeterministic choice. The Reo circuit in Figure 3 shows the *Xrouter* and other channels that are used to manage the coordination and facilitate the communication among rebecs.

For communication between rebecs, we need FIFO and filter channels. The message queues of rebecs are modeled by FIFO channels. We need to design a circuit to allow only the messages that are sent to a specific rebec to get into its queue, and filter out all other messages. To have an elegant design, we consider a consistent pattern of wiring between components. In Figure 3, there are fork nodes named F_i, and merge nodes named M_i. All messages that are sent by a rebec $rebec_i$ get out of its port *send*, then pass a *Sync* channel and enter the corresponding fork node F_i. Here, a message is copied into all the source channel ends of the outgoing *Sync* channels that are merged again in the node M_i. For a model with n rebecs, there are n *Sync* channels that connect each rebec to all other rebecs and carry the messages. Following each merge node M_i there is a *Filter* channel whose filter pattern is the ID of the receiver rebec. So, the filter following the node M_i filters out every message whose receiver is not $rebec_i$,

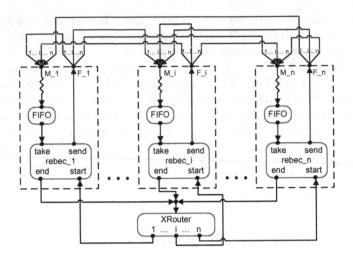

Fig. 3. Modeling Rebeca in Reo

allowing only the proper messages to pass through and get into the message queue of the rebec (the FIFO in Figure 3).

Upon receiving a *start* signal, a rebec takes a message from its queue by enabling the *take* port, and then executes the corresponding message server. During this execution, the messages that are sent, flow out of the rebec component through its *send* port, and arrive at the message queue of the destination rebec properly, passing the fork node, the merge node, and the filter channel.

Now, we have a Reo circuit that models a Rebeca model. But, to be able to construct the compositional semantics of a model and verify its properties we need to have a proper semantics for this Reo circuit and also for the rebecs. Constraint automata [19] are presented as a compositional semantics for Reo circuits and can be used to model components and the glue code circuit in a consistent way. They also provide verification facilities.

Looking more carefully, we see that by adding or removing rebecs the Reo circuit in Figure 3 which acts as the glue code will be changed. Our goal in obtaining the compositional semantics of the model is to be able to reuse the constraint automata of the parts of the Reo model that are not changed and not to construct the constraint automata of the whole Reo model from scratch. Observing that the glue code will change with a single change in the set of constituent rebecs, we can see that there is no gain in this way of constructing the compositional semantics. Although, the constraint automata for each rebec does not change and can be reused, all the join operations must be done again.

This is a good example to show how the modules in an object-based model are more tightly coupled than the modules in a component-based model. We changed our Reo circuit in Figure 3 to the circuit in Figure 4 to gain more modifiability and reusability. Here, the coordination part which is an *Xrouter* in Figure 3 is replaced with a compositional variant in Figure 4. Also, the communication part is changed to the simple circuit shown in Figure 4. This simplification is only

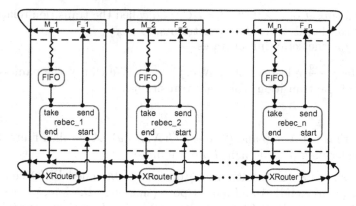

Fig. 4. Compositional modeling of Rebeca in Reo

valid because of the interleaved execution of each rebec and the fact that there is only one message carried through the *Sync* channels in each atomic step. In this way we have each rebec and its coordination and communication part as a component which can be plugged into or removed from a model without changing the rest of the model. Hence, by adding or removing a rebec, the entire model will not change. Note that our goal here is not to achieve exogenous coordination, because in Rebeca (like other object oriented models) the driving control and coordination are built in the code of rebecs and the message passing pattern.

5   Constraint Automata: Compositional Semantics of Reo

Constraint automata are presented in [19] to model Reo connectors. We use constraint automata to model the components, yielding Rebeca models fully as constraint automata. In this section, we explain the definition of constraint automata and how the constraint automata of a Reo circuit is constructed compositionally.

Using constraint automata as an operational model for Reo connectors, the automata-states stand for the possible configurations (e.g., the contents of the FIFO-channels of a Reo-connector) while the automata-transitions represent the possible data flow and its effect on these configurations. The operational semantics for Reo presented in [16] can be reformulated in terms of constraint automata. Constraint automaton of a given Reo connector can also be defined in a *compositional* way. For this, the composition operator for constraint automata and the constraint automata for a set of Reo connector primitives are presented in [19].

Definition 1. *[Constraint automata]* A constraint automaton (over the data domain *Data*) is a tuple $\mathcal{A} = (Q, \mathcal{N}ames, \longrightarrow, Q_0)$ where

- Q is a set of states,
- $\mathcal{N}ames$ is a finite set of names,

– $\longrightarrow$ is a subset of $Q \times 2^{Names} \times DC \times Q$, called the transition relation of $\mathcal{A}$, where DC is the set of data constraints,
– $Q_0 \subseteq Q$ is the set of initial states.

We write $q \xrightarrow{N,g} p$ instead of $(q, N, g, p) \in \longrightarrow$. We call N the name-set and g the guard of the transition. For every transition

$$q \xrightarrow{N,g} p$$

we require that (1) $N \neq \emptyset$ and (2) $g \in DC(N, Data)$. $\mathcal{A}$ is called finite iff Q, $\longrightarrow$ and the underlying data domain $Data$ are finite.   □

Figure 5.a shows a constraint automaton for a 1-bounded FIFO channel with input port (source end) A and output port (sink end) B. Here, we assume that the data domain consists of two data items 0 and 1. Intuitively, the initial state q_0 stands for the configuration where the buffer is empty, while the states p_0 and p_1 represent the configurations where the buffer is filled with one or the other data item.

We now explain how constraint automata can be used to model the possible data flow of a given Reo circuit. The nodes of a Reo-circuit play the role of the ports in the constraint automata. To provide a *compositional* semantics for Reo circuits, we need constraint automata for all basic channel connectors and automata-operations to mimic the composition offered by the Reo-operations for join and hiding.

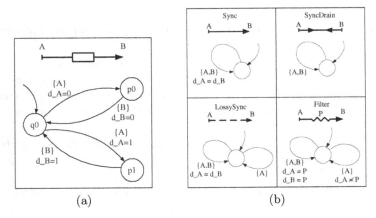

(a)   (b)

Fig. 5. (a) Deterministic constraint automaton for a 1-bounded FIFO channel; and, (b) Deterministic constraint automaton for some other channels

Figure 5.b shows the constraint automata for some of the standard basic channel types: a synchronous channel, a synchronous drain, a lossy synchronous channel, and a filter with pattern P. In every case, one single state is sufficient. Moreover, the automata are deterministic. There are operators defined on constraint automata that capture the meaning of Reo's join and hiding operators [19].

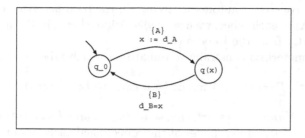

Fig. 6. Parameterized constraint automaton for a 1-bounded FIFO channel

Parameterized Constraint Automata. To simplify the pictures for constraint automata for data-dependent connectors, we use a parameterized notation for constraint automata, as proposed in [22]. For example, Figure 6 shows a parameterized constraint automata for a FIFO1 channel with source A and sink B. Thus, $q(x)$ in Figure 6 represents the states $q(d)$ for $d \in Data$. The transition from q_0 to $q(x)$ in the picture is a short-hand notation for the transitions from q_0 to $q(d)$ with the name-set $\{A\}$ and the data constraint $d = d_A$ where d ranges over all data elements in $Data$.

Formally, a *parameterized constraint automaton* is defined as a tuple

$$\mathcal{P} = (Loc, Var, v, \mathcal{N}ames, \rightsquigarrow, Loc_0, init)$$

where

- Loc is a set of locations,
- Var is a set of variables,
- $v : Loc \rightarrow 2^{Var}$ assigns to any location ℓ a (possibly empty) set of variables,
- $\mathcal{N}ames$ is a finite set of names (like in constraint automata),
- $\rightsquigarrow$ is a subset of $Loc \times 2^{\mathcal{N}ames} \times PDC \times X \times Loc$, called the transition relation of $\mathcal{P}$, where PDC is the set of parameterized data constraints and X is the function showing assignments to variables,
- $Loc_0 \subseteq Loc$ is a set of initial locations,
- $init$ is a function that assigns to any initial location $\ell \in Loc_0$ a condition for the variables.

$v(\ell)$ can be viewed as the parameter list of location ℓ. For instance, in Figure 6 we use $q(x)$ to denote that q is a location with parameter list $v(q) = \{x\}$, while q_0 is a location with an empty parameter list. The initial condition for q_0 is omitted which denotes that $init(q_0) = \mathsf{true}$.

6   Compositional Semantics of Rebeca Using Constraint Automata

To obtain the constraint automata of the coordination and communication parts of the Rebeca model, which are modeled in Reo, we use the join and hide operations on constraint automata. For specifying the semantics of rebecs we need parameterized constraint automata. To obtain the parameterized constraint automaton (PCA) of each rebec, we use an algorithm, shown in Figure 7, to extract the PCA directly from the Rebeca code.

In the parameterized constraint automaton for each rebec i,

$$\mathcal{P}_i = (Loc_i, Var_i, v_i, \mathcal{N}ames_i, \rightsquigarrow_i, Loc_{0i}, init_i)$$

where we have $\mathcal{N}ames_i = \{start, end, send, take\}$, and $Loc_{0i} = \{idle\}$. For each rebec Var_i includes state variables of the rebec, local variables of each method, and $sender$ variable which holds the ID of the sender of each message.

VARS: sender; {state variables}; {local variables};

BEGIN

    Create locations: $Idle$, $Dispatch$

    Create transitions:

        $Idle \xrightarrow{\{start\}} Dispatch$

        $Dispatch \xrightarrow{\{take, end\}, d_{take} \cdot msg=empty} Idle$

    FOR each message server $\mathcal{M}$ **DO**

        Create transition: $Dispatch \xrightarrow[sender := d_{take} \cdot sender]{\{take\}, d_{take} \cdot msg= \mathcal{M}} start_{\mathcal{M}}$

        Create $control\ graph$ from $start_{\mathcal{M}}$ to $end_{\mathcal{M}}$

        Create transition: $end_{\mathcal{M}} \xrightarrow{\{end\}} Idle$

    OD

END

Fig. 7. Algorithm to construct parameterized constraint automaton from a rebec code

The initial state of the PCA (Parameterized Constraint Automaton) of each rebec is denoted as the $idle$ state. At the beginning all rebecs are in their $idle$ states. By getting the $start$ signal as input from the $Xrouter$, a rebec moves to its $Dispatch$ state, where a message is taken from top of the corresponding queue. The data item of the port $take$ is assumed to be a tuple consisting of the $sender$ of the message and the $message\ server\ name$. According to the d_take, the next state is chosen. If the message queue is empty the transition goes back to the $idle$ state. If not, the transition goes to the state which is the beginning of the execution of a message server. In fact, the second item of d_take which is the $message\ server\ name$ specifies the next state. Suppose the message $\mathcal{M}$ is taken from the queue. This causes a transition to state $start_{\mathcal{M}}$, which denotes the beginning of the execution of the message server of $\mathcal{M}$.

The execution of each message server can be shown with a $control\ graph$ representing its different branches and assignments. In this control graph, each send statement contributes to a transition. The name of this transition is $send$, and its data constraint is a tuple containing the name of the message being sent, the ID of the receiving rebec, and the ID of the sender which is $self$. In this phase, since the automata are created for the reactive classes and not the rebecs, the receiving rebec is chosen as one of the known rebecs. This ID is

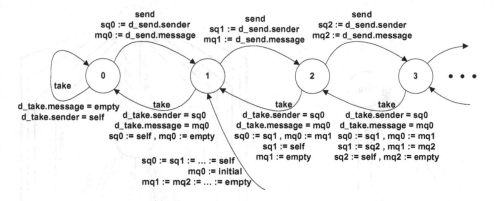

Fig. 8. Constraint automaton for a message queue channel

used by the designated *filter* of each rebec to identify the real receiver of the message. Each transition due to a *send* should also contain all the assignments made before that send. The assignments after the last send (if any) constitute the final transition of the control graph. This is a transition with *end* signal which connects the last state of the control graph ($end_\mathcal{M}$) to the *idle* state. This transition can be combined with the last transition of the control graph (and hence removing $end_\mathcal{M}$) to reduce the number of states. We use the bridge controller example of Section 2, to explain the algorithm in more detail in the next section.

We use a special kind of a FIFO channel to model the message queue of a rebec. The main point is that we want to be able to realize the situation when the queue is empty. This cannot be done with the conventional definition of a FIFO channel in Reo [17, 16]. We assume that there is a special data denoted by *empty* that the channel emits to show that the queue is empty. We define the behavior of the message queue channel as the constraint automaton shown in Figure 8.

7   An Example: Bridge Controller

We use a bridge controller as an example to model by constraint automata. This example is described in Section 2, and its Rebeca code is shown in Figure 1.

Figure 9.a shows the constraint automaton for the trains and Figure 9.b shows the constraint automaton for the bridge controller. The initial state for a train is the *idle* state. We move to the *Dispatch* state by receiving the *start* signal. A train has four message servers: *initial*, *YouMayPass*, *Passed*, and *ReachBridge*. For each one of these message servers there is an outgoing transition from the *Dispatch* state. Each transition goes to a state that designates the start of its corresponding message server. There is also another transition that is chosen when the message queue is empty. This one goes back to the *idle* state and outputs the *end* signal.

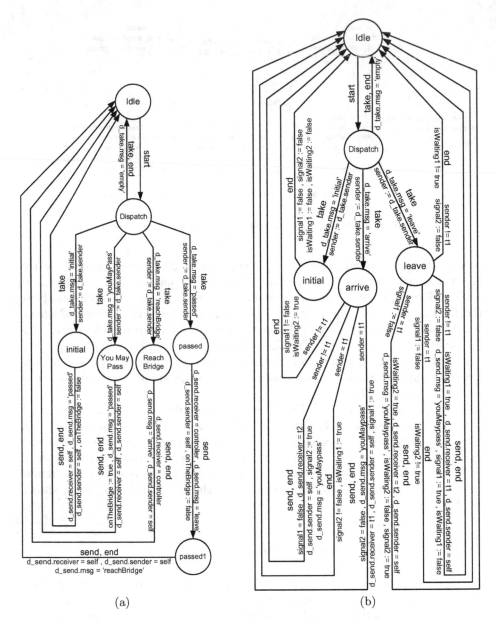

Fig. 9. Constraint Automata models for (a) Train; and, (b) Controller

As described in the algorithm of Figure 7, we must consider the different flows of control in each message server as a 'control graph'. In the message servers of the trains we have a single path in the flow of control. We partition each path by the *send* statements. For example in the message server *Passed* we have two fragments. We have two transitions corresponding to the *send* statements in Figure 9.a. The *end* signal is added to the last transition, which can be considered as an optimization issue. Considering the controller, we have conditional statements in message servers *Arrive* and *Leave*, and hence more than one possible path in the flow of control. The transitions generated for different flows of controls can be seen in Figure 9.b.

The mapping presented in Section 4 and Figure 4 allow us to first construct the constraint automata of the communication and coordination parts, which can be reused in all Rebeca models. We can subsequently compose the constraint automata of the rebecs with these constraint automata. Thus, we obtain the constraint automaton of the whole system which shows the behavior of the model and can also be used for model checking purposes. We have already developed a tool to automate the specified mapping [23], and we have used it to map a few case studies in Rebeca into constraint automata. In this tool a set of heuristic rules are used to sequence a compositional construction of constraint automata that help to prevent the state space explosion problem.

Our compositional semantics allows a natural modular mapping from the problem space into the model space. To better show the benefit of this mapping, consider a modified version of the bridge controller problem, where more than one train can arrive from each side of the bridge (on multiple tracks). To avoid "hard-coding" the number of trains in this example, it is more appropriate to use a more component-based style model, where a queue on each side of the bridge keeps the passage requests. The Rebeca code for this version of bridge controller can be found on the Rebeca home page [24]. In this model, trains can be plugged in, and the derived constraint automata can be reused and composed together with the constraint automata of the new trains.

8   Conclusion and Future Work

We use the coordination language Reo to build a compositional semantics for the actor-based language, Rebeca. We modified the Reo circuit from its primary and natural layout to a more compositional and hence more reusable variant. Constraint automata are the essential devices in building this compositional semantics. The work presented in this paper can be used for both modeling and verification purposes. In general, for the object-based models that are written in a component-based paradigm, the compositional semantics presented here can be fully exploited and the unchanged parts can be completely reused. For all kinds of models, the constraint automata of the coordination and communication parts and the individual rebecs can be reused.

Our work can also be regarded as a good example where constraint automata are used for modeling components and connectors in a consistent manner, allowing to derive the behavior of a whole system as a composition of the behavior of its constituents. The differences between objects and components, and the challenges in moving from objects to components are illustrated in this work.

In our future work, we intend to use the tool in [23] for further experiments. We will continue our investigation of mapping reactive objects to components in order to characterize the patterns in the behavior of rebecs that make a model more modifiable and the rebecs more reusable. Another direction in our future work is to consider dynamic rebec creation and dynamic changing topology in the mapping, although dynamic features are not yet supported by constraint automata they are present in Reo. A formal proof for our mapping algorithm will also be provided.

References

1. de Boer, F.S., Bonsangue, M.M., Graf, S., de Roever, W.P., eds.: Formal Methods for Components and Objects, International Symposium, FMCO'02, Leiden, The Netherlands, November 2002, Revised Lectures. Volume 2852 of LNCS, Springer-Verlag, Germany (2003)
2. de Roever, W.P., Langmaack, h., Pnueli, A., eds.: Compositionality: The Significant Difference, International Symposium, COMPOS'97, Bad Malente, Germany, September 1997, Revised Lectures. Volume 1536 of LNCS, Springer-Verlag, Germany (1998)
3. Lamport, L.: Composition: A way to make proofs harder. In: Proceedings of COMPOS: International Symposium on Compositionality: The Significant Difference. Volume 1536 of LNCS, (Springer-Verlag, Germany, 1997) 402–407
4. Lynch, N.A., Tuttle, M.R.: Hierarchical correctness proofs for distributed algorithms. Technical Report MIT/LCS/TR-387, MIT (1987)
5. Abadi, M., Lamport, L.: Composing specifications. In Jagadish, H.V., Mumick, I.S., eds.: Proceedings of the 1996 ACM SIGMOD International Conference on Management of Data, Montreal, Canada, ACM Press, USA, (1996) 365–376
6. Talcott, C.: Composable semantic models for actor theories. Higher-Order and Symbolic Computation **11** (1998) 281–343
7. Sirjani, M., Movaghar, A., Shali, A., de Boer, F.: Modeling and verification of reactive systems using Rebeca. Fundamenta Informatica **63** (Dec. 2004) 385–410
8. Sirjani, M., Movaghar, A.: An actor-based model for formal modelling of reactive systems: Rebeca. Technical Report CS-TR-80-01, Tehran, Iran (2001)
9. Sirjani, M., Movaghar, A., Mousavi, M.: Compositional verification of an object-based reactive system. In: Proceedings of AVoCS'01, Oxford, UK (2001) 114–118
10. Hewitt, C.: Description and theoretical analysis (using schemata) of PLANNER: A language for proving theorems and manipulating models in a robot. MIT Artificial Intelligence Technical Report 258, Department of Computer Science, MIT (1972)
11. Agha, G.: Actors: A Model of Concurrent Computation in Distributed Systems. MIT Press, Cambridge, MA, USA (1990)
12. Sirjani, M., Movaghar, A., Shali, A., de Boer, F.: Model checking, automated abstraction, and compositional verification of Rebeca models. Journal of Universal Computer Science **11** (2005) 1054–1082
13. Sirjani, M., Shali, A., Jaghoori, M., Iravanchi, H., Movaghar, A.: A front-end tool for automated abstraction and modular verification of actor-based models. In: Proceedings of ACSD'04, (IEEE Computer Society, 2004) 145–148
14. Jaghoori, M.M., Sirjani, M., Mousavi, M.R., Movaghar, A.: Efficient symmetry reduction for an actor-based model. In: 2nd International Conference on Distributed Computing and Internet Technology. Volume 3816 of LNCS. (2005) 494–507
15. Jaghoori, M.M., Movaghar, A., Sirjani, M.: Modere: The model-checking engine of Rebeca. In: ACM Symposium on Applied Computing - Software Verificatin Track. (2006) to appear.

16. Arbab, F.: Reo: A channel-based coordination model for component composition. Mathematical Structures in Computer Science **14** (2004) 329–366
17. Arbab, F., Rutten, J.J.: A coinductive calculus of component connectors. Technical Report SEN-R0216, CWI (Centre for Mathematics and Computer Science), Amsterdam, The Netherlands (2002)
18. Arbab, F.: Abstract behavior types: A foundation model for components and their composition. In: Proceedings of FMCO'03. Volume 2852 of LNCS. (2003) 33–70
19. Arbab, F., Baier, C., Rutten, J.J., Sirjani, M.: Modeling component connectors in Reo by constraint automata. In: Proceedings of FOCLASA'03. Volume 97 of ENTCS., Elsevier (2004) 25–46
20. Sirjani, M., de Boer, F.S., Movaghar, A., Shali, A.: Extended Rebeca: A component-based actor language with synchronous message passing. In: Proceedings of ACSD'05, IEEE Computer Society (2005) 212–221
21. Sirjani, M., de Boer, F.S., Movaghar, A.: Modular verification of a component-based actor language. Journal of Universal Computer Science **11** (2005) 1695–1717
22. Baier, C., Sirjani, M., Arbab, F., Rutten, J.J.: Modeling component connectors in Reo by constraint automata. (Science of Computer Programming) accepted 2005, to appear.
23. Farrokhian, M.: Automating the mapping of Rebeca to constraint automata. Master Thesis, Sharif University of Technology (2006)
24. Rebeca home page: Available through http://khorshid.ut.ac.ir/~rebeca.

Author Index

Lecture Notes in Computer Science

For information about Vols. 1–3956

please contact your bookseller or Springer

Vol. 3998: T. Calamoneri, I. Finocchi, G.F. Italiano (Eds.), Algorithms and Complexity. XII, 394 pages. 2006.

Vol. 3997: W. Grieskamp, C. Weise (Eds.), Formal Approaches to Software Testing. XII, 219 pages. 2006.

Vol. 3996: A. Keller, J.-P. Martin-Flatin (Eds.), Self-Managed Networks, Systems, and Services. X, 185 pages. 2006.

Vol. 3995: G. Müller (Ed.), Emerging Trends in Information and Communication Security. XX, 524 pages. 2006.

Vol. 3994: V.N. Alexandrov, G.D. van Albada, P.M.A. Sloot, J. Dongarra (Eds.), Computational Science – ICCS 2006, Part IV. XXXV, 1096 pages. 2006.

Vol. 3993: V.N. Alexandrov, G.D. van Albada, P.M.A. Sloot, J. Dongarra (Eds.), Computational Science – ICCS 2006, Part III. XXXVI, 1136 pages. 2006.

Vol. 3992: V.N. Alexandrov, G.D. van Albada, P.M.A. Sloot, J. Dongarra (Eds.), Computational Science – ICCS 2006, Part II. XXXV, 1122 pages. 2006.

Vol. 3991: V.N. Alexandrov, G.D. van Albada, P.M.A. Sloot, J. Dongarra (Eds.), Computational Science – ICCS 2006, Part I. LXXXI, 1096 pages. 2006.

Vol. 3990: J. C. Beck, B.M. Smith (Eds.), Integration of AI and OR Techniques in Constraint Programming for Combinatorial Optimization Problems. X, 301 pages. 2006.

Vol. 3989: J. Zhou, M. Yung, F. Bao, Applied Cryptography and Network Security. XIV, 488 pages. 2006.

Vol. 3987: M. Hazas, J. Krumm, T. Strang (Eds.), Location- and Context-Awareness. X, 289 pages. 2006.

Vol. 3986: K. Stølen, W.H. Winsborough, F. Martinelli, F. Massacci (Eds.), Trust Management. XIV, 474 pages. 2006.

Vol. 3984: M. Gavrilova, O. Gervasi, V. Kumar, C.J. K. Tan, D. Taniar, A. Laganà, Y. Mun, H. Choo (Eds.), Computational Science and Its Applications - ICCSA 2006, Part V. XXV, 1045 pages. 2006.

Vol. 3983: M. Gavrilova, O. Gervasi, V. Kumar, C.J. K. Tan, D. Taniar, A. Laganà, Y. Mun, H. Choo (Eds.), Computational Science and Its Applications - ICCSA 2006, Part IV. XXVI, 1191 pages. 2006.

Vol. 3982: M. Gavrilova, O. Gervasi, V. Kumar, C.J. K. Tan, D. Taniar, A. Laganà, Y. Mun, H. Choo (Eds.), Computational Science and Its Applications - ICCSA 2006, Part III. XXV, 1243 pages. 2006.

Vol. 3981: M. Gavrilova, O. Gervasi, V. Kumar, C.J. K. Tan, D. Taniar, A. Laganà, Y. Mun, H. Choo (Eds.), Computational Science and Its Applications - ICCSA 2006, Part II. XXVI, 1255 pages. 2006.

Vol. 3980: M. Gavrilova, O. Gervasi, V. Kumar, C.J. K. Tan, D. Taniar, A. Laganà, Y. Mun, H. Choo (Eds.), Computational Science and Its Applications - ICCSA 2006, Part I. LXXV, 1199 pages. 2006.

Vol. 3979: T.S. Huang, N. Sebe, M.S. Lew, V. Pavlović, M. Kölsch, A. Galata, B. Kisačanin (Eds.), Computer Vision in Human-Computer Interaction. XII, 121 pages. 2006.

Vol. 3978: B. Hnich, M. Carlsson, F. Fages, F. Rossi (Eds.), Recent Advances in Constraints. VIII, 179 pages. 2006. (Sublibrary LNAI).

Vol. 3977: N. Fuhr, M. Lalmas, S. Malik, G. Kazai (Eds.), Advances in XML Information Retrieval and Evaluation. XII, 556 pages. 2006.

Vol. 3976: F. Boavida, T. Plagemann, B. Stiller, C. Westphal, E. Monteiro (Eds.), Networking 2006. Networking Technologies, Services, and Protocols; Performance of Computer and Communication Networks; Mobile and Wireless Communications Systems. XXVI, 1276 pages. 2006.

Vol. 3975: S. Mehrotra, D.D. Zeng, H. Chen, B.M. Thuraisingham, F.-Y. Wang (Eds.), Intelligence and Security Informatics. XXII, 772 pages. 2006.

Vol. 3973: J. Wang, Z. Yi, J.M. Zurada, B.-L. Lu, H. Yin (Eds.), Advances in Neural Networks - ISNN 2006, Part III. XXIX, 1402 pages. 2006.

Vol. 3972: J. Wang, Z. Yi, J.M. Zurada, B.-L. Lu, H. Yin (Eds.), Advances in Neural Networks - ISNN 2006, Part II. XXVII, 1444 pages. 2006.

Vol. 3971: J. Wang, Z. Yi, J.M. Zurada, B.-L. Lu, H. Yin (Eds.), Advances in Neural Networks - ISNN 2006, Part I. LXVII, 1442 pages. 2006.

Vol. 3970: T. Braun, G. Carle, S. Fahmy, Y. Koucheryavy (Eds.), Wired/Wireless Internet Communications. XIV, 350 pages. 2006.

Vol. 3969: Ø. Ytrehus (Ed.), Coding and Cryptography. XI, 443 pages. 2006.

Vol. 3968: K.P. Fishkin, B. Schiele, P. Nixon, A. Quigley (Eds.), Pervasive Computing. XV, 402 pages. 2006.

Vol. 3967: D. Grigoriev, J. Harrison, E.A. Hirsch (Eds.), Computer Science – Theory and Applications. XVI, 684 pages. 2006.

Vol. 3966: Q. Wang, D. Pfahl, D.M. Raffo, P. Wernick (Eds.), Software Process Change. XIV, 356 pages. 2006.

Vol. 3965: M. Bernardo, A. Cimatti (Eds.), Formal Methods for Hardware Verification. VII, 243 pages. 2006.

Vol. 3964: M. Ü. Uyar, A.Y. Duale, M.A. Fecko (Eds.), Testing of Communicating Systems. XI, 373 pages. 2006.

Vol. 3963: O. Dikenelli, M.-P. Gleizes, A. Ricci (Eds.), Engineering Societies in the Agents World VI. XII, 303 pages. 2006. (Sublibrary LNAI).

Vol. 3962: W. IJsselsteijn, Y. de Kort, C. Midden, B. Eggen, E. van den Hoven (Eds.), Persuasive Technology. XII, 216 pages. 2006.

Vol. 3960: R. Vieira, P. Quaresma, M.d.G.V. Nunes, N.J. Mamede, C. Oliveira, M.C. Dias (Eds.), Computational Processing of the Portuguese Language. XII, 274 pages. 2006. (Sublibrary LNAI).

Vol. 3959: J.-Y. Cai, S. B. Cooper, A. Li (Eds.), Theory and Applications of Models of Computation. XV, 794 pages. 2006.

Vol. 3958: M. Yung, Y. Dodis, A. Kiayias, T. Malkin (Eds.), Public Key Cryptography - PKC 2006. XIV, 543 pages. 2006.